INJUSTICE 2

VOLUME 4

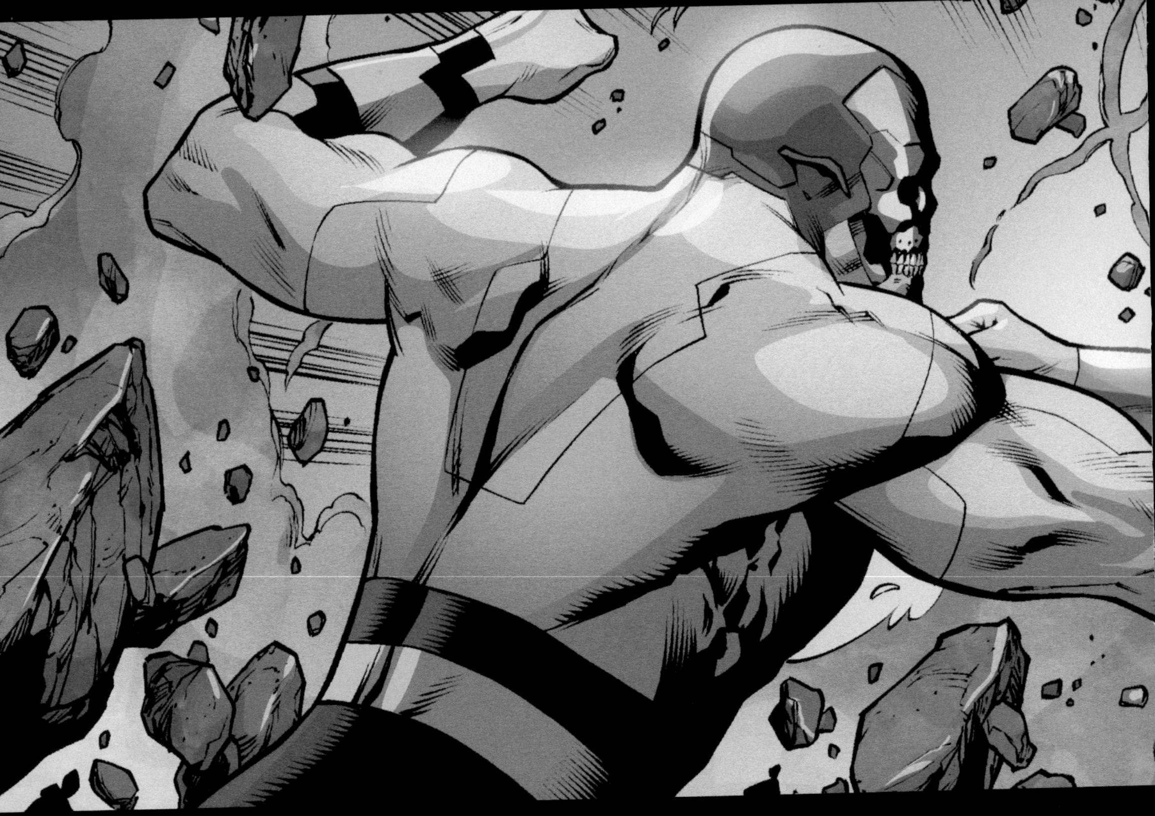

TOM TAYLOR
writer

BRUNO REDONDO   DANIEL SAMPERE   MIKE S. MILLER
XERMANICO   JUAN ALBARRAN
artists

REX LOKUS   J. NANJAN
colorists

TICE™ 2

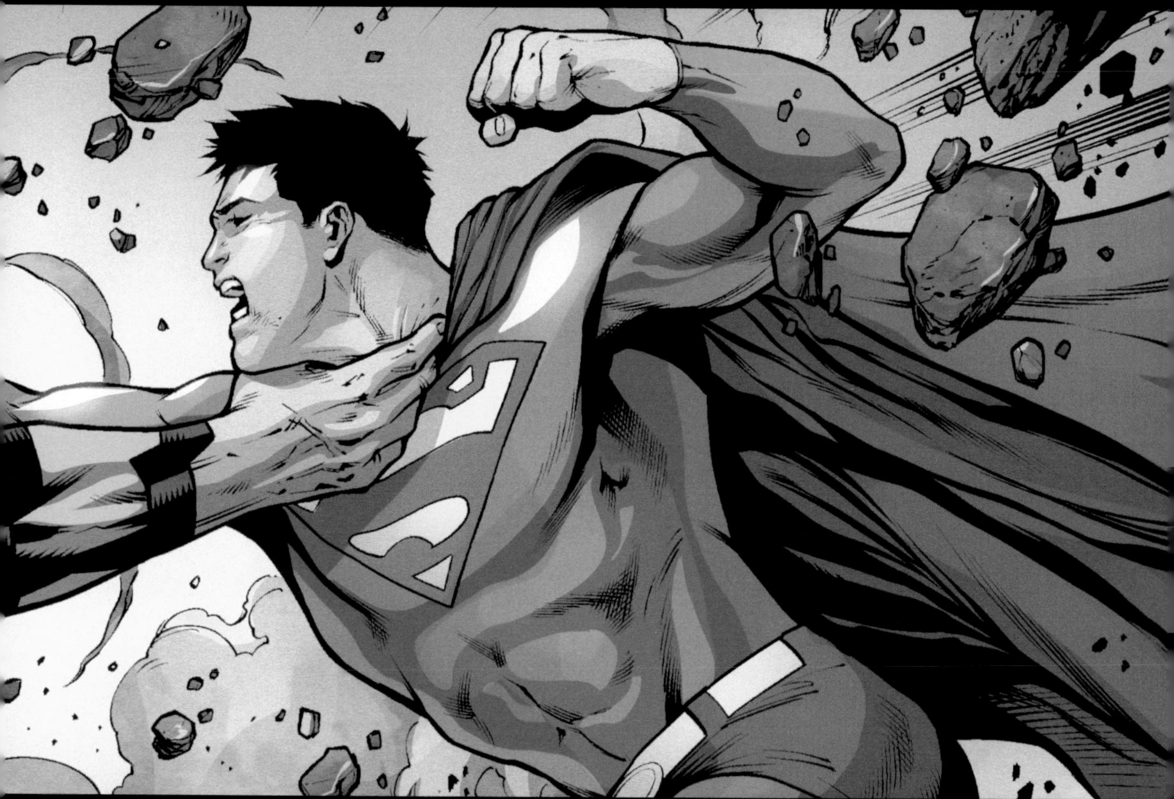

VOLUME 4

SUPERMAN created by JERRY SIEGEL and JOE SHUSTER
SUPERGIRL based on the characters created by JERRY SIEGEL and JOE SHUSTER
SUPERBOY created by JERRY SIEGEL
By special arrangement with the Jerry Siegel family

WONDER WOMAN created by WILLIAM MOULTON MARSTON

JIM CHADWICK Editor – Original Series
LIZ ERICKSON Assistant Editor – Original Series
JEB WOODARD Group Editor – Collected Editions
ALEX GALER Editor – Collected Edition
STEVE COOK Design Director – Books
MEGEN BELLERSEN Publication Design

BOB HARRAS Senior VP – Editor-in-Chief, DC Comics
PAT McCALLUM Executive Editor, DC Comics

DAN DiDIO Publisher
JIM LEE Publisher & Chief Creative Officer
AMIT DESAI Executive VP – Business & Marketing Strategy,
    Direct to Consumer & Global Franchise Management
BOBBIE CHASE VP & Executive Editor, Young Reader & Talent Development
MARK CHIARELLO Senior VP – Art, Design & Collected Editions
JOHN CUNNINGHAM Senior VP – Sales & Trade Marketing
BRIAR DARDEN VP – Business Affairs
ANNE DePIES Senior VP – Business Strategy, Finance & Administration
DON FALLETTI VP – Manufacturing Operations
LAWRENCE GANEM VP – Editorial Administration & Talent Relations
ALISON GILL Senior VP – Manufacturing & Operations
JASON GREENBERG VP – Business Strategy & Finance
HANK KANALZ Senior VP – Editorial Strategy & Administration
JAY KOGAN Senior VP – Legal Affairs
NICK J. NAPOLITANO VP – Manufacturing Administration
LISETTE OSTERLOH VP – Digital Marketing & Events
EDDIE SCANNELL VP – Consumer Marketing
COURTNEY SIMMONS Senior VP – Publicity & Communications
JIM (SKI) SOKOLOWSKI VP – Comic Book Specialty Sales & Trade Marketing
NANCY SPEARS VP – Mass, Book, Digital Sales & Trade Marketing
MICHELE R. WELLS VP – Content Strategy

INJUSTICE 2 VOL. 4

DC Comics, 2900 West Alameda Ave., Burbank, CA 91505
Printed by LSC Communications, Kendallville, IN, USA.
11/2/18. First Printing.
ISBN: 978-1-4012-8533-3

Library of Congress Cataloging-in-Publication Data is available.

PEFC Certified

Printed on paper from
sustainably managed
forests and controlled
sources

PEFC/29-31-337   www.pefc.org

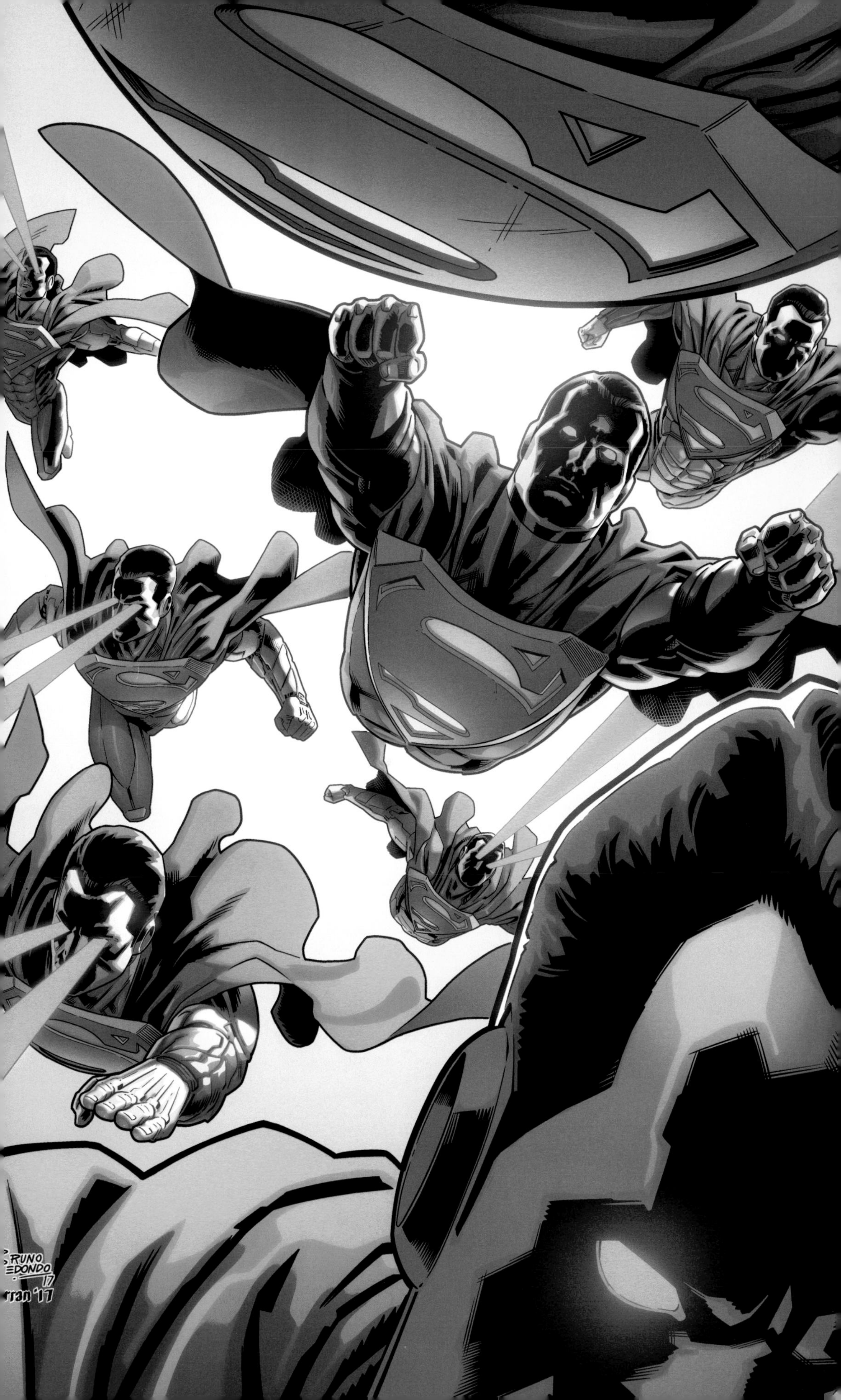

"Arctic Assault"

Tom Taylor Writer **Xermanico** Artist **J. Nanjan** Colorist **Wes Abbott** Letterer

Cover art by **Bruno Redondo**, **Juan Albarran** and **Alejandro Sanchez**

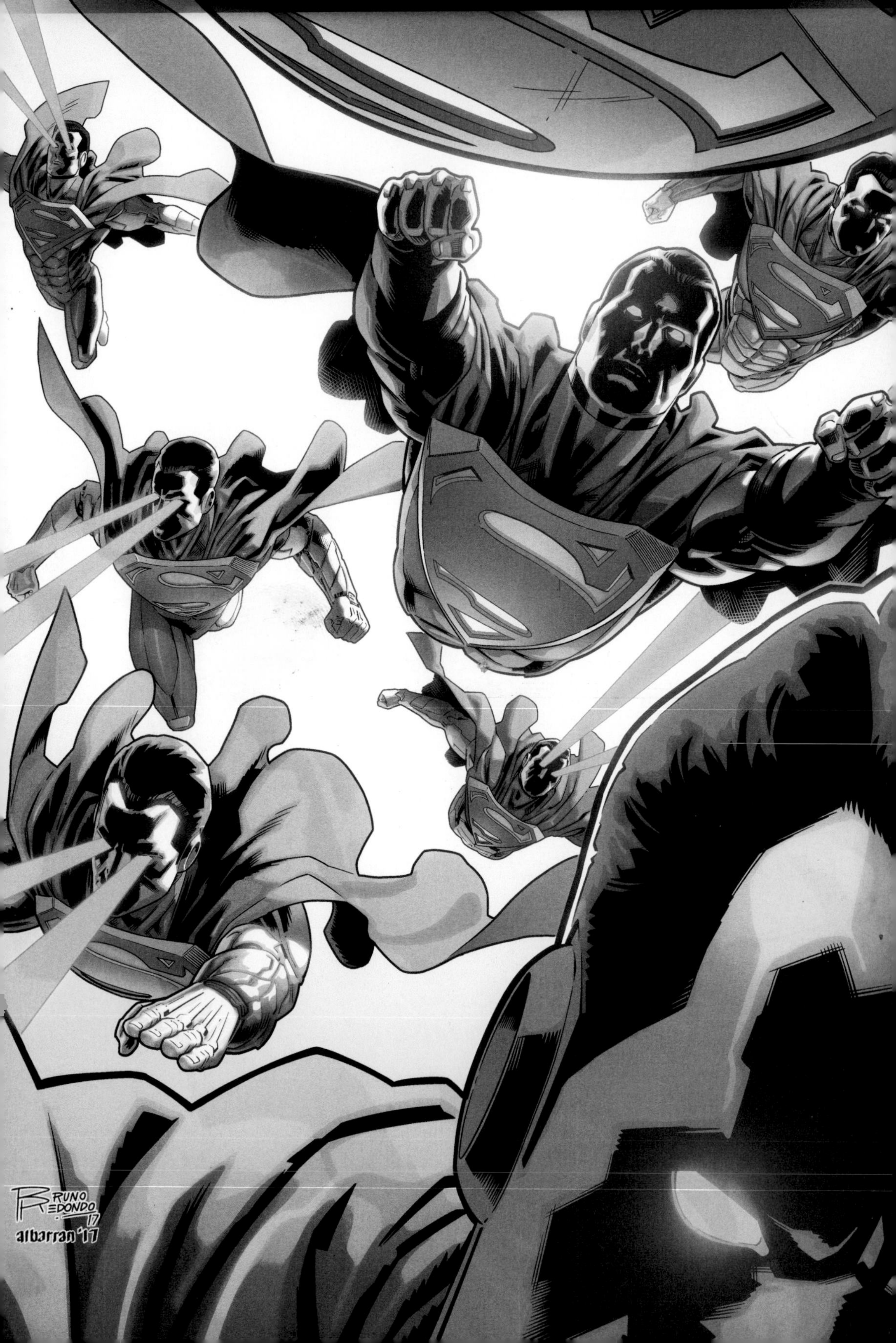
BRUNO REDONDO '17
albarran '17

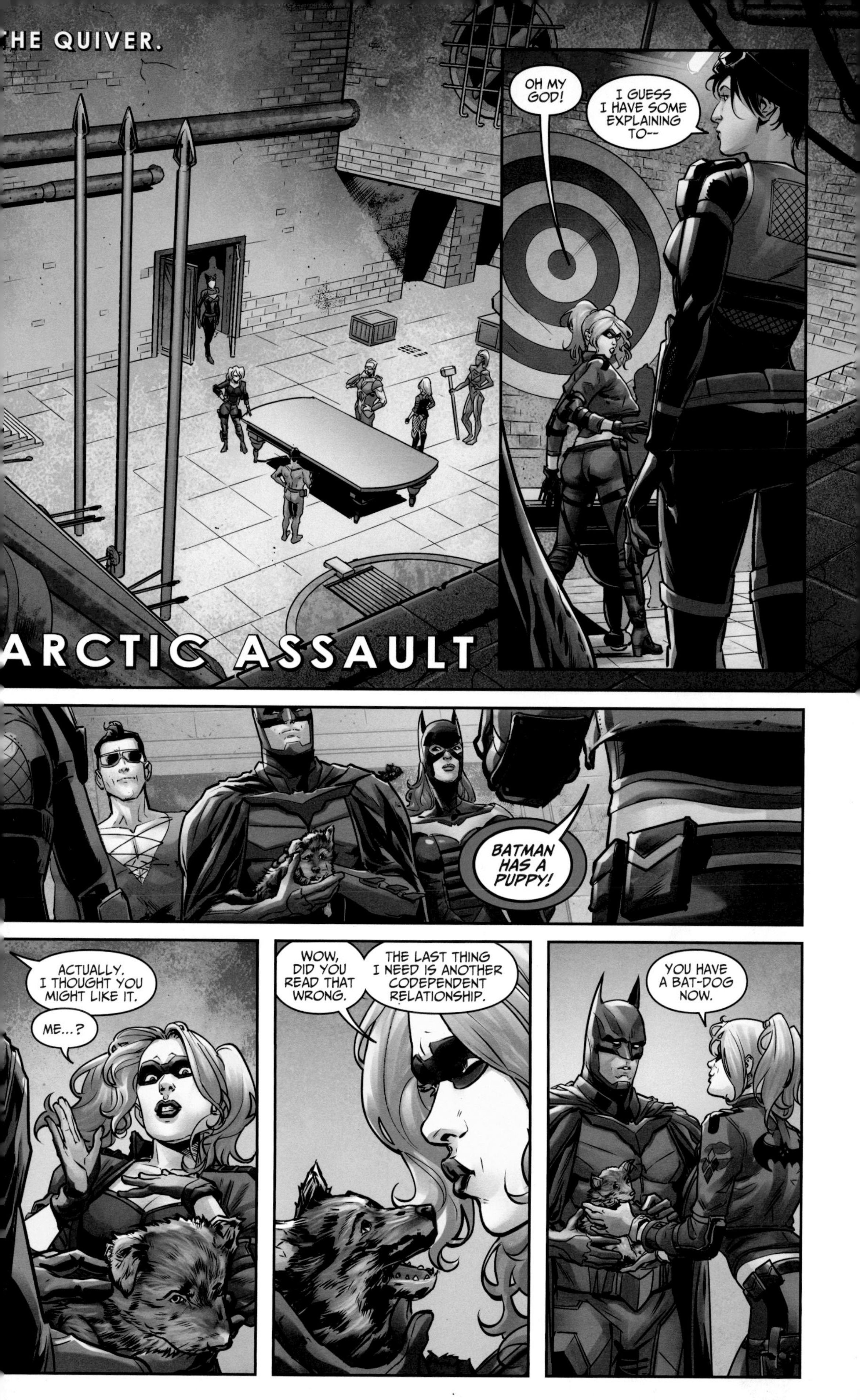
THE QUIVER.
OH MY GOD!
I GUESS I HAVE SOME EXPLAINING TO--
ARCTIC ASSAULT
BATMAN HAS A PUPPY!
ACTUALLY. I THOUGHT YOU MIGHT LIKE IT.
ME...?
WOW, DID YOU READ THAT WRONG.
THE LAST THING I NEED IS ANOTHER CODEPENDENT RELATIONSHIP.
YOU HAVE A BAT-DOG NOW.

WHAT ARE YOU DOING HERE, BRUCE?

THERE WAS AN ATTACK. WE NEED TO--

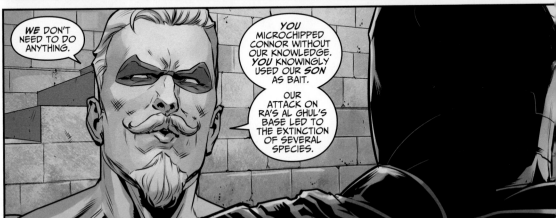

WE DON'T NEED TO DO ANYTHING.

YOU MICROCHIPPED CONNOR WITHOUT OUR KNOWLEDGE. YOU KNOWINGLY USED OUR SON AS BAIT.

OUR ATTACK ON RA'S AL GHUL'S BASE LED TO THE EXTINCTION OF SEVERAL SPECIES.

AND UNDER YOUR LEADERSHIP, THE U.S. LOST ITS GOVERNMENT AND ALL OF ITS LIVING PRESIDENTS.

AM I MISSING SOMETHING?

NO. THAT ABOUT COVERS IT.

AND, EVEN IF YOU HADN'T PISSED ME OFF SO MUCH, WHILE YOU'RE UNDER SUCH PUBLIC INVESTIGATION FOR YOUR ACTIONS, THE JUSTICE LEAGUE TASK FORCE CAN'T POSSIBLY HAVE YOU ON THE TEAM.

YOU WOULD TARNISH US ALL.

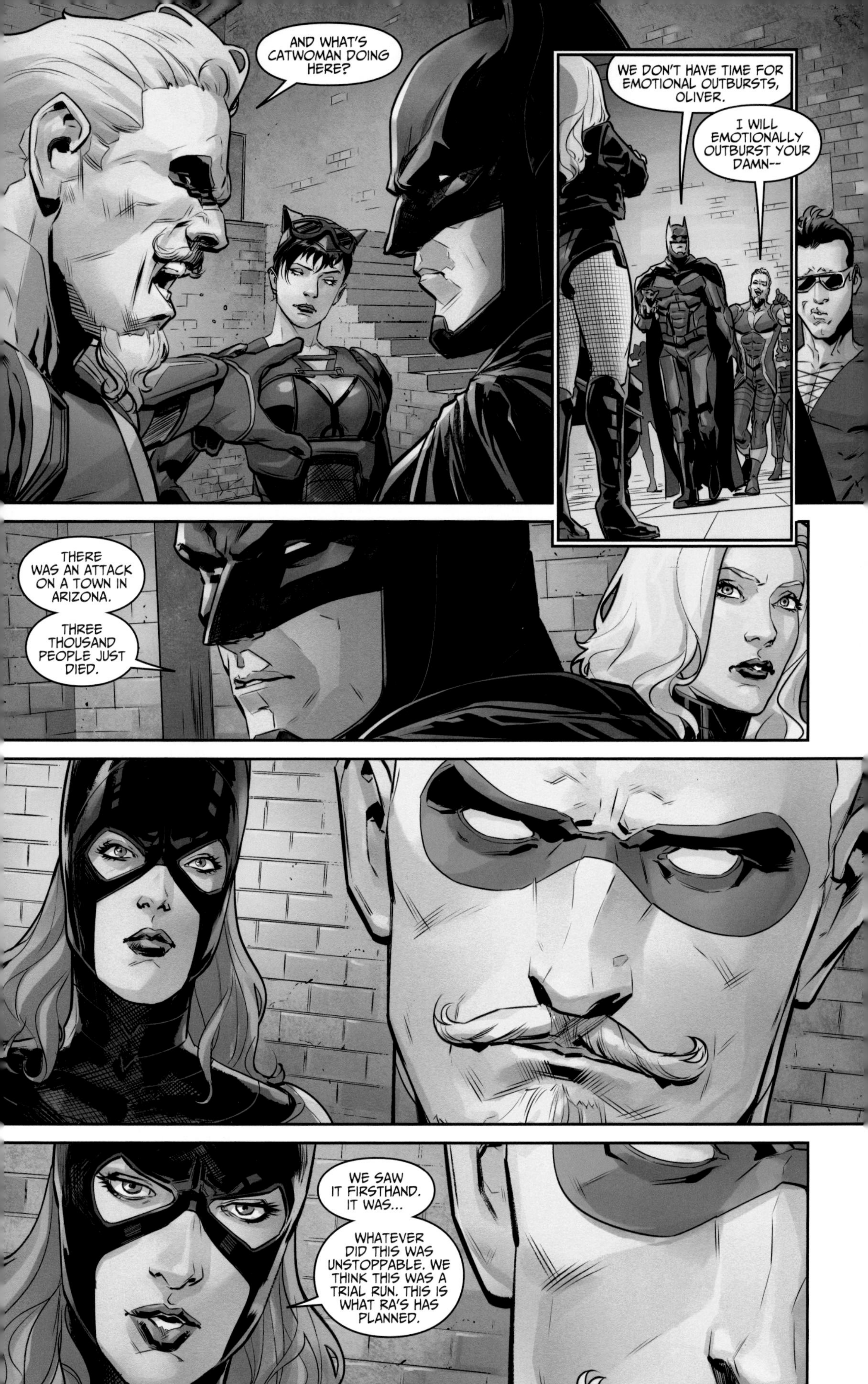
AND WHAT'S CATWOMAN DOING HERE?
WE DON'T HAVE TIME FOR EMOTIONAL OUTBURSTS, OLIVER.
I WILL EMOTIONALLY OUTBURST YOUR DAMN--
THERE WAS AN ATTACK ON A TOWN IN ARIZONA.
THREE THOUSAND PEOPLE JUST DIED.
WE SAW IT FIRSTHAND. IT WAS...
WHATEVER DID THIS WAS UNSTOPPABLE. WE THINK THIS WAS A TRIAL RUN. THIS IS WHAT RA'S HAS PLANNED.

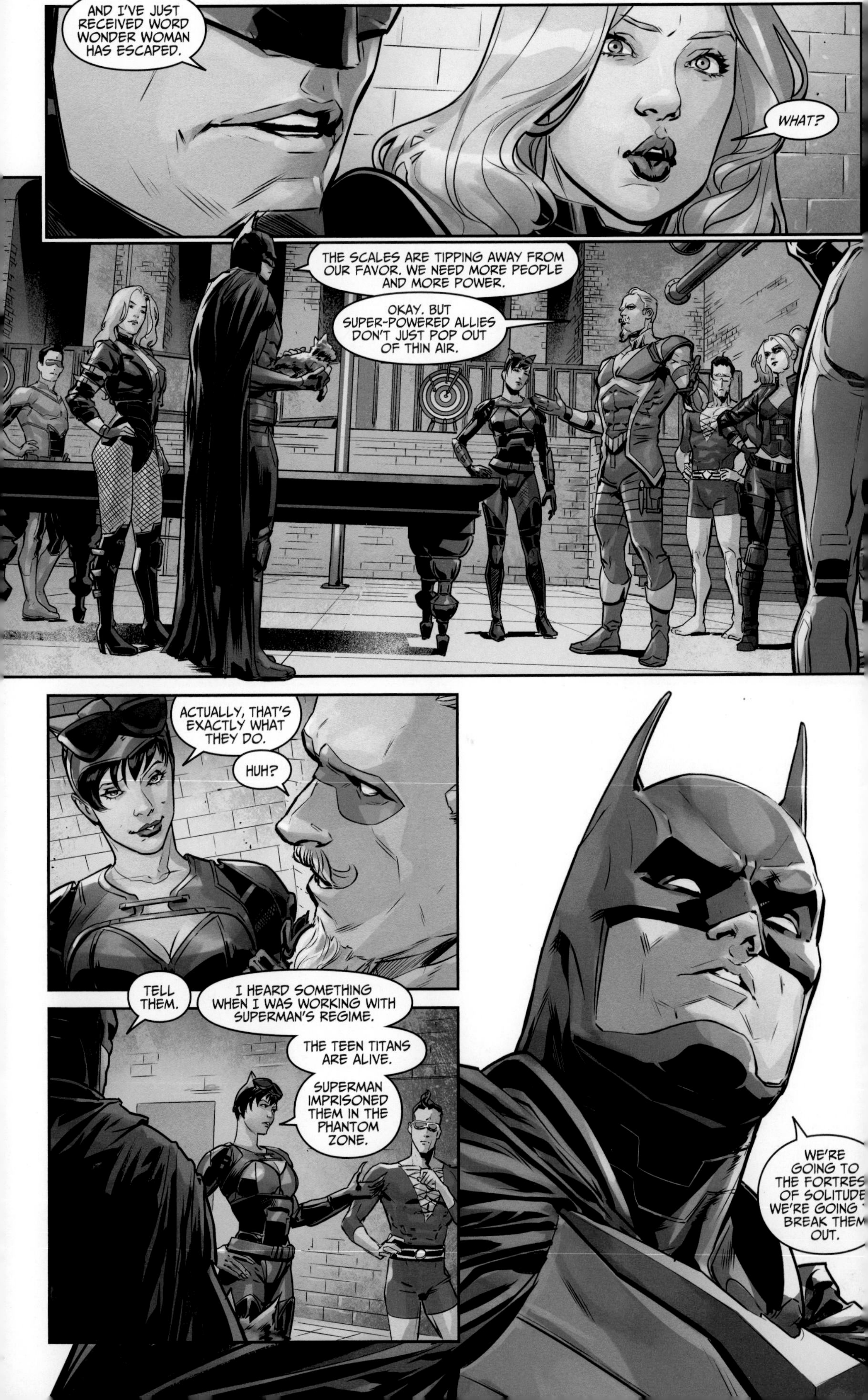
AND I'VE JUST RECEIVED WORD WONDER WOMAN HAS ESCAPED.
WHAT?
THE SCALES ARE TIPPING AWAY FROM OUR FAVOR. WE NEED MORE PEOPLE AND MORE POWER.
OKAY. BUT SUPER-POWERED ALLIES DON'T JUST POP OUT OF THIN AIR.
ACTUALLY, THAT'S EXACTLY WHAT THEY DO.
HUH?
TELL THEM.
I HEARD SOMETHING WHEN I WAS WORKING WITH SUPERMAN'S REGIME.
THE TEEN TITANS ARE ALIVE.
SUPERMAN IMPRISONED THEM IN THE PHANTOM ZONE.
WE'RE GOING TO THE FORTRES OF SOLITUDE WE'RE GOING BREAK THEM OUT.

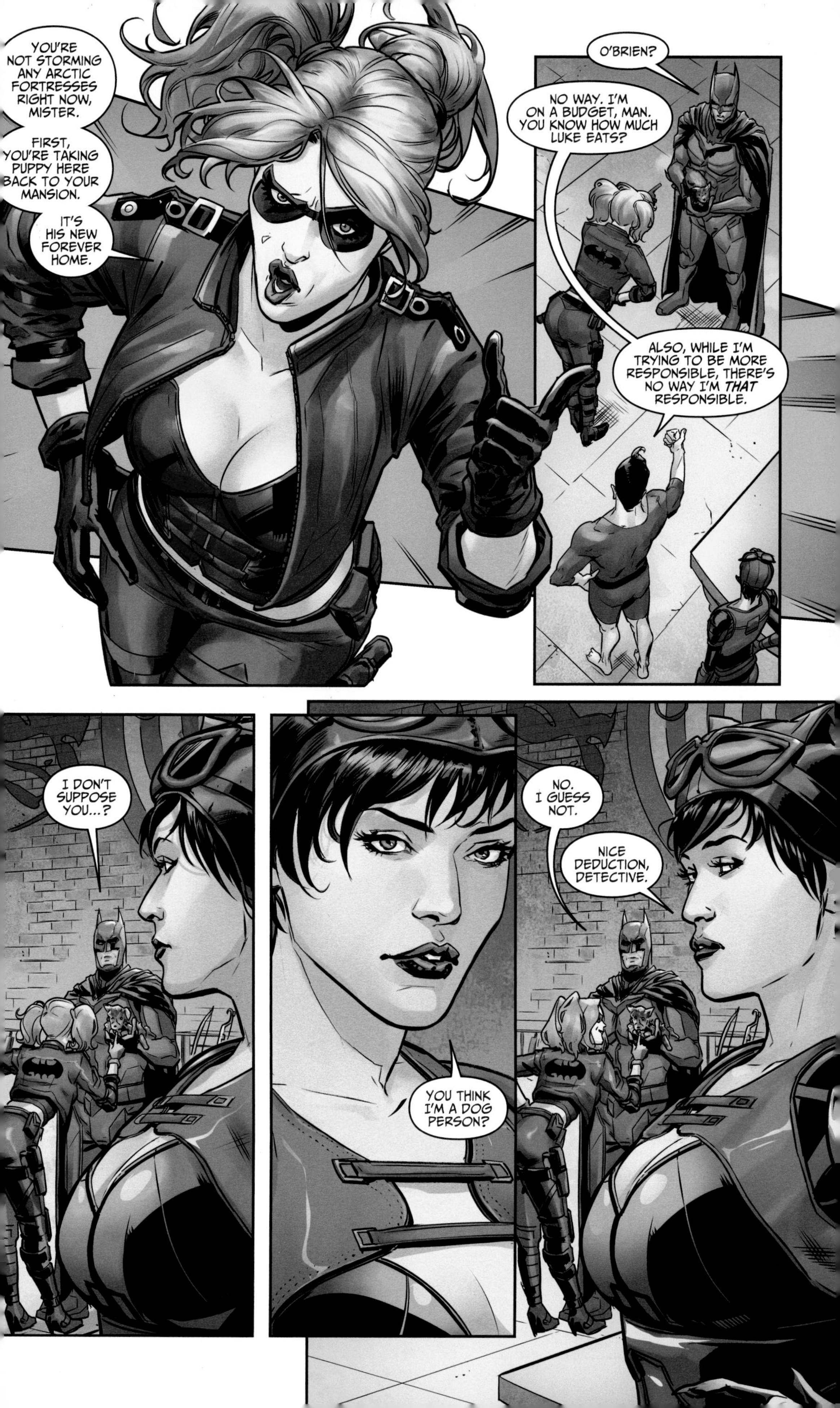

YOU'RE NOT STORMING ANY ARCTIC FORTRESSES RIGHT NOW, MISTER.
FIRST, YOU'RE TAKING PUPPY HERE BACK TO YOUR MANSION.
IT'S HIS NEW FOREVER HOME.
O'BRIEN?
NO WAY. I'M ON A BUDGET, MAN. YOU KNOW HOW MUCH LUKE EATS?
ALSO, WHILE I'M TRYING TO BE MORE RESPONSIBLE, THERE'S NO WAY I'M *THAT* RESPONSIBLE.
I DON'T SUPPOSE YOU...?
YOU THINK I'M A DOG PERSON?
NO. I GUESS NOT.
NICE DEDUCTION, DETECTIVE.

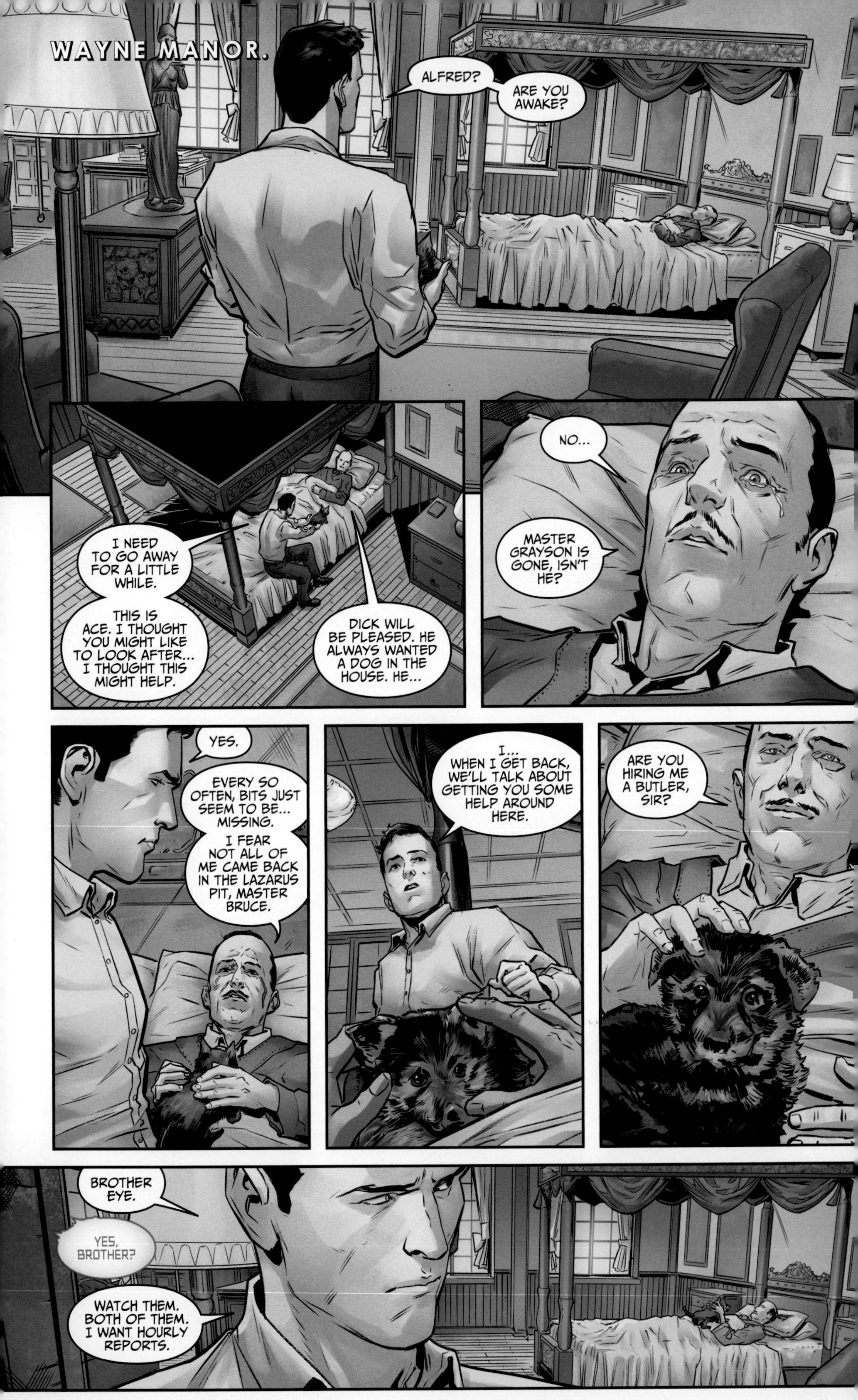
WAYNE MANOR.
ALFRED?
ARE YOU AWAKE?
I NEED TO GO AWAY FOR A LITTLE WHILE.
THIS IS ACE. I THOUGHT YOU MIGHT LIKE TO LOOK AFTER... I THOUGHT THIS MIGHT HELP.
DICK WILL BE PLEASED. HE ALWAYS WANTED A DOG IN THE HOUSE. HE...
NO...
MASTER GRAYSON IS GONE, ISN'T HE?
YES.
EVERY SO OFTEN, BITS JUST SEEM TO BE... MISSING.
I FEAR NOT ALL OF ME CAME BACK IN THE LAZARUS PIT, MASTER BRUCE.
I... WHEN I GET BACK, WE'LL TALK ABOUT GETTING YOU SOME HELP AROUND HERE.
ARE YOU HIRING ME A BUTLER, SIR?
BROTHER EYE.
YES, BROTHER?
WATCH THEM. BOTH OF THEM. I WANT HOURLY REPORTS.

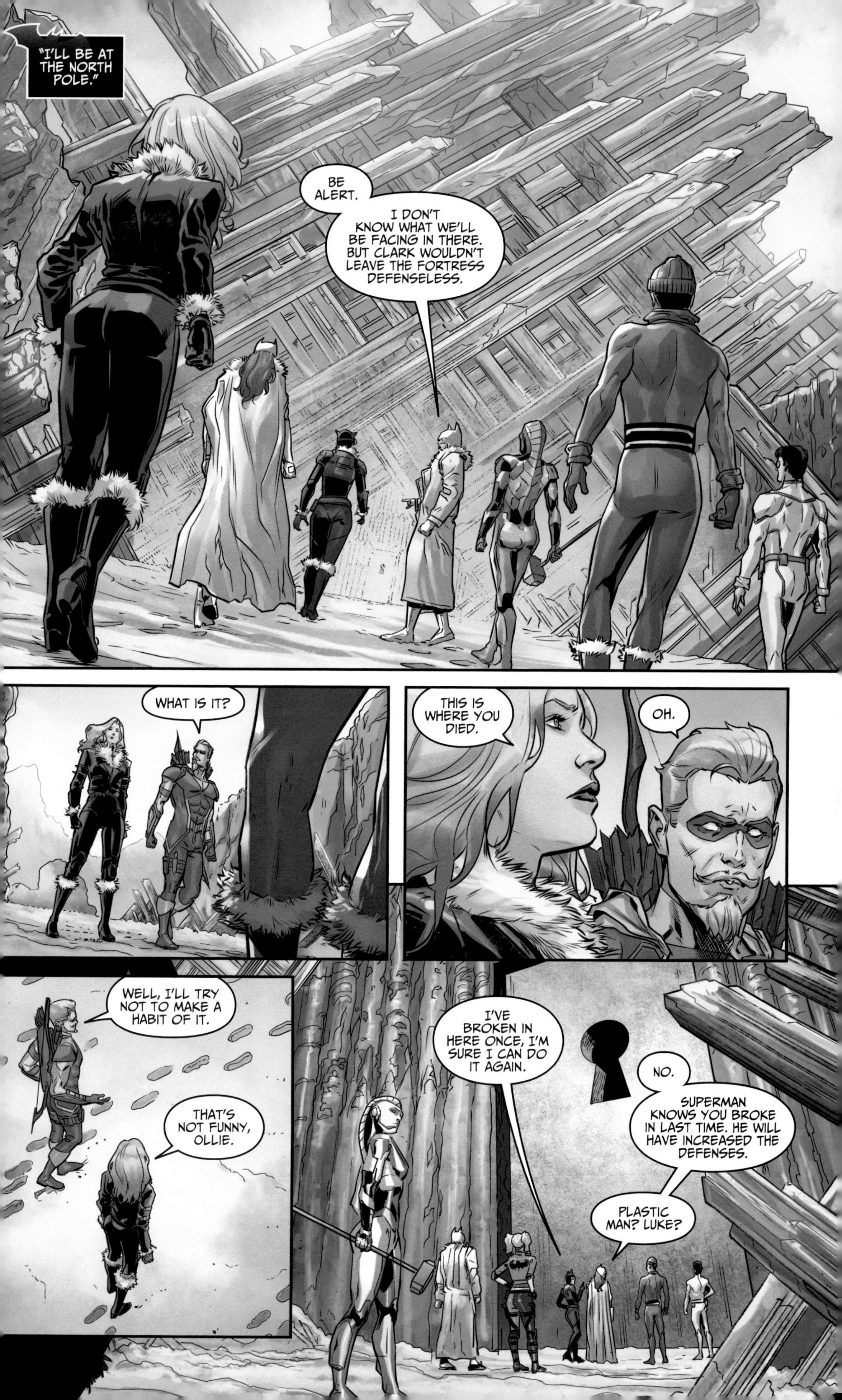
"I'LL BE AT THE NORTH POLE."
BE ALERT.
I DON'T KNOW WHAT WE'LL BE FACING IN THERE. BUT CLARK WOULDN'T LEAVE THE FORTRESS DEFENSELESS.
WHAT IS IT?
THIS IS WHERE YOU DIED.
OH.
WELL, I'LL TRY NOT TO MAKE A HABIT OF IT.
THAT'S NOT FUNNY, OLLIE.
I'VE BROKEN IN HERE ONCE, I'M SURE I CAN DO IT AGAIN.
NO.
SUPERMAN KNOWS YOU BROKE IN LAST TIME. HE WILL HAVE INCREASED THE DEFENSES.
PLASTIC MAN? LUKE?

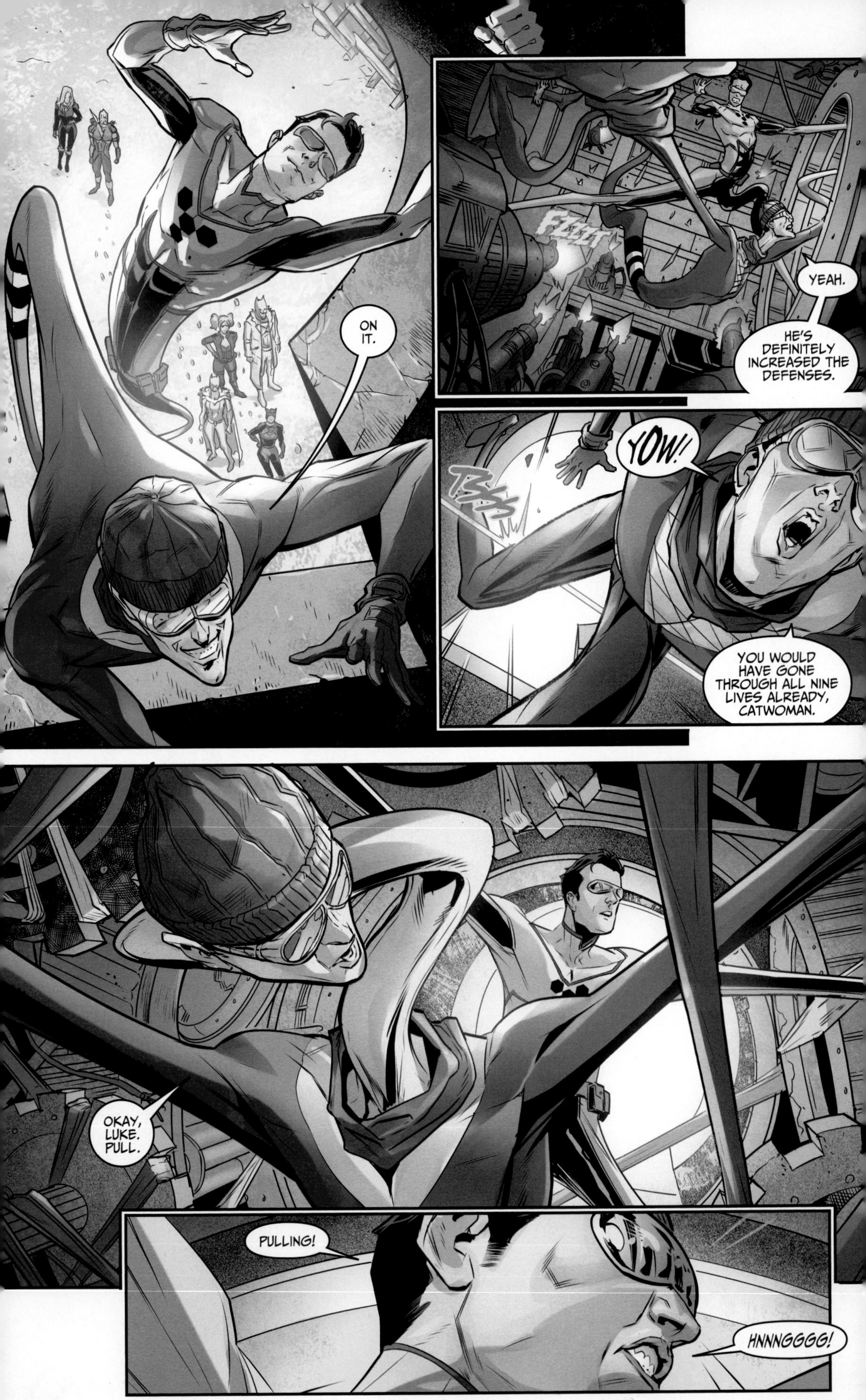
ON IT.
FZZZT
YEAH.
HE'S DEFINITELY INCREASED THE DEFENSES.
TSSS
YOW!
YOU WOULD HAVE GONE THROUGH ALL NINE LIVES ALREADY, CATWOMAN.
OKAY, LUKE. PULL.
PULLING!
HNNNGGGG!

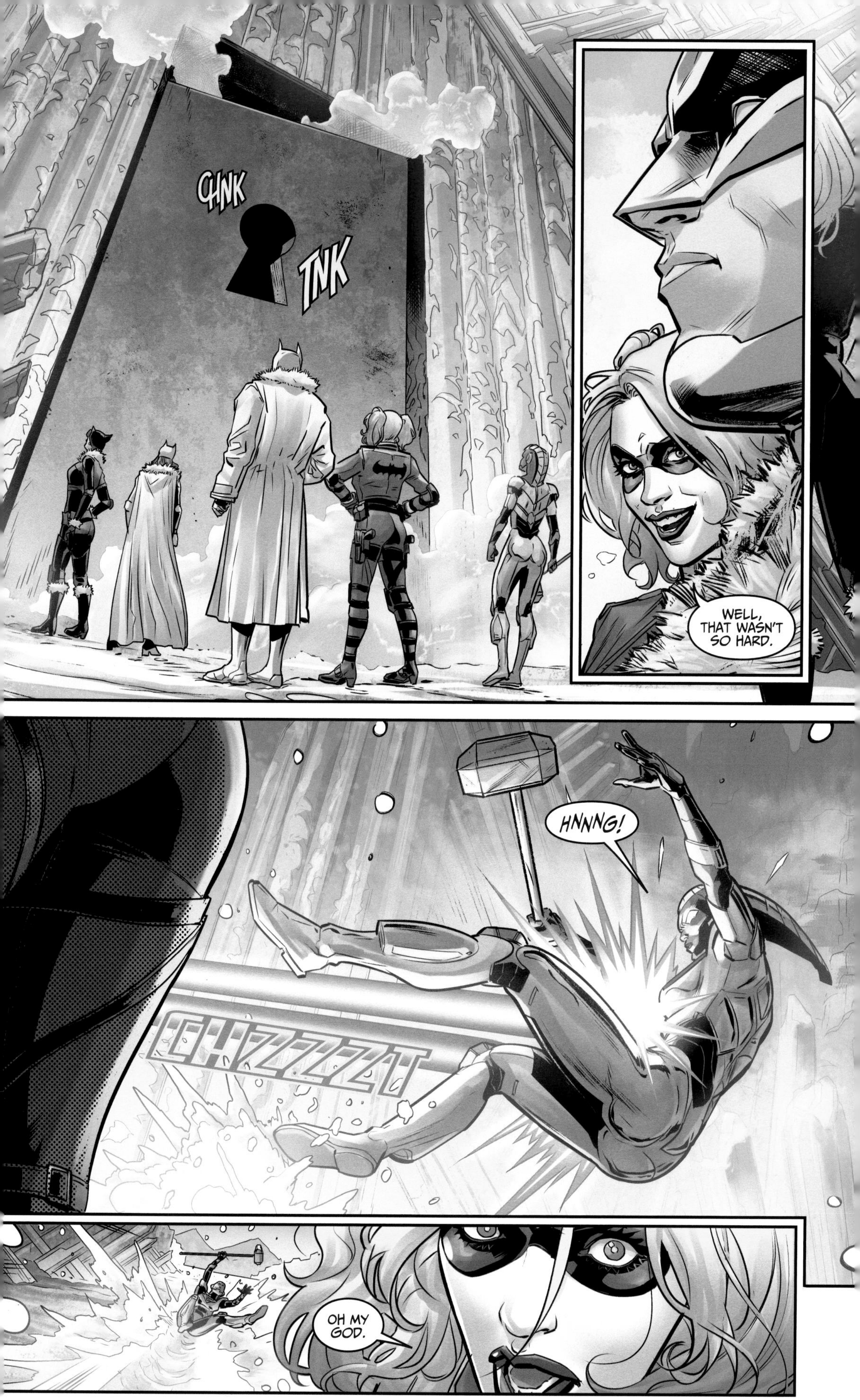
CHNK
TNK
WELL, THAT WASN'T SO HARD.
HNNNG!
CHZZZZT
OH MY GOD.

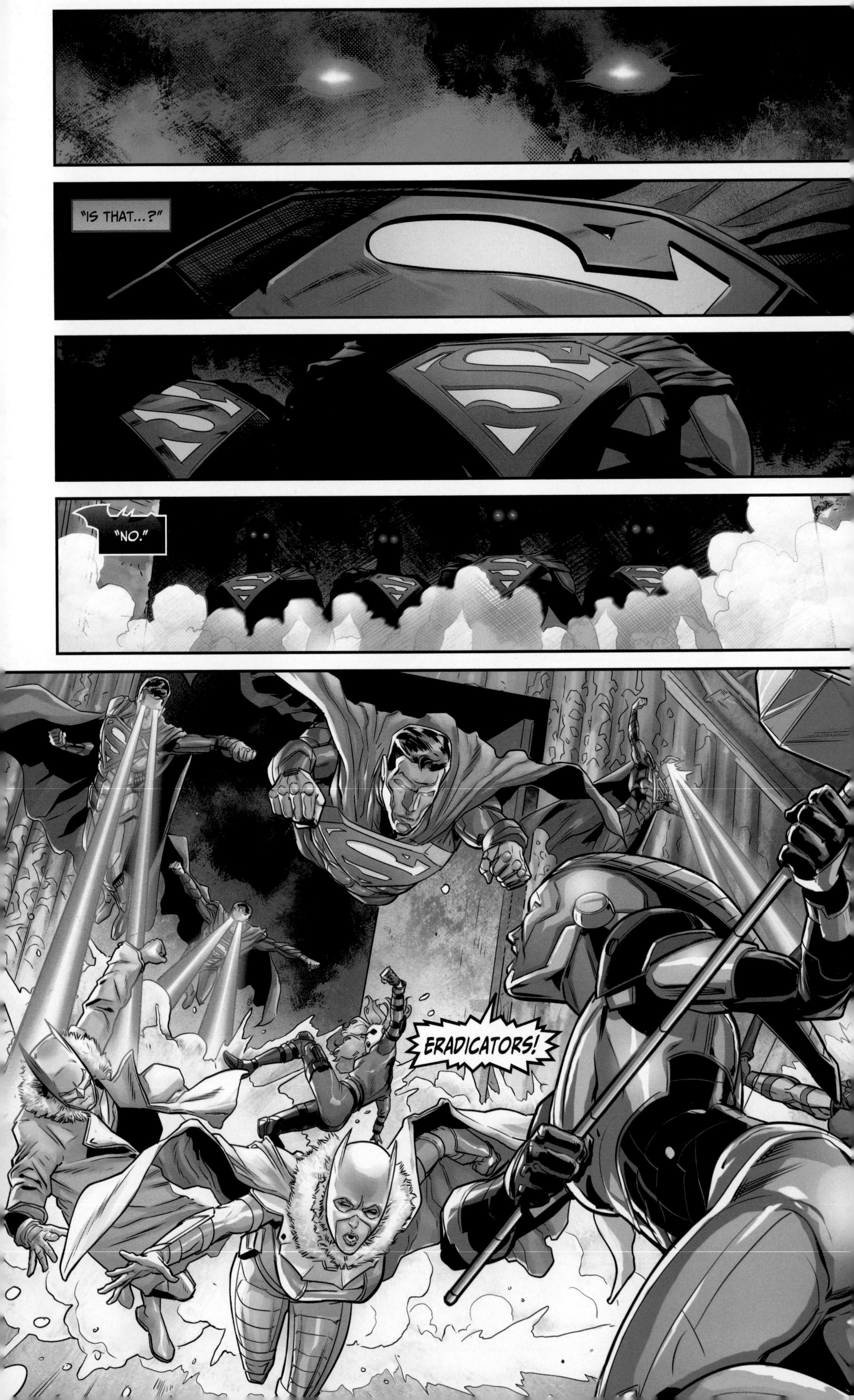
"IS THAT...?"
"NO."
ERADICATORS!

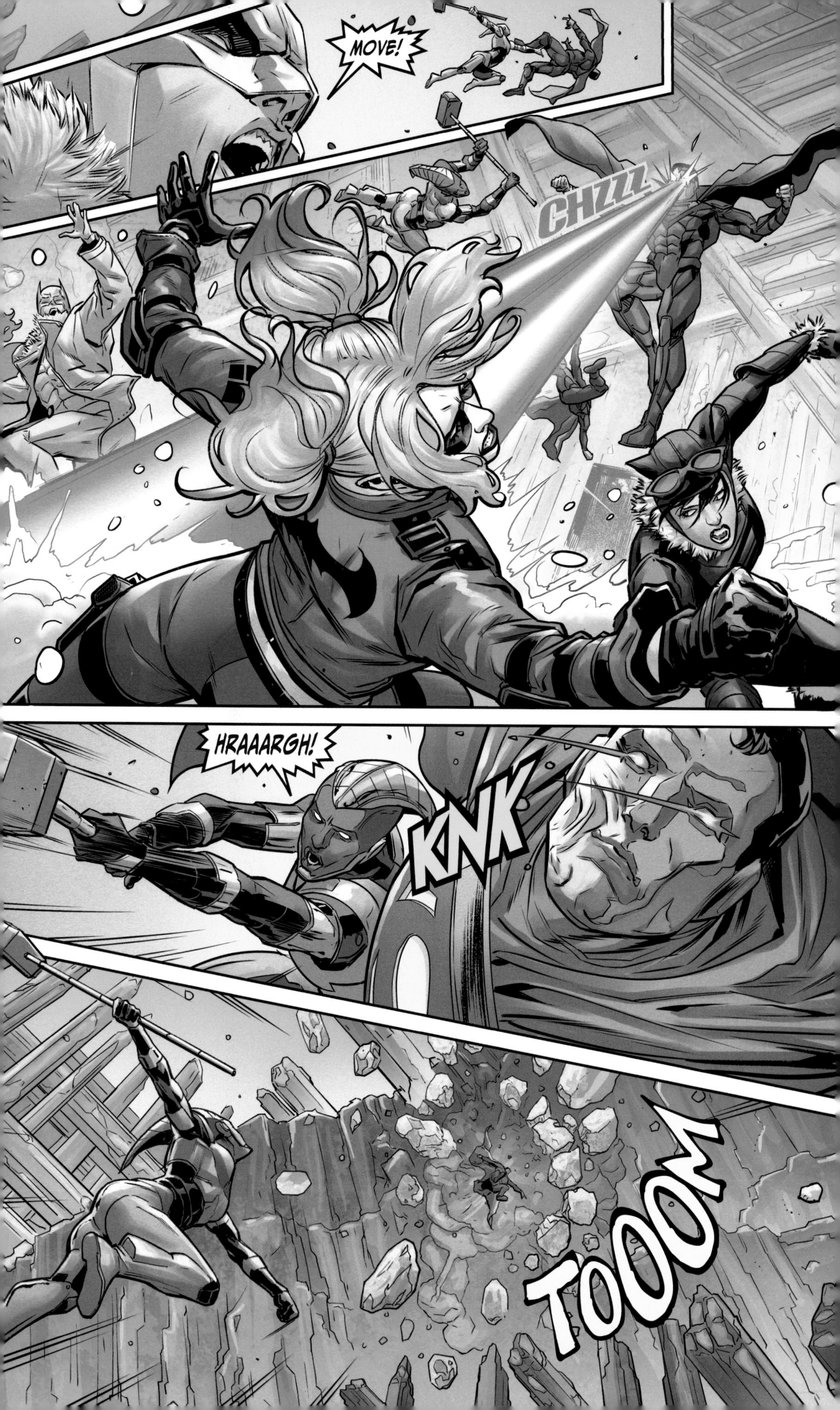
MOVE!
CHZZZ
HRAAARGH!
KNK
TOOOM

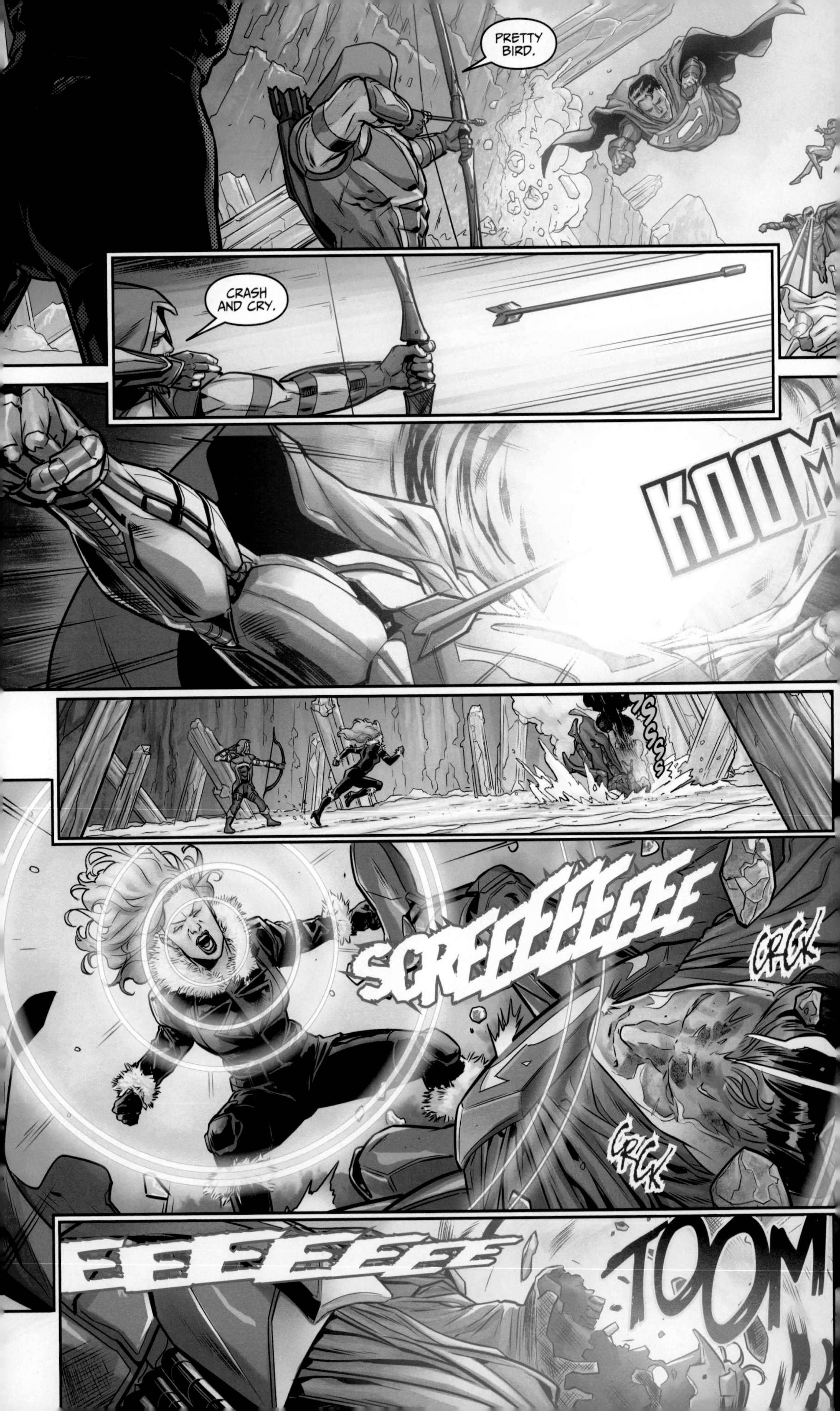
PRETTY BIRD.
CRASH AND CRY.
KOOM
SCREEEEEEEE
CRCK
CRCK
EEEEEEEE
TOOM

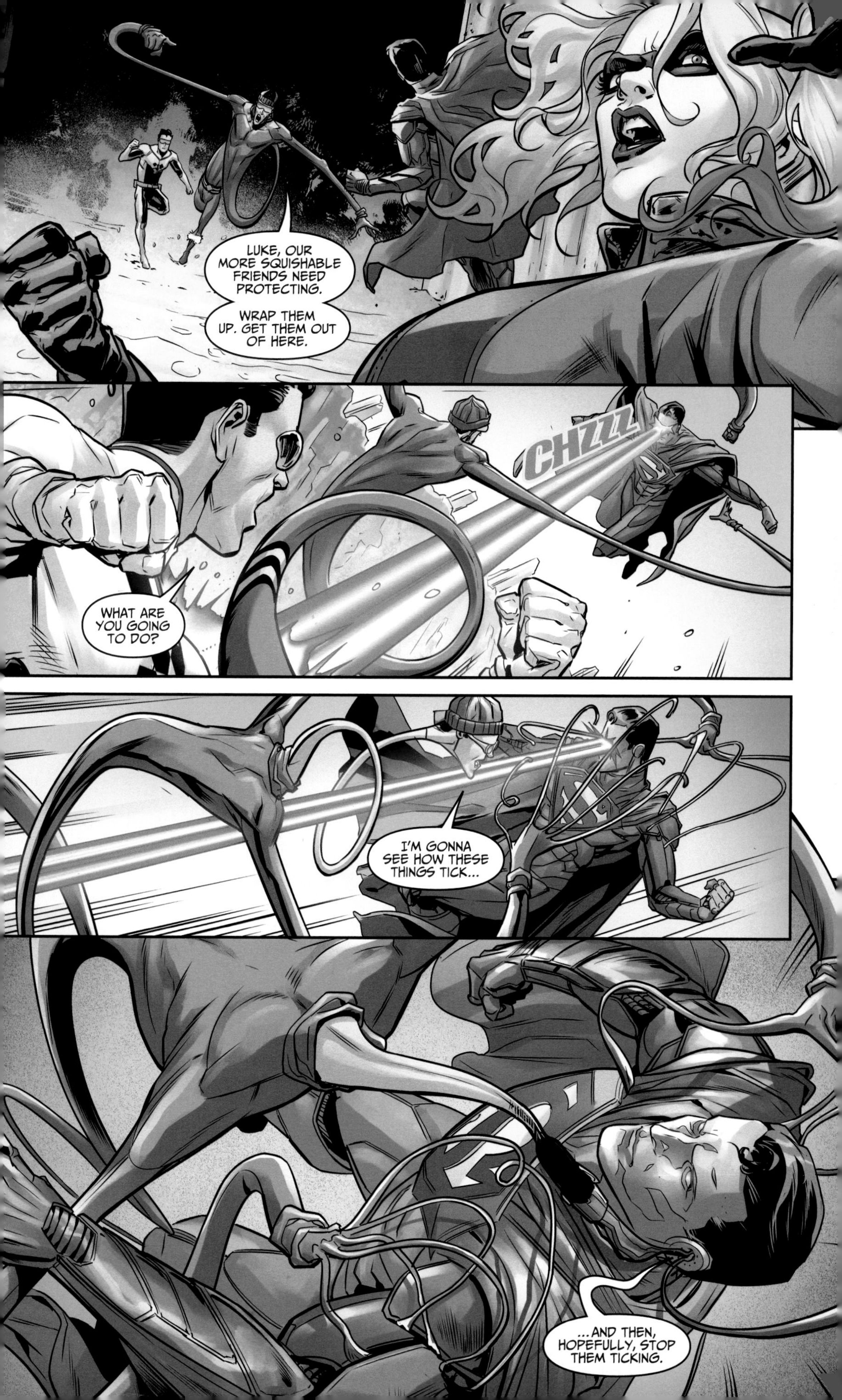
LUKE, OUR MORE SQUISHABLE FRIENDS NEED PROTECTING.
WRAP THEM UP. GET THEM OUT OF HERE.
CHZZZ
WHAT ARE YOU GOING TO DO?
I'M GONNA SEE HOW THESE THINGS TICK...
...AND THEN, HOPEFULLY, STOP THEM TICKING.

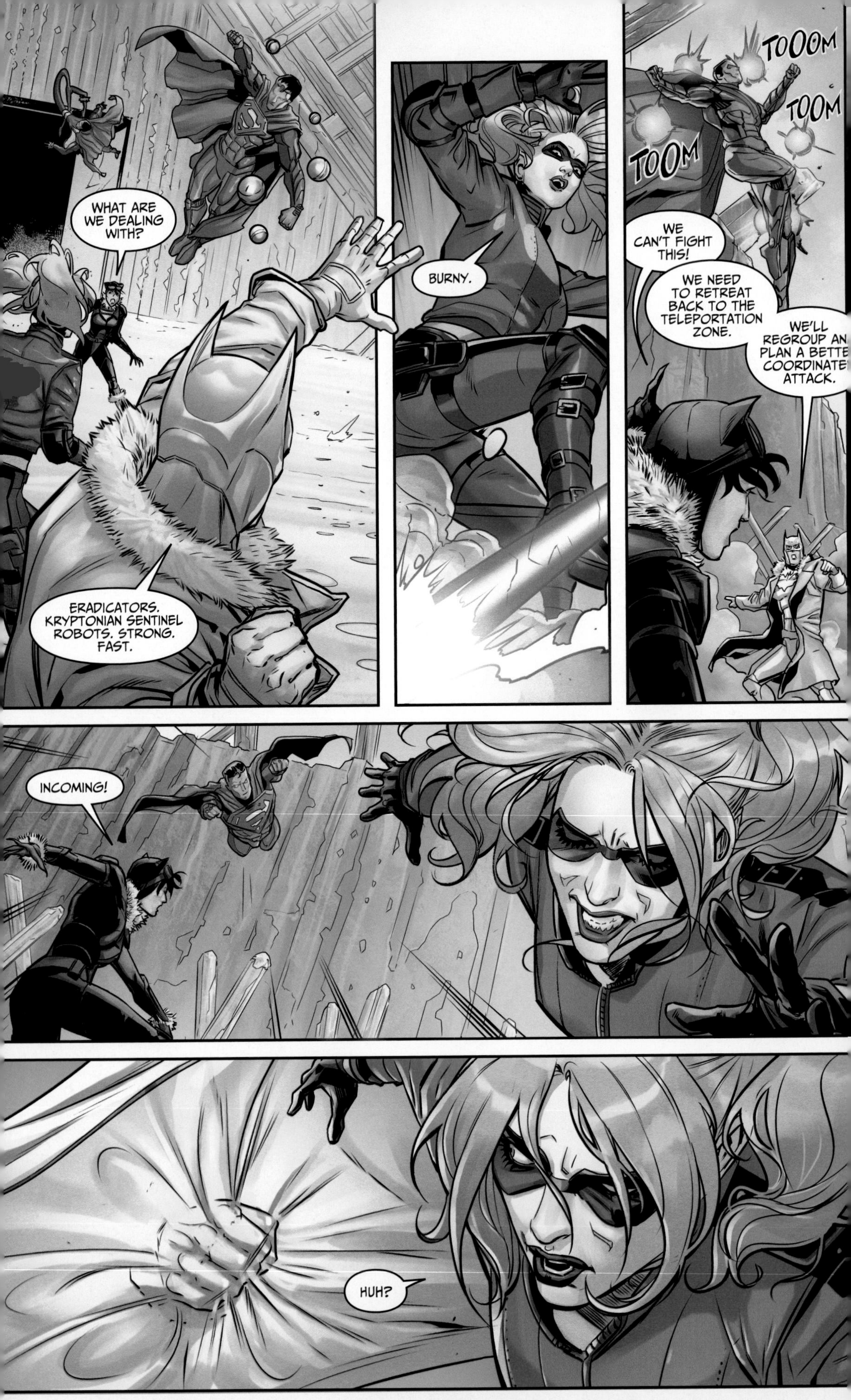
WHAT ARE WE DEALING WITH?
ERADICATORS. KRYPTONIAN SENTINEL ROBOTS. STRONG. FAST.
BURNY.
TOOOM
TOOM
TOOM
WE CAN'T FIGHT THIS!
WE NEED TO RETREAT BACK TO THE TELEPORTATION ZONE.
WE'LL REGROUP AN PLAN A BETTE COORDINATE ATTACK.
INCOMING!
HUH?

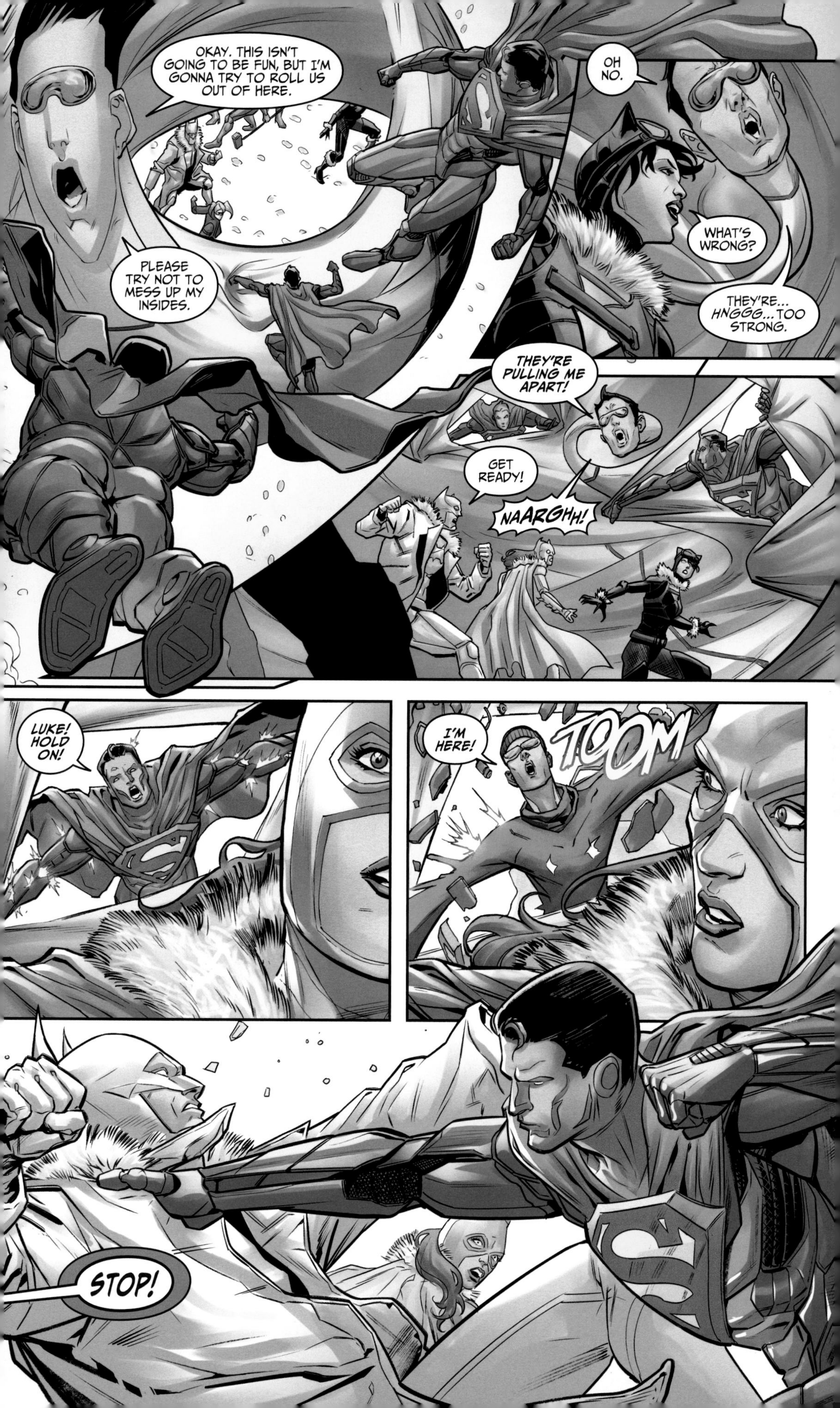
OKAY. THIS ISN'T GOING TO BE FUN, BUT I'M GONNA TRY TO ROLL US OUT OF HERE.
PLEASE TRY NOT TO MESS UP MY INSIDES.
OH NO.
WHAT'S WRONG?
THEY'RE... HNGGG...TOO STRONG.
THEY'RE PULLING ME APART!
GET READY!
NAARGHH!
LUKE! HOLD ON!
I'M HERE!
TOOM
STOP!

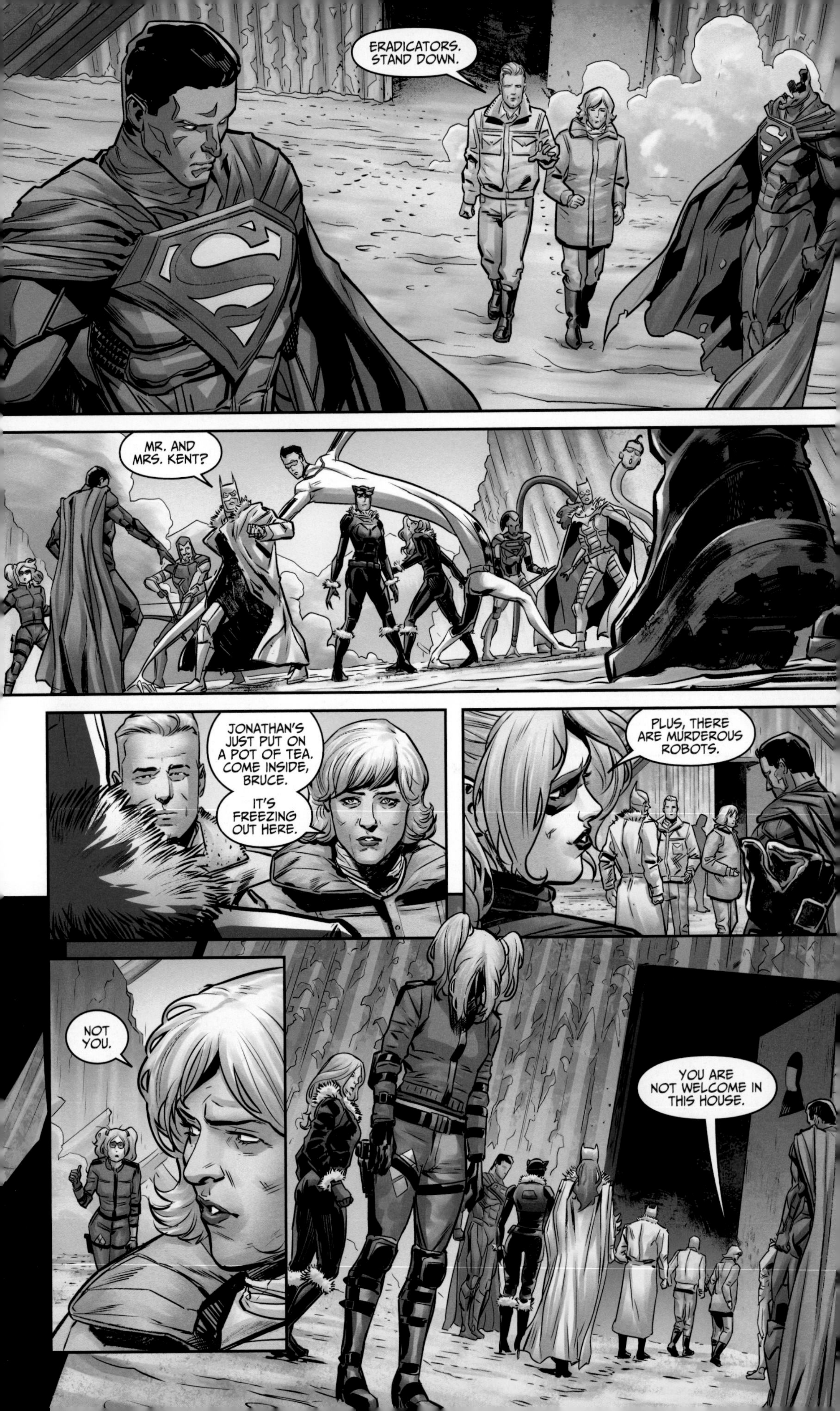
ERADICATORS. STAND DOWN.
MR. AND MRS. KENT?
JONATHAN'S JUST PUT ON A POT OF TEA. COME INSIDE, BRUCE.
IT'S FREEZING OUT HERE.
PLUS, THERE ARE MURDEROUS ROBOTS.
NOT YOU.
YOU ARE NOT WELCOME IN THIS HOUSE.

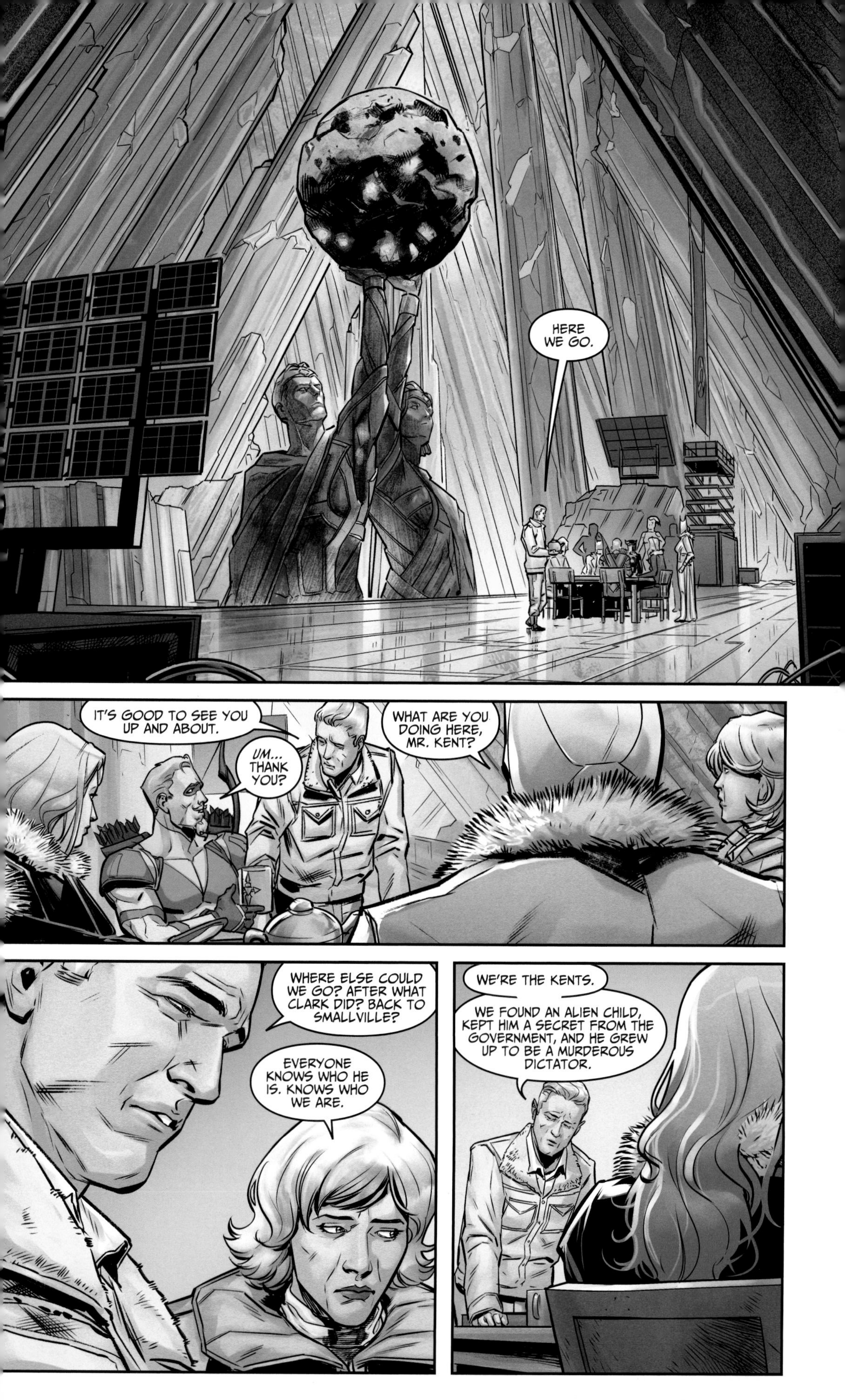
HERE WE GO.
IT'S GOOD TO SEE YOU UP AND ABOUT.
UM... THANK YOU?
WHAT ARE YOU DOING HERE, MR. KENT?
WHERE ELSE COULD WE GO? AFTER WHAT CLARK DID? BACK TO SMALLVILLE?
EVERYONE KNOWS WHO HE IS. KNOWS WHO WE ARE.
WE'RE THE KENTS.
WE FOUND AN ALIEN CHILD, KEPT HIM A SECRET FROM THE GOVERNMENT, AND HE GREW UP TO BE A MURDEROUS DICTATOR.

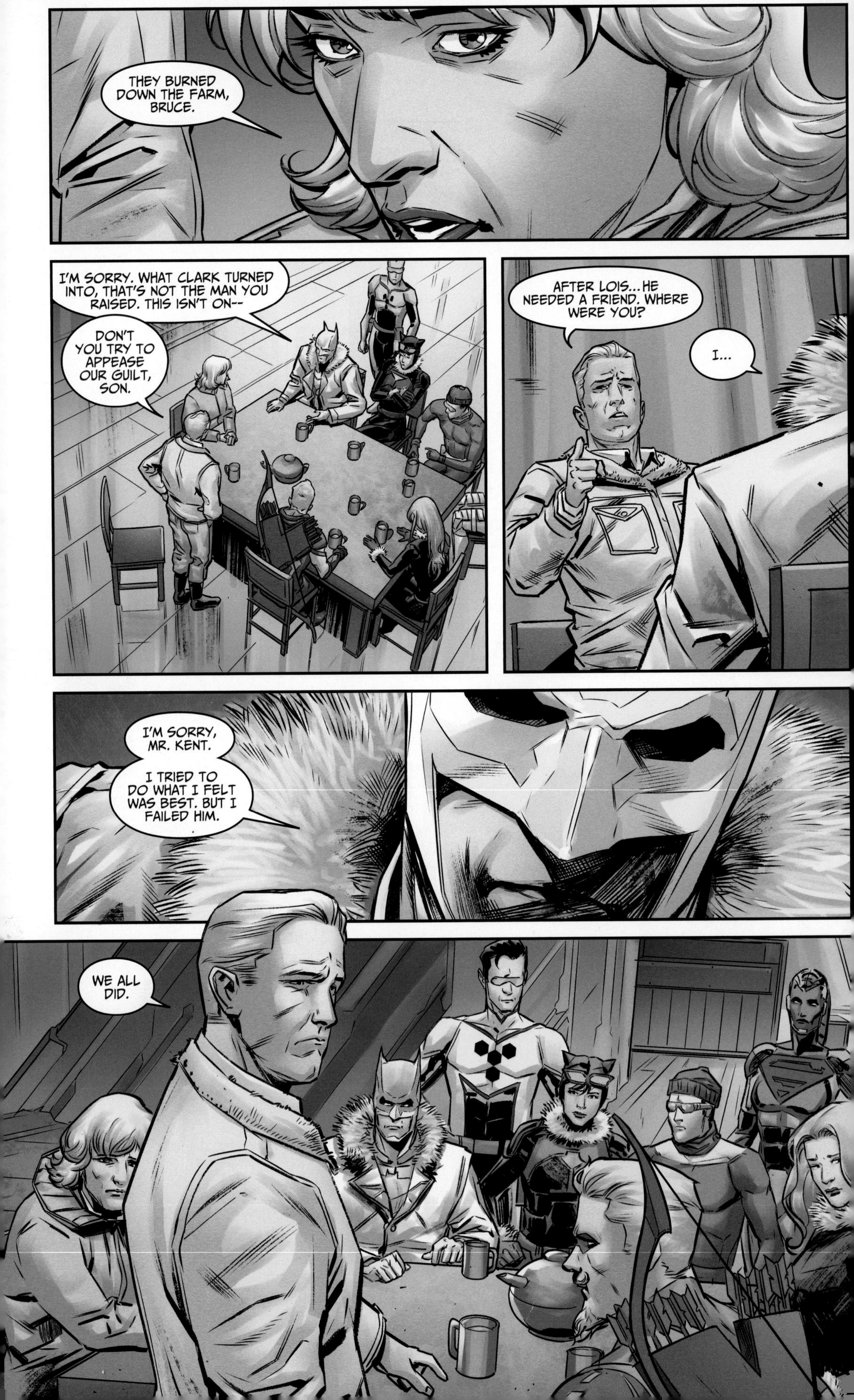
THEY BURNED DOWN THE FARM, BRUCE.
I'M SORRY. WHAT CLARK TURNED INTO, THAT'S NOT THE MAN YOU RAISED. THIS ISN'T ON--
DON'T YOU TRY TO APPEASE OUR GUILT, SON.
AFTER LOIS... HE NEEDED A FRIEND. WHERE WERE YOU?
I...
I'M SORRY, MR. KENT.
I TRIED TO DO WHAT I FELT WAS BEST. BUT I FAILED HIM.
WE ALL DID.

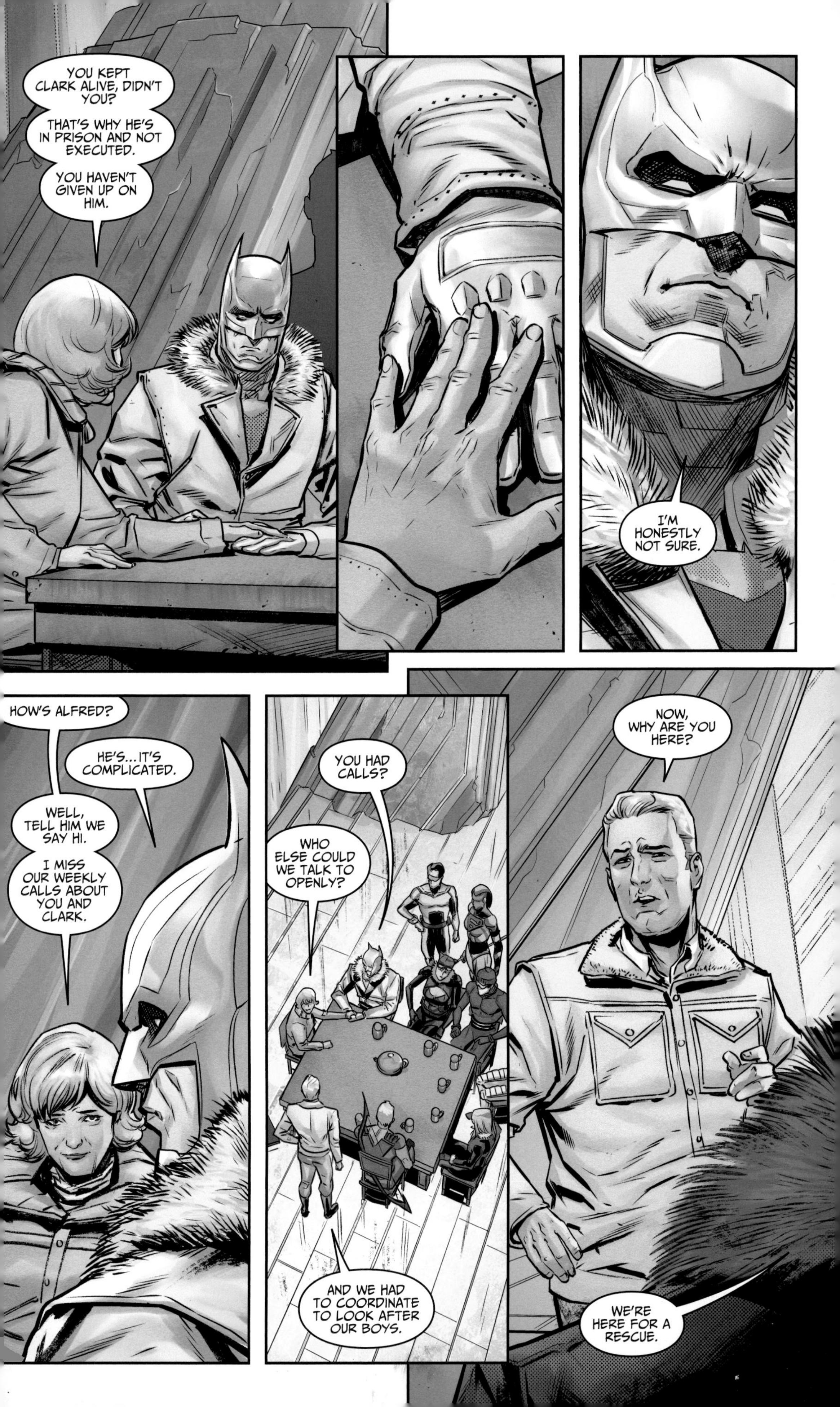
YOU KEPT CLARK ALIVE, DIDN'T YOU?
THAT'S WHY HE'S IN PRISON AND NOT EXECUTED.
YOU HAVEN'T GIVEN UP ON HIM.
I'M HONESTLY NOT SURE.
HOW'S ALFRED?
HE'S...IT'S COMPLICATED.
WELL, TELL HIM WE SAY HI.
I MISS OUR WEEKLY CALLS ABOUT YOU AND CLARK.
YOU HAD CALLS?
WHO ELSE COULD WE TALK TO OPENLY?
AND WE HAD TO COORDINATE TO LOOK AFTER OUR BOYS.
NOW, WHY ARE YOU HERE?
WE'RE HERE FOR A RESCUE.

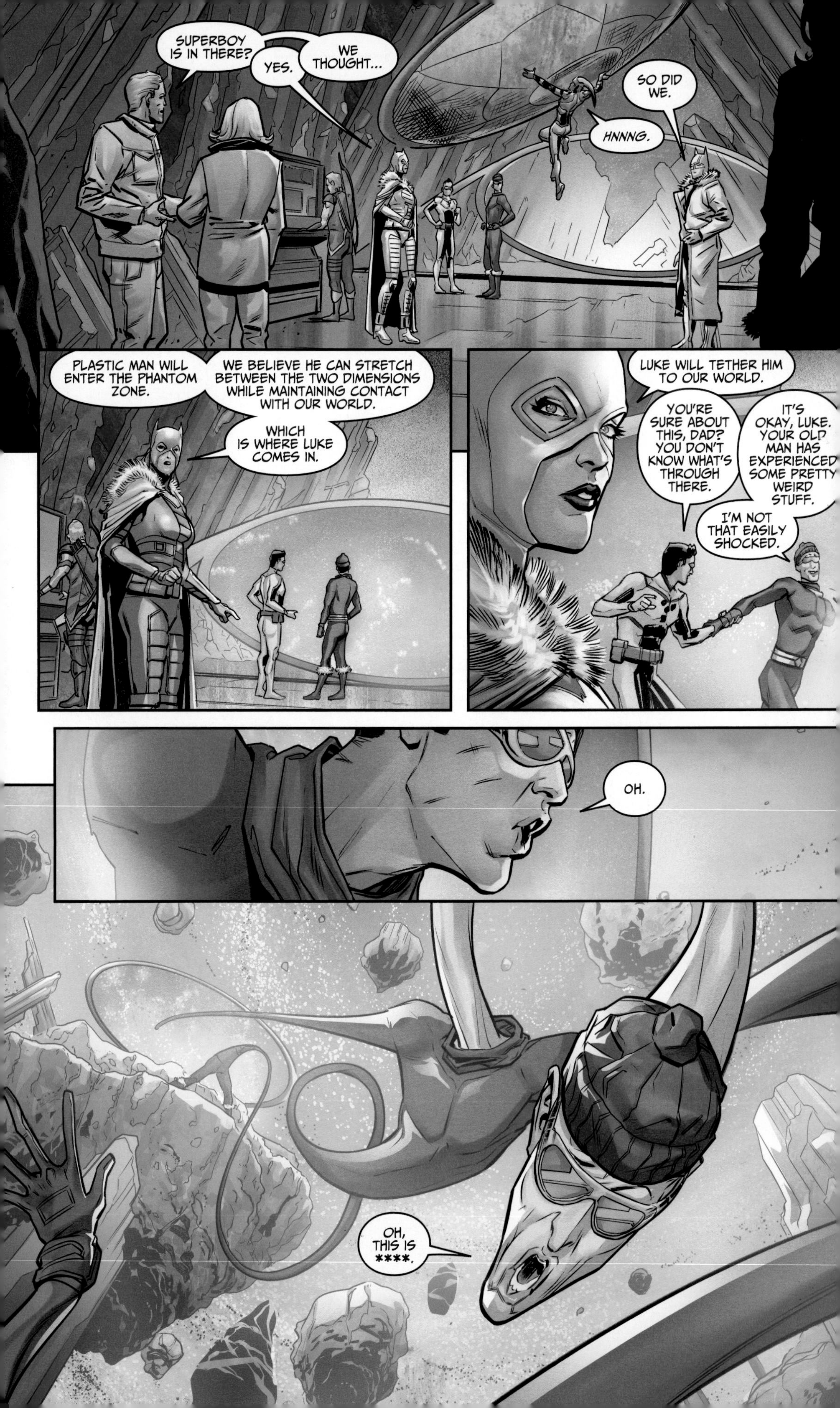
SUPERBOY IS IN THERE?
YES.
WE THOUGHT...
SO DID WE.
HNNNG.
PLASTIC MAN WILL ENTER THE PHANTOM ZONE.
WE BELIEVE HE CAN STRETCH BETWEEN THE TWO DIMENSIONS WHILE MAINTAINING CONTACT WITH OUR WORLD.
WHICH IS WHERE LUKE COMES IN.
LUKE WILL TETHER HIM TO OUR WORLD.
YOU'RE SURE ABOUT THIS, DAD? YOU DON'T KNOW WHAT'S THROUGH THERE.
IT'S OKAY, LUKE. YOUR OLD MAN HAS EXPERIENCED SOME PRETTY WEIRD STUFF.
I'M NOT THAT EASILY SHOCKED.
OH.
OH, THIS IS ****.

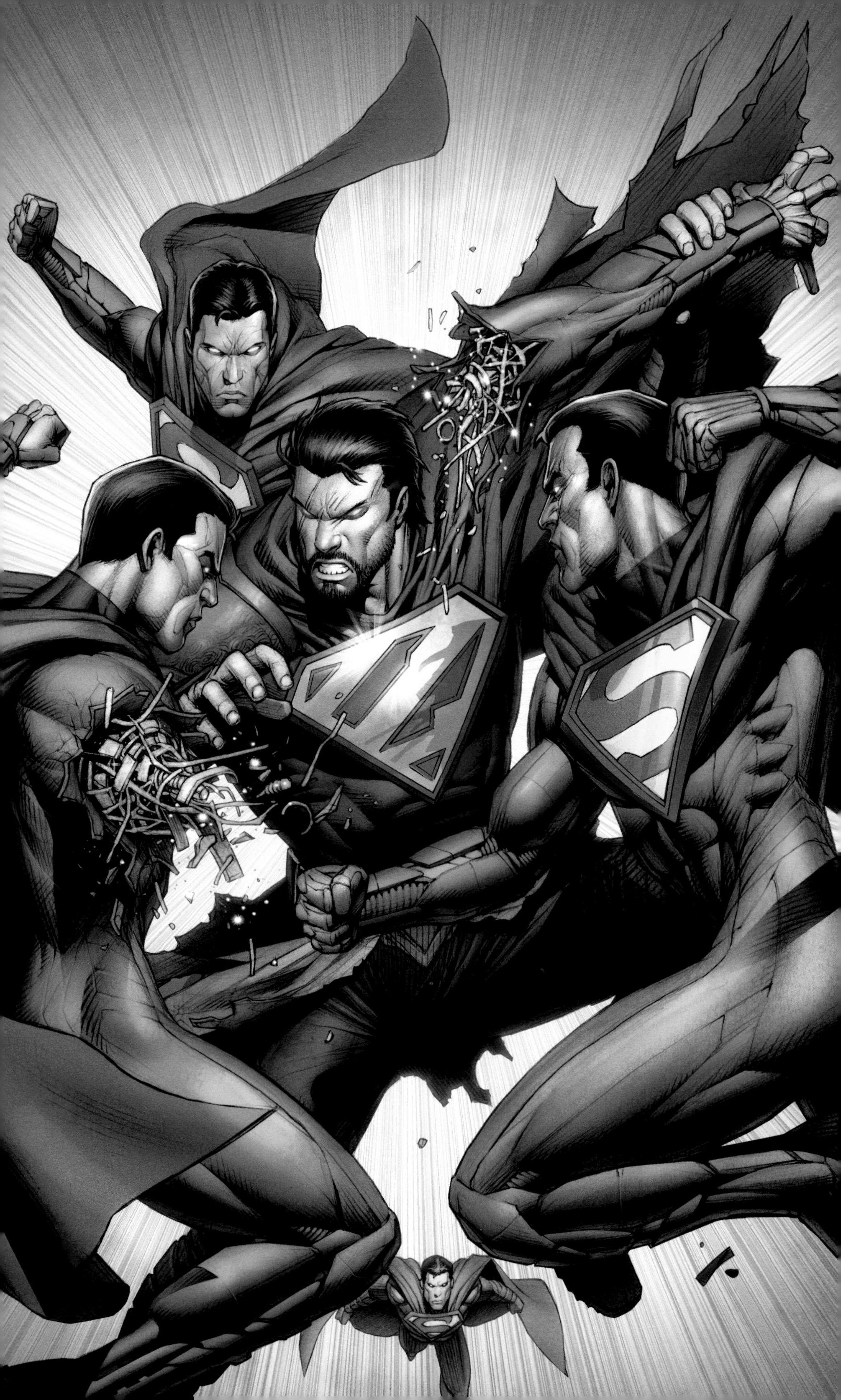

"Zod Unleashed"

Tom Taylor Writer **Daniel Sampere** Artist **Rex Lokus** Colorist **Wes Abbott** Letterer

Cover art by **Dale Keown**

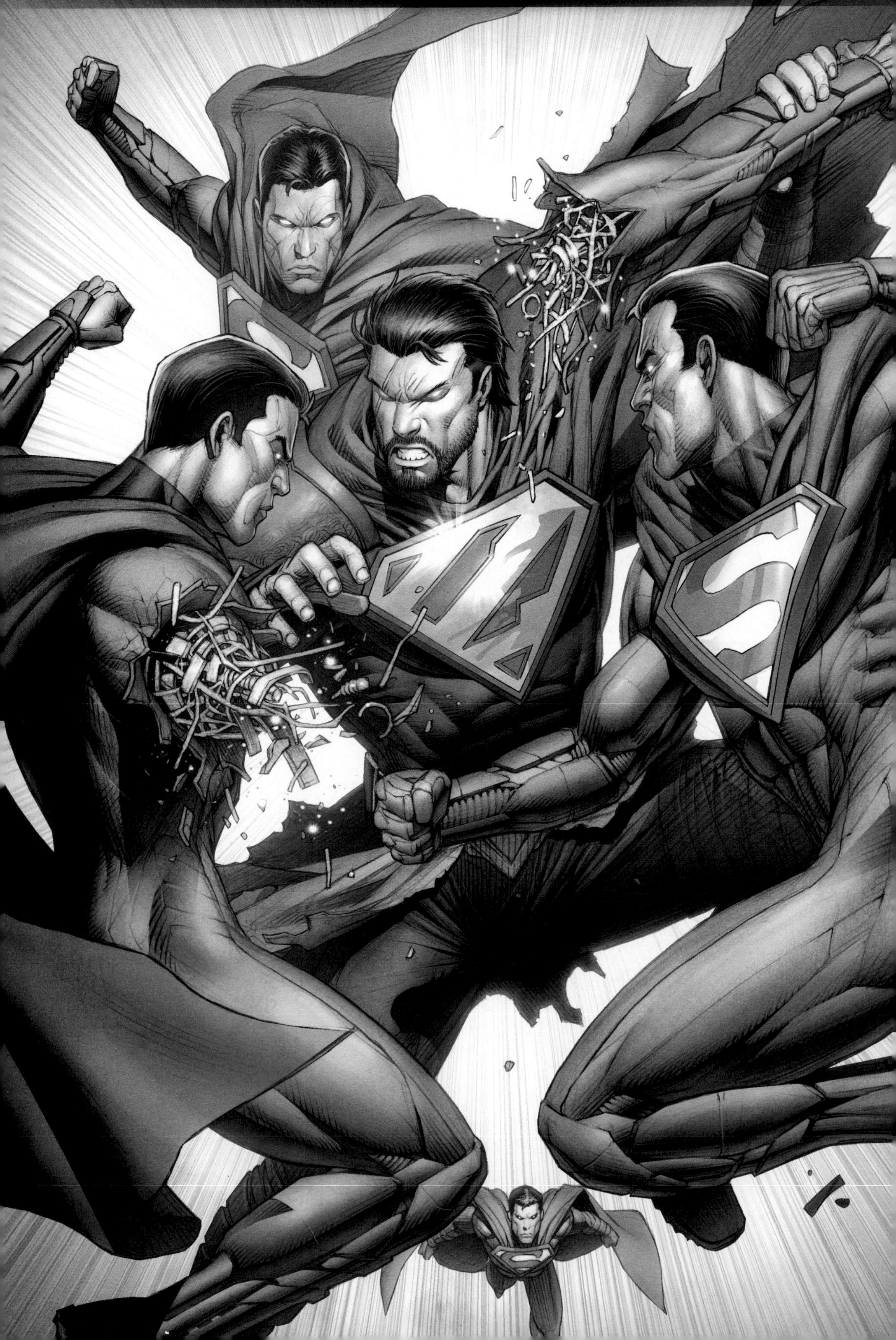

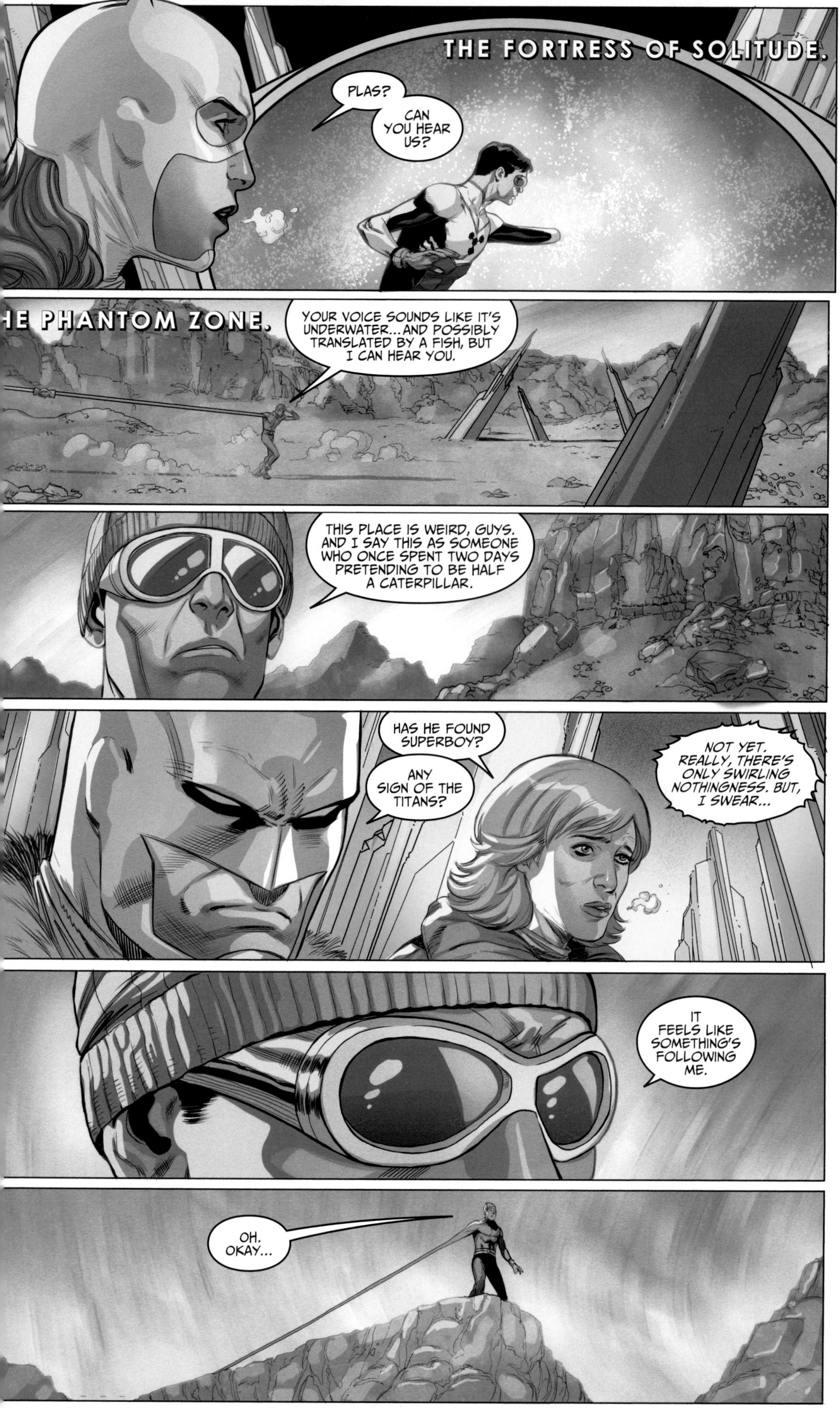
THE FORTRESS OF SOLITUDE.
PLAS?
CAN YOU HEAR US?
HE PHANTOM ZONE.
YOUR VOICE SOUNDS LIKE IT'S UNDERWATER...AND POSSIBLY TRANSLATED BY A FISH, BUT I CAN HEAR YOU.
THIS PLACE IS WEIRD, GUYS. AND I SAY THIS AS SOMEONE WHO ONCE SPENT TWO DAYS PRETENDING TO BE HALF A CATERPILLAR.
HAS HE FOUND SUPERBOY?
ANY SIGN OF THE TITANS?
NOT YET. REALLY, THERE'S ONLY SWIRLING NOTHINGNESS. BUT, I SWEAR...
IT FEELS LIKE SOMETHING'S FOLLOWING ME.
OH. OKAY...

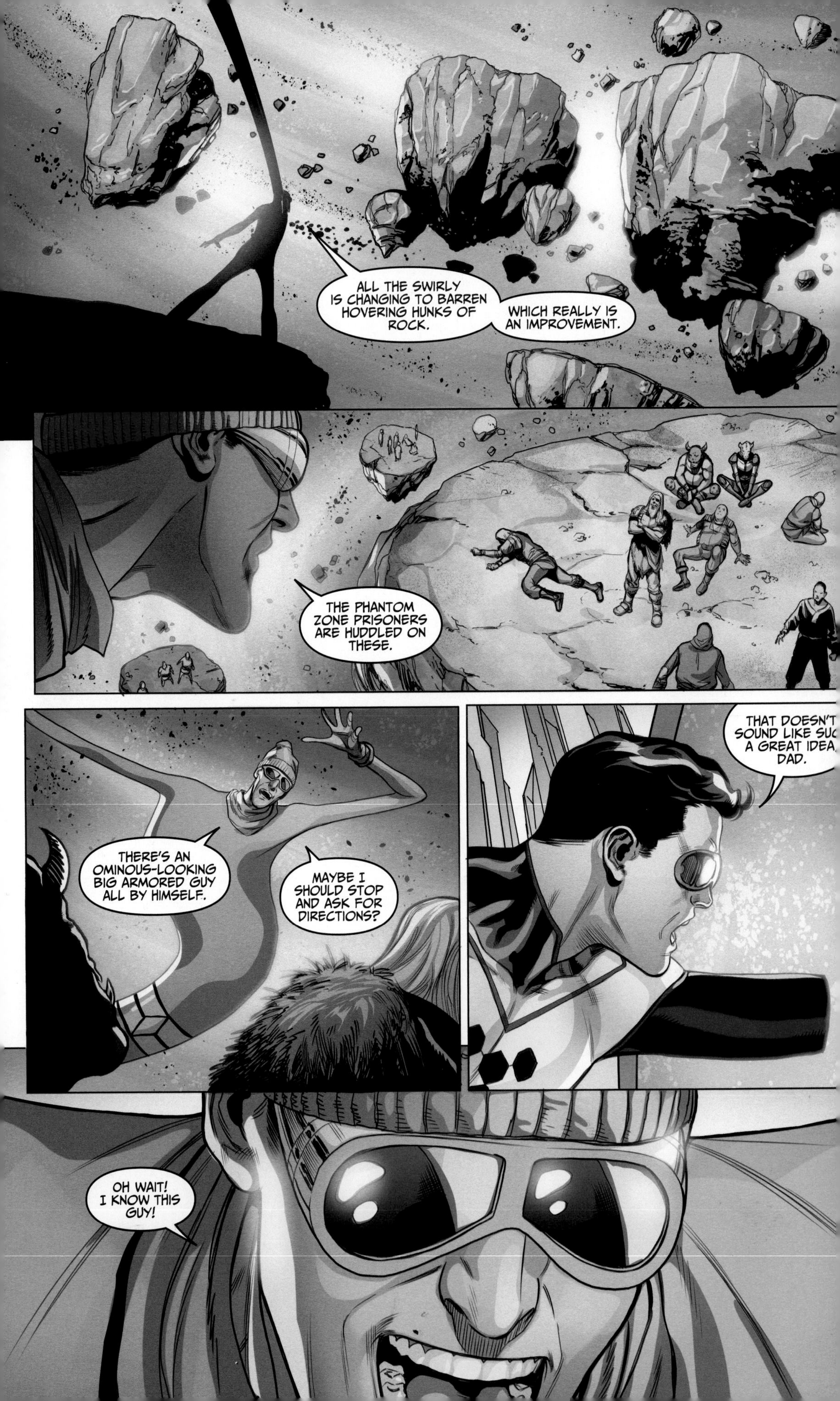
ALL THE SWIRLY IS CHANGING TO BARREN HOVERING HUNKS OF ROCK.
WHICH REALLY IS AN IMPROVEMENT.
THE PHANTOM ZONE PRISONERS ARE HUDDLED ON THESE.
THERE'S AN OMINOUS-LOOKING BIG ARMORED GUY ALL BY HIMSELF.
MAYBE I SHOULD STOP AND ASK FOR DIRECTIONS?
THAT DOESN'T SOUND LIKE SUC A GREAT IDEA DAD.
OH WAIT! I KNOW THIS GUY!

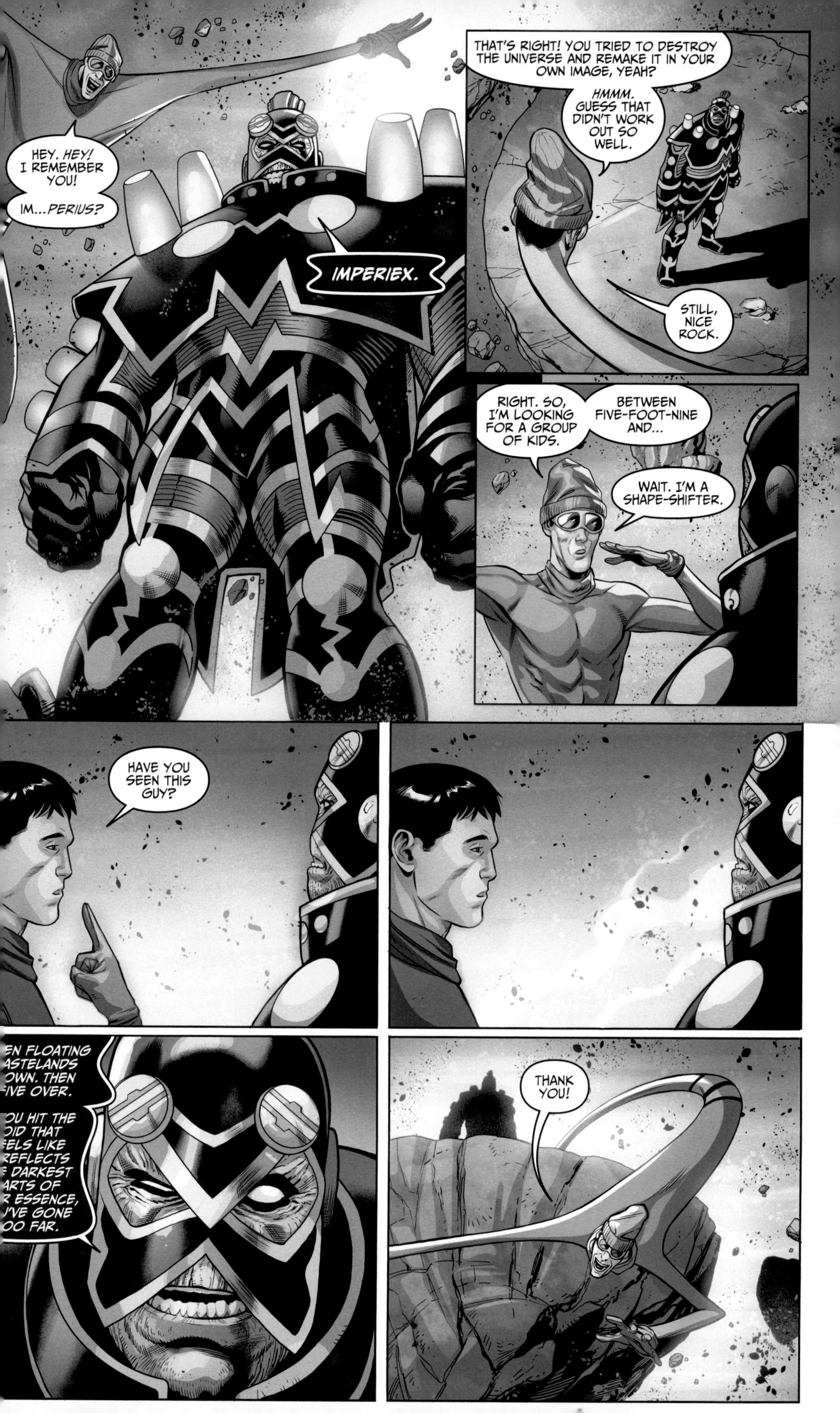
HEY. HEY! I REMEMBER YOU!
IM...PERIUS?
IMPERIEX.
THAT'S RIGHT! YOU TRIED TO DESTROY THE UNIVERSE AND REMAKE IT IN YOUR OWN IMAGE, YEAH?
HMMM. GUESS THAT DIDN'T WORK OUT SO WELL.
STILL, NICE ROCK.
RIGHT. SO, I'M LOOKING FOR A GROUP OF KIDS.
BETWEEN FIVE-FOOT-NINE AND...
WAIT. I'M A SHAPE-SHIFTER.
HAVE YOU SEEN THIS GUY?
THANK YOU!

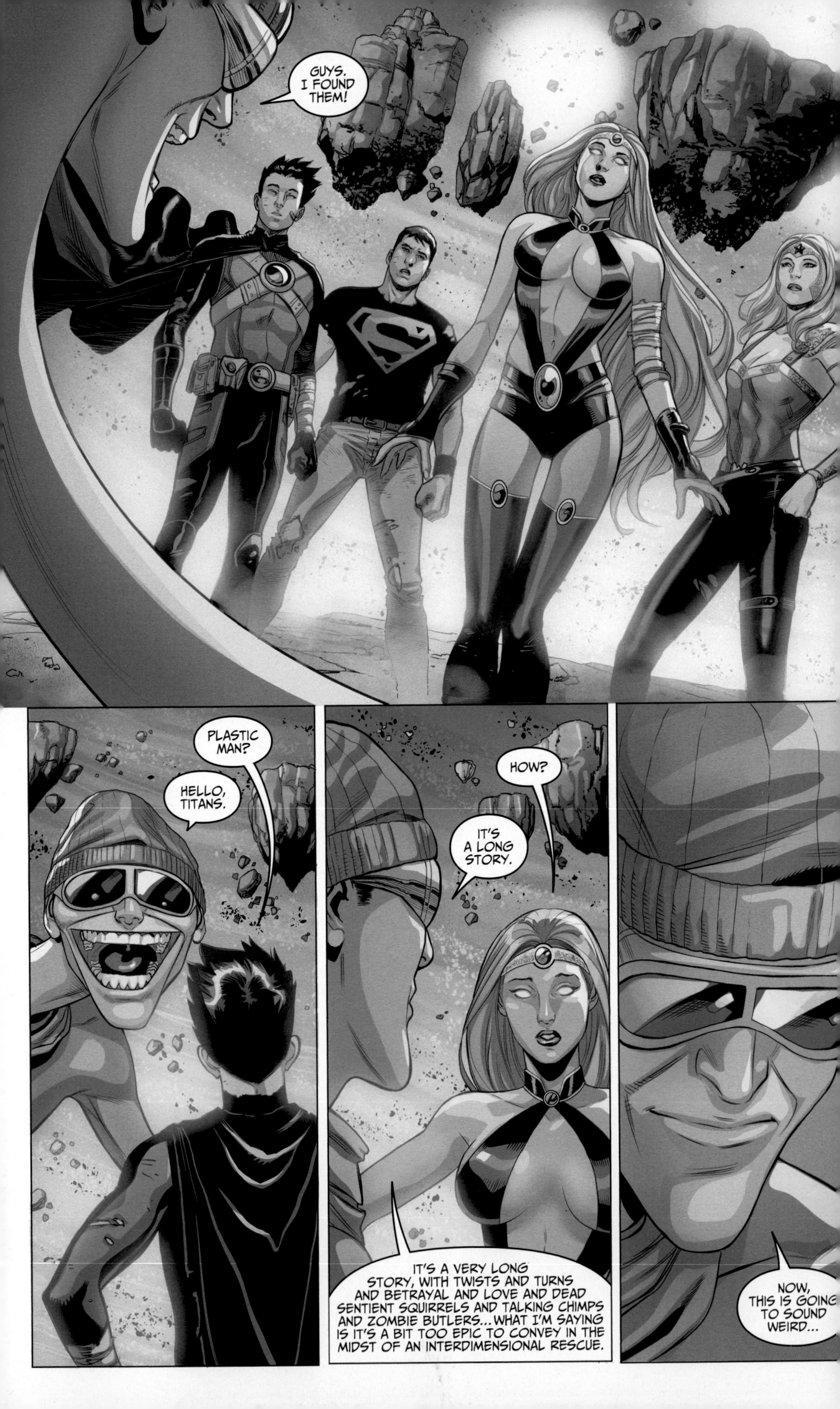
GUYS. I FOUND THEM!
PLASTIC MAN?
HELLO, TITANS.
HOW?
IT'S A LONG STORY.
IT'S A VERY LONG STORY, WITH TWISTS AND TURNS AND BETRAYAL AND LOVE AND DEAD SENTIENT SQUIRRELS AND TALKING CHIMPS AND ZOMBIE BUTLERS...WHAT I'M SAYING IS IT'S A BIT TOO EPIC TO CONVEY IN THE MIDST OF AN INTERDIMENSIONAL RESCUE.
NOW, THIS IS GOING TO SOUND WEIRD...

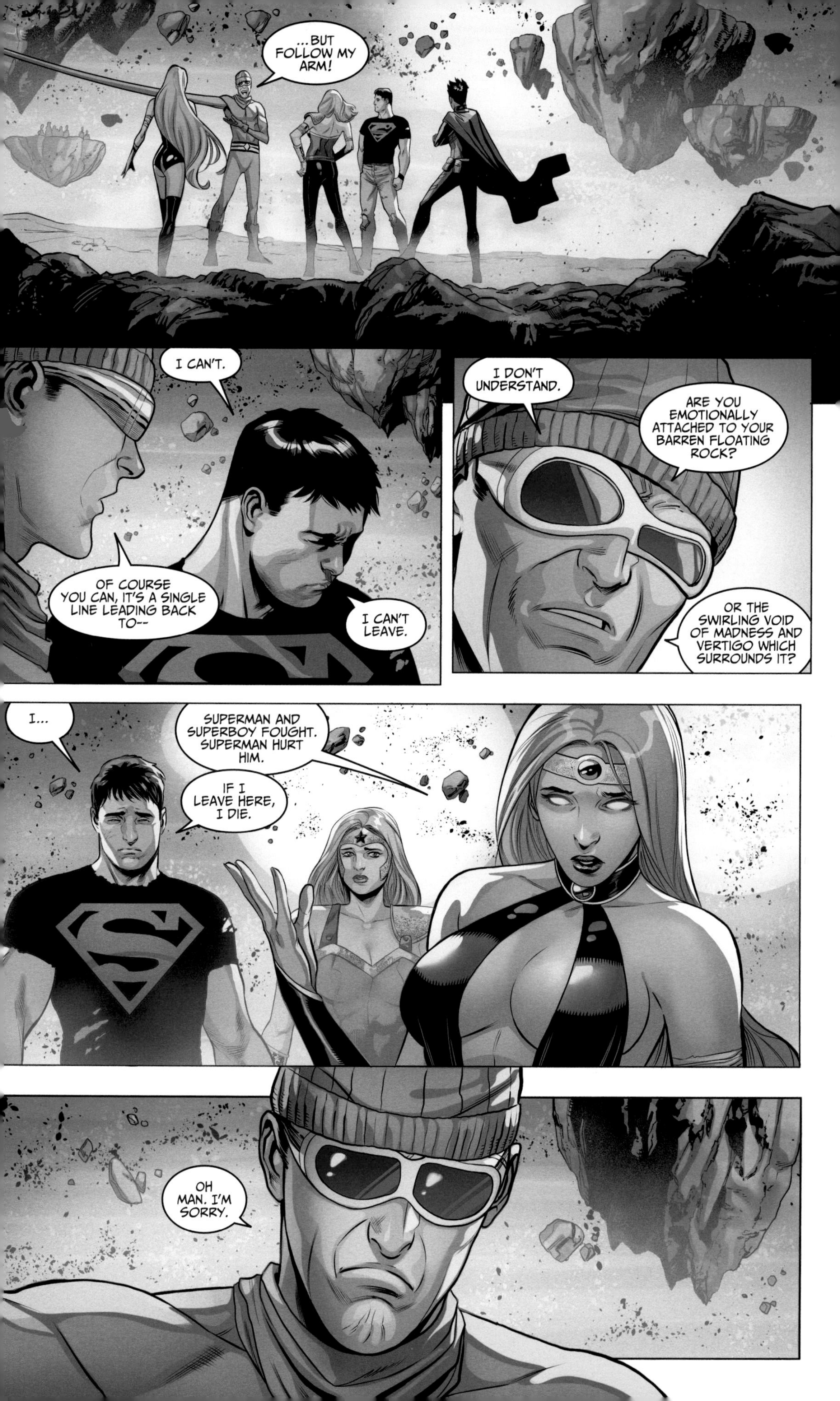

...BUT FOLLOW MY ARM!
I CAN'T.
OF COURSE YOU CAN, IT'S A SINGLE LINE LEADING BACK TO--
I CAN'T LEAVE.
I DON'T UNDERSTAND.
ARE YOU EMOTIONALLY ATTACHED TO YOUR BARREN FLOATING ROCK?
OR THE SWIRLING VOID OF MADNESS AND VERTIGO WHICH SURROUNDS IT?
I...
SUPERMAN AND SUPERBOY FOUGHT. SUPERMAN HURT HIM.
IF I LEAVE HERE, I DIE.
OH MAN. I'M SORRY.

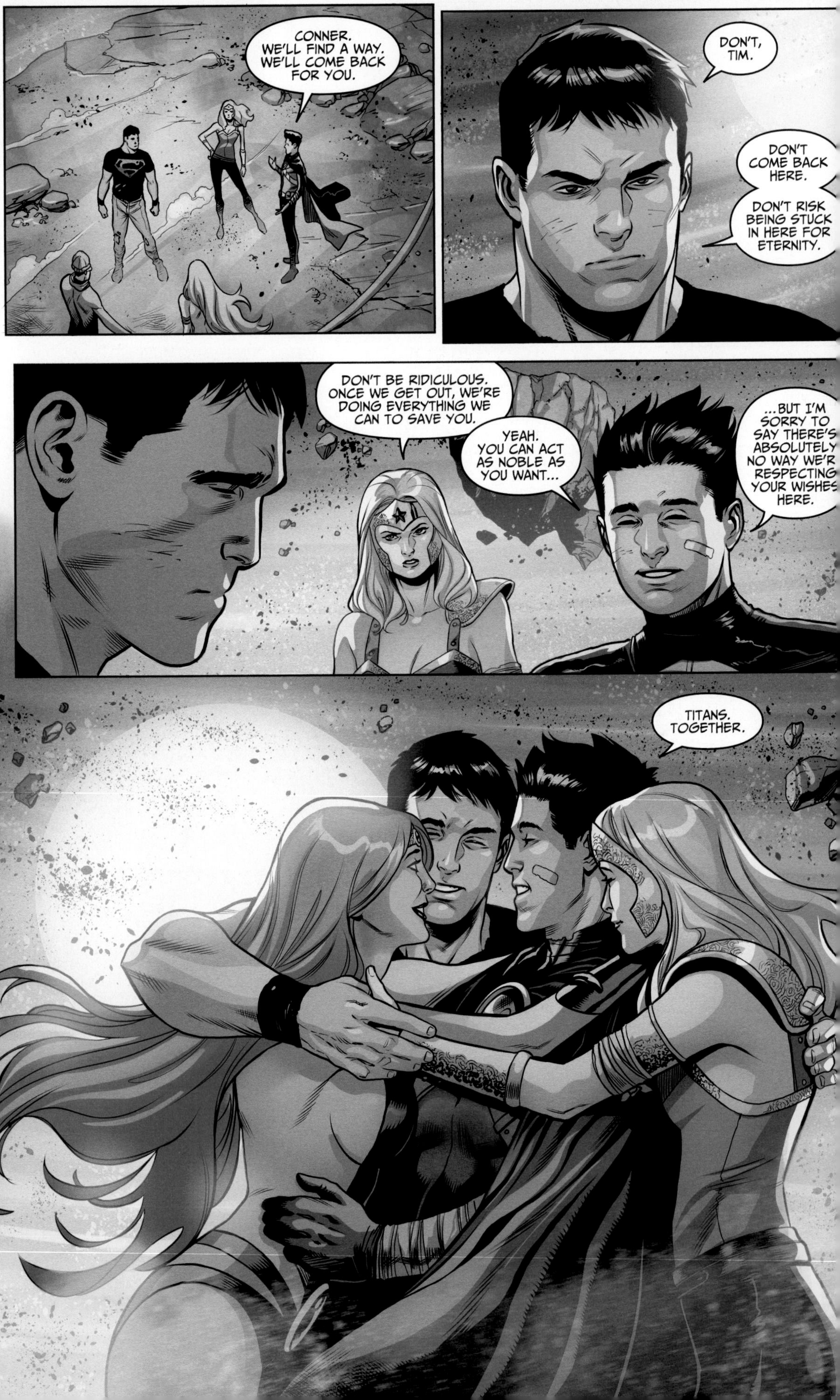
CONNER. WE'LL FIND A WAY. WE'LL COME BACK FOR YOU.
DON'T, TIM.
DON'T COME BACK HERE.
DON'T RISK BEING STUCK IN HERE FOR ETERNITY.
DON'T BE RIDICULOUS. ONCE WE GET OUT, WE'RE DOING EVERYTHING WE CAN TO SAVE YOU.
YEAH. YOU CAN ACT AS NOBLE AS YOU WANT...
...BUT I'M SORRY TO SAY THERE'S ABSOLUTELY NO WAY WE'RE RESPECTING YOUR WISHES HERE.
TITANS. TOGETHER.

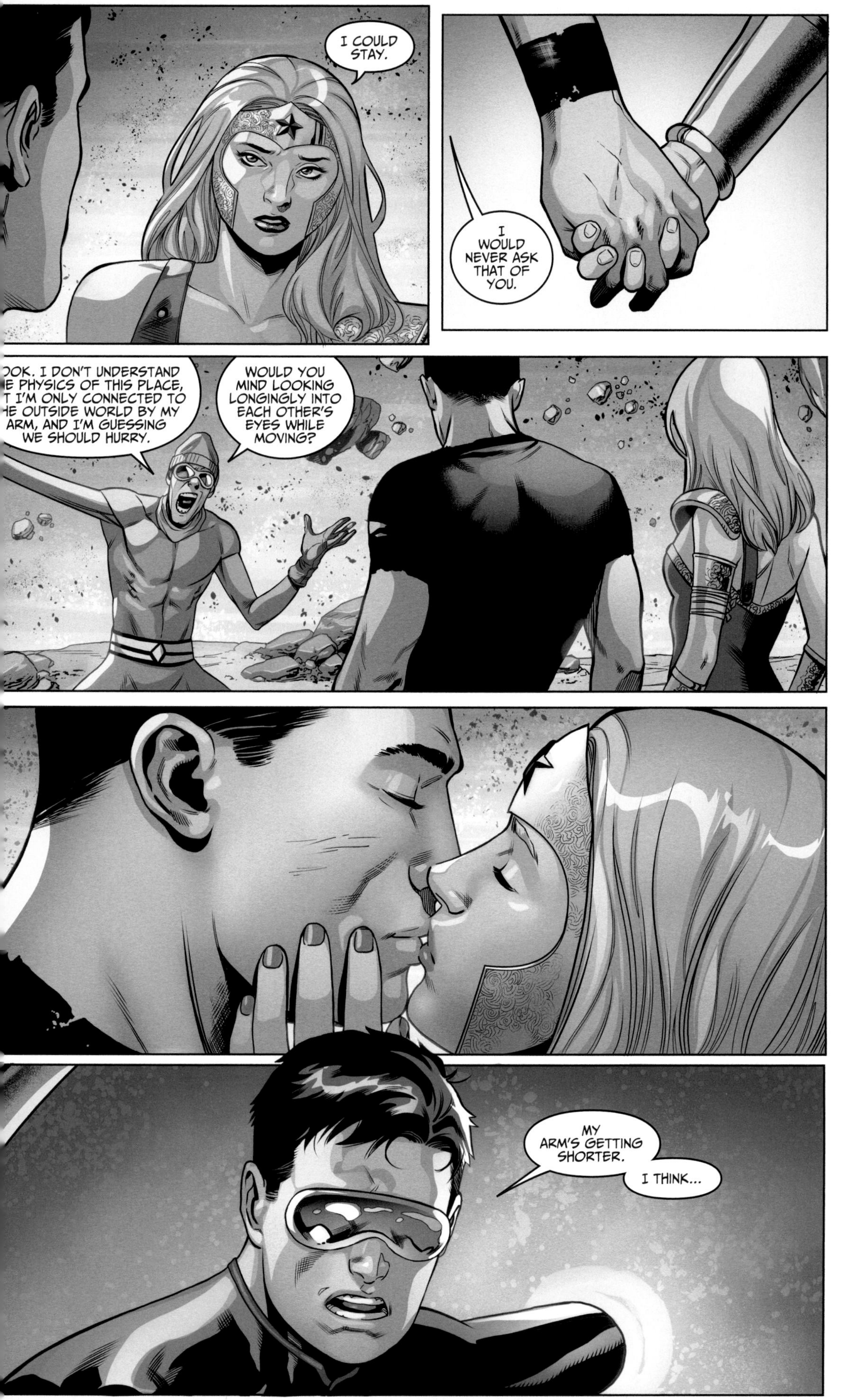
I COULD STAY.
I WOULD NEVER ASK THAT OF YOU.
OOK. I DON'T UNDERSTAND E PHYSICS OF THIS PLACE, T I'M ONLY CONNECTED TO E OUTSIDE WORLD BY MY ARM, AND I'M GUESSING WE SHOULD HURRY.
WOULD YOU MIND LOOKING LONGINGLY INTO EACH OTHER'S EYES WHILE MOVING?
MY ARM'S GETTING SHORTER.
I THINK...

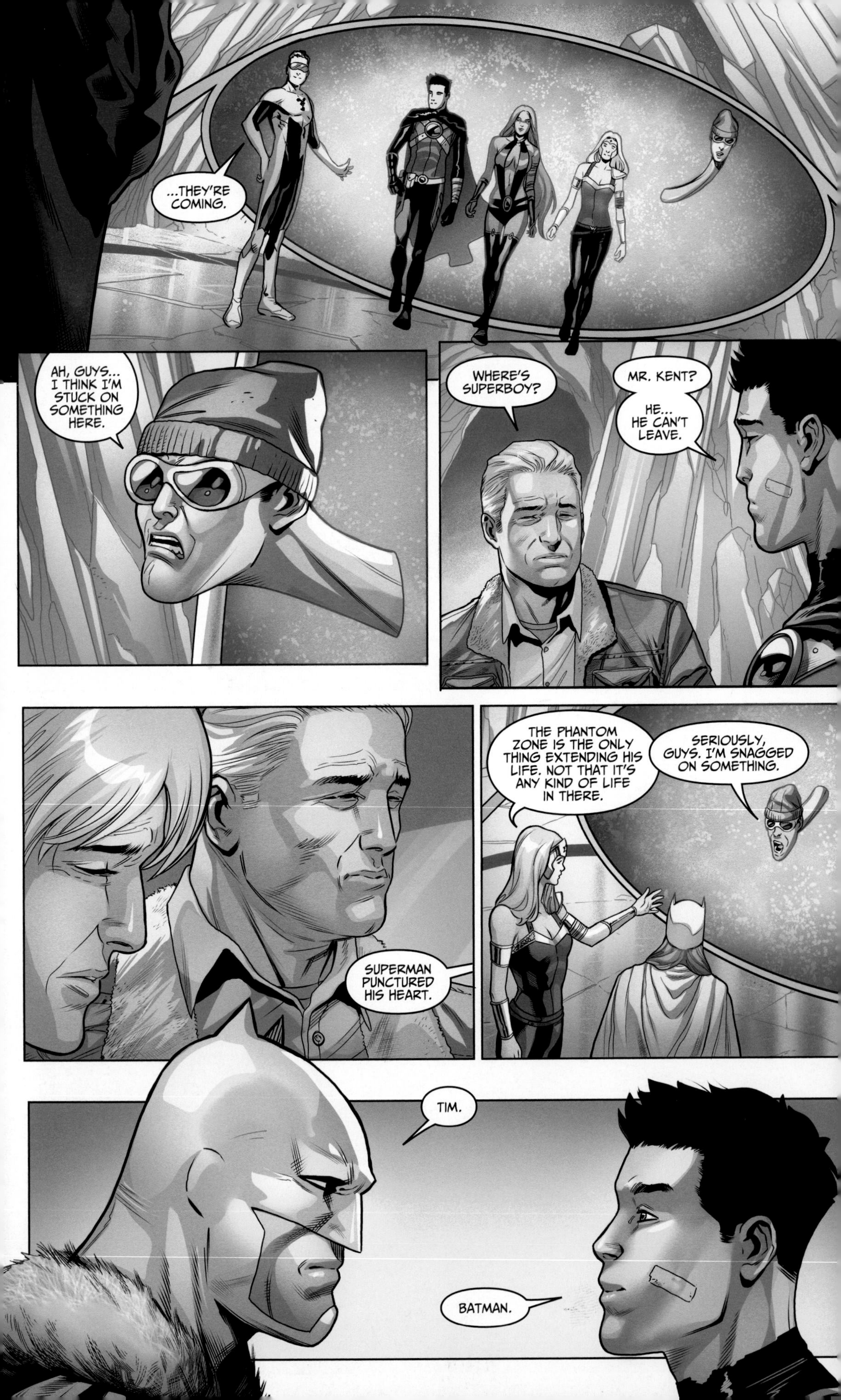

...THEY'RE COMING.
AH, GUYS... I THINK I'M STUCK ON SOMETHING HERE.
WHERE'S SUPERBOY?
MR. KENT?
HE... HE CAN'T LEAVE.
SUPERMAN PUNCTURED HIS HEART.
THE PHANTOM ZONE IS THE ONLY THING EXTENDING HIS LIFE. NOT THAT IT'S ANY KIND OF LIFE IN THERE.
SERIOUSLY, GUYS. I'M SNAGGED ON SOMETHING.
TIM.
BATMAN.

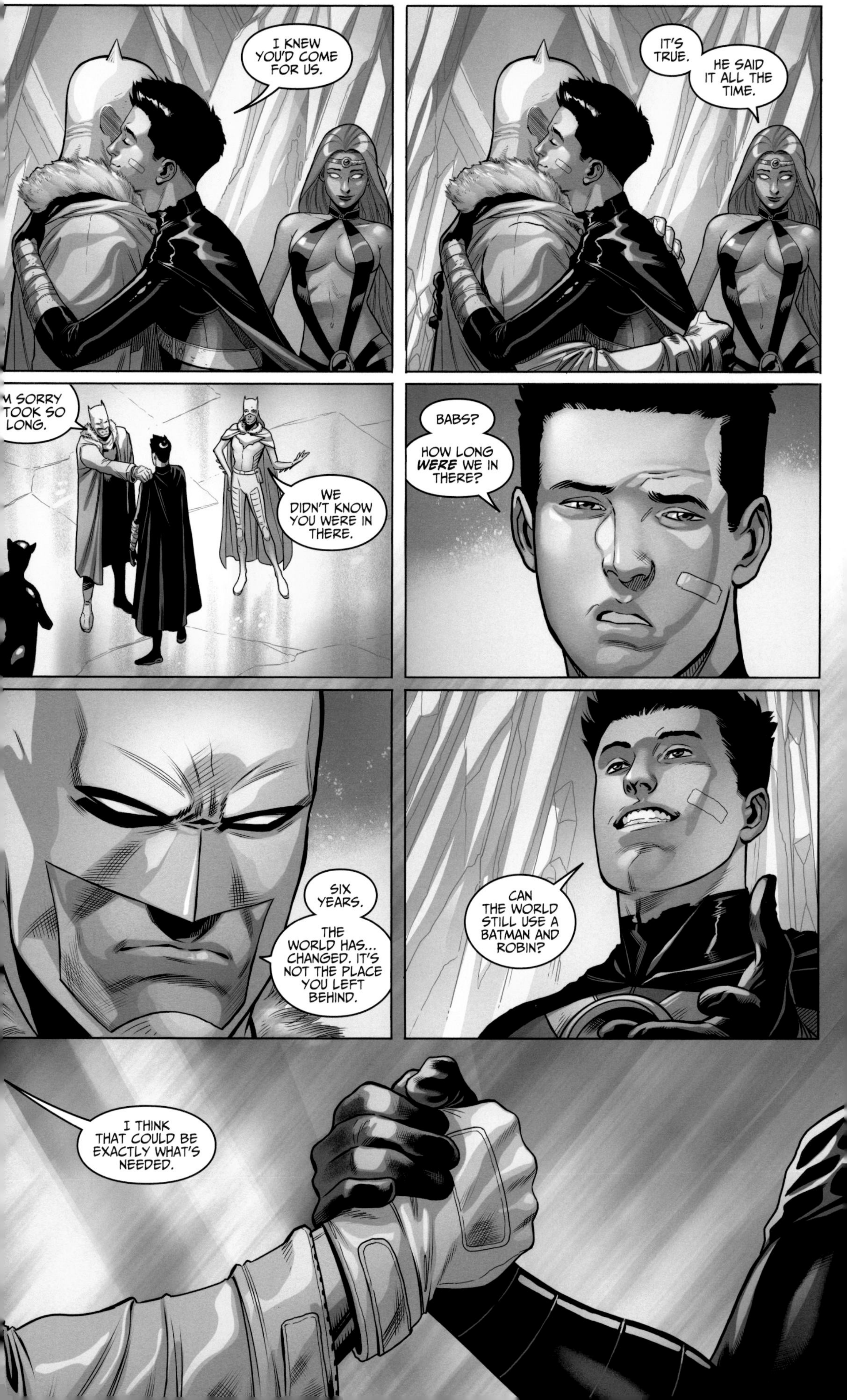
I KNEW YOU'D COME FOR US.
IT'S TRUE.
HE SAID IT ALL THE TIME.
M SORRY TOOK SO LONG.
WE DIDN'T KNOW YOU WERE IN THERE.
BABS?
HOW LONG *WERE* WE IN THERE?
SIX YEARS.
THE WORLD HAS... CHANGED. IT'S NOT THE PLACE YOU LEFT BEHIND.
CAN THE WORLD STILL USE A BATMAN AND ROBIN?
I THINK THAT COULD BE EXACTLY WHAT'S NEEDED.

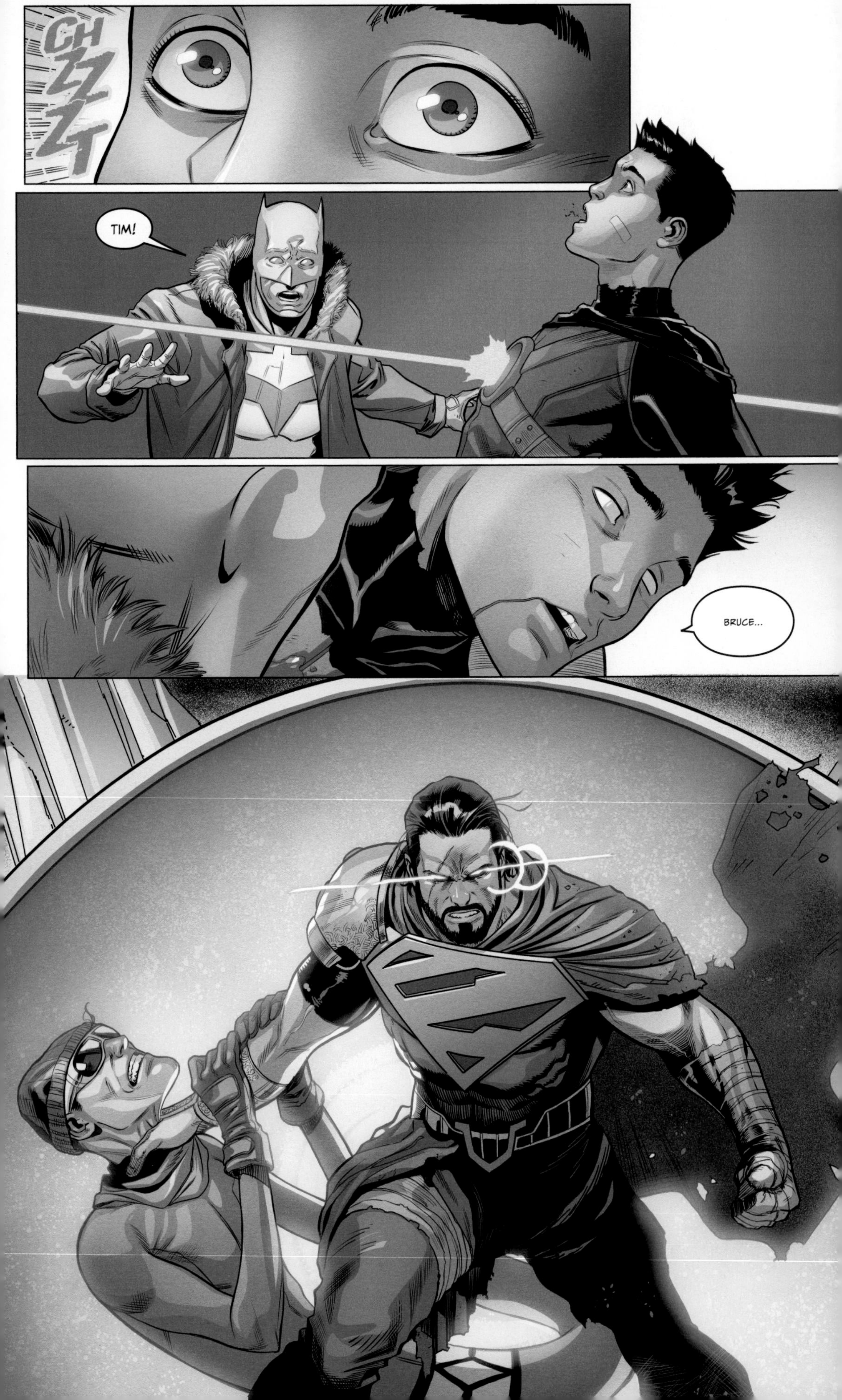
CHZZZT
TIM!
BRUCE...

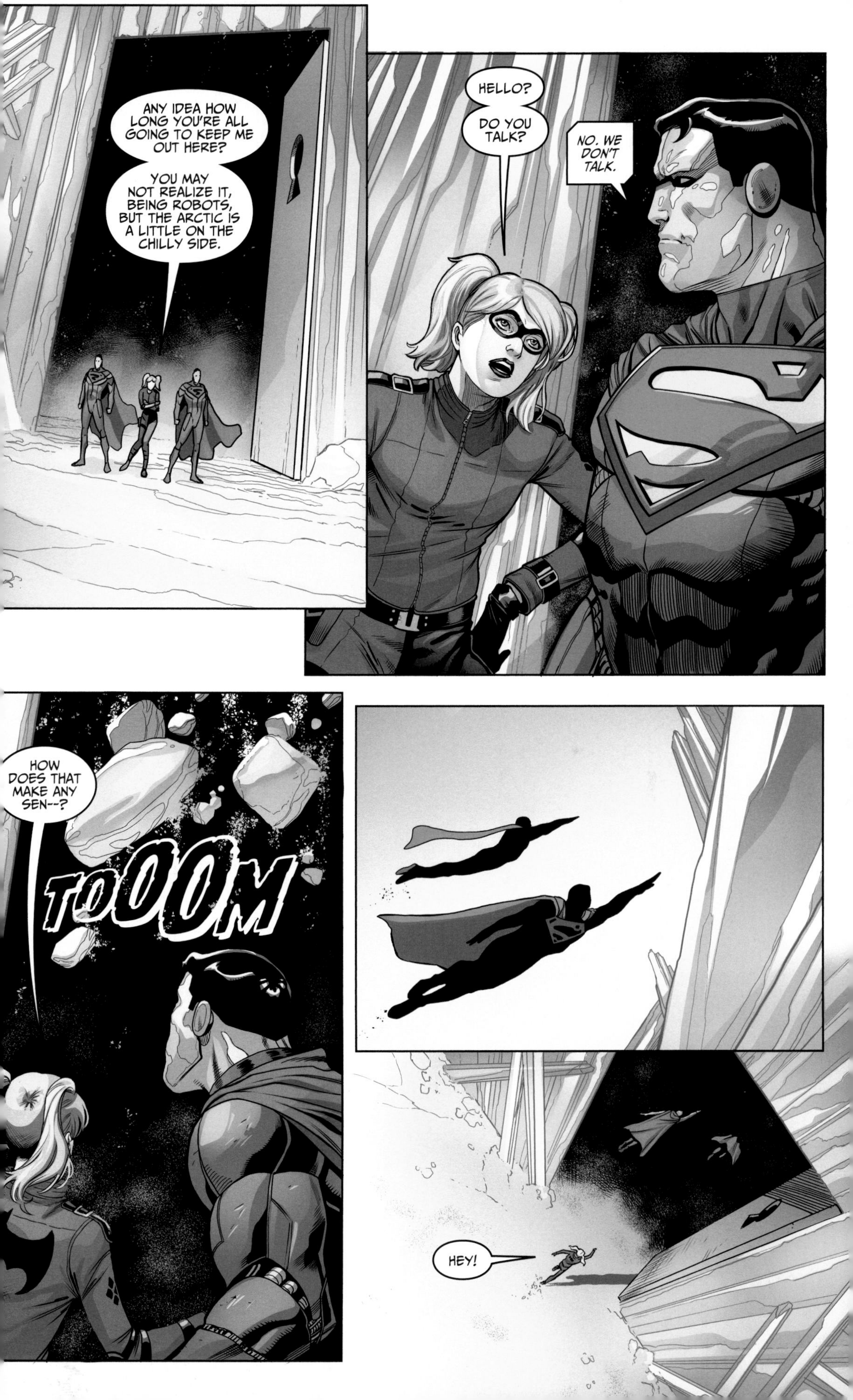

ANY IDEA HOW LONG YOU'RE ALL GOING TO KEEP ME OUT HERE?
YOU MAY NOT REALIZE IT, BEING ROBOTS, BUT THE ARCTIC IS A LITTLE ON THE CHILLY SIDE.
HELLO?
DO YOU TALK?
NO. WE DON'T TALK.
HOW DOES THAT MAKE ANY SEN--?
TOOOM
HEY!

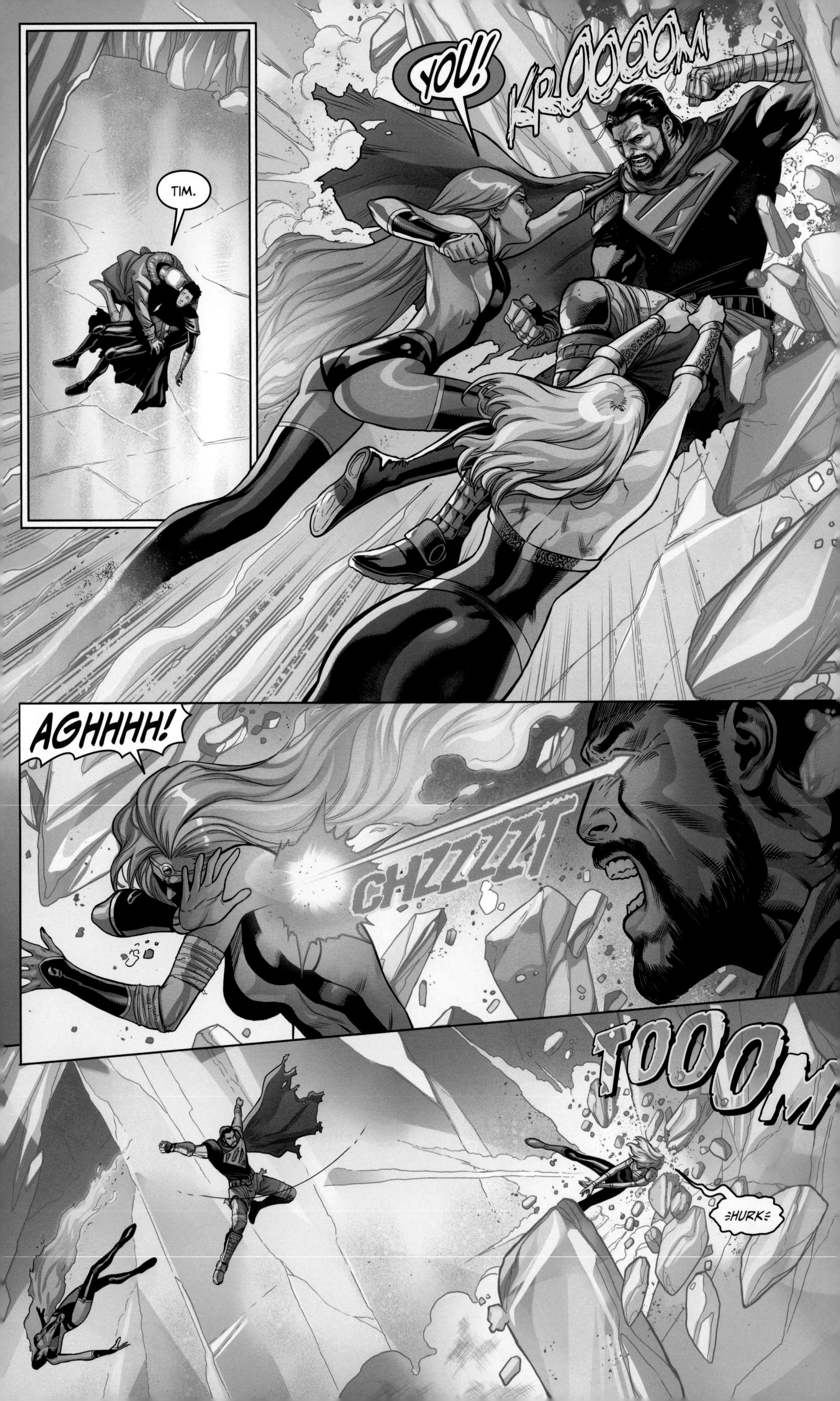
TIM.
YOU!!
KRUOOOOM
AGHHHH!
CHZZZZZT
TOOOOM
HURK

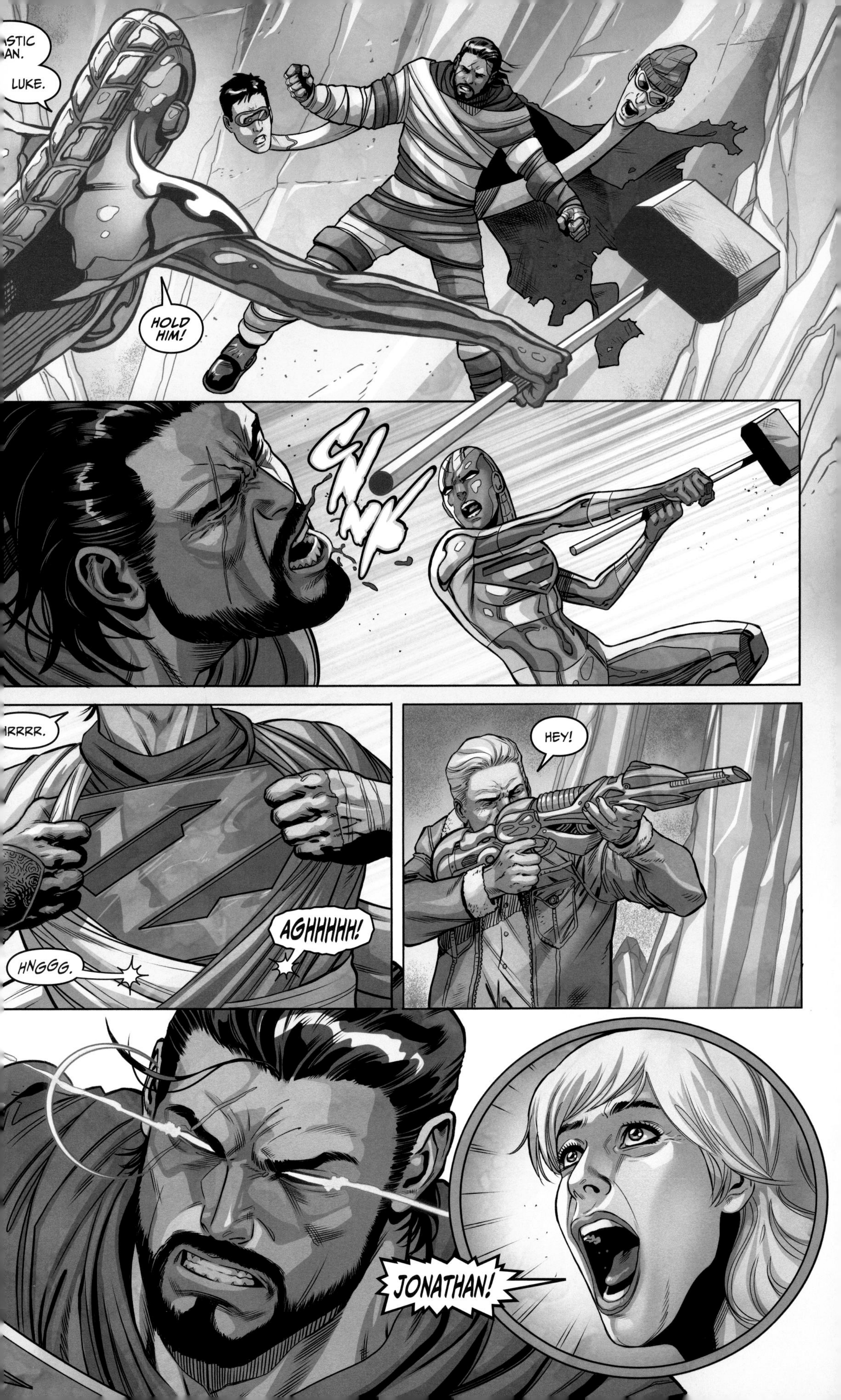

ASTIC
AN.
LUKE.
HOLD HIM!
CHNK
RRRR.
HNGGG.
AGHHHHH!
HEY!
JONATHAN!

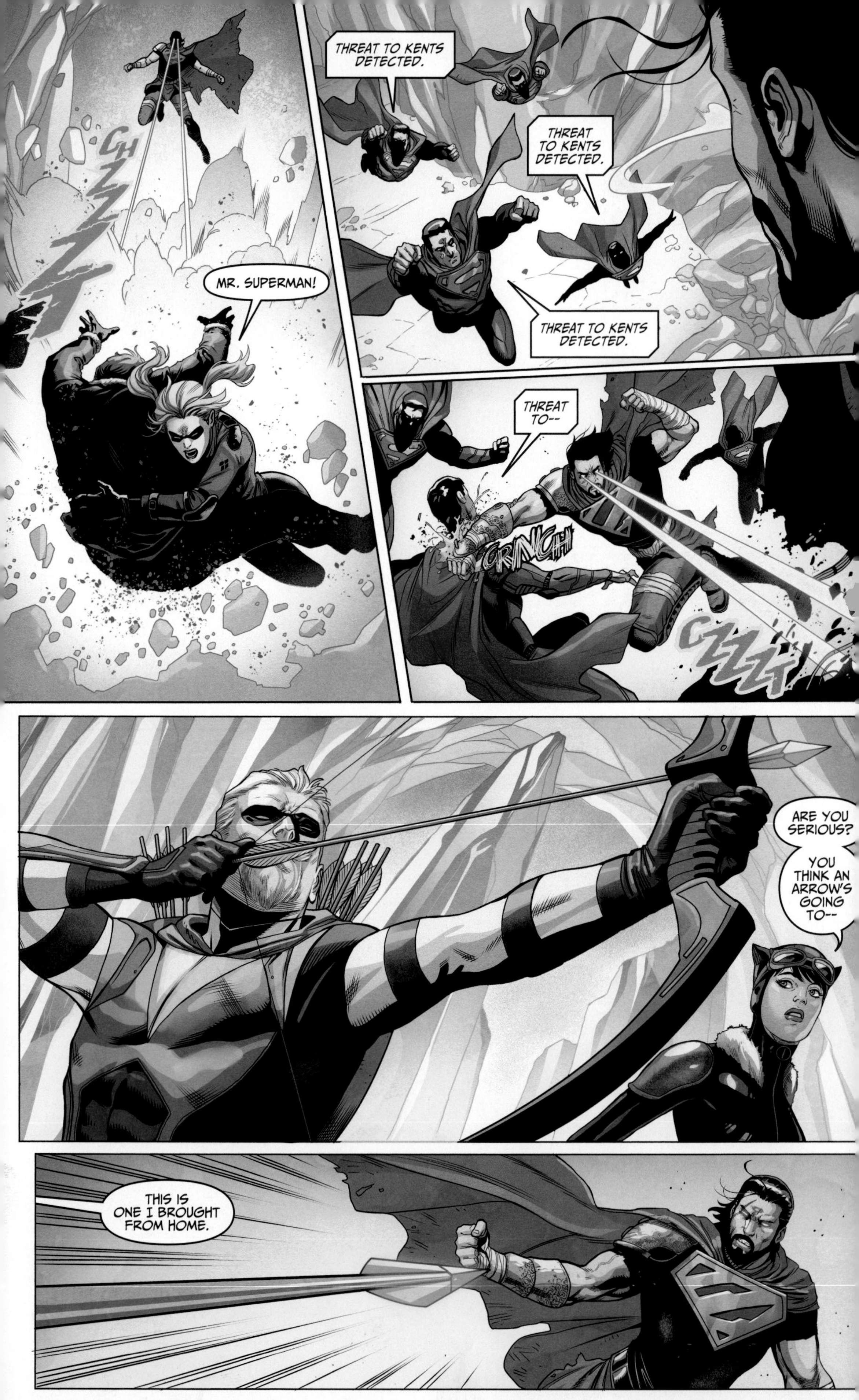

CHZZZZ
MR. SUPERMAN!
THREAT TO KENTS DETECTED.
THREAT TO KENTS DETECTED.
THREAT TO KENTS DETECTED.
THREAT TO--
CRUNCH
CZZZK
ARE YOU SERIOUS?
YOU THINK AN ARROW'S GOING TO--
THIS IS ONE I BROUGHT FROM HOME.

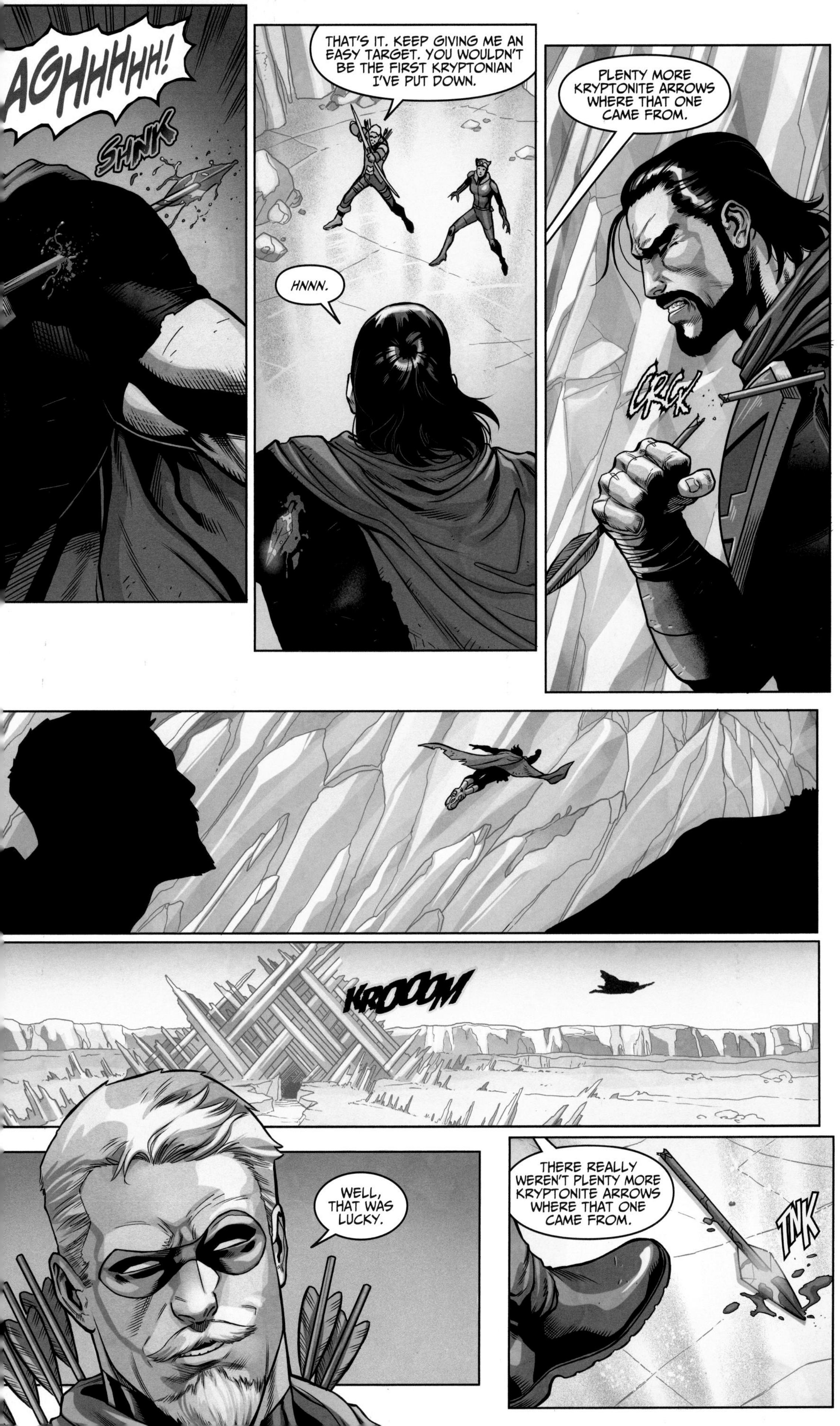
AGHHHHH!
SHNK
THAT'S IT. KEEP GIVING ME AN EASY TARGET. YOU WOULDN'T BE THE FIRST KRYPTONIAN I'VE PUT DOWN.
HNNN.
PLENTY MORE KRYPTONITE ARROWS WHERE THAT ONE CAME FROM.
CRICK
KROOOM
WELL, THAT WAS LUCKY.
THERE REALLY WEREN'T PLENTY MORE KRYPTONITE ARROWS WHERE THAT ONE CAME FROM.
TNK

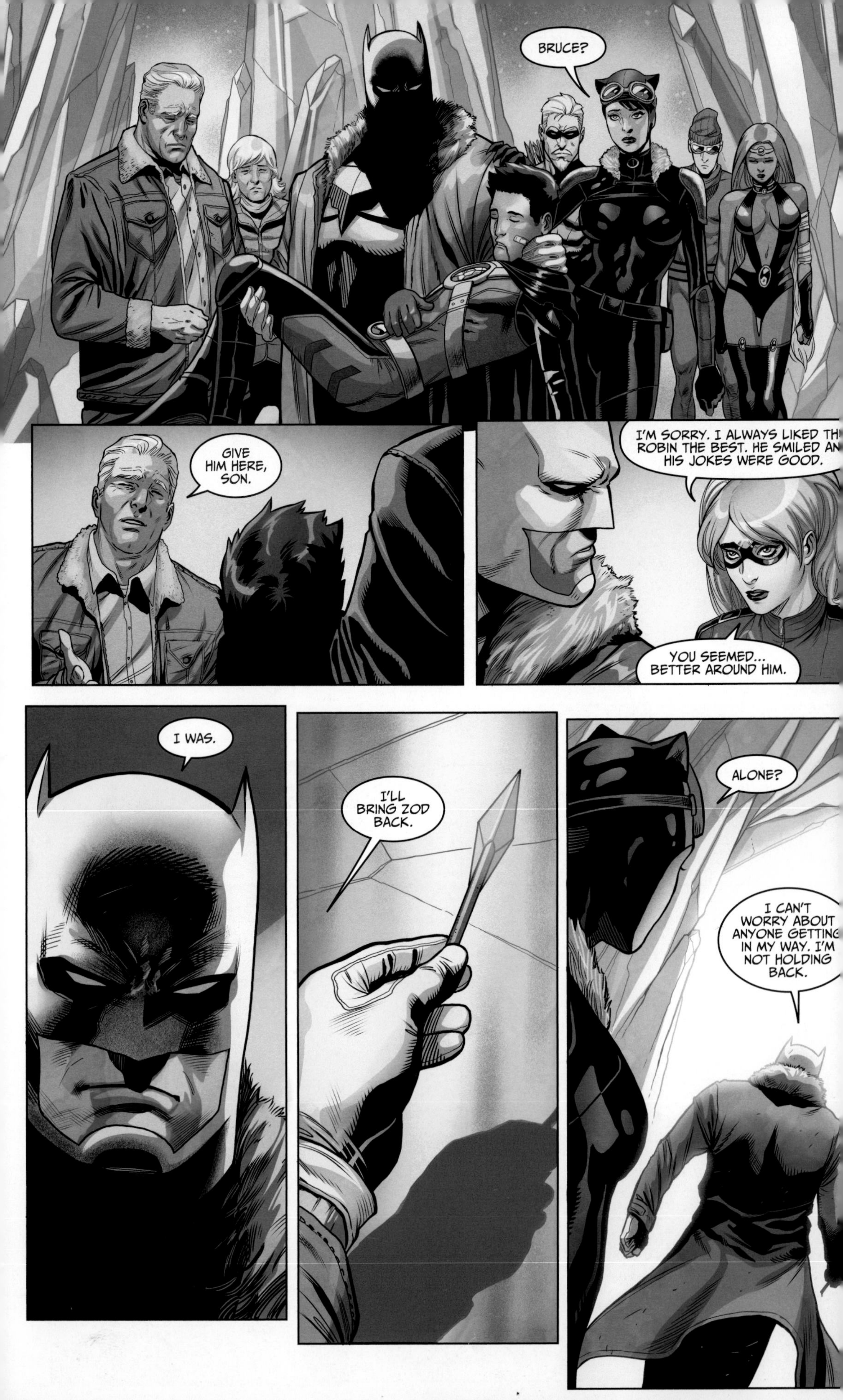
BRUCE?
GIVE HIM HERE, SON.
I'M SORRY. I ALWAYS LIKED TH ROBIN THE BEST. HE SMILED AN HIS JOKES WERE GOOD.
YOU SEEMED... BETTER AROUND HIM.
I WAS.
I'LL BRING ZOD BACK.
ALONE?
I CAN'T WORRY ABOUT ANYONE GETTING IN MY WAY. I'M NOT HOLDING BACK.

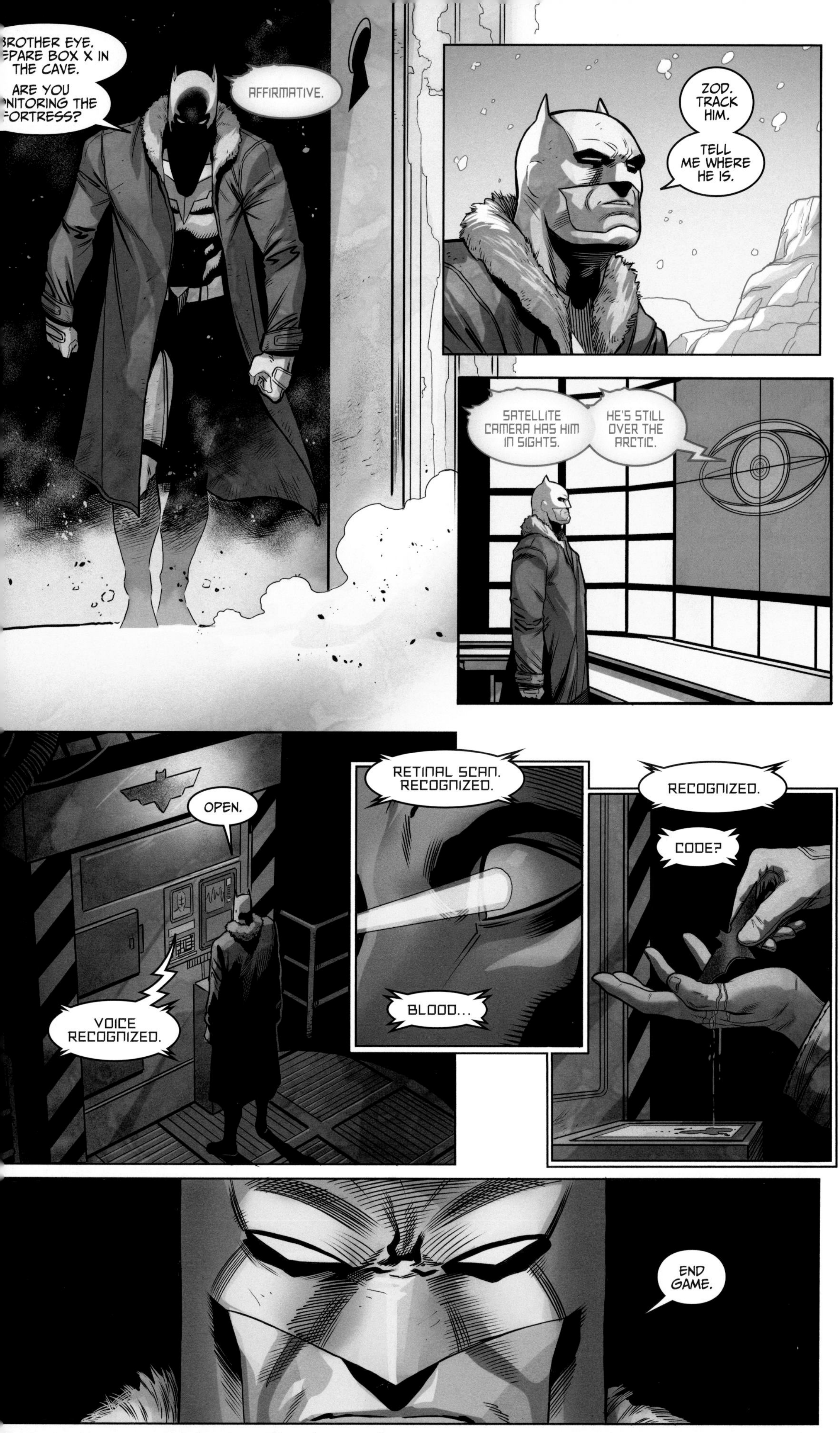
BROTHER EYE.
EPARE BOX X IN
THE CAVE.
ARE YOU
NITORING THE
FORTRESS?
AFFIRMATIVE.
ZOD.
TRACK
HIM.
TELL
ME WHERE
HE IS.
SATELLITE
CAMERA HAS HIM
IN SIGHTS.
HE'S STILL
OVER THE
ARCTIC.
OPEN.
VOICE
RECOGNIZED.
RETINAL SCAN.
RECOGNIZED.
BLOOD...
RECOGNIZED.
CODE?
END
GAME.

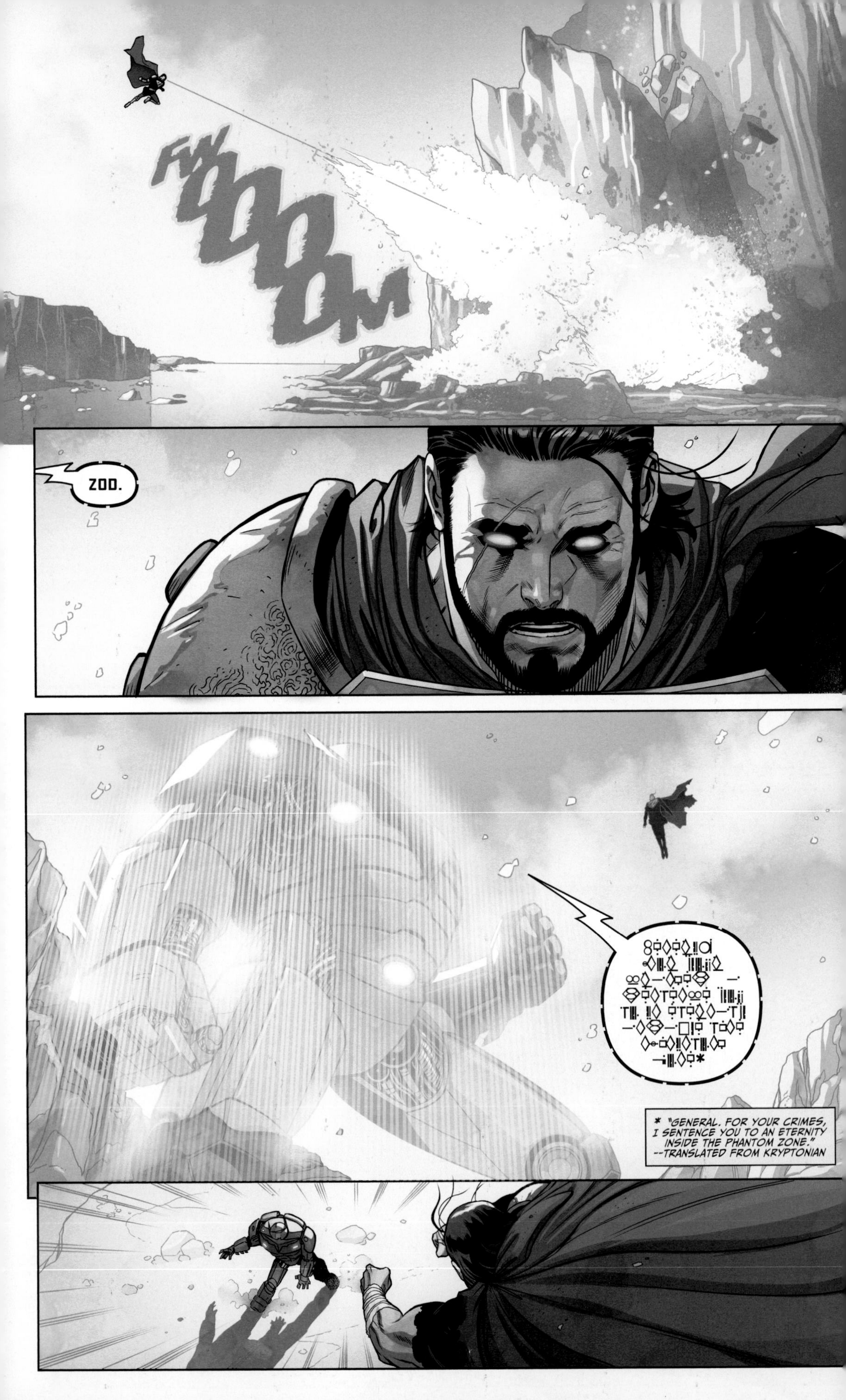
FWOOOM
ZOD.
* "GENERAL. FOR YOUR CRIMES, I SENTENCE YOU TO AN ETERNITY INSIDE THE PHANTOM ZONE." --TRANSLATED FROM KRYPTONIAN

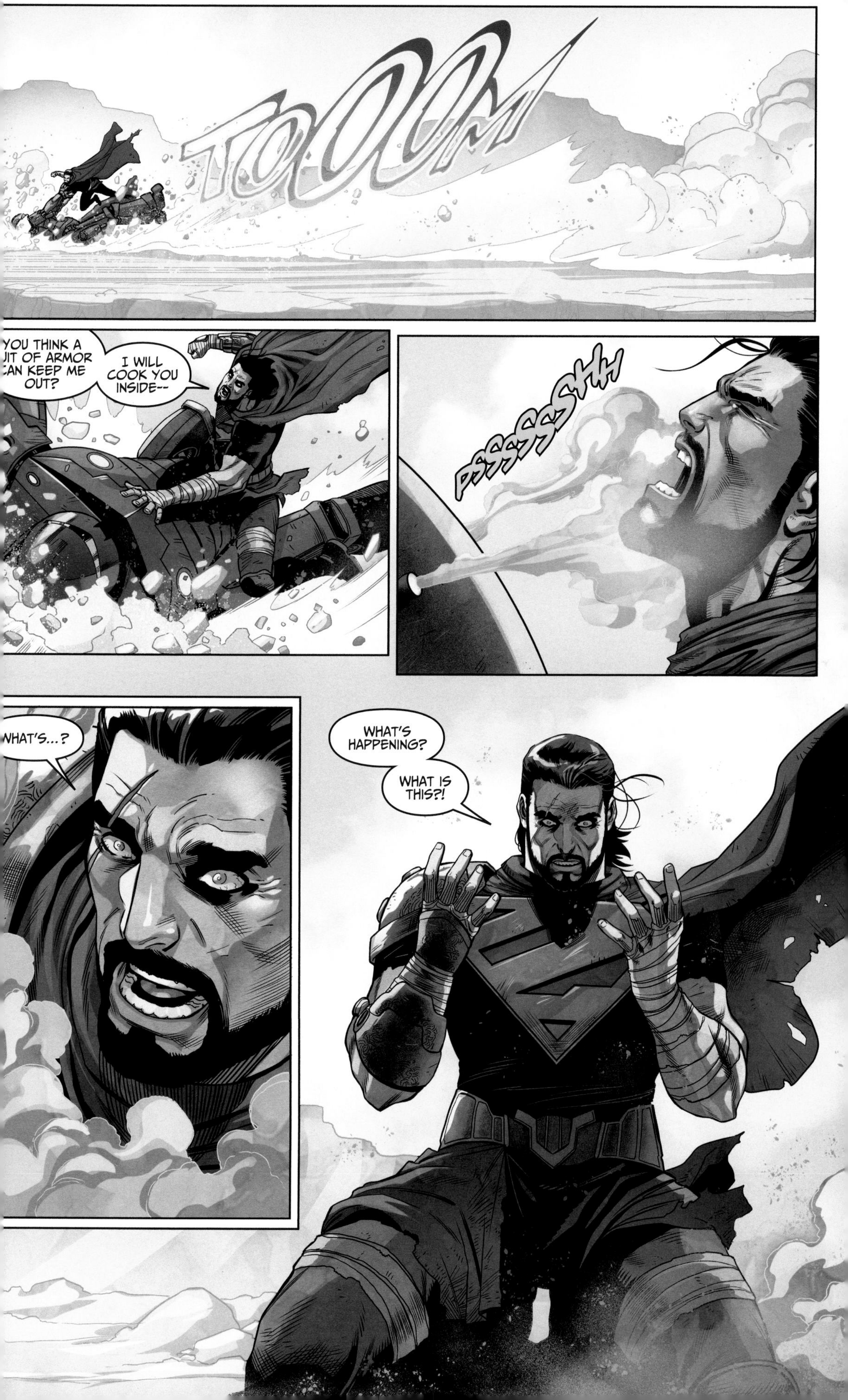
TOOOM
YOU THINK A
UIT OF ARMOR
CAN KEEP ME
OUT?
I WILL
COOK YOU
INSIDE--
PSSSSSSHH
WHAT'S...?
WHAT'S
HAPPENING?
WHAT IS
THIS?!

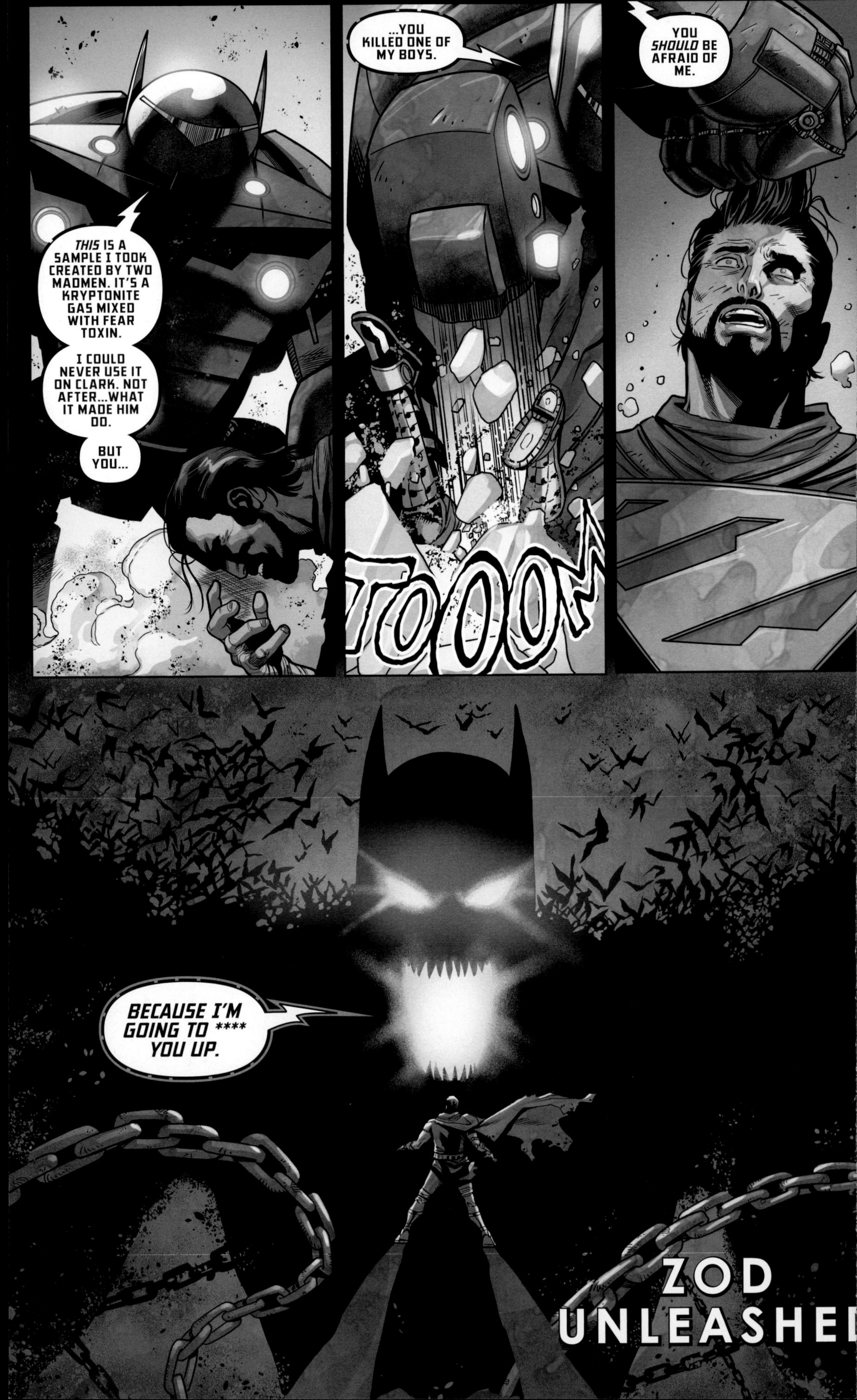
THIS IS A SAMPLE I TOOK CREATED BY TWO MADMEN. IT'S A KRYPTONITE GAS MIXED WITH FEAR TOXIN.
I COULD NEVER USE IT ON CLARK. NOT AFTER...WHAT IT MADE HIM DO.
BUT YOU...
...YOU KILLED ONE OF MY BOYS.
TOOOM
YOU SHOULD BE AFRAID OF ME.
BECAUSE I'M GOING TO **** YOU UP.
ZOD UNLEASHED

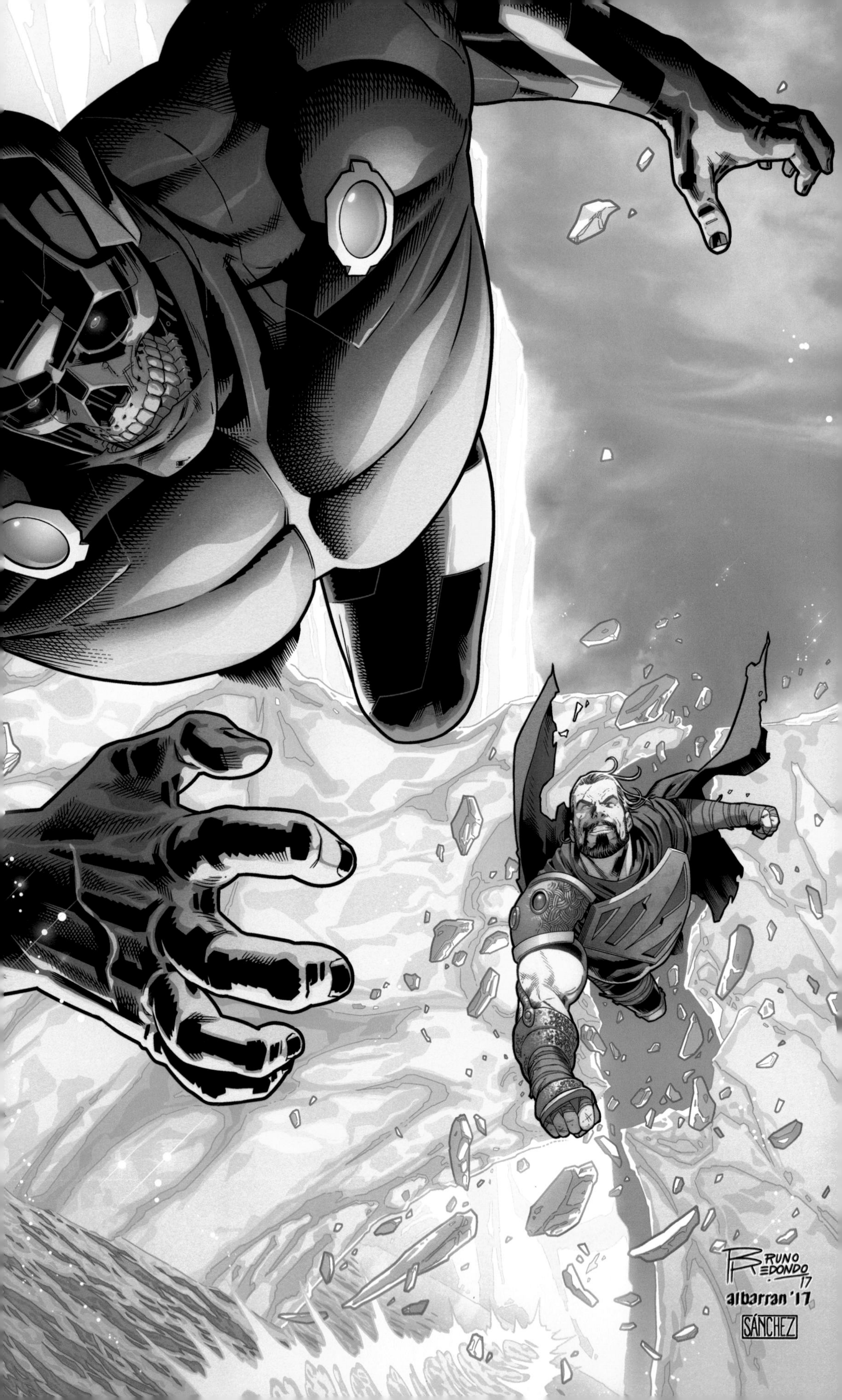
BRUNO REDONDO 17
albarran '17
SÁNCHEZ

“Long Night”

Tom Taylor Writer **Bruno Redondo** Layouts **Juan Albarran** Finishes **Rex Lokus** Colorist **Wes Abbott** Letterer

Cover art by **Bruno Redondo**, **Juan Albarran** and **Alejandro Sanchez**

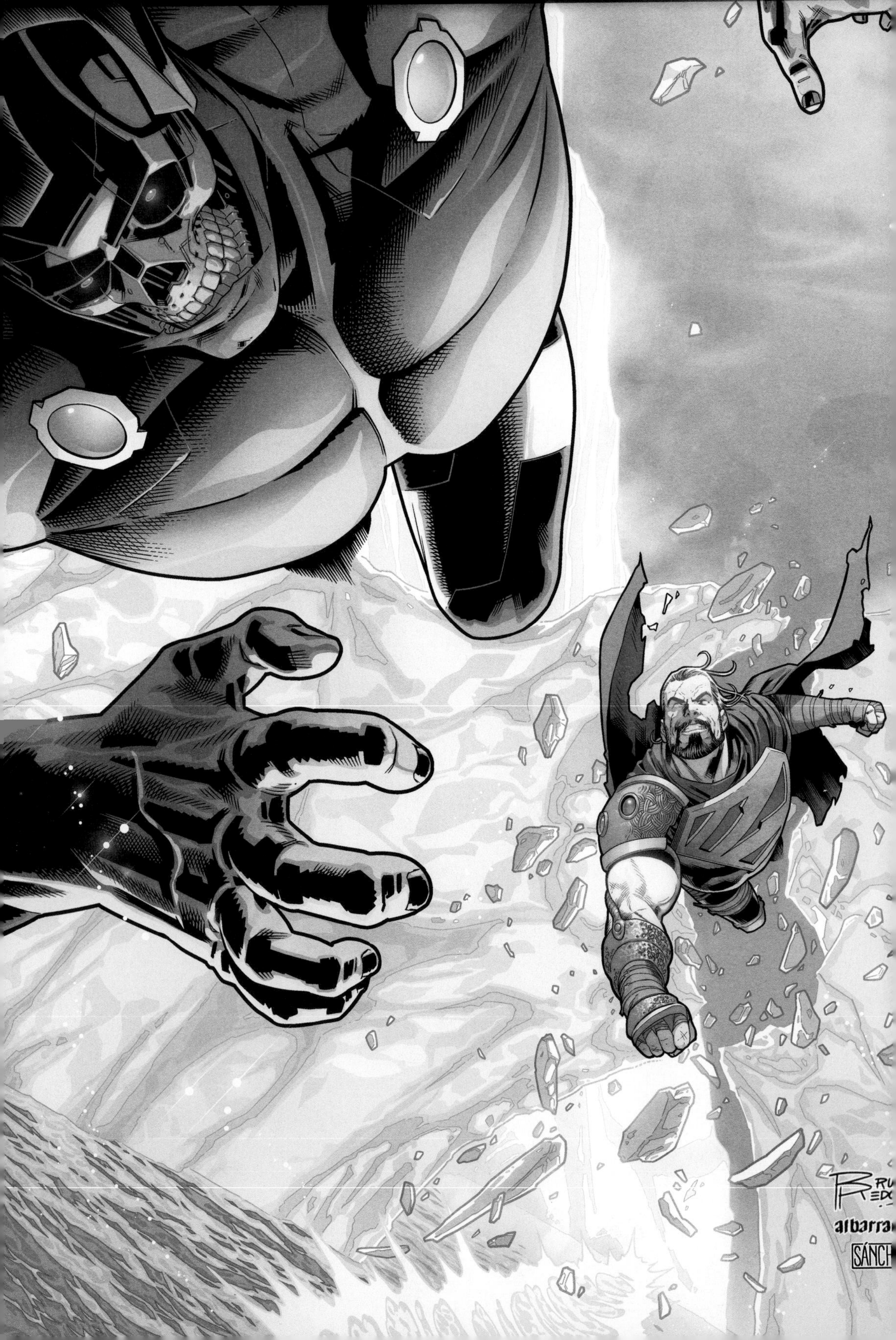

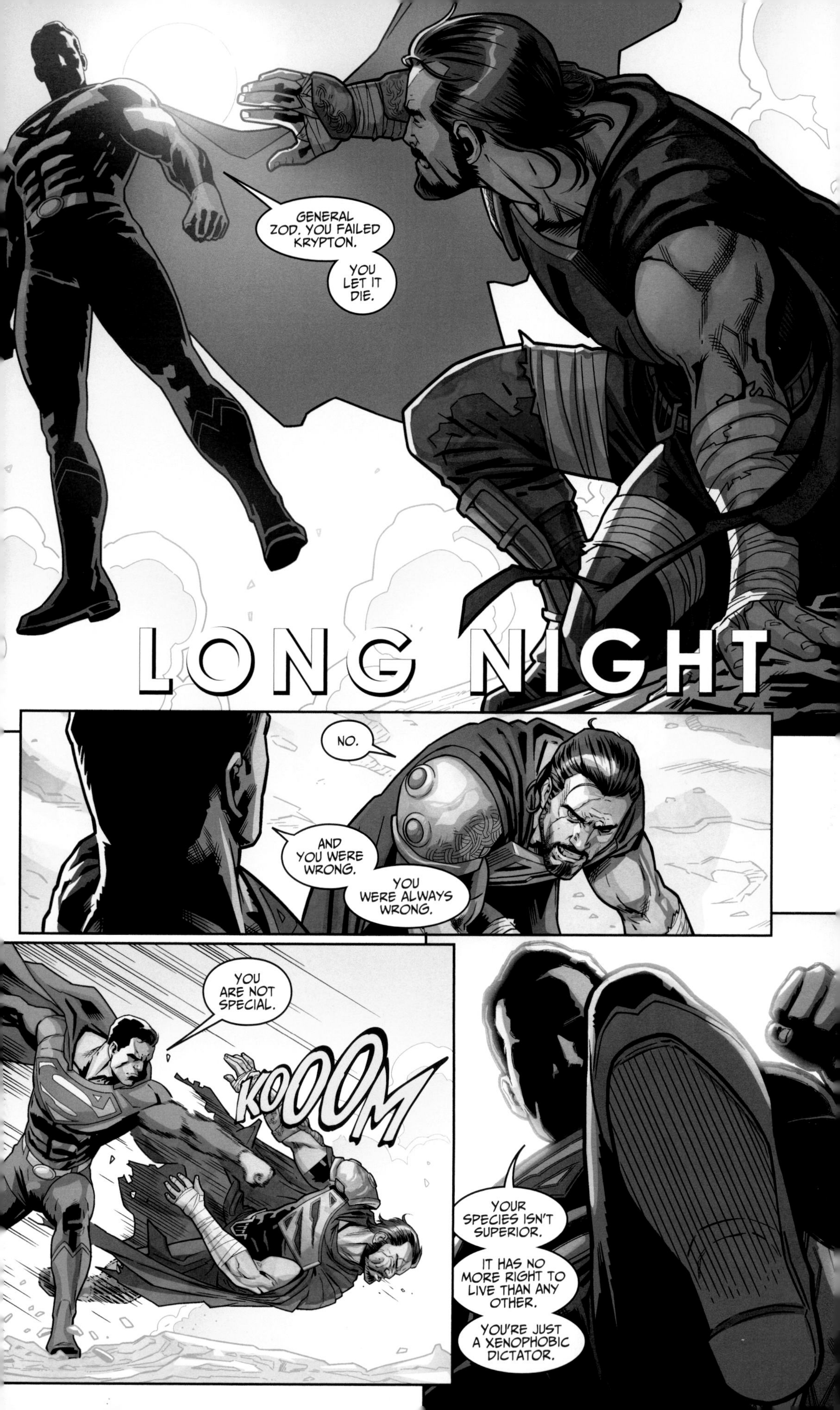

GENERAL ZOD. YOU FAILED KRYPTON.
YOU LET IT DIE.
LONG NIGHT
NO.
AND YOU WERE WRONG.
YOU WERE ALWAYS WRONG.
YOU ARE NOT SPECIAL.
KOOOM
YOUR SPECIES ISN'T SUPERIOR.
IT HAS NO MORE RIGHT TO LIVE THAN ANY OTHER.
YOU'RE JUST A XENOPHOBIC DICTATOR.

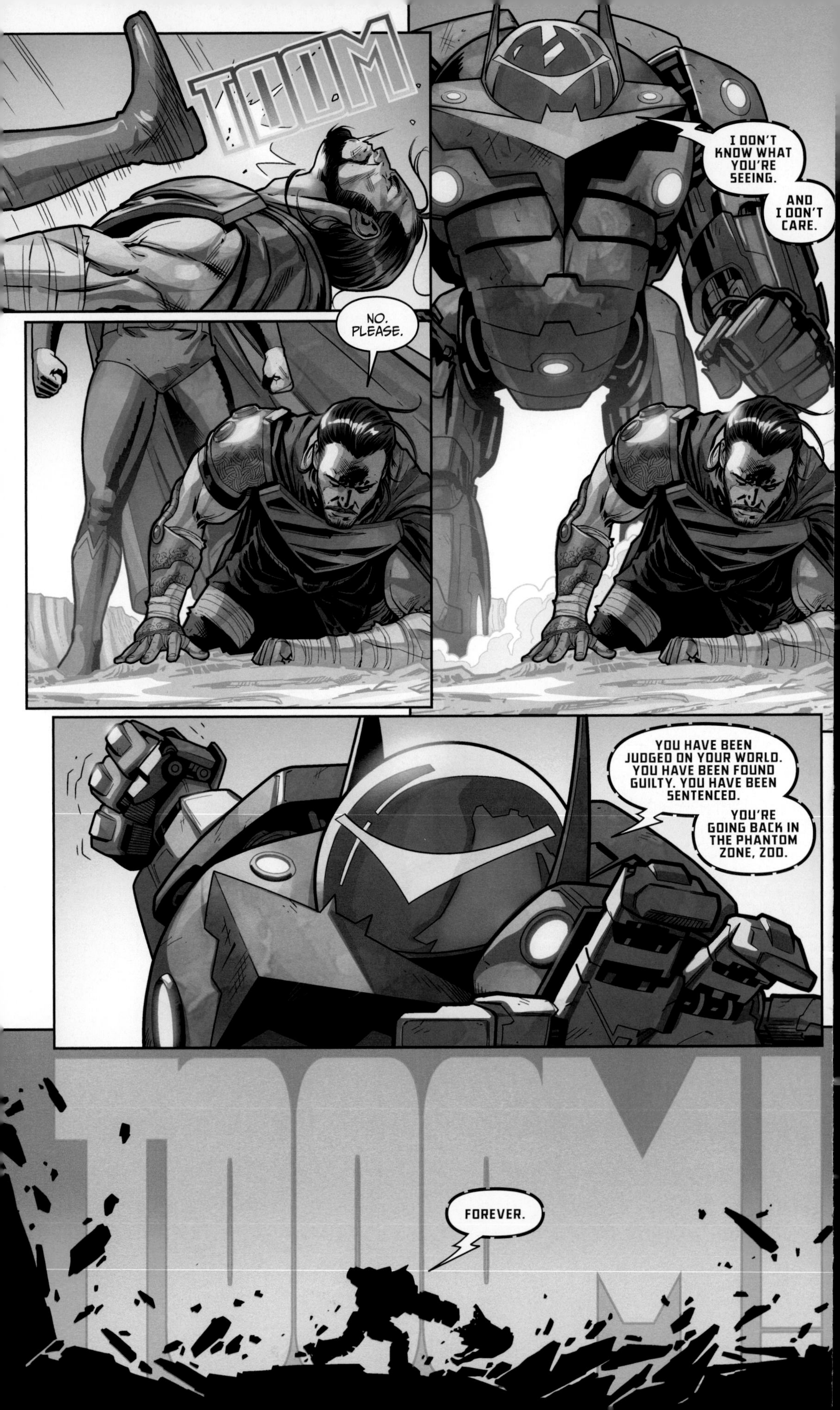
TOOM
I DON'T KNOW WHAT YOU'RE SEEING.
AND I DON'T CARE.
NO. PLEASE.
YOU HAVE BEEN JUDGED ON YOUR WORLD. YOU HAVE BEEN FOUND GUILTY. YOU HAVE BEEN SENTENCED.
YOU'RE GOING BACK IN THE PHANTOM ZONE, ZOD.
FOREVER.

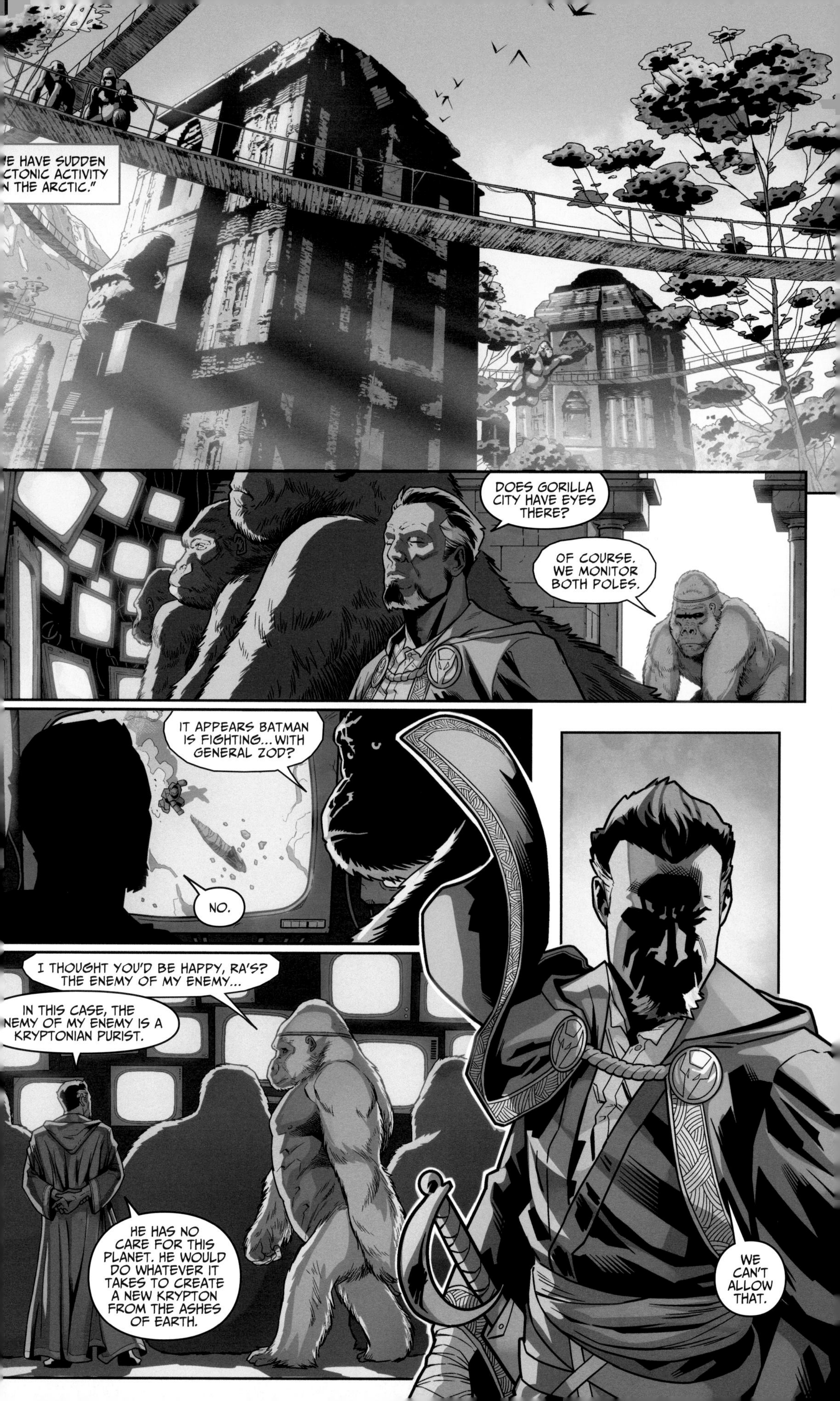

E HAVE SUDDEN CTONIC ACTIVITY N THE ARCTIC."
DOES GORILLA CITY HAVE EYES THERE?
OF COURSE. WE MONITOR BOTH POLES.
IT APPEARS BATMAN IS FIGHTING... WITH GENERAL ZOD?
NO.
I THOUGHT YOU'D BE HAPPY, RA'S? THE ENEMY OF MY ENEMY...
IN THIS CASE, THE NEMY OF MY ENEMY IS A KRYPTONIAN PURIST.
HE HAS NO CARE FOR THIS PLANET. HE WOULD DO WHATEVER IT TAKES TO CREATE A NEW KRYPTON FROM THE ASHES OF EARTH.
WE CAN'T ALLOW THAT.

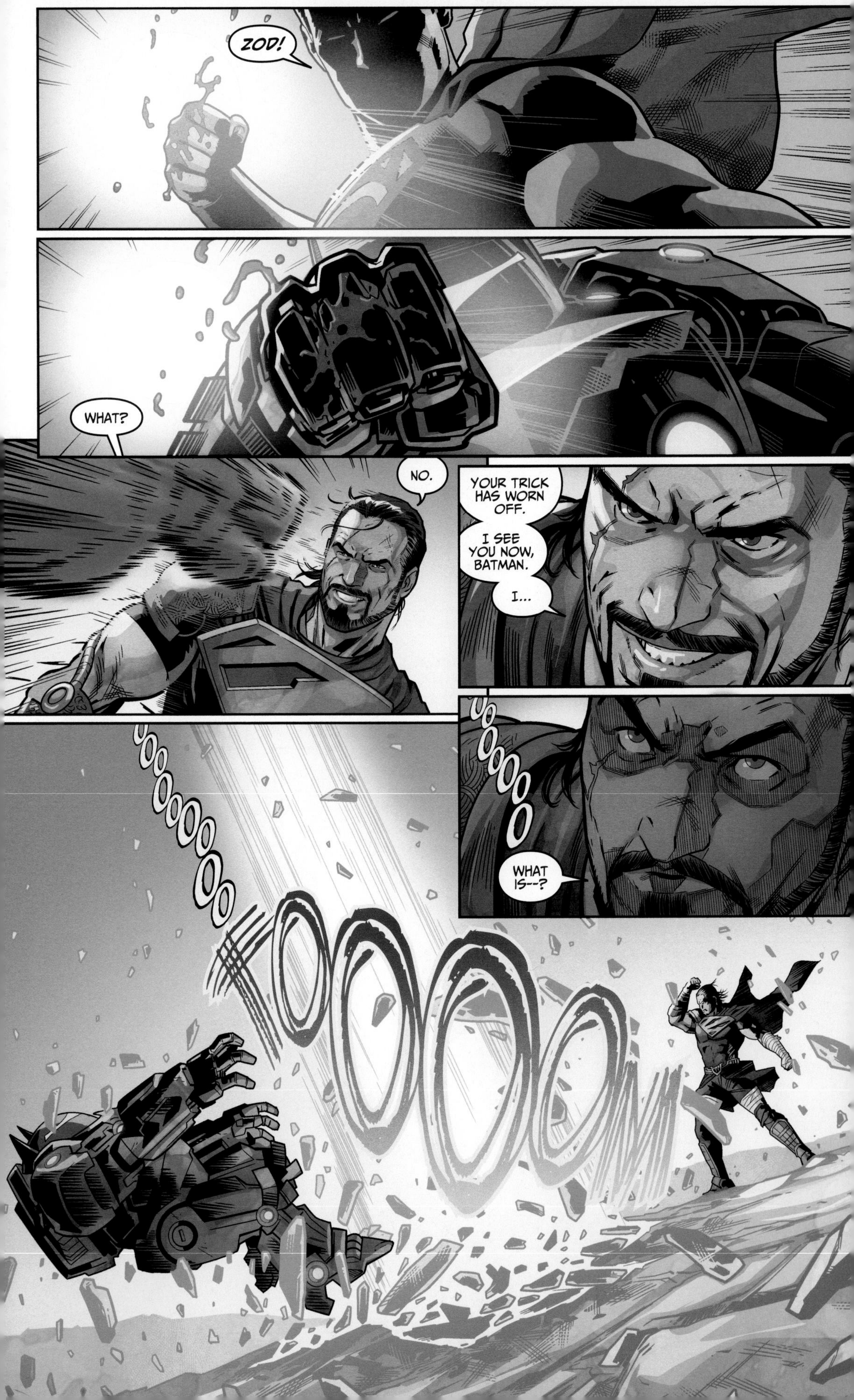

ZOD!
WHAT?
NO.
YOUR TRICK HAS WORN OFF.
I SEE YOU NOW, BATMAN.
I...
OOOOOO
WHAT IS--?
OOOOOOOOOO
TOOOOOM

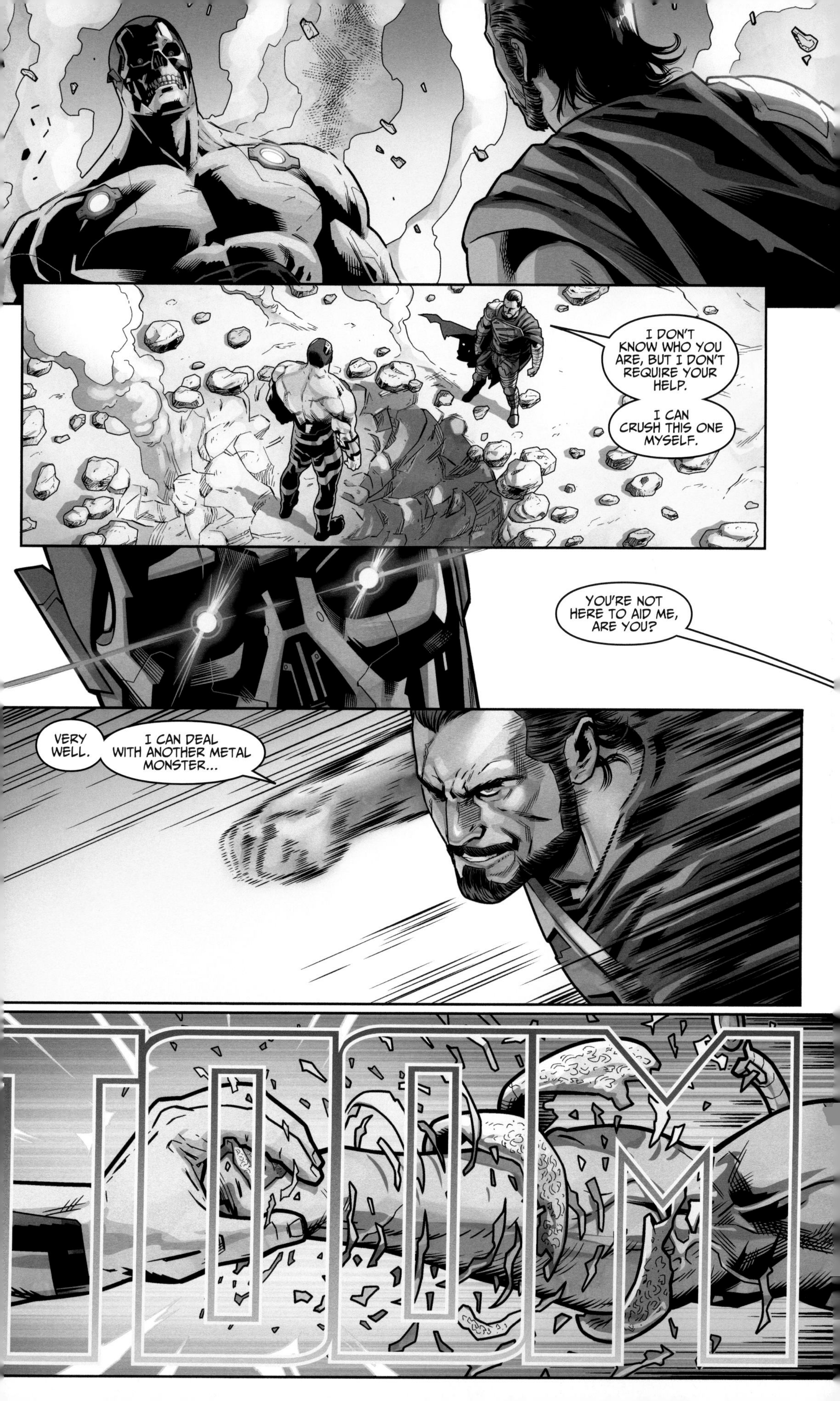
I DON'T KNOW WHO YOU ARE, BUT I DON'T REQUIRE YOUR HELP.
I CAN CRUSH THIS ONE MYSELF.
YOU'RE NOT HERE TO AID ME, ARE YOU?
VERY WELL.
I CAN DEAL WITH ANOTHER METAL MONSTER...

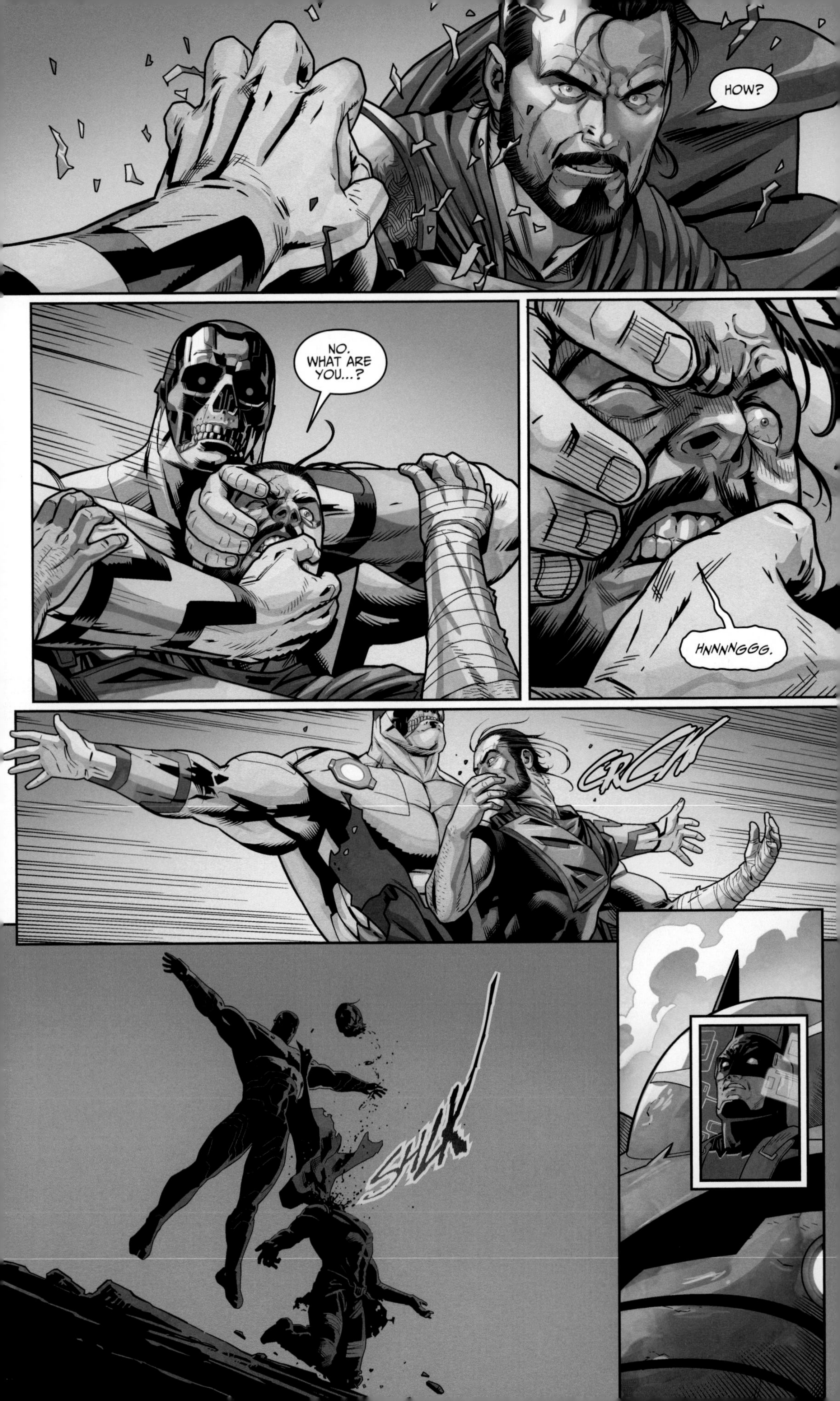
HOW?
NO. WHAT ARE YOU...?
HNNNNGGG.
CRCH
SHLK

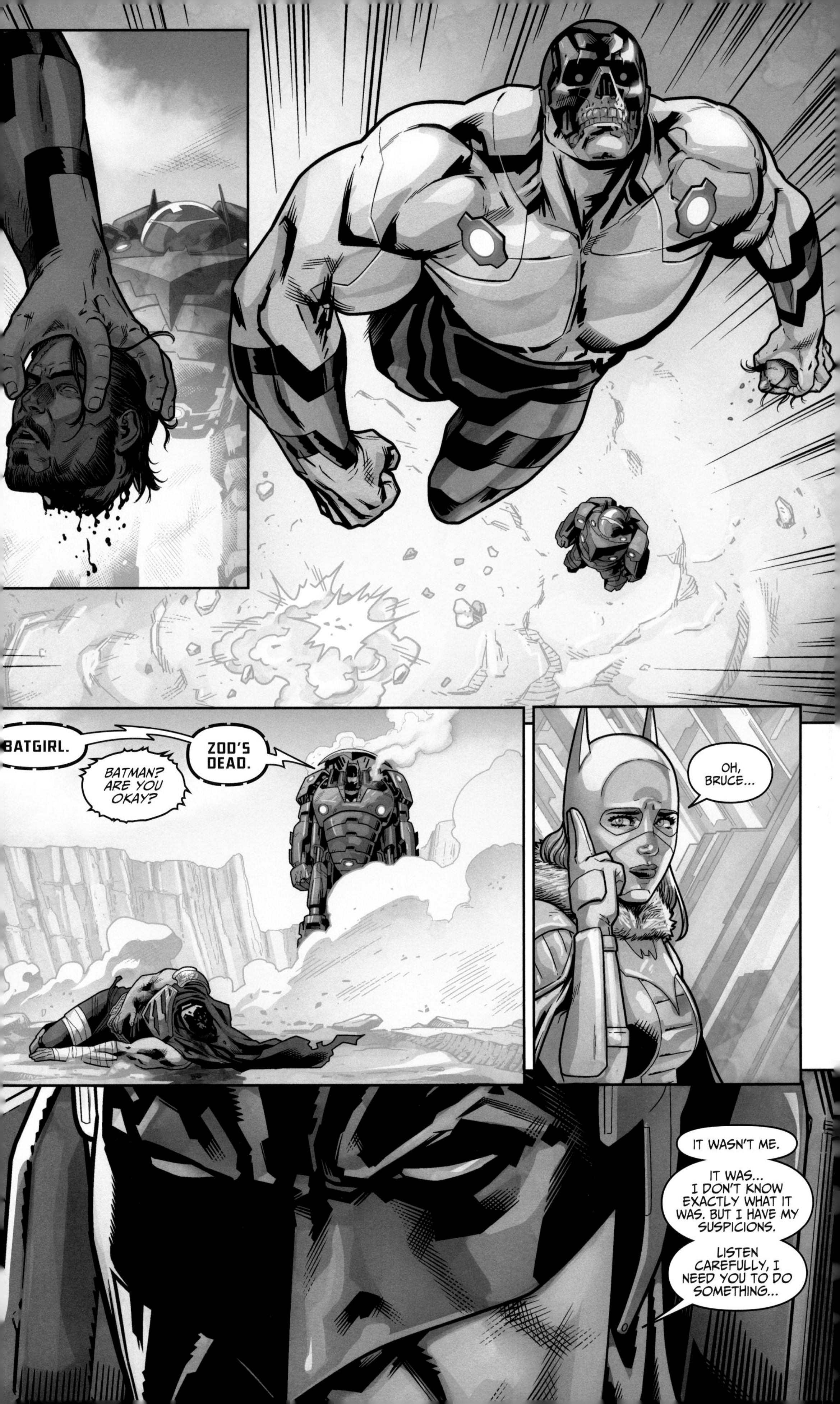
BATGIRL.
ZOD'S DEAD.
BATMAN? ARE YOU OKAY?
OH, BRUCE...
IT WASN'T ME.
IT WAS... I DON'T KNOW EXACTLY WHAT IT WAS. BUT I HAVE MY SUSPICIONS.
LISTEN CAREFULLY, I NEED YOU TO DO SOMETHING...

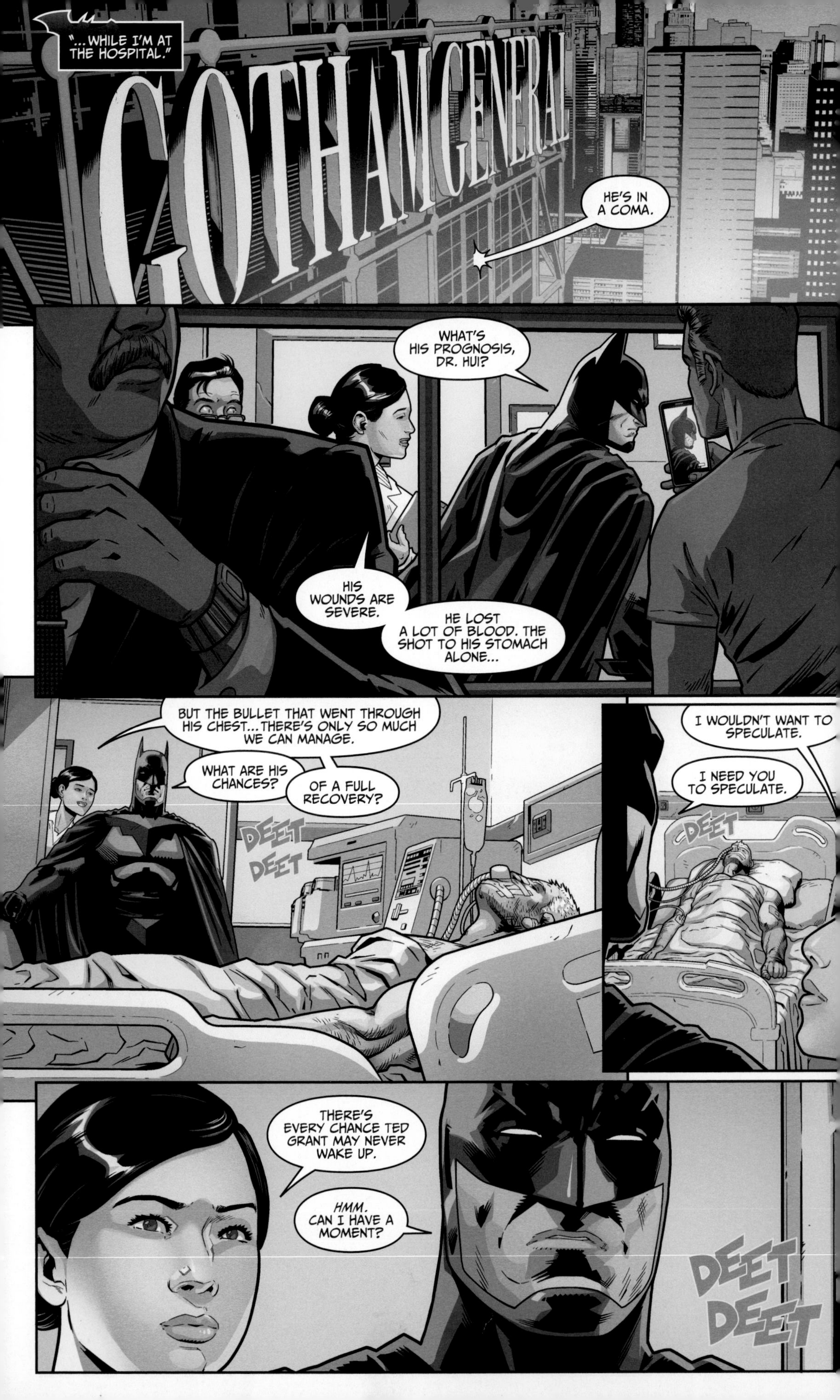
"...WHILE I'M AT THE HOSPITAL."
GOTHAM GENERAL
HE'S IN A COMA.
WHAT'S HIS PROGNOSIS, DR. HUI?
HIS WOUNDS ARE SEVERE.
HE LOST A LOT OF BLOOD. THE SHOT TO HIS STOMACH ALONE...
BUT THE BULLET THAT WENT THROUGH HIS CHEST...THERE'S ONLY SO MUCH WE CAN MANAGE.
WHAT ARE HIS CHANCES?
OF A FULL RECOVERY?
DEET DEET
I WOULDN'T WANT TO SPECULATE.
I NEED YOU TO SPECULATE.
DEET
THERE'S EVERY CHANCE TED GRANT MAY NEVER WAKE UP.
HMM. CAN I HAVE A MOMENT?
DEET DEET

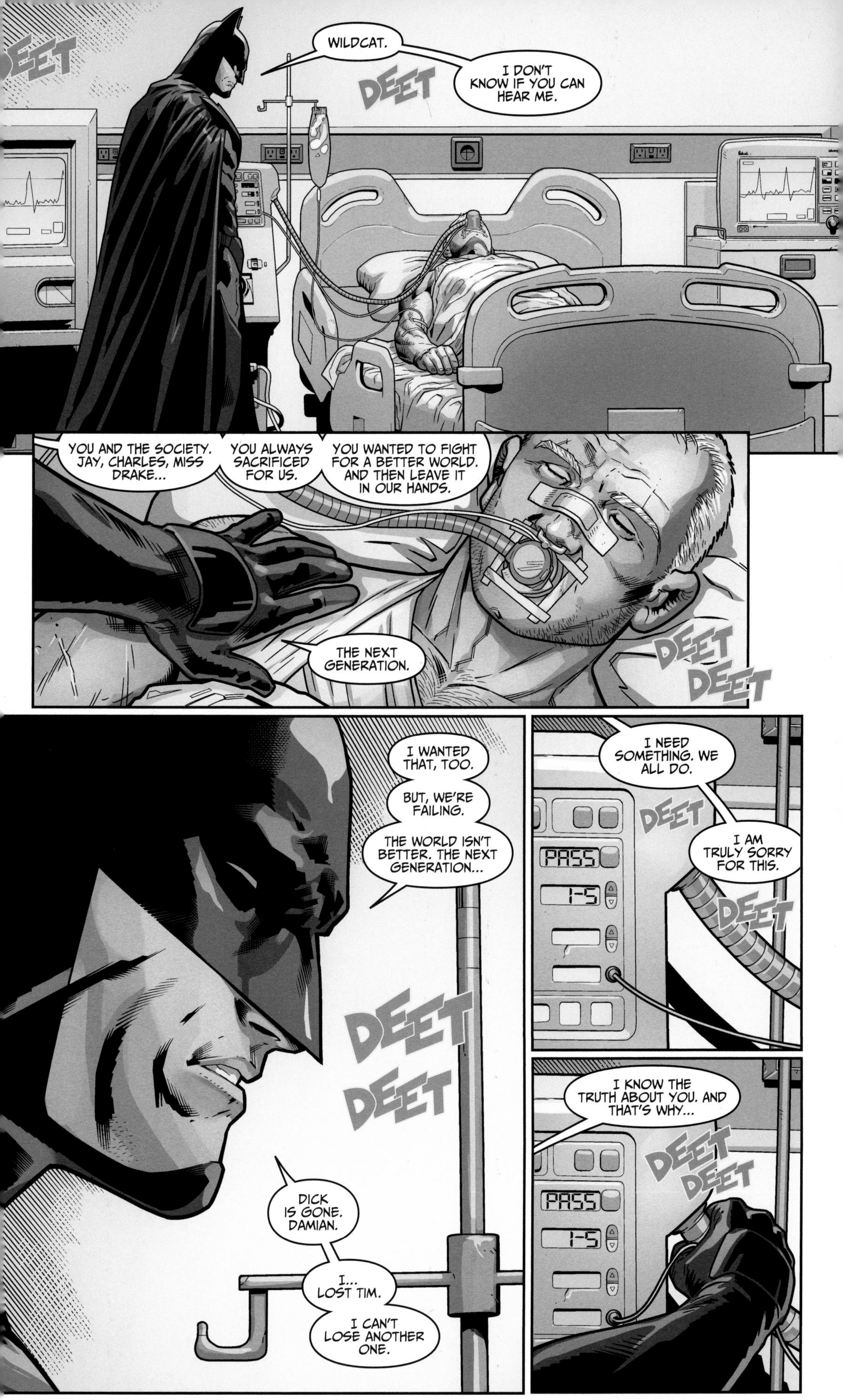
DEET
WILDCAT.
DEET
I DON'T KNOW IF YOU CAN HEAR ME.
YOU AND THE SOCIETY. JAY, CHARLES, MISS DRAKE...
YOU ALWAYS SACRIFICED FOR US.
YOU WANTED TO FIGHT FOR A BETTER WORLD. AND THEN LEAVE IT IN OUR HANDS.
THE NEXT GENERATION.
DEET DEET
I WANTED THAT, TOO.
BUT, WE'RE FAILING.
THE WORLD ISN'T BETTER. THE NEXT GENERATION...
DEET DEET
DICK IS GONE. DAMIAN.
I... LOST TIM.
I CAN'T LOSE ANOTHER ONE.
I NEED SOMETHING. WE ALL DO.
DEET
PASS
1-5
I AM TRULY SORRY FOR THIS.
DEET
I KNOW THE TRUTH ABOUT YOU. AND THAT'S WHY...
DEET DEET
PASS
1-5

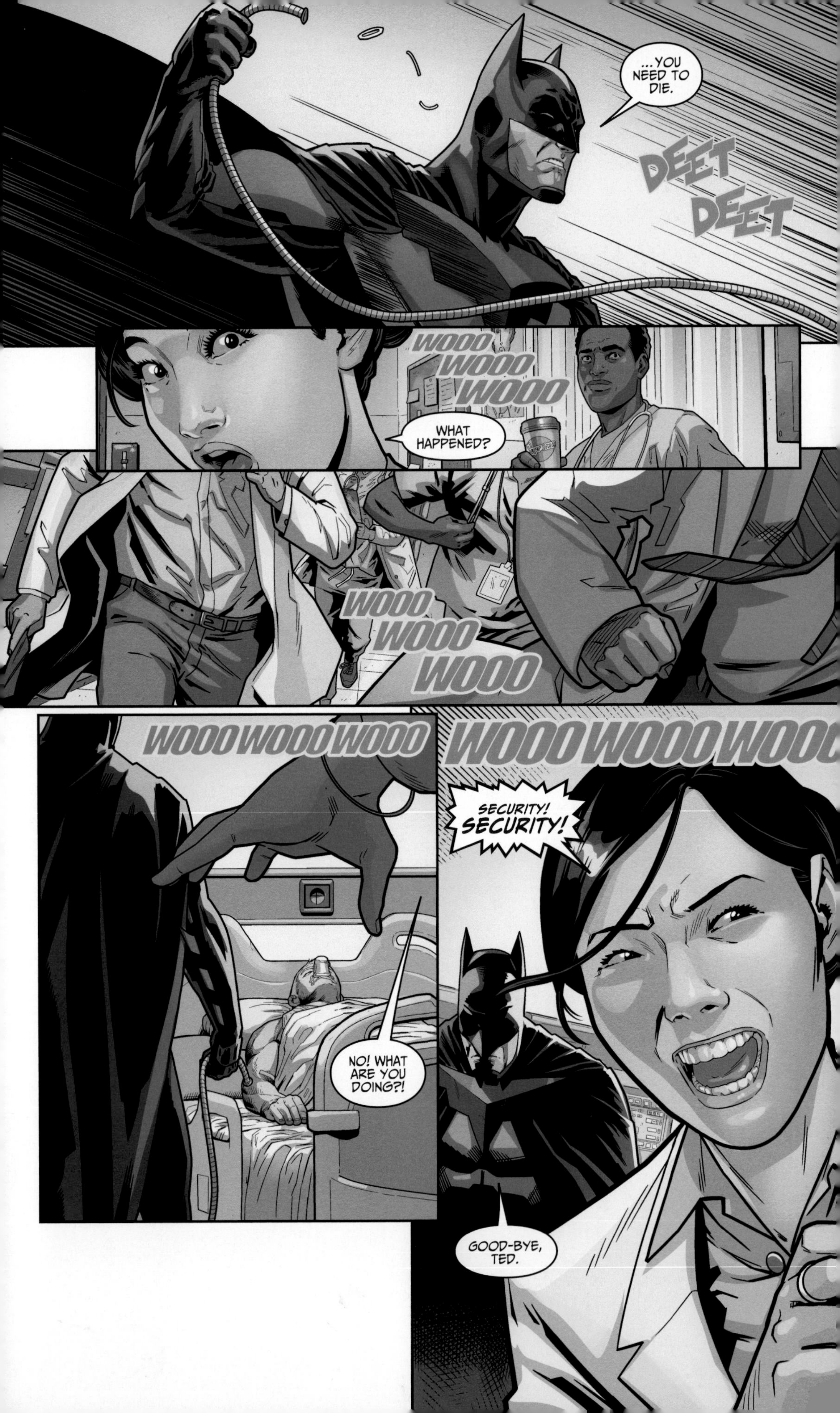
...YOU NEED TO DIE.
DEET DEET
WOOO WOOO WOOO
WHAT HAPPENED?
WOOO WOOO WOOO
WOOO WOOO WOOO
NO! WHAT ARE YOU DOING?!
WOOO WOOO WOOO
SECURITY! SECURITY!
GOOD-BYE, TED.

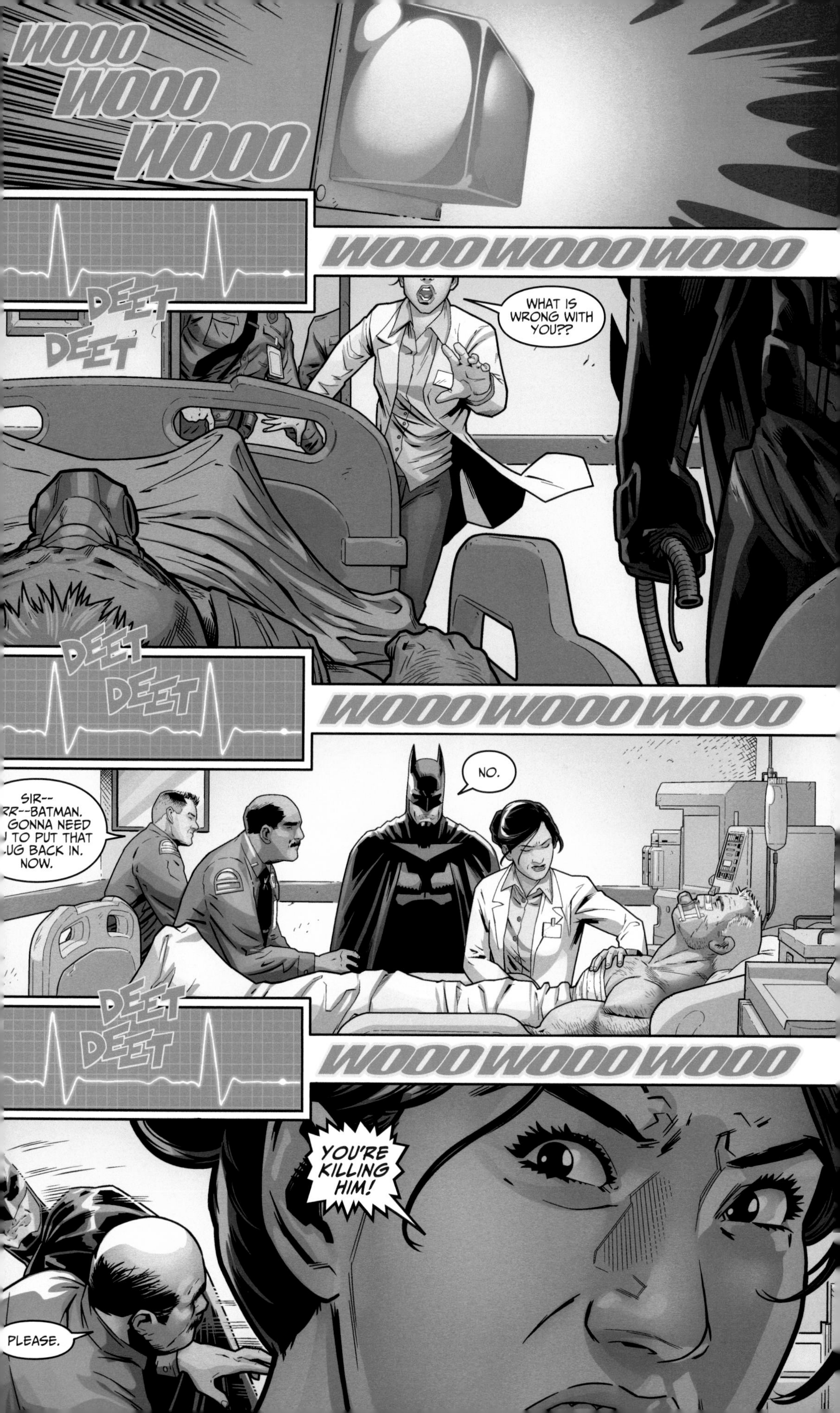
WOOO
WOOO
WOOO
WOOO WOOO WOOO
DEET
DEET
WHAT IS WRONG WITH YOU??
DEET
DEET
WOOO WOOO WOOO
SIR-- RR--BATMAN. GONNA NEED TO PUT THAT UG BACK IN. NOW.
NO.
DEET
DEET
WOOO WOOO WOOO
YOU'RE KILLING HIM!
PLEASE.

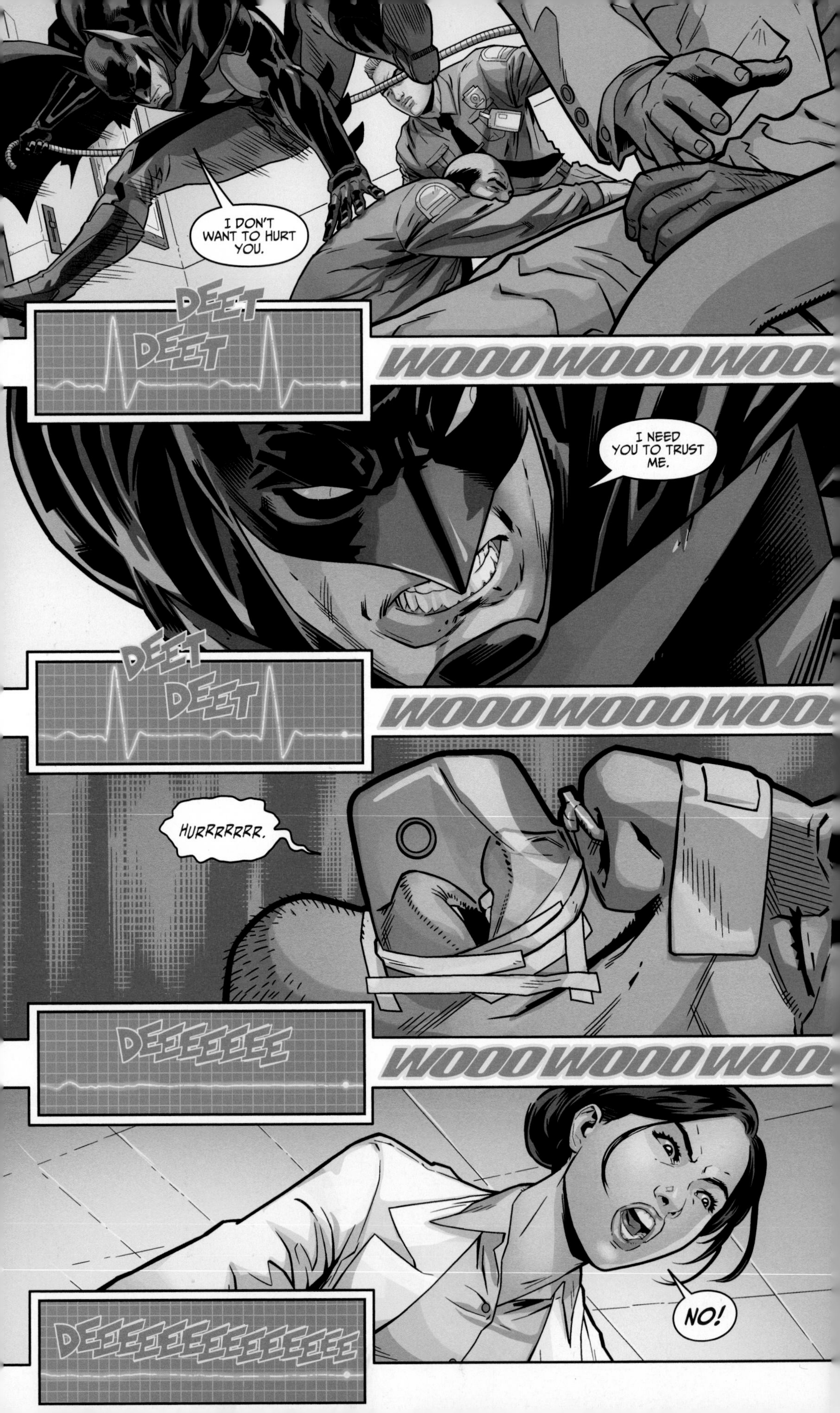
I DON'T WANT TO HURT YOU.
DEET
DEET
WOOO WOOO WOO
I NEED YOU TO TRUST ME.
DEET
DEET
WOOO WOOO WOO
HURRRRRR.
DEEEEEEE
WOOO WOOO WOO
NO!
DEEEEEEEEEEEEEE

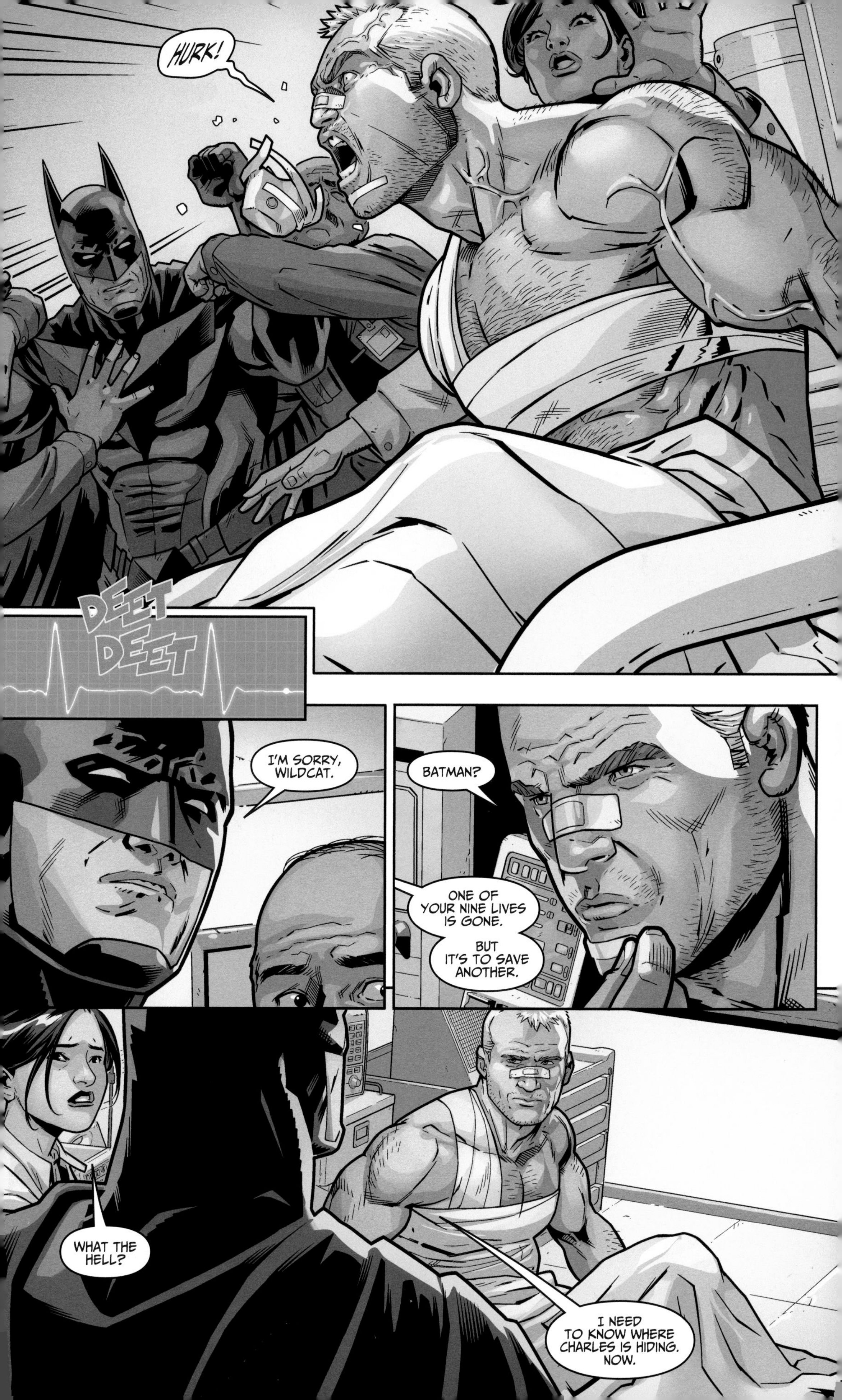
HURK!
DEET
DEET
I'M SORRY, WILDCAT.
BATMAN?
ONE OF YOUR NINE LIVES IS GONE.
BUT IT'S TO SAVE ANOTHER.
WHAT THE HELL?
I NEED TO KNOW WHERE CHARLES IS HIDING. NOW.

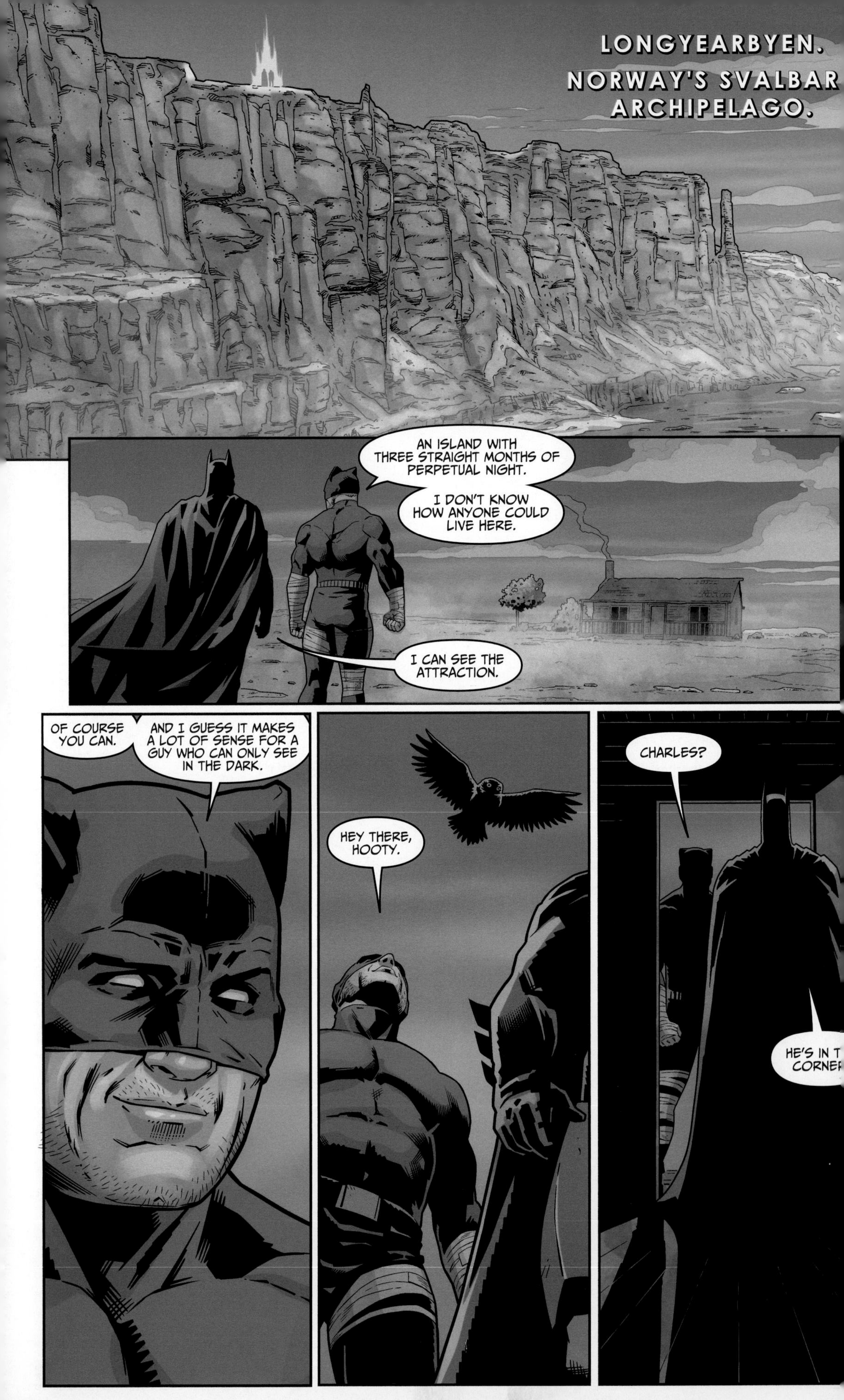

LONGYEARBYEN.
NORWAY'S SVALBAR
ARCHIPELAGO.
AN ISLAND WITH THREE STRAIGHT MONTHS OF PERPETUAL NIGHT.
I DON'T KNOW HOW ANYONE COULD LIVE HERE.
I CAN SEE THE ATTRACTION.
OF COURSE YOU CAN.
AND I GUESS IT MAKES A LOT OF SENSE FOR A GUY WHO CAN ONLY SEE IN THE DARK.
HEY THERE, HOOTY.
CHARLES?
HE'S IN T
CORNEF

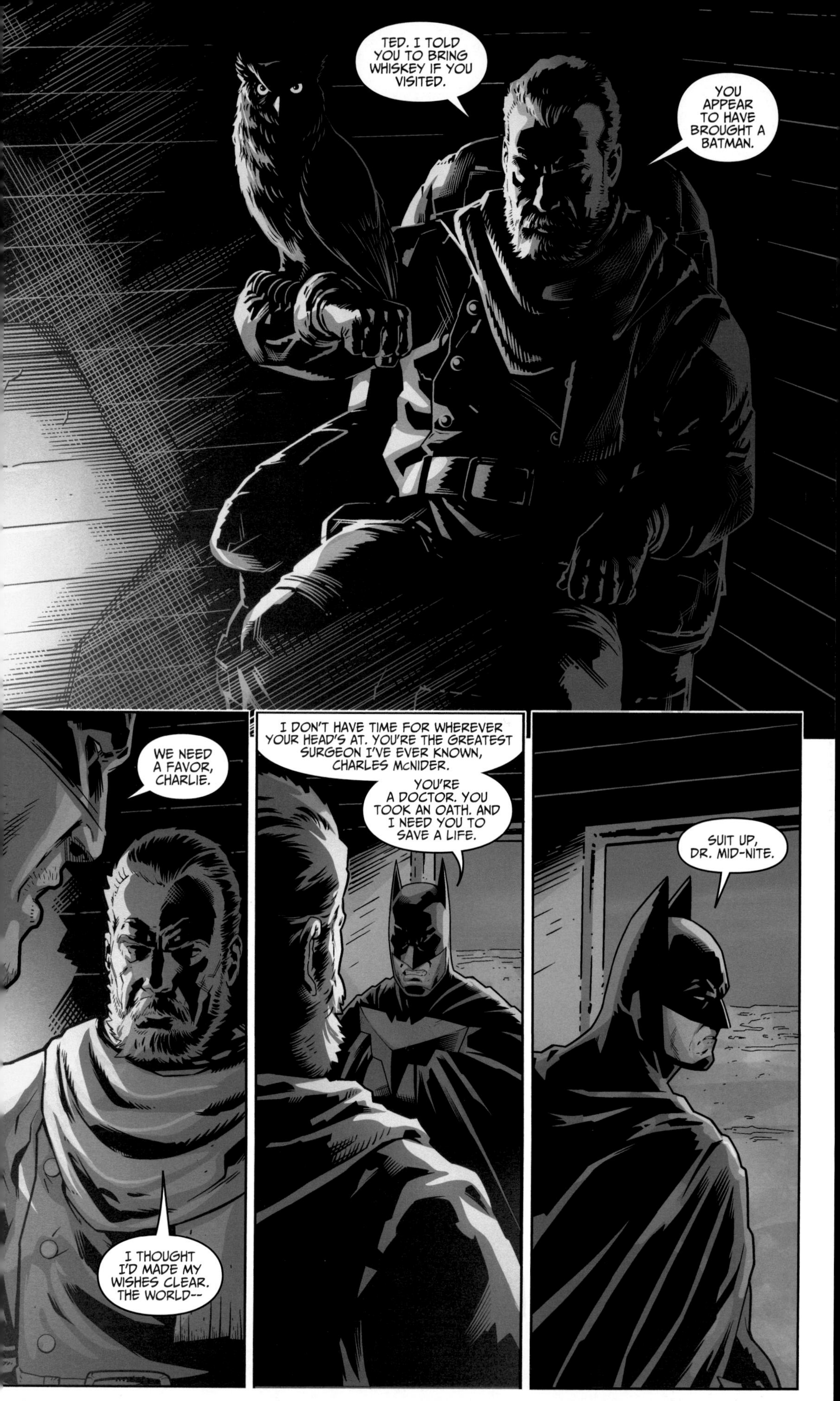
TED. I TOLD YOU TO BRING WHISKEY IF YOU VISITED.
YOU APPEAR TO HAVE BROUGHT A BATMAN.
WE NEED A FAVOR, CHARLIE.
I THOUGHT I'D MADE MY WISHES CLEAR. THE WORLD--
I DON'T HAVE TIME FOR WHEREVER YOUR HEAD'S AT. YOU'RE THE GREATEST SURGEON I'VE EVER KNOWN, CHARLES McNIDER.
YOU'RE A DOCTOR. YOU TOOK AN OATH. AND I NEED YOU TO SAVE A LIFE.
SUIT UP, DR. MID-NITE.

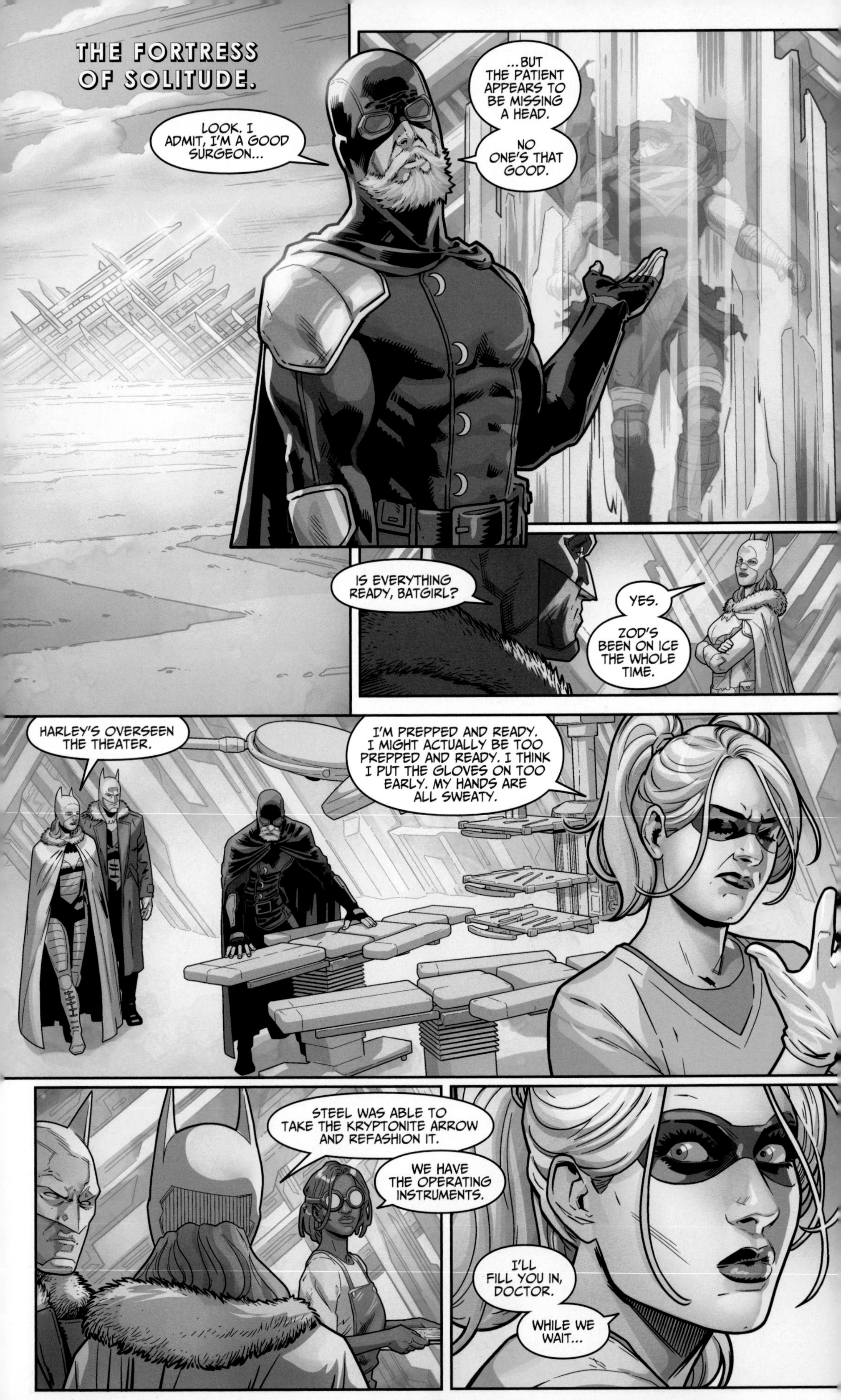
THE FORTRESS OF SOLITUDE.
LOOK. I ADMIT, I'M A GOOD SURGEON...
...BUT THE PATIENT APPEARS TO BE MISSING A HEAD.
NO ONE'S THAT GOOD.
IS EVERYTHING READY, BATGIRL?
YES.
ZOD'S BEEN ON ICE THE WHOLE TIME.
HARLEY'S OVERSEEN THE THEATER.
I'M PREPPED AND READY. I MIGHT ACTUALLY BE TOO PREPPED AND READY. I THINK I PUT THE GLOVES ON TOO EARLY. MY HANDS ARE ALL SWEATY.
STEEL WAS ABLE TO TAKE THE KRYPTONITE ARROW AND REFASHION IT.
WE HAVE THE OPERATING INSTRUMENTS.
I'LL FILL YOU IN, DOCTOR.
WHILE WE WAIT...

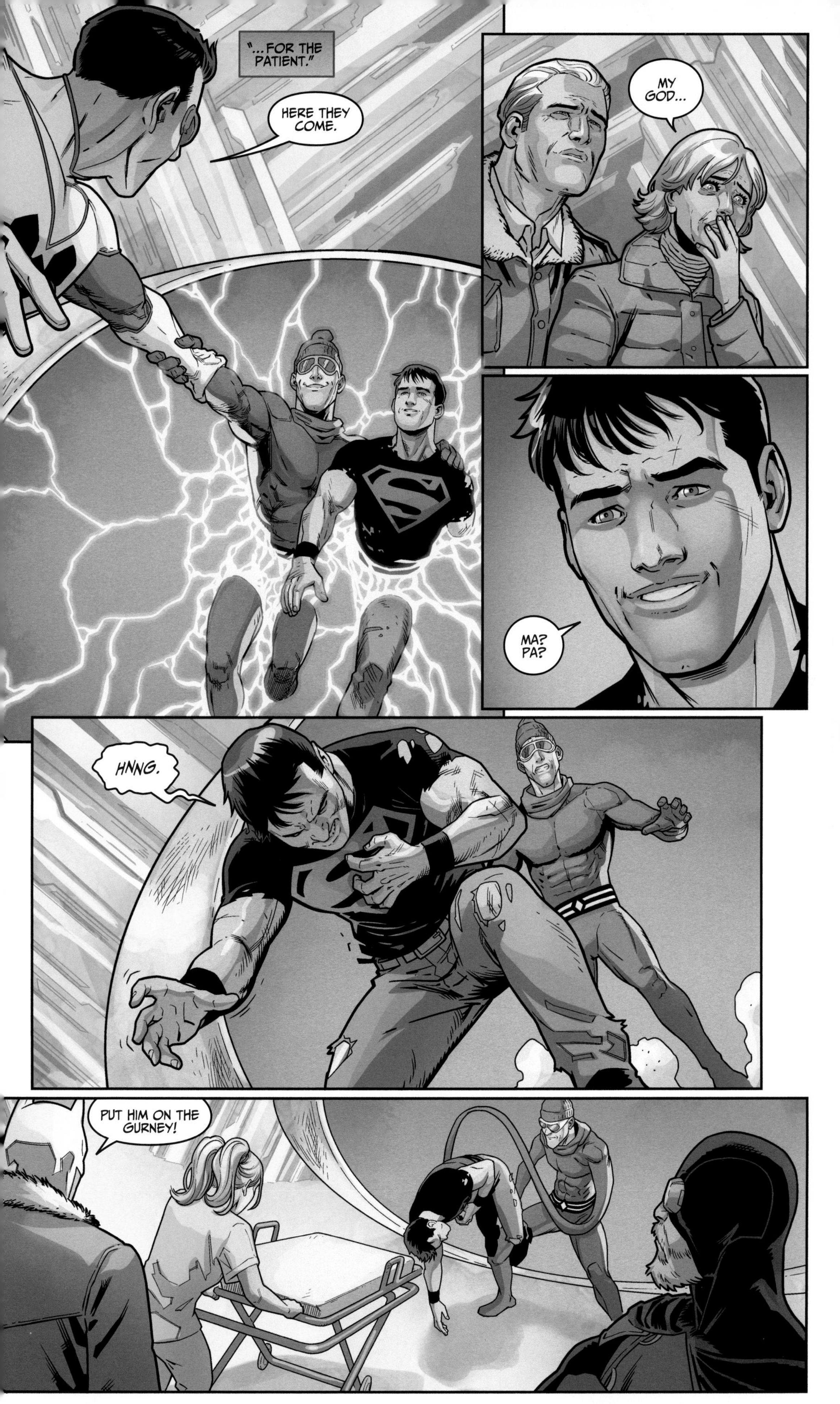
"...FOR THE PATIENT."
HERE THEY COME.
MY GOD...
MA? PA?
HNNG.
PUT HIM ON THE GURNEY!

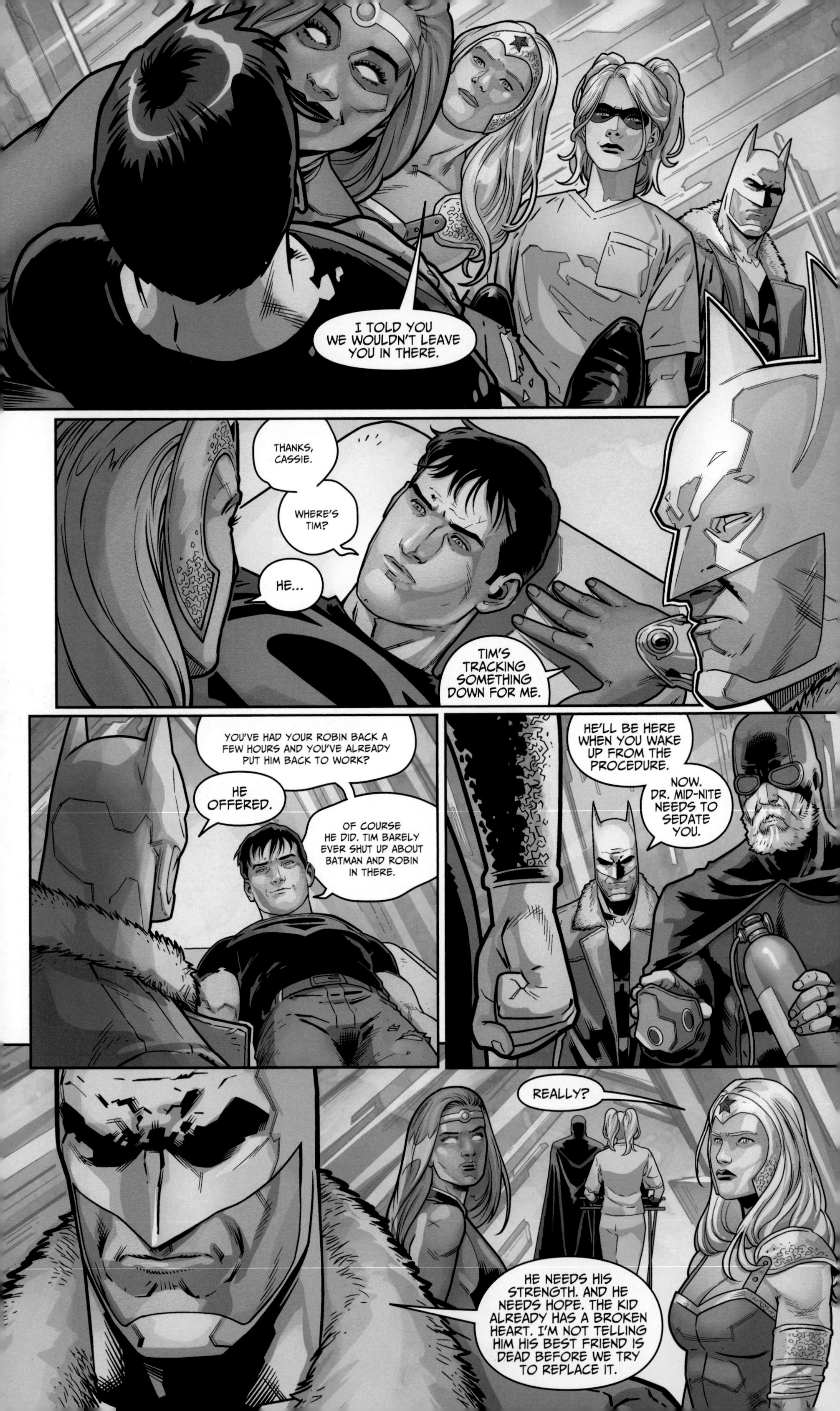
I TOLD YOU WE WOULDN'T LEAVE YOU IN THERE.
THANKS, CASSIE.
WHERE'S TIM?
HE...
TIM'S TRACKING SOMETHING DOWN FOR ME.
YOU'VE HAD YOUR ROBIN BACK A FEW HOURS AND YOU'VE ALREADY PUT HIM BACK TO WORK?
HE OFFERED.
OF COURSE HE DID. TIM BARELY EVER SHUT UP ABOUT BATMAN AND ROBIN IN THERE.
HE'LL BE HERE WHEN YOU WAKE UP FROM THE PROCEDURE.
NOW. DR. MID-NITE NEEDS TO SEDATE YOU.
REALLY?
HE NEEDS HIS STRENGTH. AND HE NEEDS HOPE. THE KID ALREADY HAS A BROKEN HEART. I'M NOT TELLING HIM HIS BEST FRIEND IS DEAD BEFORE WE TRY TO REPLACE IT.

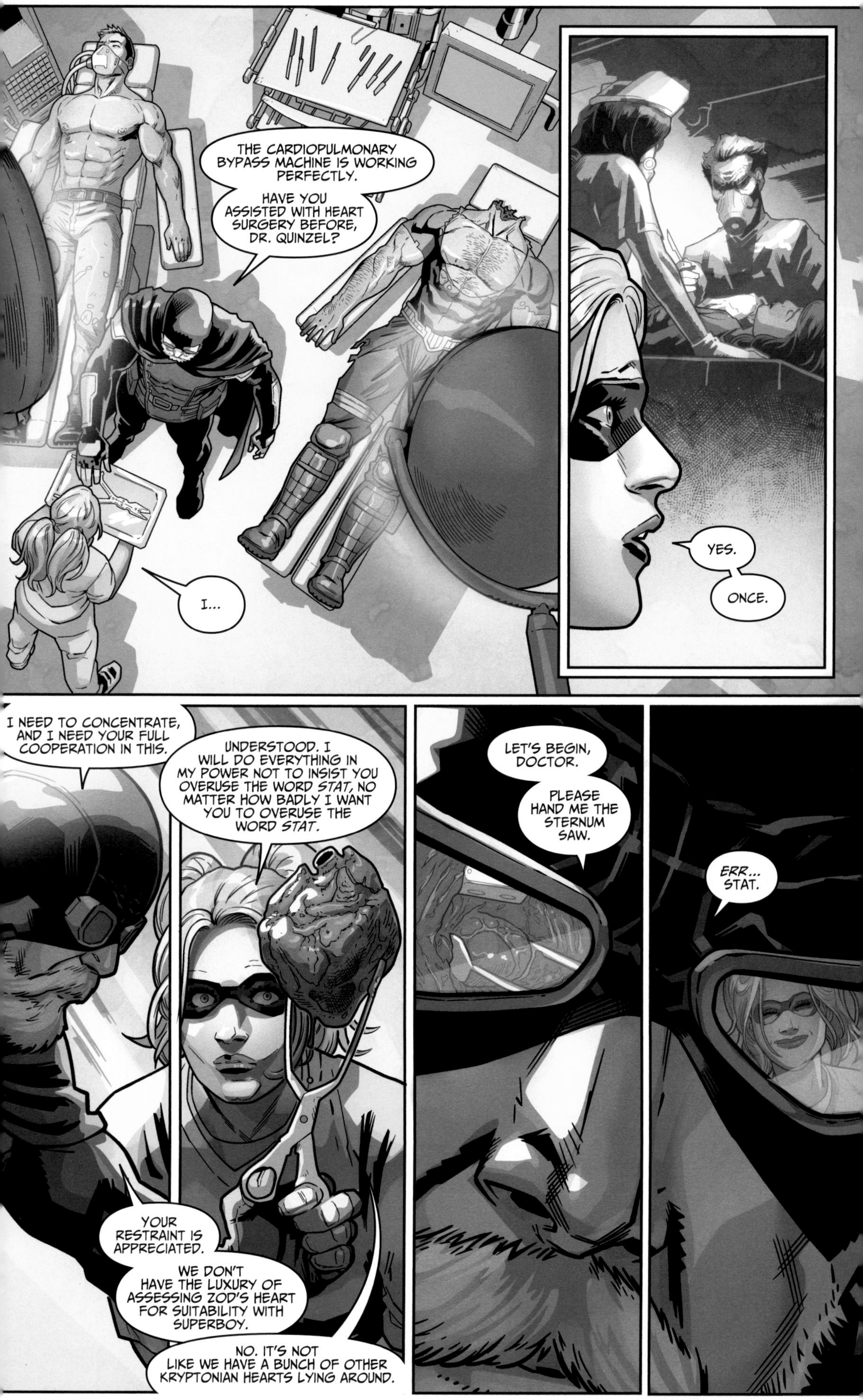
THE CARDIOPULMONARY BYPASS MACHINE IS WORKING PERFECTLY.
HAVE YOU ASSISTED WITH HEART SURGERY BEFORE, DR. QUINZEL?
I...
YES.
ONCE.
I NEED TO CONCENTRATE, AND I NEED YOUR FULL COOPERATION IN THIS.
UNDERSTOOD. I WILL DO EVERYTHING IN MY POWER NOT TO INSIST YOU OVERUSE THE WORD *STAT*, NO MATTER HOW BADLY I WANT YOU TO OVERUSE THE WORD *STAT*.
YOUR RESTRAINT IS APPRECIATED.
WE DON'T HAVE THE LUXURY OF ASSESSING ZOD'S HEART FOR SUITABILITY WITH SUPERBOY.
NO. IT'S NOT LIKE WE HAVE A BUNCH OF OTHER KRYPTONIAN HEARTS LYING AROUND.
LET'S BEGIN, DOCTOR.
PLEASE HAND ME THE STERNUM SAW.
ERR... STAT.

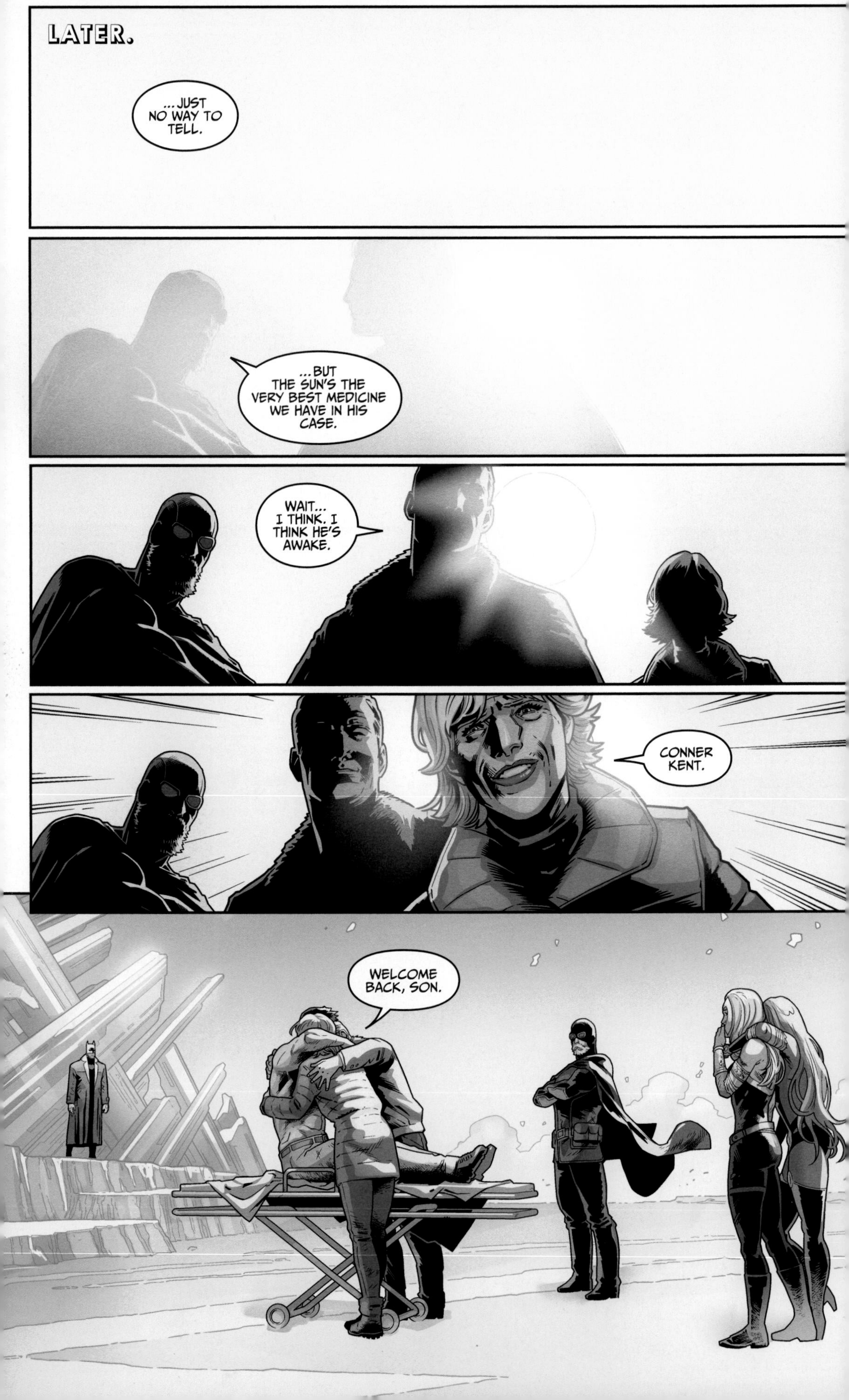
LATER.
...JUST NO WAY TO TELL.
...BUT THE SUN'S THE VERY BEST MEDICINE WE HAVE IN HIS CASE.
WAIT... I THINK. I THINK HE'S AWAKE.
CONNER KENT.
WELCOME BACK, SON.

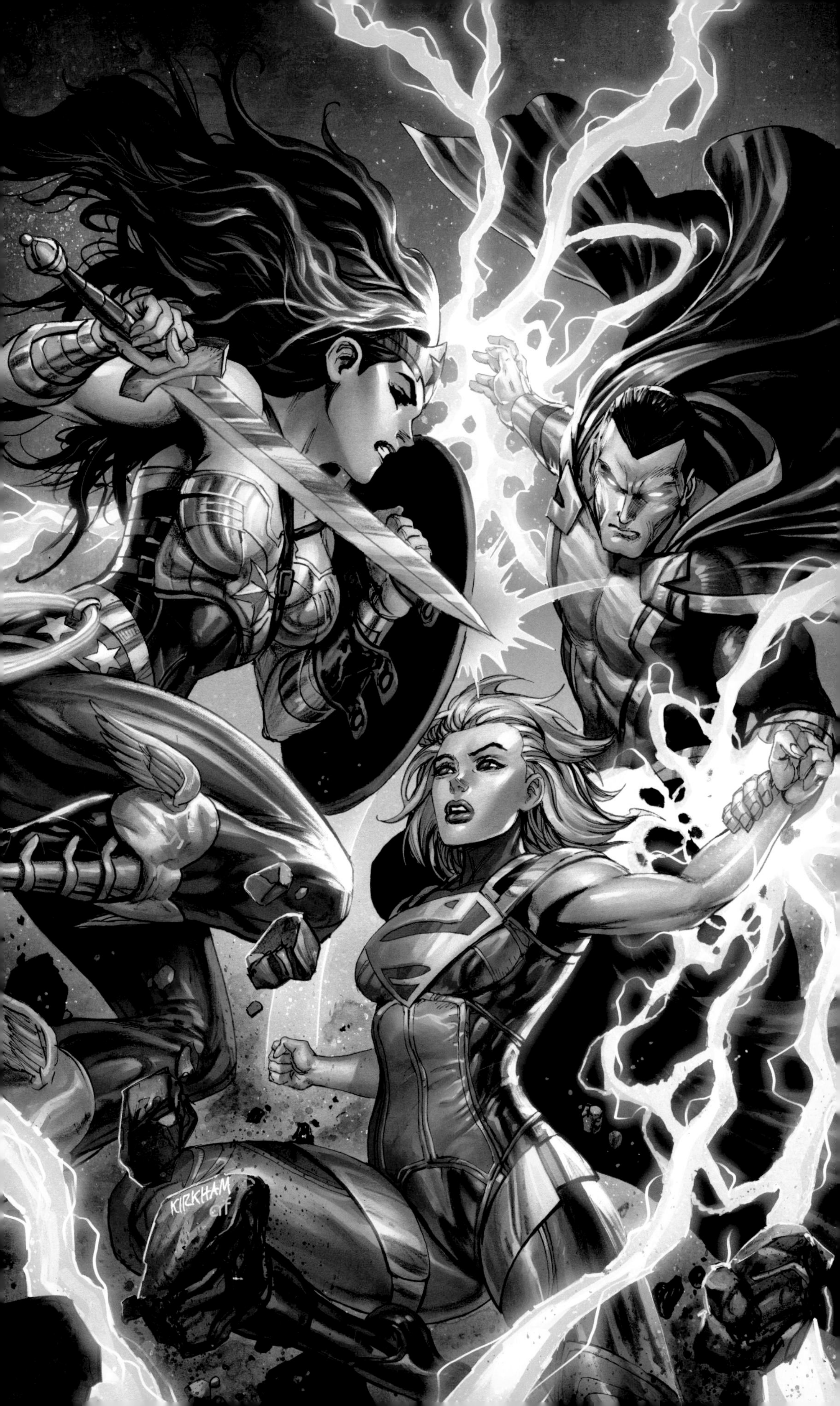
KIRKHAM

"Rapunzel"

Tom Taylor Writer **Daniel Sampere** and **Mike S. Miller** (pages 1-3, 8-10) Artists
Rex Lokus and **J. Nanjan** (pages 1-3, 8-10) Colorists **Wes Abbott** Letterer

Cover art by **Tyler Kirkham** and **Arif Prianto**

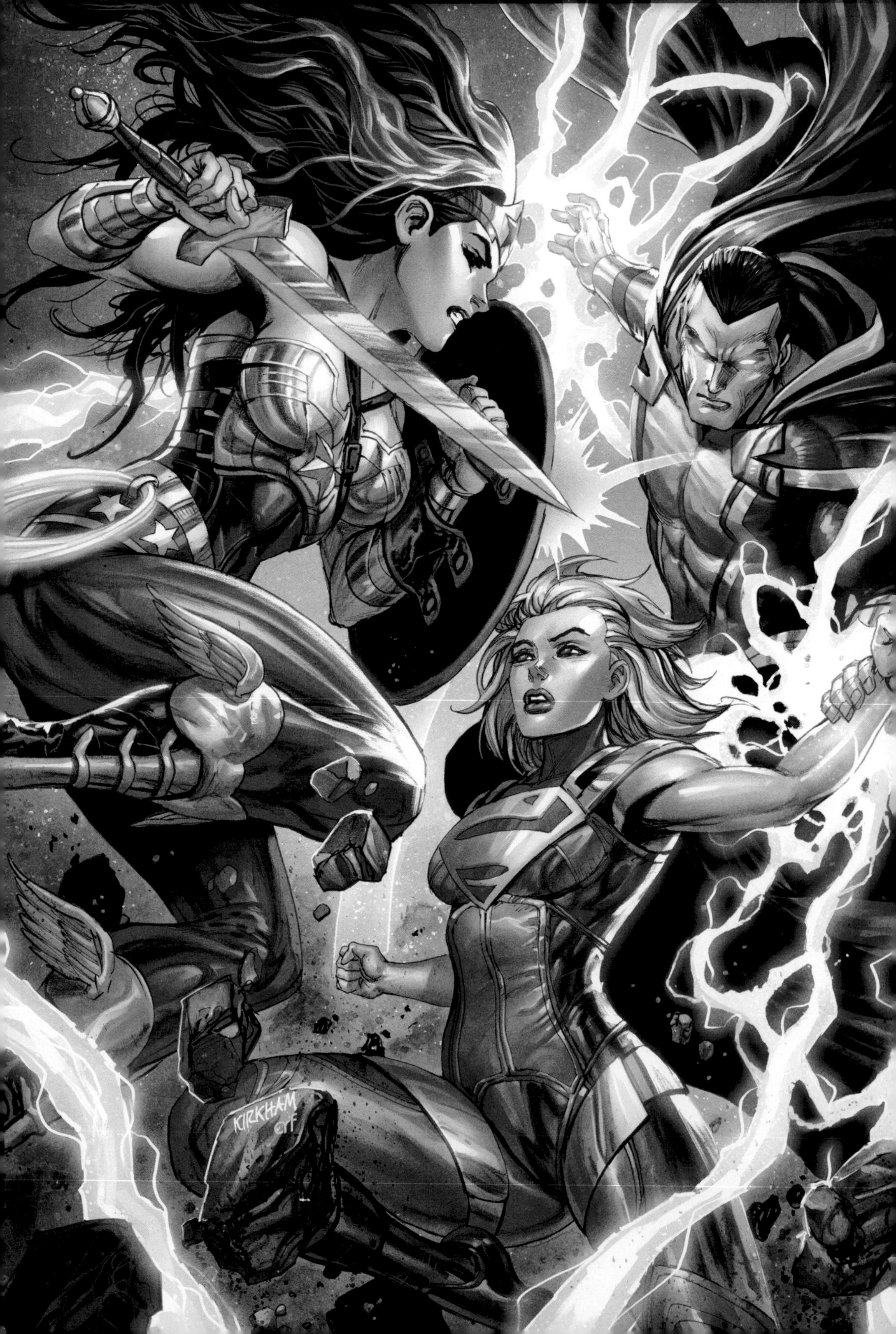
KIRKHAM

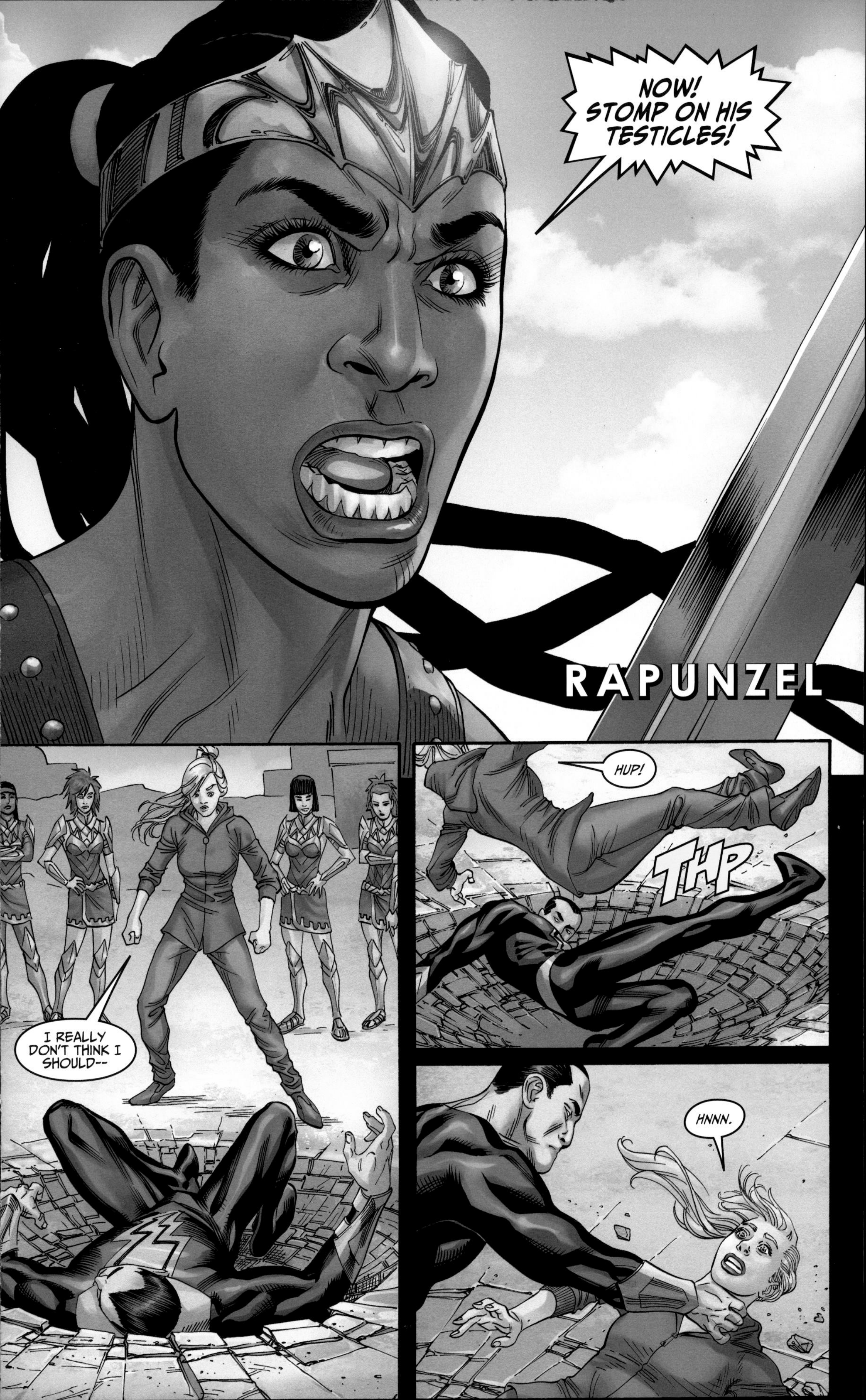
NOW! STOMP ON HIS TESTICLES!
RAPUNZEL
I REALLY DON'T THINK I SHOULD--
HUP!
THP
HNNN.

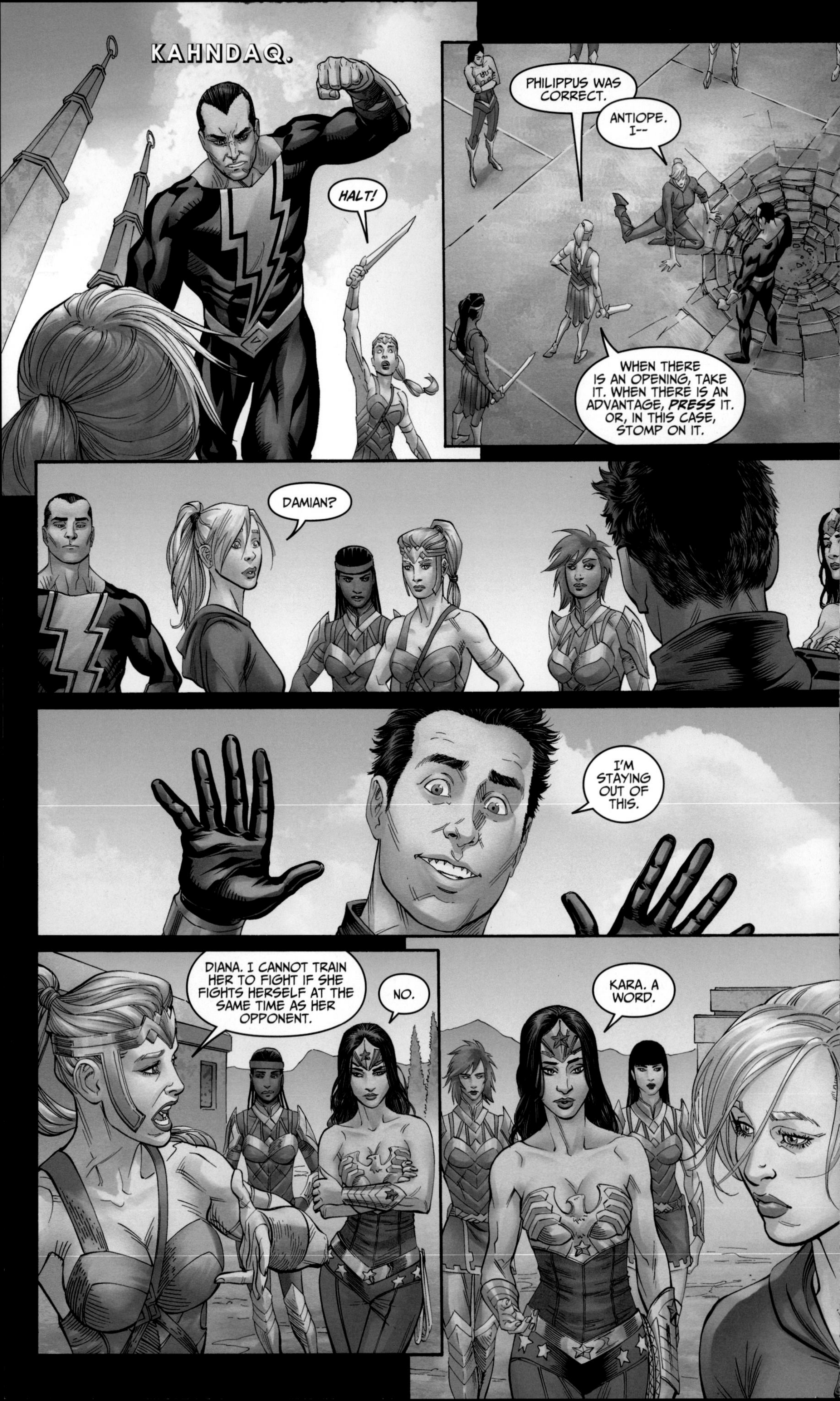
KAHNDAQ.
HALT!
PHILIPPUS WAS CORRECT.
ANTIOPE. I--
WHEN THERE IS AN OPENING, TAKE IT. WHEN THERE IS AN ADVANTAGE, PRESS IT. OR, IN THIS CASE, STOMP ON IT.
DAMIAN?
I'M STAYING OUT OF THIS.
DIANA. I CANNOT TRAIN HER TO FIGHT IF SHE FIGHTS HERSELF AT THE SAME TIME AS HER OPPONENT.
NO.
KARA. A WORD.

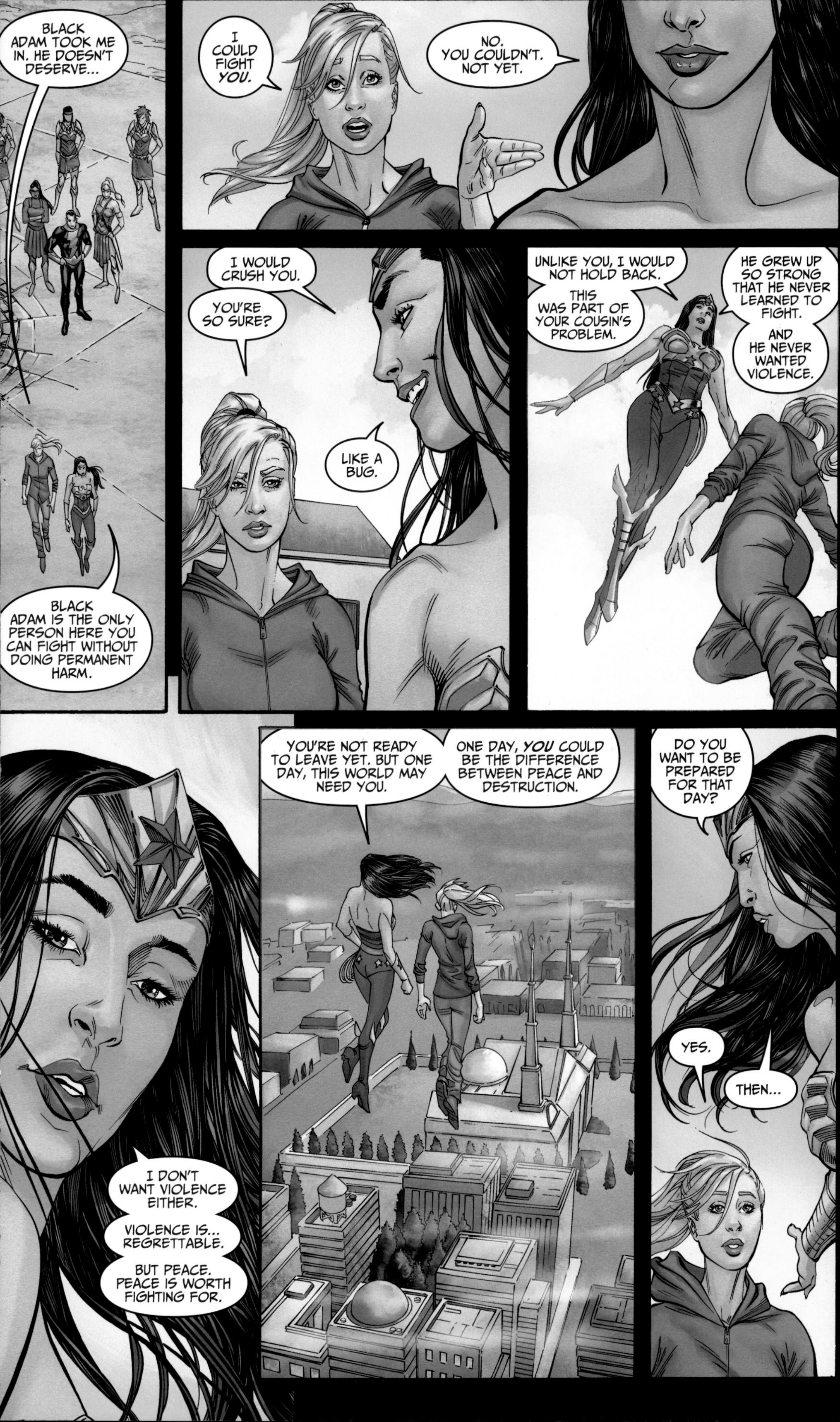
BLACK ADAM TOOK ME IN. HE DOESN'T DESERVE...
BLACK ADAM IS THE ONLY PERSON HERE YOU CAN FIGHT WITHOUT DOING PERMANENT HARM.
I COULD FIGHT *YOU.*
NO. YOU COULDN'T. NOT YET.
I WOULD CRUSH YOU.
YOU'RE SO SURE?
LIKE A BUG.
UNLIKE YOU, I WOULD NOT HOLD BACK.
THIS WAS PART OF YOUR COUSIN'S PROBLEM.
HE GREW UP SO STRONG THAT HE NEVER LEARNED TO FIGHT.
AND HE NEVER WANTED VIOLENCE.
I DON'T WANT VIOLENCE EITHER.
VIOLENCE IS... REGRETTABLE.
BUT PEACE. PEACE IS WORTH FIGHTING FOR.
YOU'RE NOT READY TO LEAVE YET. BUT ONE DAY, THIS WORLD MAY NEED YOU.
ONE DAY, *YOU* COULD BE THE DIFFERENCE BETWEEN PEACE AND DESTRUCTION.
DO YOU WANT TO BE PREPARED FOR THAT DAY?
YES.
THEN...

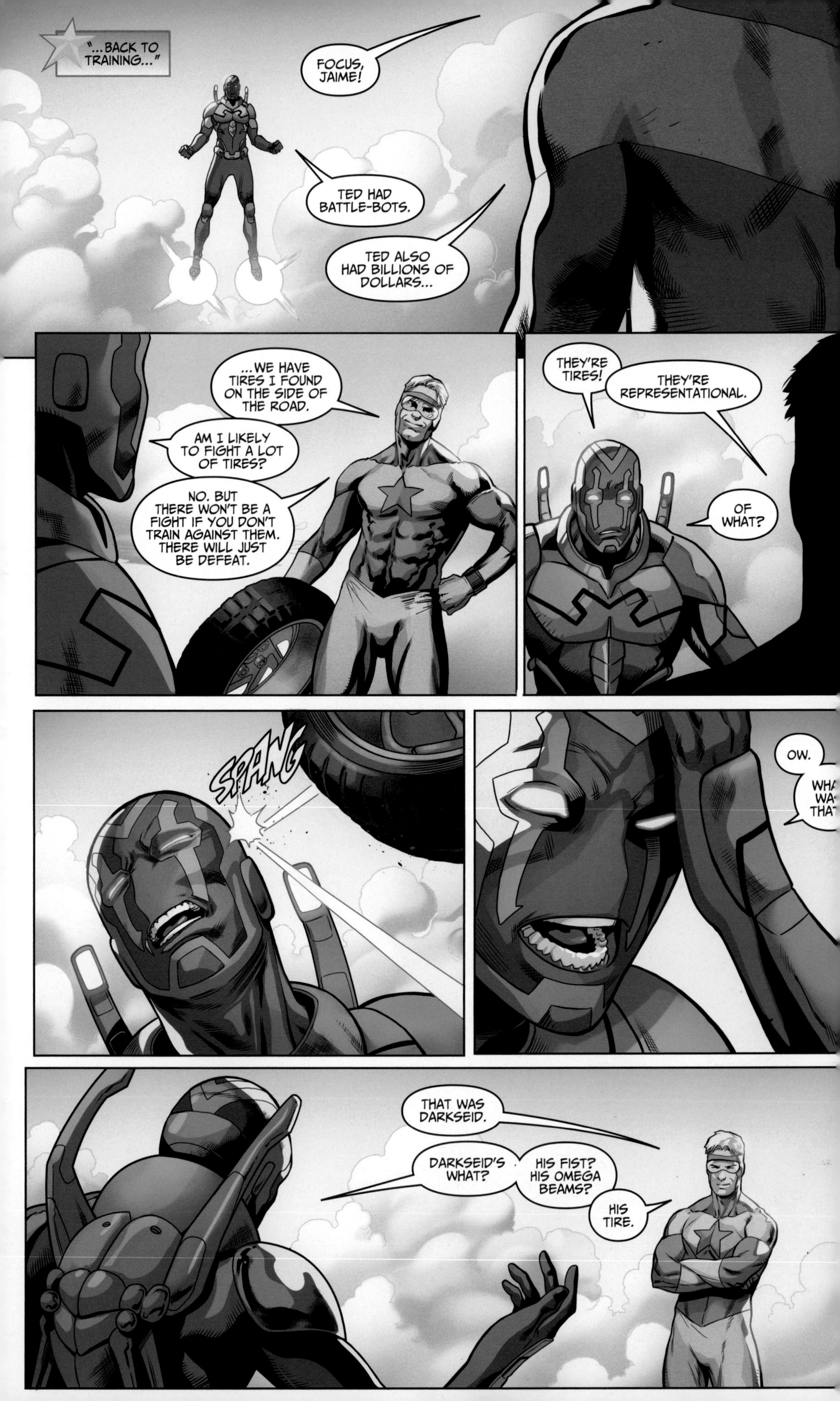
"...BACK TO TRAINING..."
FOCUS, JAIME!
TED HAD BATTLE-BOTS.
TED ALSO HAD BILLIONS OF DOLLARS...
...WE HAVE TIRES I FOUND ON THE SIDE OF THE ROAD.
AM I LIKELY TO FIGHT A LOT OF TIRES?
NO. BUT THERE WON'T BE A FIGHT IF YOU DON'T TRAIN AGAINST THEM. THERE WILL JUST BE DEFEAT.
THEY'RE TIRES!
THEY'RE REPRESENTATIONAL.
OF WHAT?
SPANG
OW.
THAT WAS DARKSEID.
DARKSEID'S WHAT?
HIS FIST? HIS OMEGA BEAMS?
HIS TIRE.

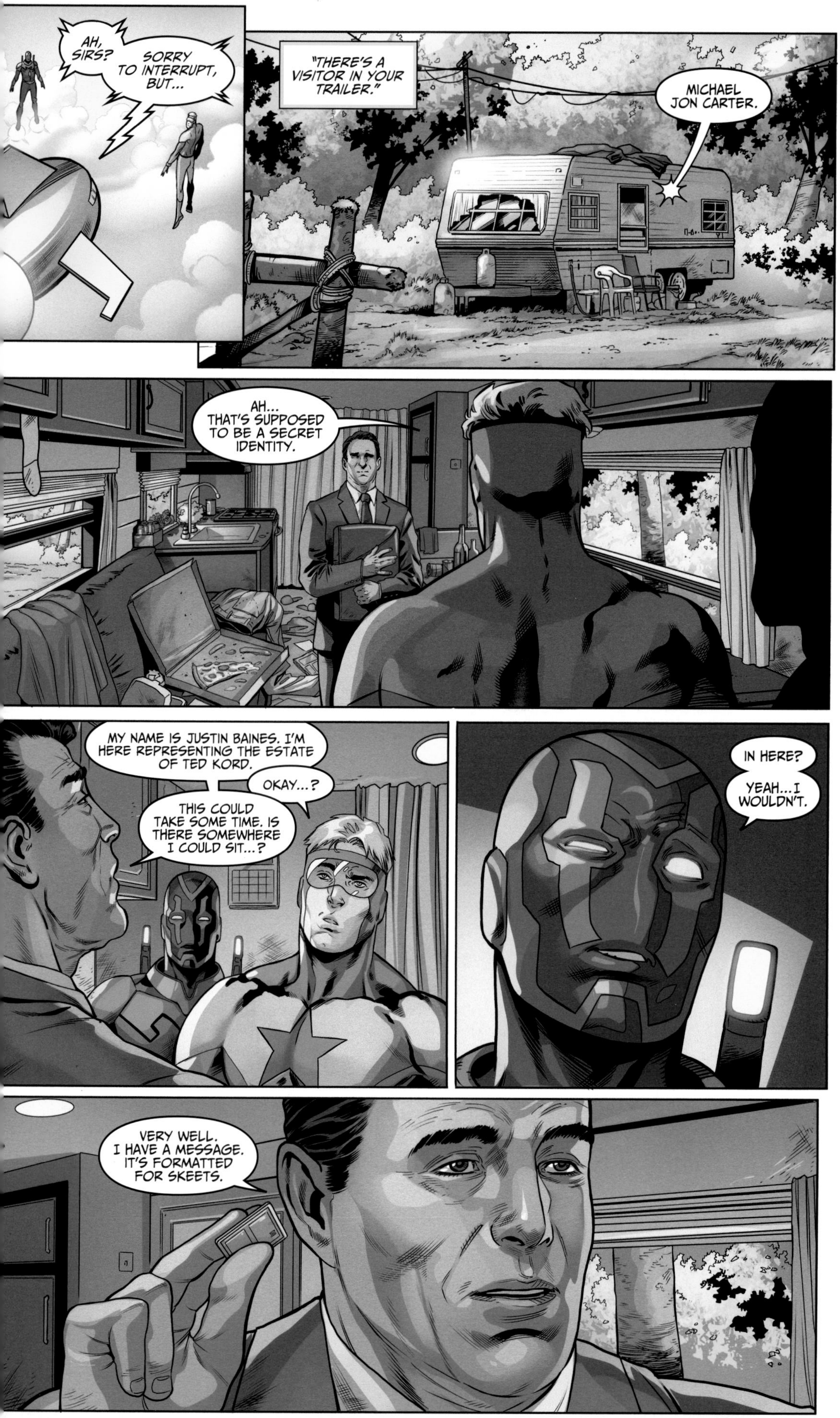

AH, SIRS?
SORRY TO INTERRUPT, BUT...
"THERE'S A VISITOR IN YOUR TRAILER."
MICHAEL JON CARTER.
AH... THAT'S SUPPOSED TO BE A SECRET IDENTITY.
MY NAME IS JUSTIN BAINES. I'M HERE REPRESENTING THE ESTATE OF TED KORD.
OKAY...?
THIS COULD TAKE SOME TIME. IS THERE SOMEWHERE I COULD SIT...?
IN HERE?
YEAH...I WOULDN'T.
VERY WELL. I HAVE A MESSAGE. IT'S FORMATTED FOR SKEETS.

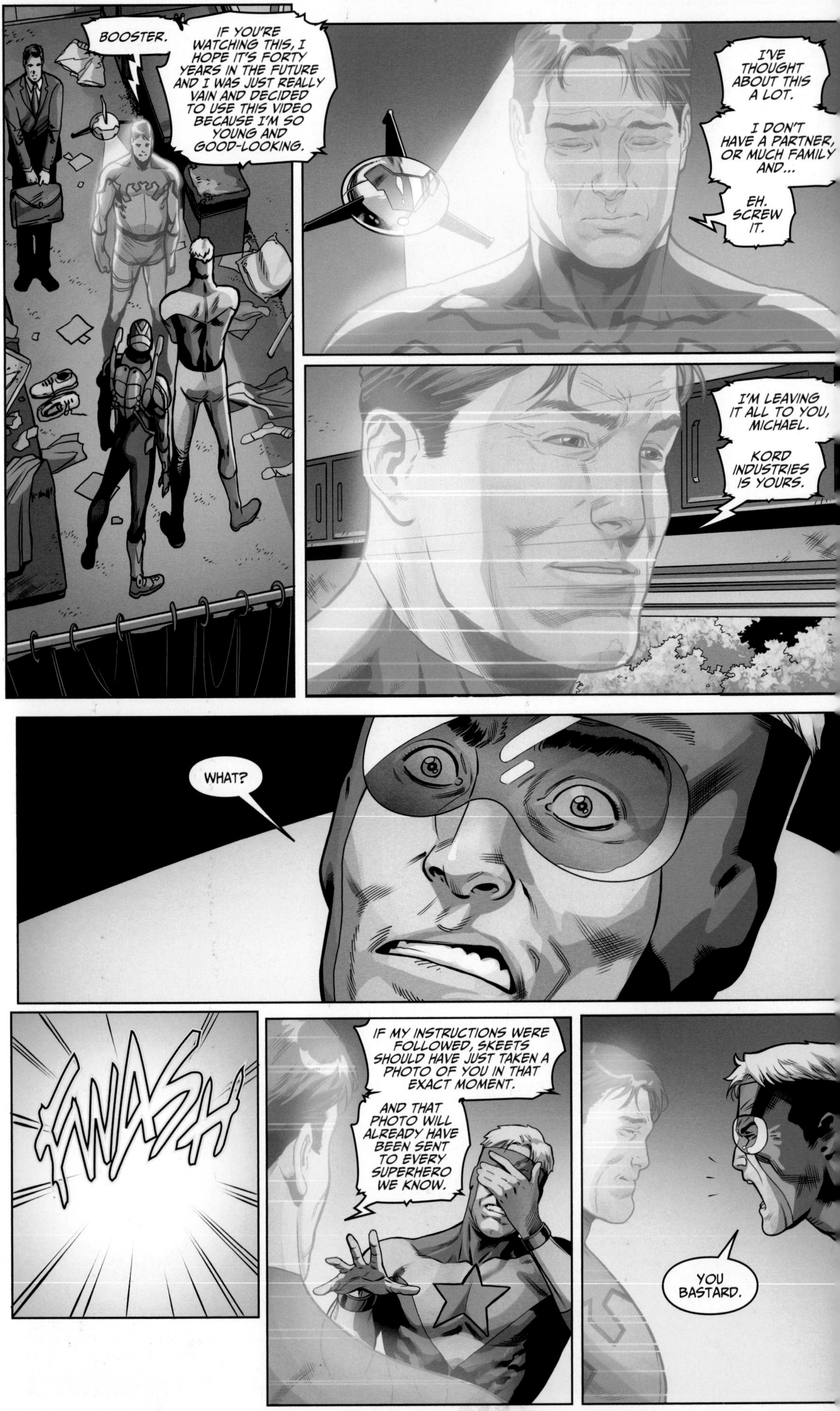
BOOSTER.
IF YOU'RE WATCHING THIS, I HOPE IT'S FORTY YEARS IN THE FUTURE AND I WAS JUST REALLY VAIN AND DECIDED TO USE THIS VIDEO BECAUSE I'M SO YOUNG AND GOOD-LOOKING.
I'VE THOUGHT ABOUT THIS A LOT.
I DON'T HAVE A PARTNER, OR MUCH FAMILY AND...
EH. SCREW IT.
I'M LEAVING IT ALL TO YOU, MICHAEL.
KORD INDUSTRIES IS YOURS.
WHAT?
FWASH
IF MY INSTRUCTIONS WERE FOLLOWED, SKEETS SHOULD HAVE JUST TAKEN A PHOTO OF YOU IN THAT EXACT MOMENT.
AND THAT PHOTO WILL ALREADY HAVE BEEN SENT TO EVERY SUPERHERO WE KNOW.
YOU BASTARD.

ERE'S OTHER HING.

I PUT SOME MONEY IN A LONG-TERM SAVINGS ACCOUNT. THE ACCOUNT HAD STRICT PAYMENT INSTRUCTIONS FOR WHEN IT REACHED A CERTAIN AMOUNT.

IF MY CALCULATIONS ARE CORRECT-- AND, LET'S FACE IT, THEY WILL BE--

ENOUGH MONEY WILL HAVE ACCRUED BY YOUR TIME TO PAY FOR THE SUIT YOU STOLE FROM THE MUSEUM. AND THE PAYMENT WILL HAVE BEEN AUTOMATICALLY MADE IN THE FUTURE.

NO MORE IMPOSTER SYNDROME. YOUR SUIT IS LEGALLY YOURS, BOOSTER.

NOW IT'S ALL ABOUT WHAT YOU'RE GOING TO DO WITH IT.

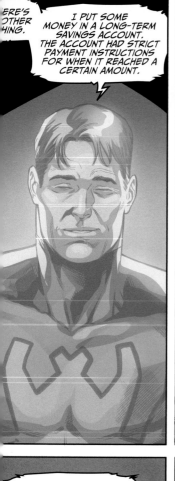

SPEAKING OF WHICH, THERE'S THIS KID. JAIME. HE'S SPECIAL.

YOU CAN SEE IT. HE'S ACTUALLY GONNA BE THE KIND OF HERO WE ALWAYS PRETENDED WE'D BE ONE DAY.

LOOK AFTER HIM, YEAH?

I REALIZE THIS IS BIG, AND I ALWAYS RIB YOU FOR BEING USELESS. UT I NEVER REALLY THOUGHT YOU WERE. I TRUST YOU TO STEP UP.

LOVE YA, MAN.

WELL?

UM...IT'S A LOT TO TAKE IN.

I THINK THE FIRST THING TO DO WOULD BE TO MOVE. YOU CAN LIVE ANYWHERE, SIR.

WELL, YEAH. OF COURSE I CAN. THAT'S KIND OF THE POINT OF A TRAILER. THAT'S WHY IT HAS WHEELS.

I DIDN'T MEAN...

YOU ARE NOW A BILLIONAIRE, MR. CARTER. YOU CAN LIVE IN PRETTY MUCH ANY HOUSE YOU WANT.

OH.

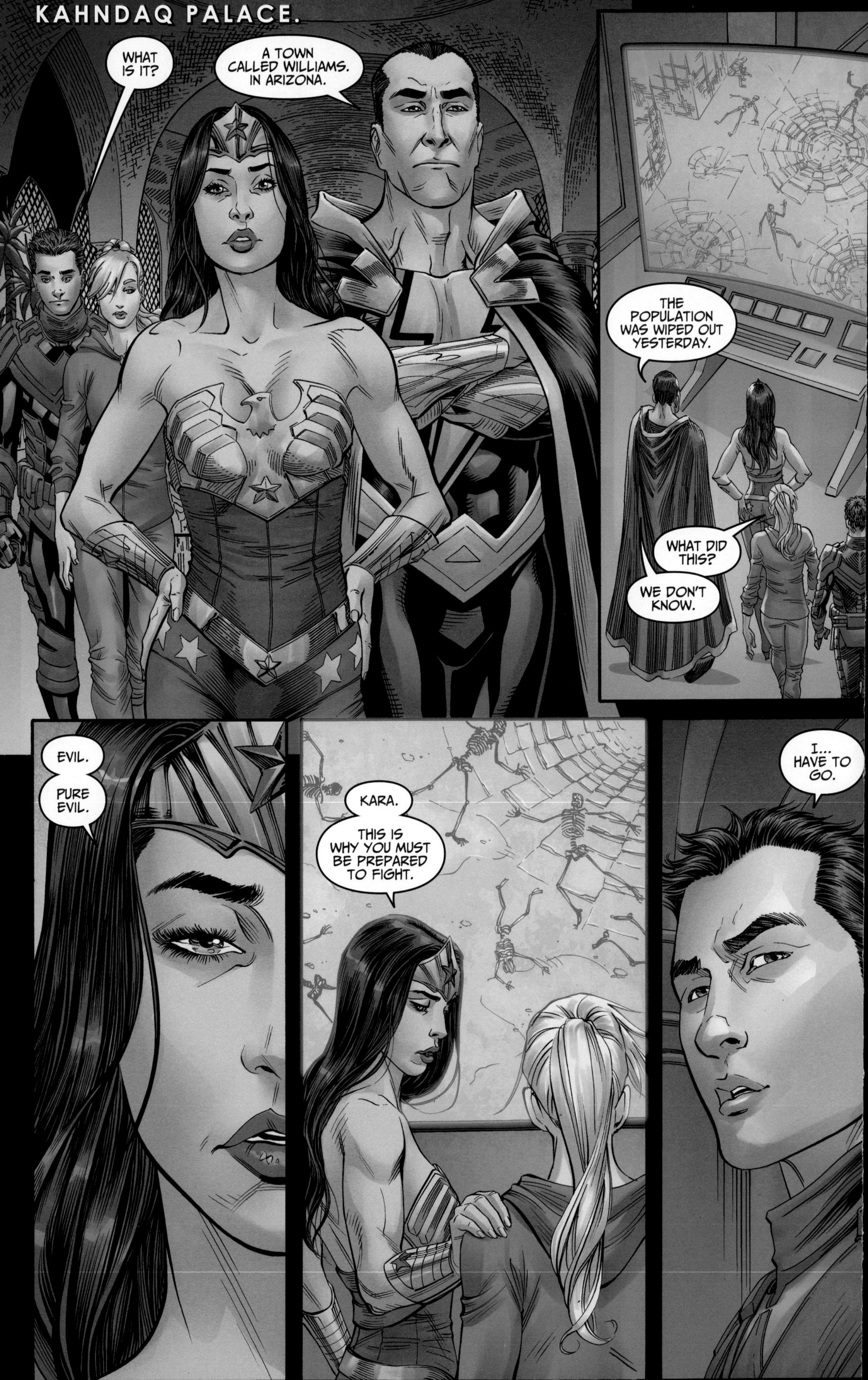
KAHNDAQ PALACE.
WHAT IS IT?
A TOWN CALLED WILLIAMS. IN ARIZONA.
THE POPULATION WAS WIPED OUT YESTERDAY.
WHAT DID THIS?
WE DON'T KNOW.
EVIL.
PURE EVIL.
KARA.
THIS IS WHY YOU MUST BE PREPARED TO FIGHT.
I... HAVE TO GO.

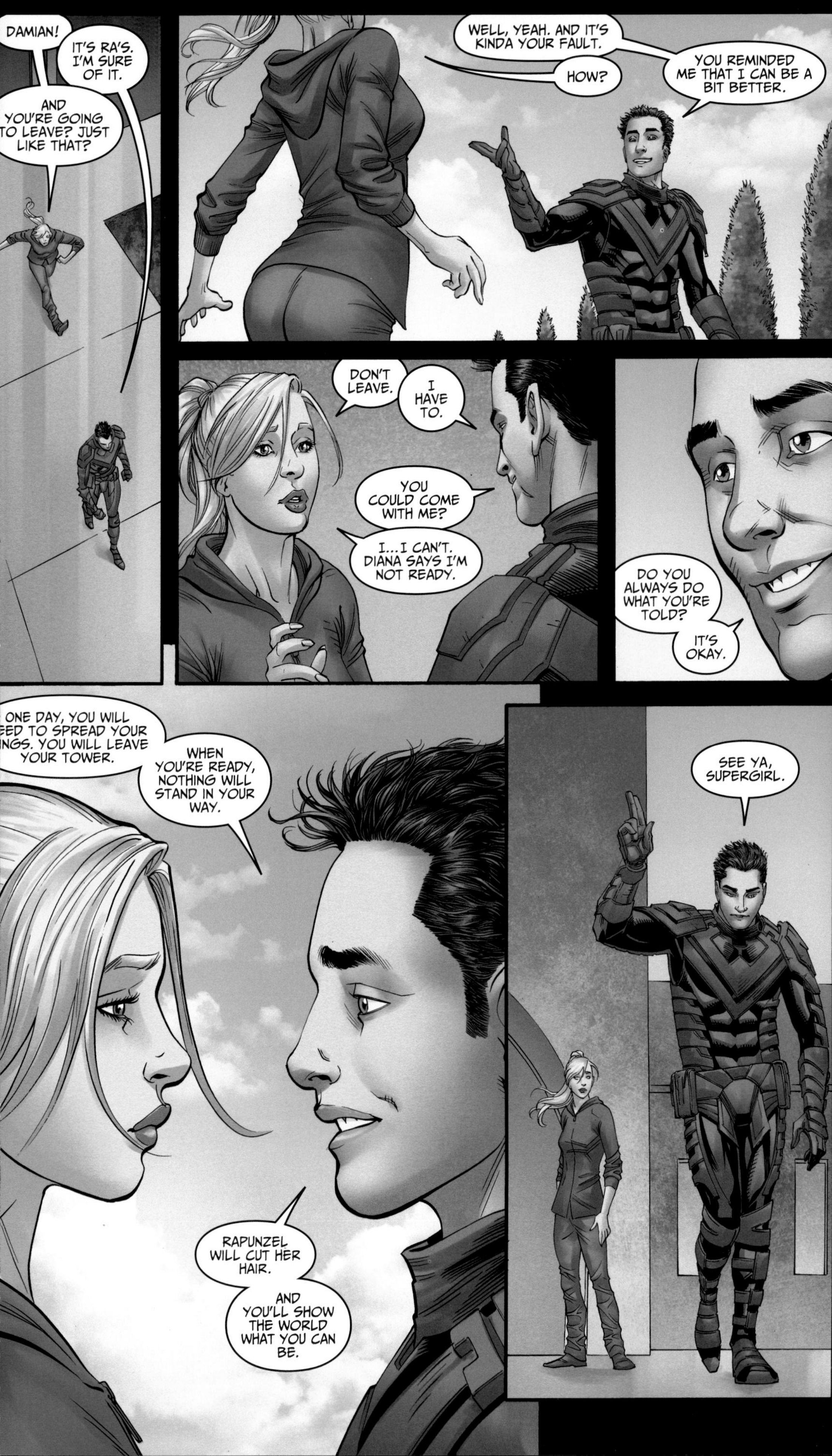

DAMIAN!
IT'S RA'S. I'M SURE OF IT.
AND YOU'RE GOING TO LEAVE? JUST LIKE THAT?
WELL, YEAH. AND IT'S KINDA YOUR FAULT.
HOW?
YOU REMINDED ME THAT I CAN BE A BIT BETTER.
DON'T LEAVE.
I HAVE TO.
YOU COULD COME WITH ME?
I...I CAN'T. DIANA SAYS I'M NOT READY.
DO YOU ALWAYS DO WHAT YOU'RE TOLD?
IT'S OKAY.
ONE DAY, YOU WILL EED TO SPREAD YOUR INGS. YOU WILL LEAVE YOUR TOWER.
WHEN YOU'RE READY, NOTHING WILL STAND IN YOUR WAY.
RAPUNZEL WILL CUT HER HAIR.
AND YOU'LL SHOW THE WORLD WHAT YOU CAN BE.
SEE YA, SUPERGIRL.

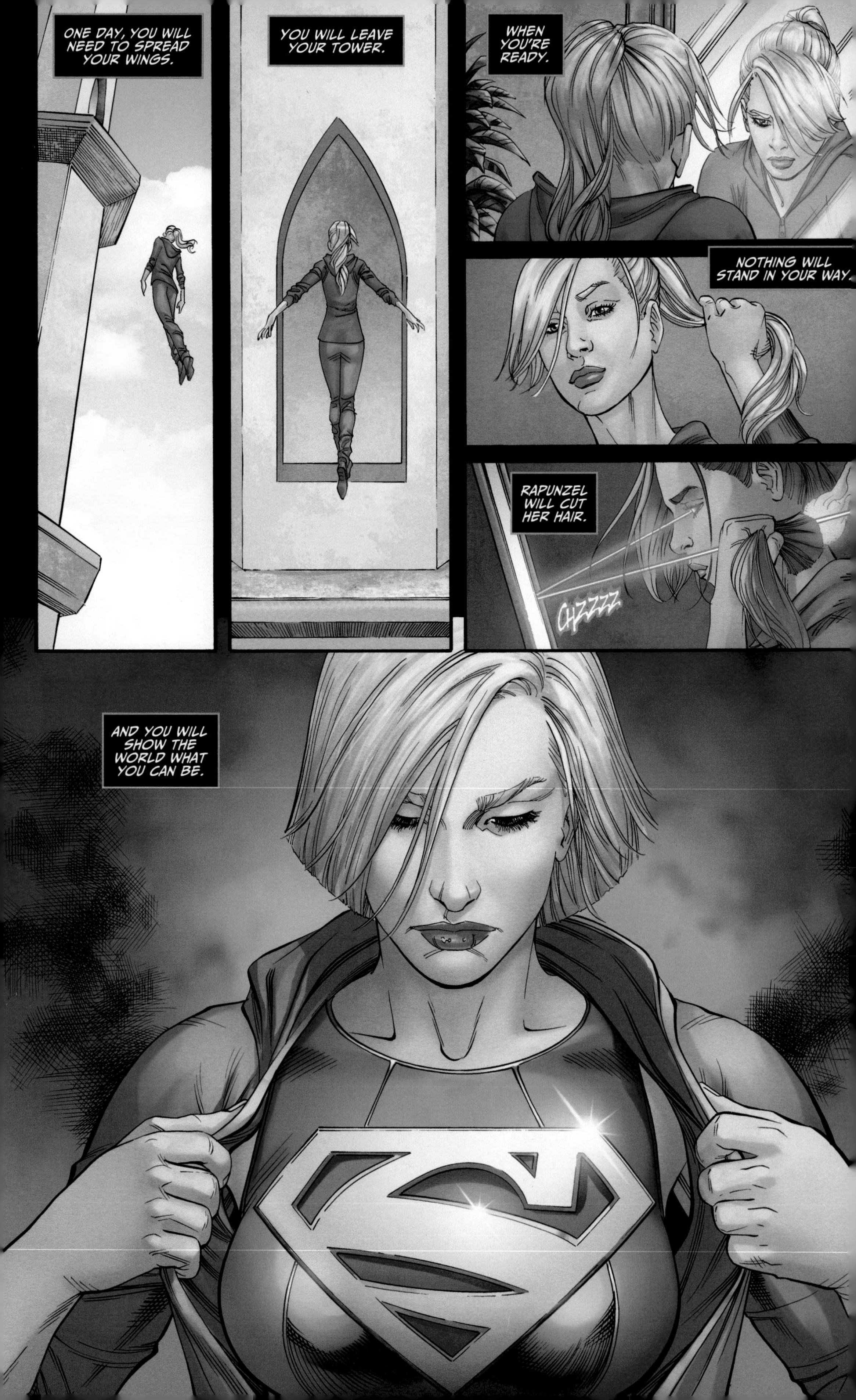
ONE DAY, YOU WILL NEED TO SPREAD YOUR WINGS.
YOU WILL LEAVE YOUR TOWER.
WHEN YOU'RE READY.
NOTHING WILL STAND IN YOUR WAY.
RAPUNZEL WILL CUT HER HAIR.
CHZZZZ
AND YOU WILL SHOW THE WORLD WHAT YOU CAN BE.

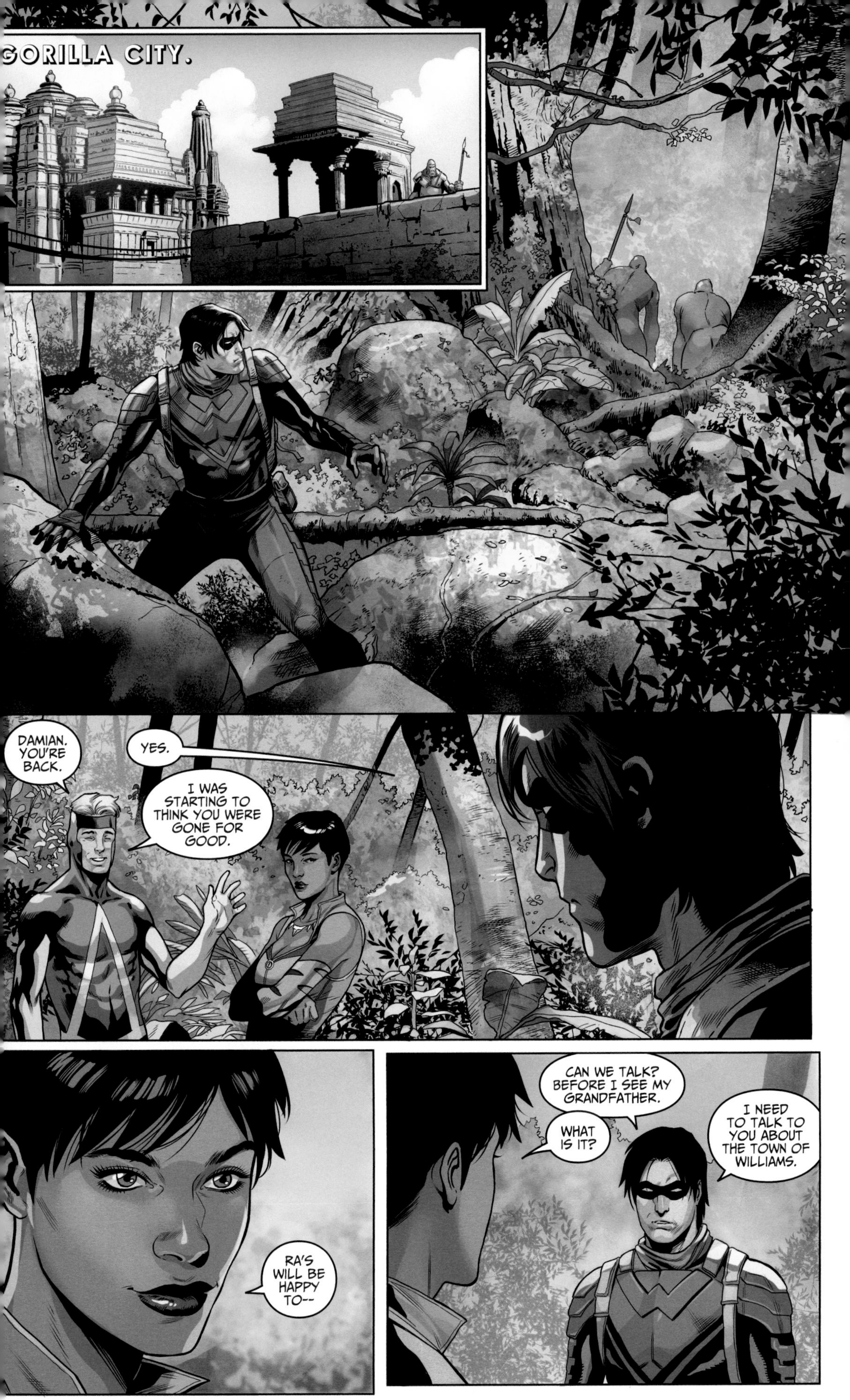
GORILLA CITY.
DAMIAN. YOU'RE BACK.
YES.
I WAS STARTING TO THINK YOU WERE GONE FOR GOOD.
RA'S WILL BE HAPPY TO--
CAN WE TALK? BEFORE I SEE MY GRANDFATHER.
WHAT IS IT?
I NEED TO TALK TO YOU ABOUT THE TOWN OF WILLIAMS.

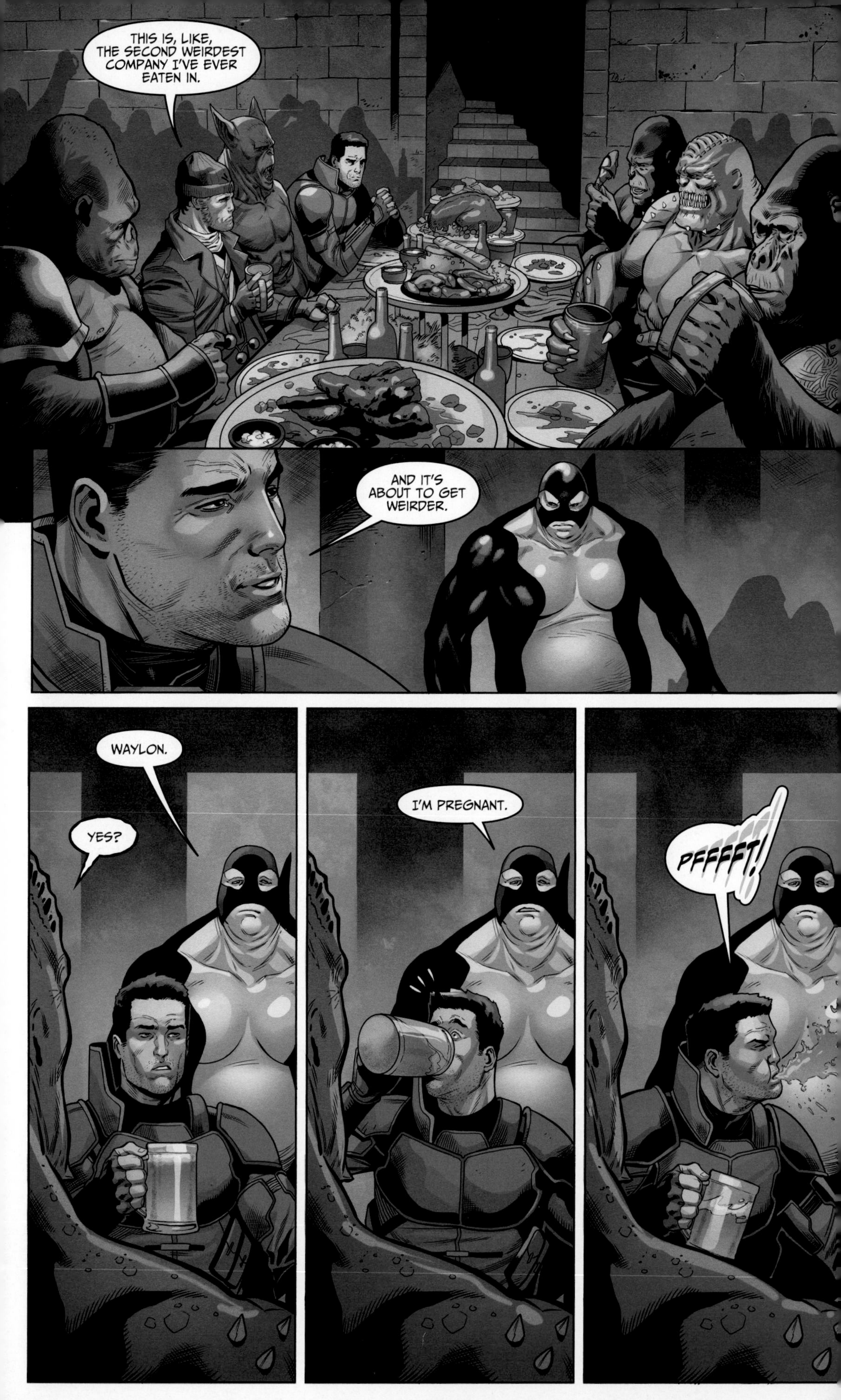
THIS IS, LIKE, THE SECOND WEIRDEST COMPANY I'VE EVER EATEN IN.
AND IT'S ABOUT TO GET WEIRDER.
WAYLON.
YES?
I'M PREGNANT.
PFFFFT!

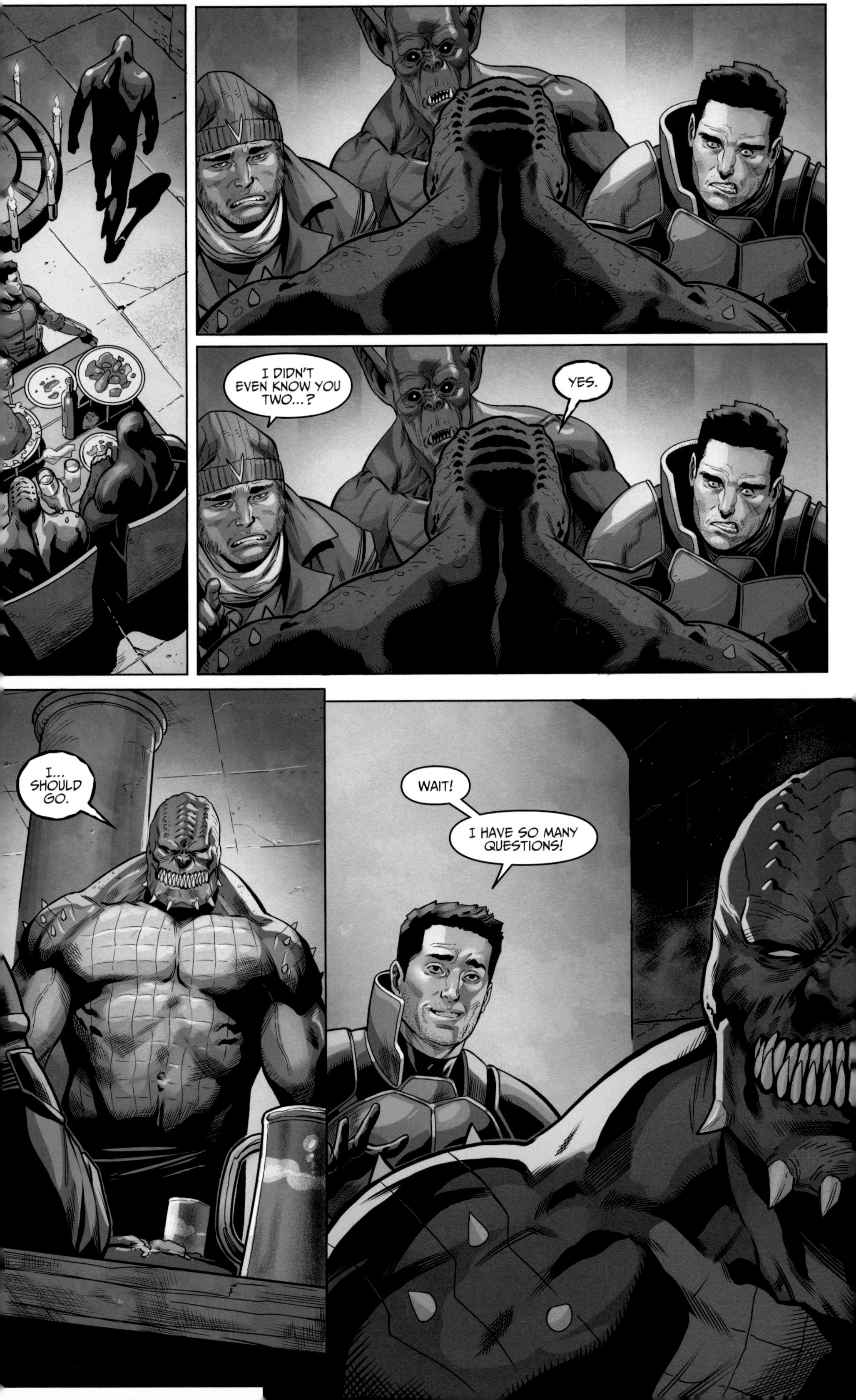
I DIDN'T EVEN KNOW YOU TWO...?
YES.
I... SHOULD GO.
WAIT!
I HAVE SO MANY QUESTIONS!

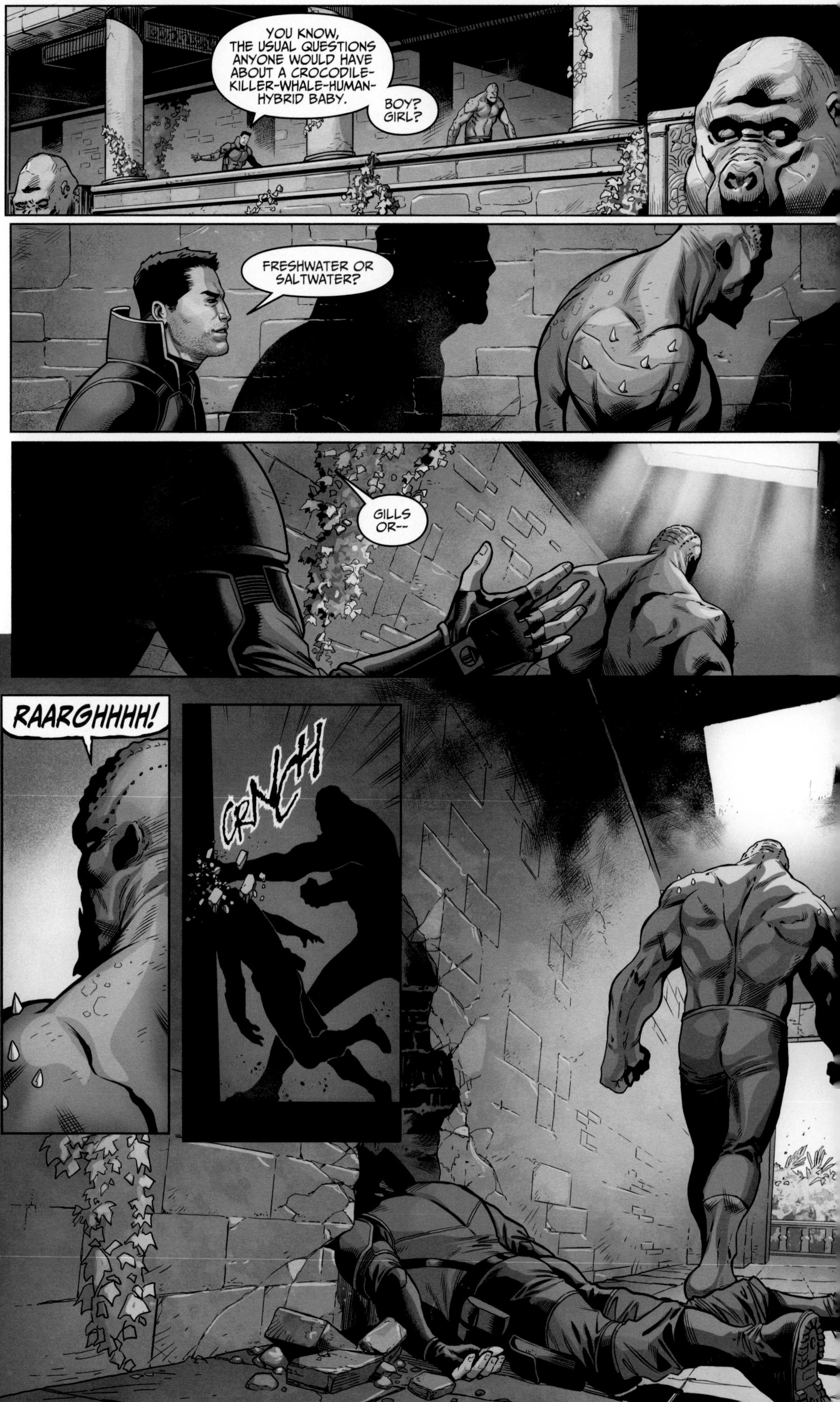
YOU KNOW, THE USUAL QUESTIONS ANYONE WOULD HAVE ABOUT A CROCODILE-KILLER-WHALE-HUMAN-HYBRID BABY.
BOY? GIRL?
FRESHWATER OR SALTWATER?
GILLS OR--
RAARGHHHH!
CRNCH

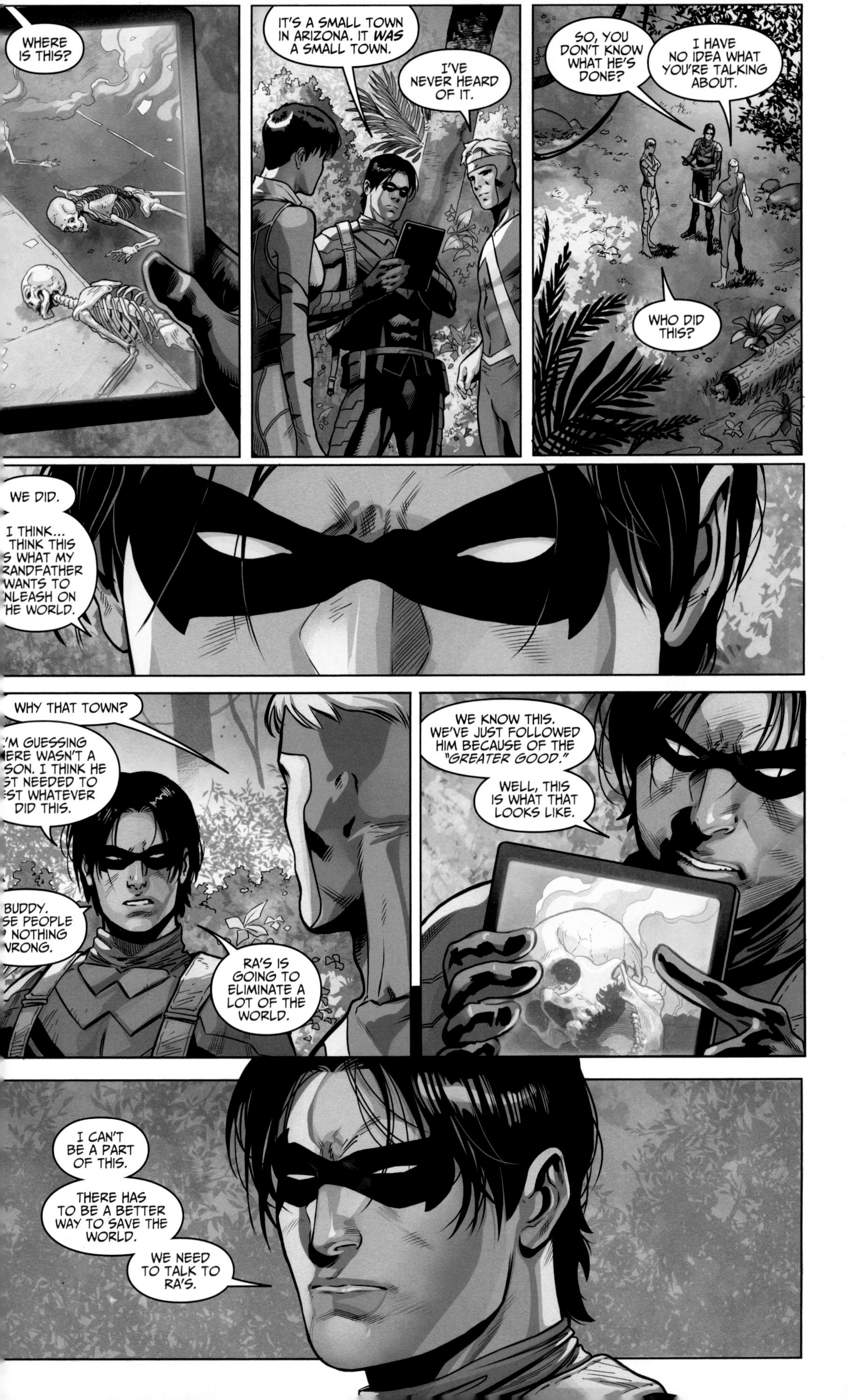

WHERE IS THIS?
IT'S A SMALL TOWN IN ARIZONA. IT *WAS* A SMALL TOWN.
I'VE NEVER HEARD OF IT.
SO, YOU DON'T KNOW WHAT HE'S DONE?
I HAVE NO IDEA WHAT YOU'RE TALKING ABOUT.
WHO DID THIS?
WE DID.
I THINK... THINK THIS S WHAT MY RANDFATHER WANTS TO NLEASH ON HE WORLD.
WHY THAT TOWN?
'M GUESSING ERE WASN'T A SON. I THINK HE ST NEEDED TO ST WHATEVER DID THIS.
BUDDY. SE PEOPLE NOTHING VRONG.
RA'S IS GOING TO ELIMINATE A LOT OF THE WORLD.
WE KNOW THIS. WE'VE JUST FOLLOWED HIM BECAUSE OF THE "GREATER GOOD."
WELL, THIS IS WHAT THAT LOOKS LIKE.
I CAN'T BE A PART OF THIS.
THERE HAS TO BE A BETTER WAY TO SAVE THE WORLD.
WE NEED TO TALK TO RA'S.

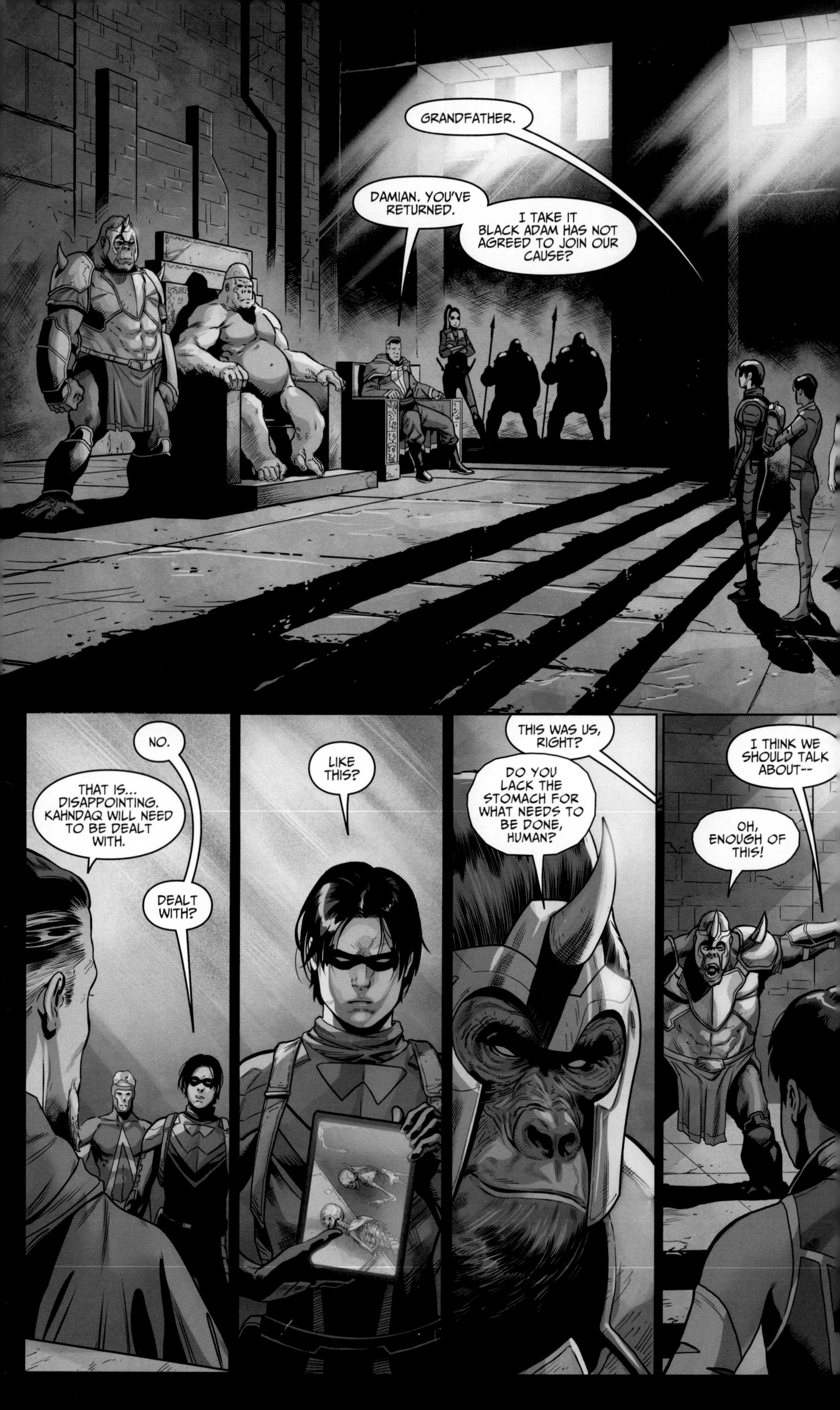

GRANDFATHER.
DAMIAN. YOU'VE RETURNED.
I TAKE IT BLACK ADAM HAS NOT AGREED TO JOIN OUR CAUSE?
NO.
THAT IS... DISAPPOINTING. KAHNDAQ WILL NEED TO BE DEALT WITH.
DEALT WITH?
LIKE THIS?
THIS WAS US, RIGHT?
DO YOU LACK THE STOMACH FOR WHAT NEEDS TO BE DONE, HUMAN?
I THINK WE SHOULD TALK ABOUT--
OH, ENOUGH OF THIS!

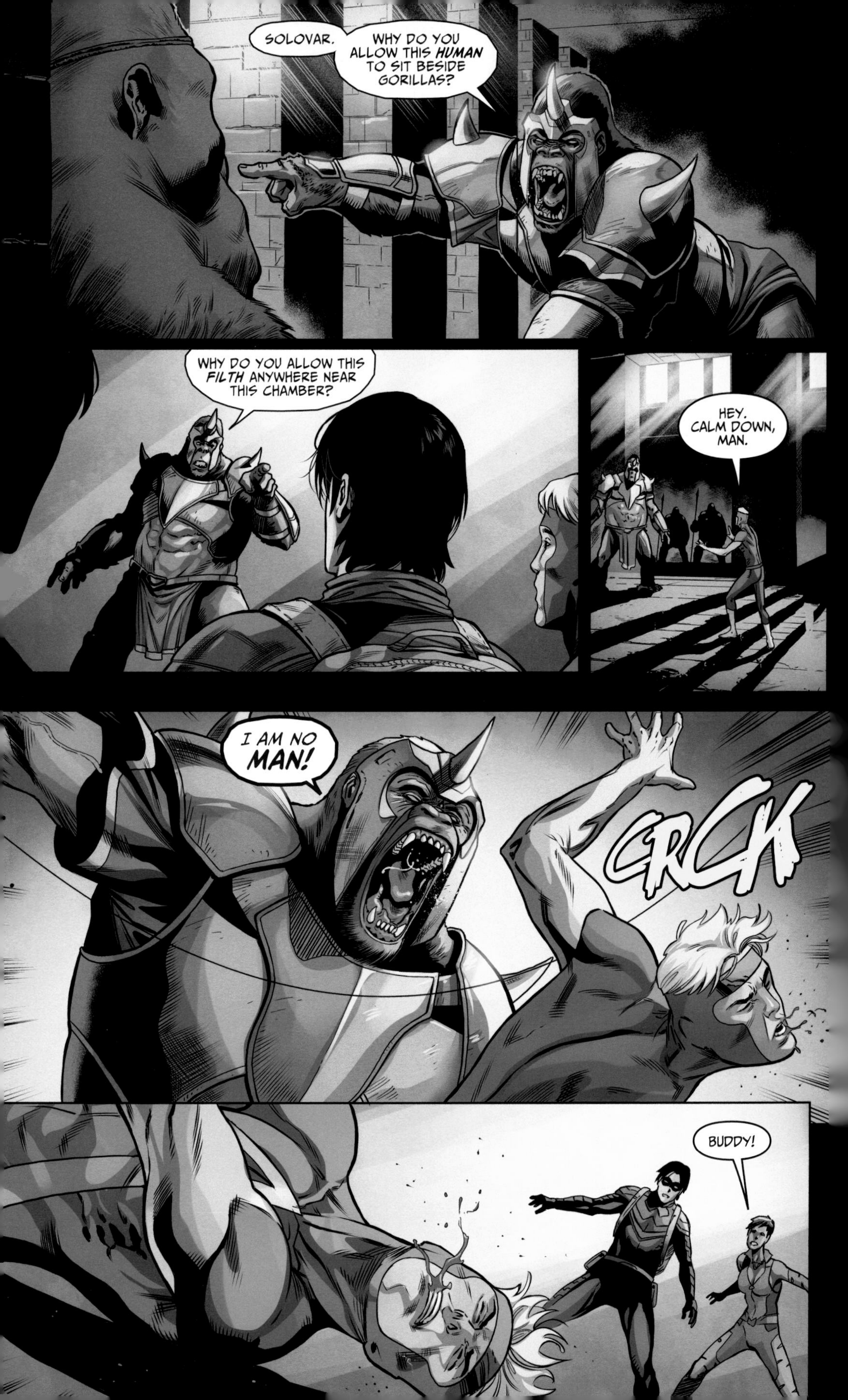
SOLOVAR.
WHY DO YOU ALLOW THIS HUMAN TO SIT BESIDE GORILLAS?
WHY DO YOU ALLOW THIS FILTH ANYWHERE NEAR THIS CHAMBER?
HEY. CALM DOWN, MAN.
I AM NO MAN!
CRCK
BUDDY!

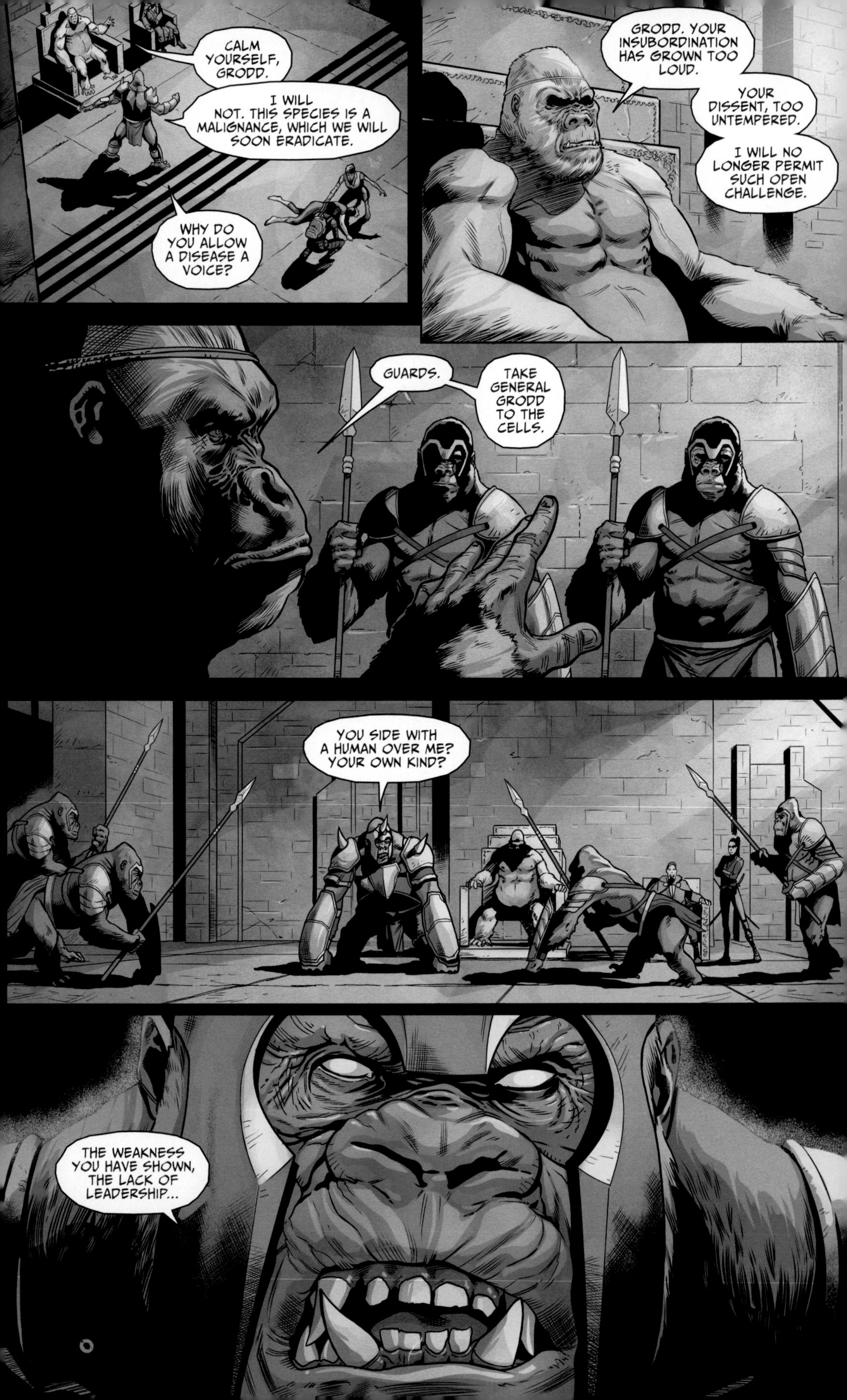
CALM YOURSELF, GRODD.
I WILL NOT. THIS SPECIES IS A MALIGNANCE, WHICH WE WILL SOON ERADICATE.
WHY DO YOU ALLOW A DISEASE A VOICE?
GRODD. YOUR INSUBORDINATION HAS GROWN TOO LOUD.
YOUR DISSENT, TOO UNTEMPERED.
I WILL NO LONGER PERMIT SUCH OPEN CHALLENGE.
GUARDS.
TAKE GENERAL GRODD TO THE CELLS.
YOU SIDE WITH A HUMAN OVER ME? YOUR OWN KIND?
THE WEAKNESS YOU HAVE SHOWN, THE LACK OF LEADERSHIP...

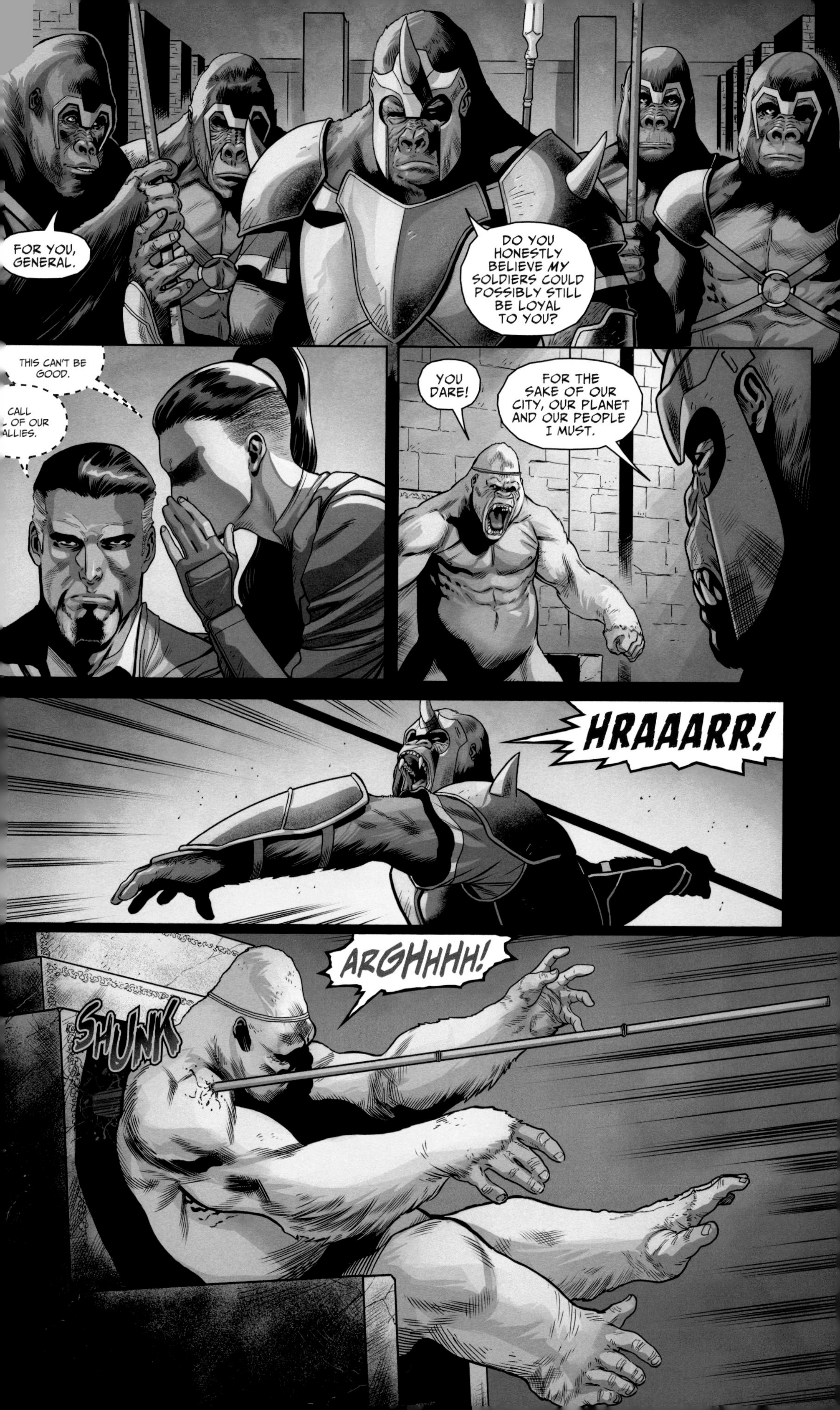
FOR YOU, GENERAL.
DO YOU HONESTLY BELIEVE MY SOLDIERS COULD POSSIBLY STILL BE LOYAL TO YOU?
THIS CAN'T BE GOOD.
CALL OF OUR ALLIES.
YOU DARE!
FOR THE SAKE OF OUR CITY, OUR PLANET AND OUR PEOPLE I MUST.
HRAAARR!
ARGHHHH!
SHUNK

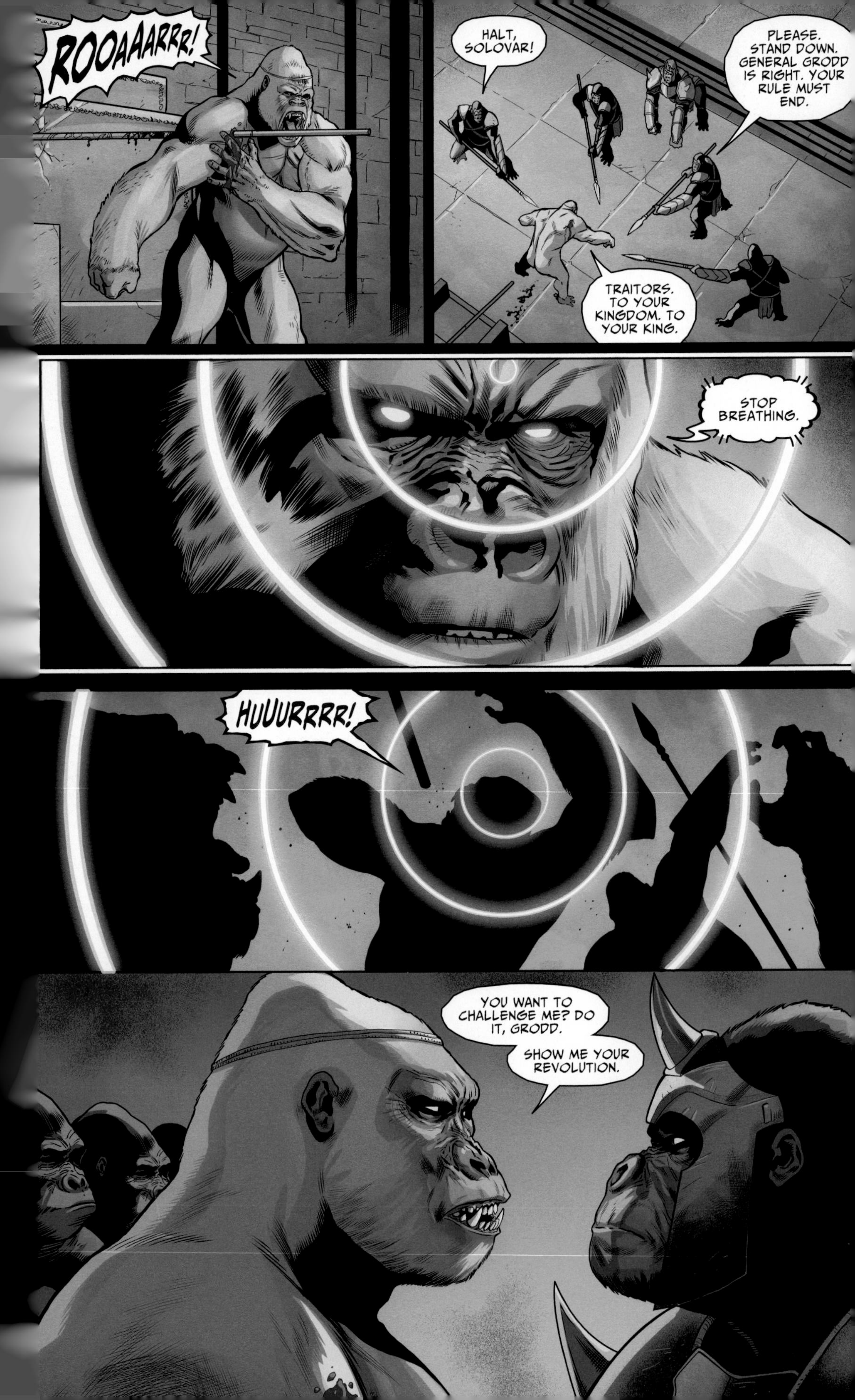
ROOAAARRR!
HALT, SOLOVAR!
PLEASE. STAND DOWN. GENERAL GRODD IS RIGHT. YOUR RULE MUST END.
TRAITORS. TO YOUR KINGDOM. TO YOUR KING.
STOP BREATHING.
HUUURRRR!
YOU WANT TO CHALLENGE ME? DO IT, GRODD.
SHOW ME YOUR REVOLUTION.

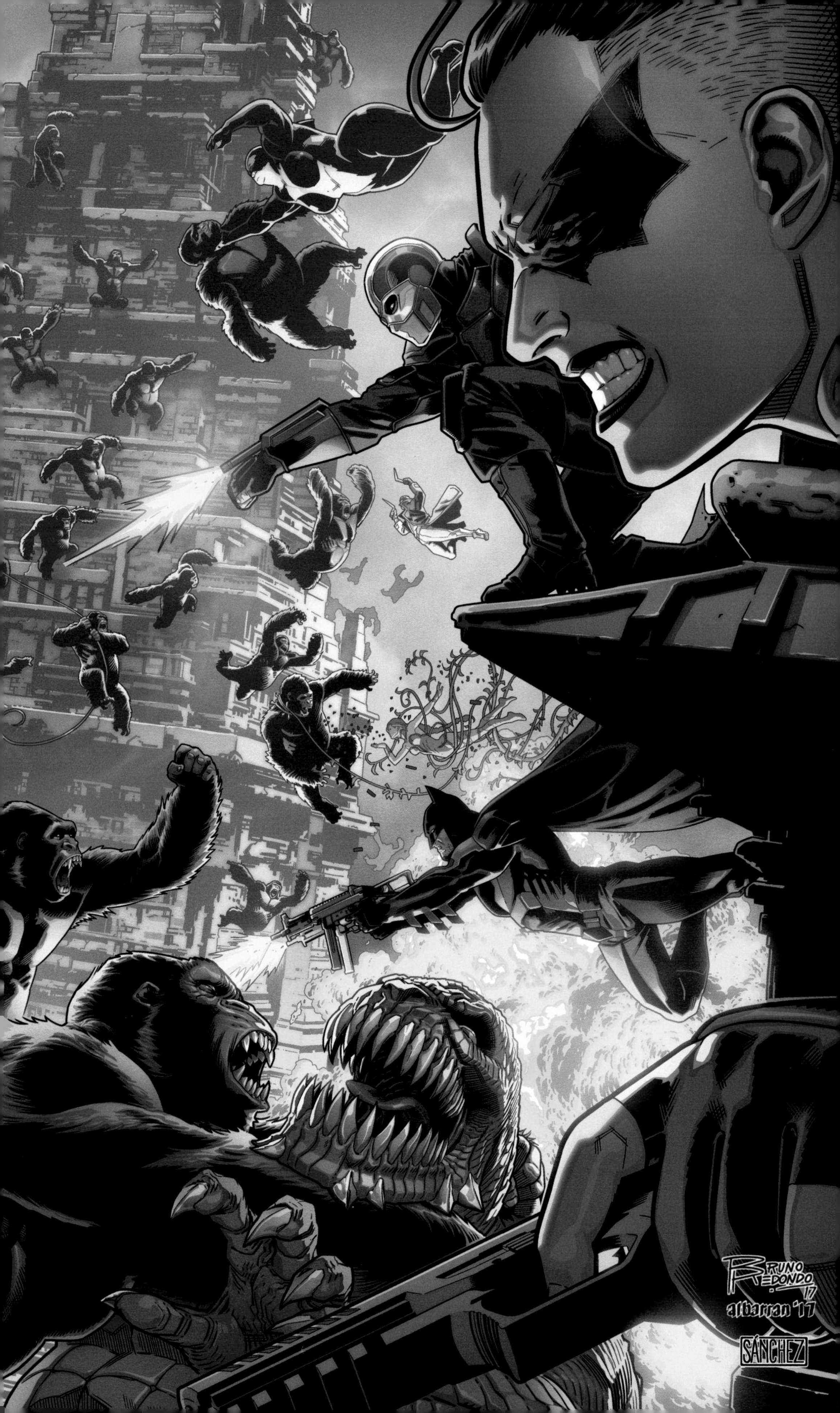
BRUNO REDONDO '17
albarran '17
SÁNCHEZ

“Gorilla Rebellion”
Tom Taylor Writer **Bruno Redondo** and **Mike S. Miller** (Kahndaq sequence) Pencillers
Juan Albarran and **Mike S. Miller** (Kahndaq sequence) Inkers
Rex Lokus and **J. Nanjan** (Kahndaq sequence) Colorists **Wes Abbott** Letterer

Cover art by **Bruno Redondo**, **Juan Albarran** and **Alejandro Sanchez**

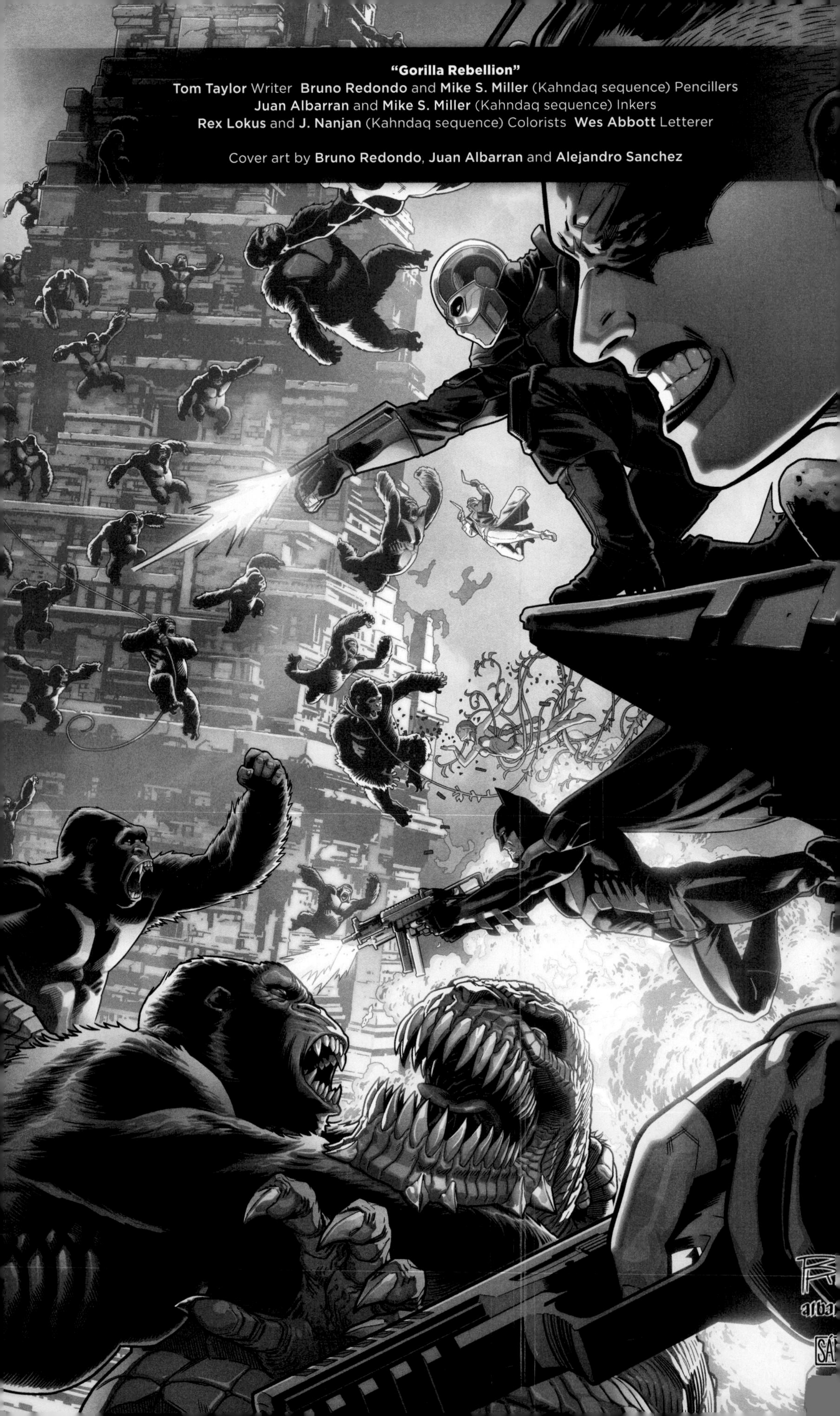

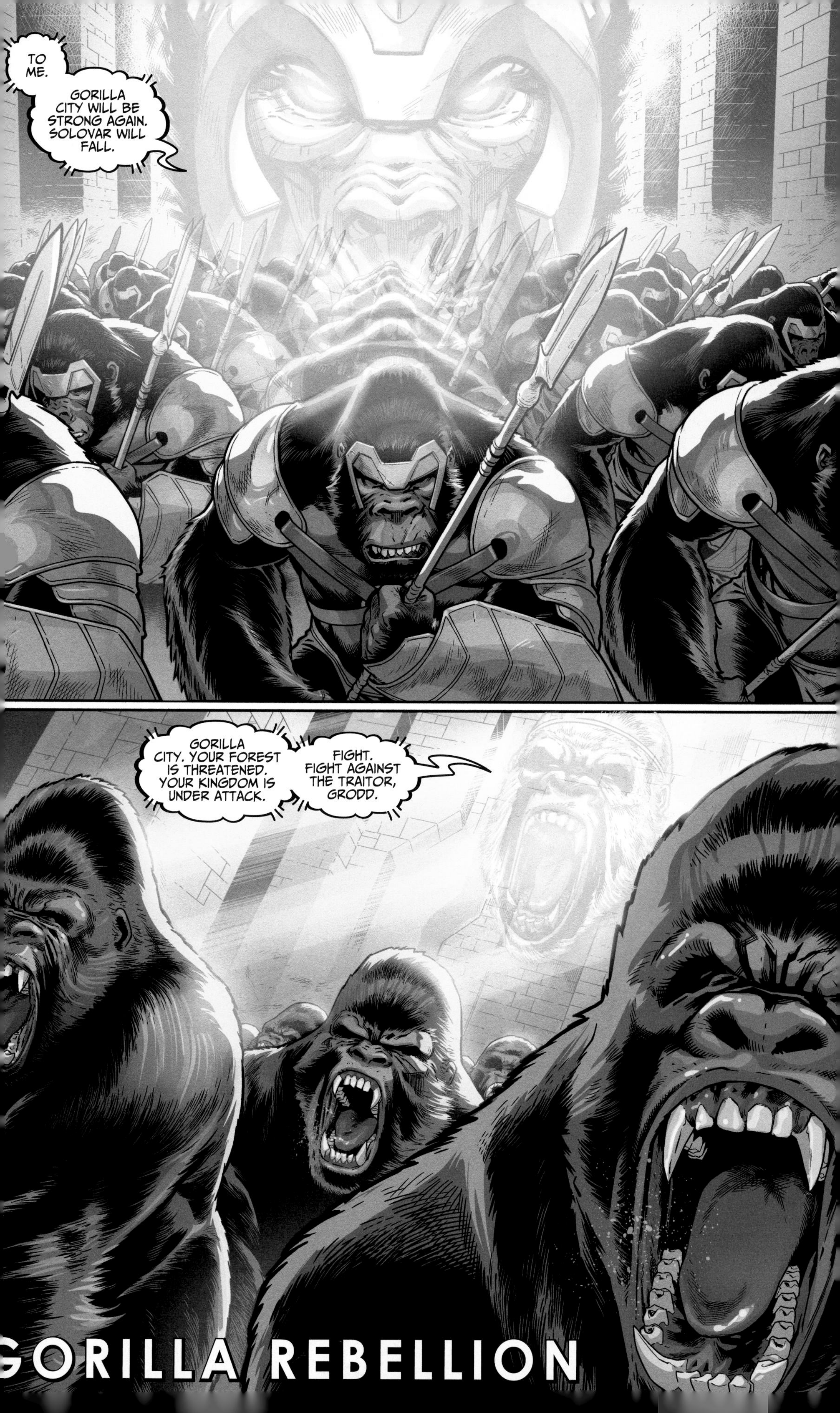
TO ME.
GORILLA CITY WILL BE STRONG AGAIN. SOLOVAR WILL FALL.
GORILLA CITY. YOUR FOREST IS THREATENED. YOUR KINGDOM IS UNDER ATTACK.
FIGHT. FIGHT AGAINST THE TRAITOR, GRODD.
GORILLA REBELLION

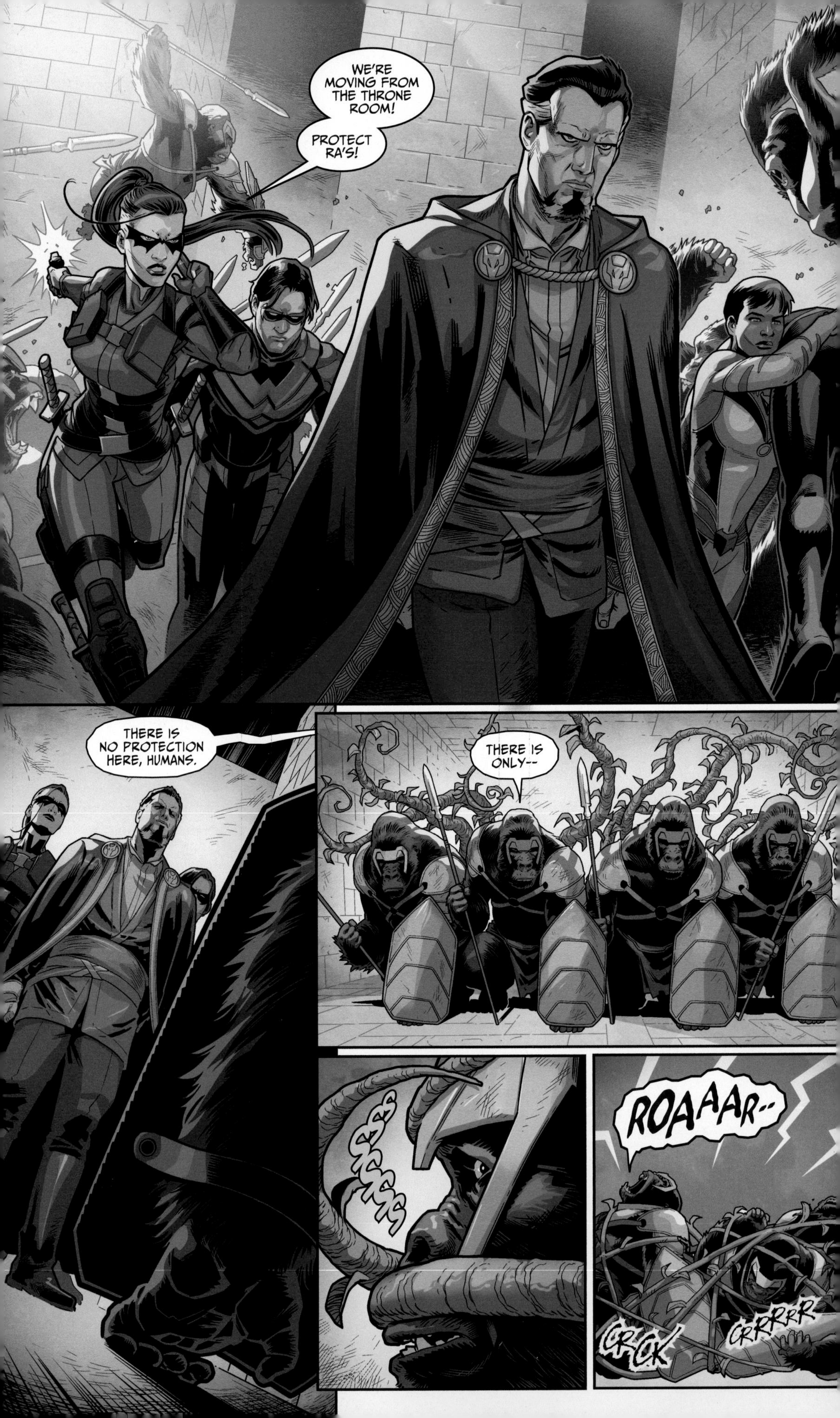

WE'RE MOVING FROM THE THRONE ROOM!
PROTECT RA'S!
THERE IS NO PROTECTION HERE, HUMANS.
THERE IS ONLY--
SSSSSS
ROAAAR--
CRCK
CRRRRR

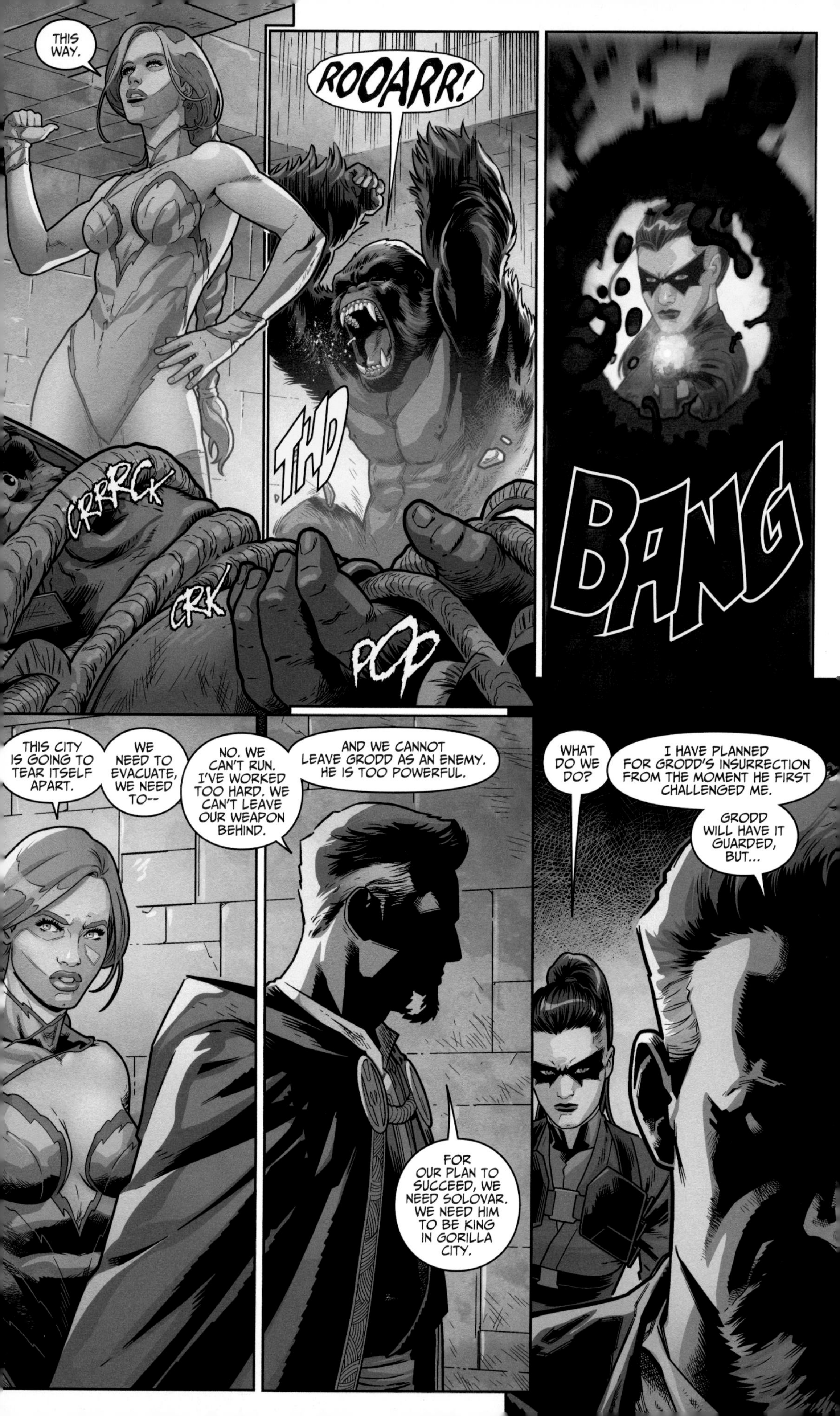
THIS WAY.
ROOARR!
THD
CRRRCK
CRK
POP
BANG
THIS CITY IS GOING TO TEAR ITSELF APART.
WE NEED TO EVACUATE, WE NEED TO--
NO. WE CAN'T RUN. I'VE WORKED TOO HARD. WE CAN'T LEAVE OUR WEAPON BEHIND.
AND WE CANNOT LEAVE GRODD AS AN ENEMY. HE IS TOO POWERFUL.
FOR OUR PLAN TO SUCCEED, WE NEED SOLOVAR. WE NEED HIM TO BE KING IN GORILLA CITY.
WHAT DO WE DO?
I HAVE PLANNED FOR GRODD'S INSURRECTION FROM THE MOMENT HE FIRST CHALLENGED ME.
GRODD WILL HAVE IT GUARDED, BUT...

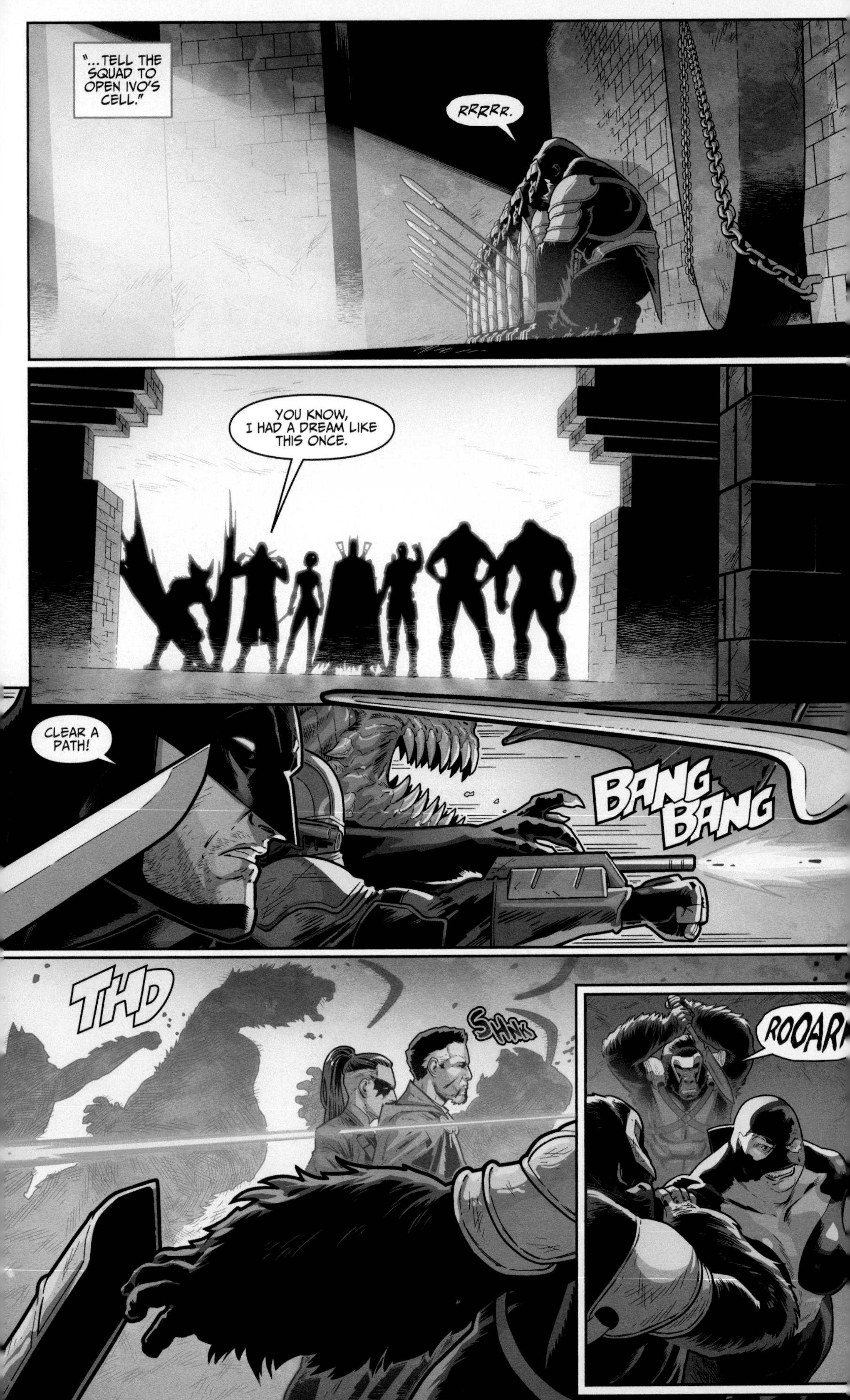
"...TELL THE SQUAD TO OPEN IVO'S CELL."
RRRRR.
YOU KNOW, I HAD A DREAM LIKE THIS ONCE.
CLEAR A PATH!
BANG BANG
THD
SHNK
ROOAR

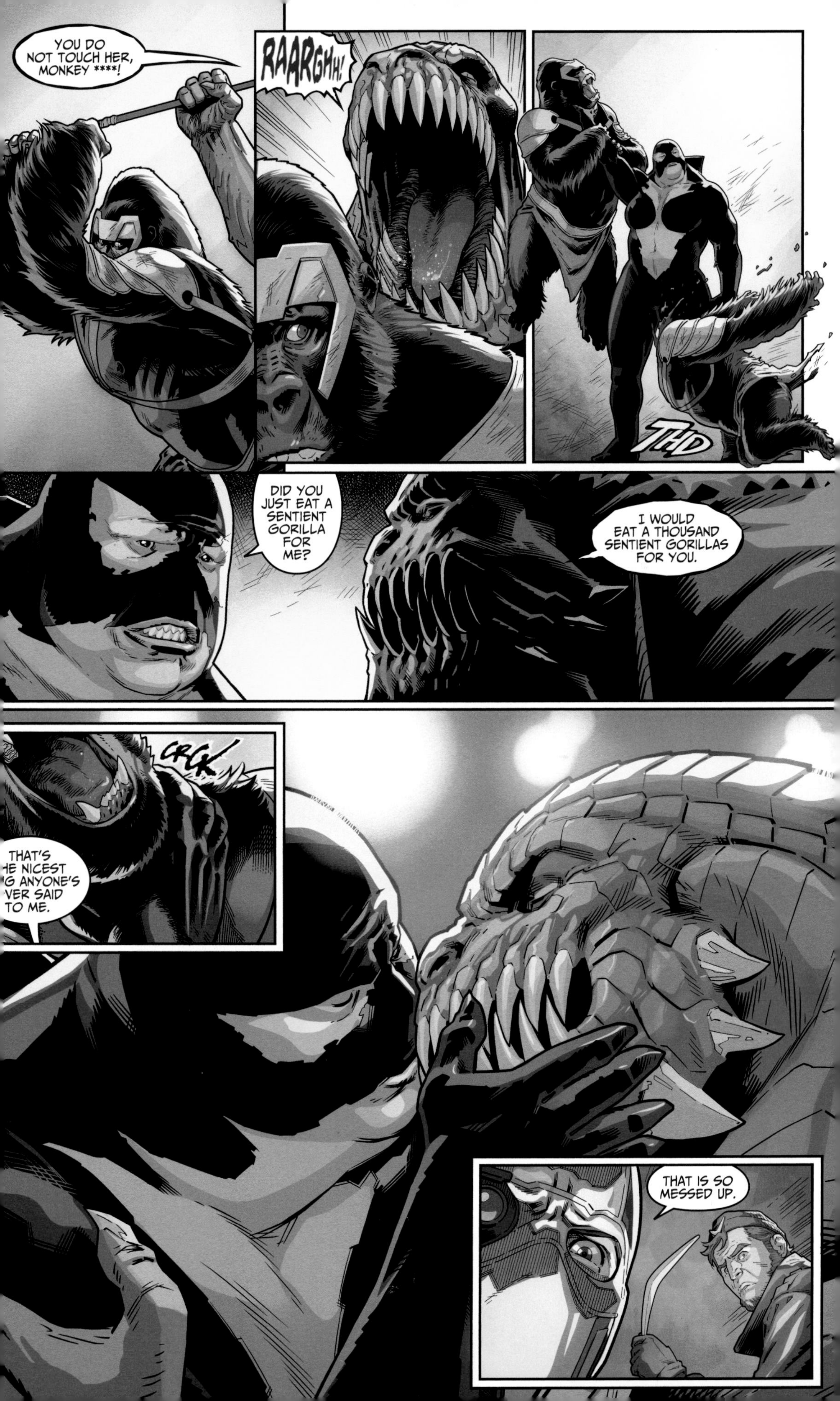
YOU DO NOT TOUCH HER, MONKEY ****!
RAARGHH!
THD
DID YOU JUST EAT A SENTIENT GORILLA FOR ME?
I WOULD EAT A THOUSAND SENTIENT GORILLAS FOR YOU.
CRCK
THAT'S
THE NICEST
G ANYONE'S
VER SAID
TO ME.
THAT IS SO MESSED UP.

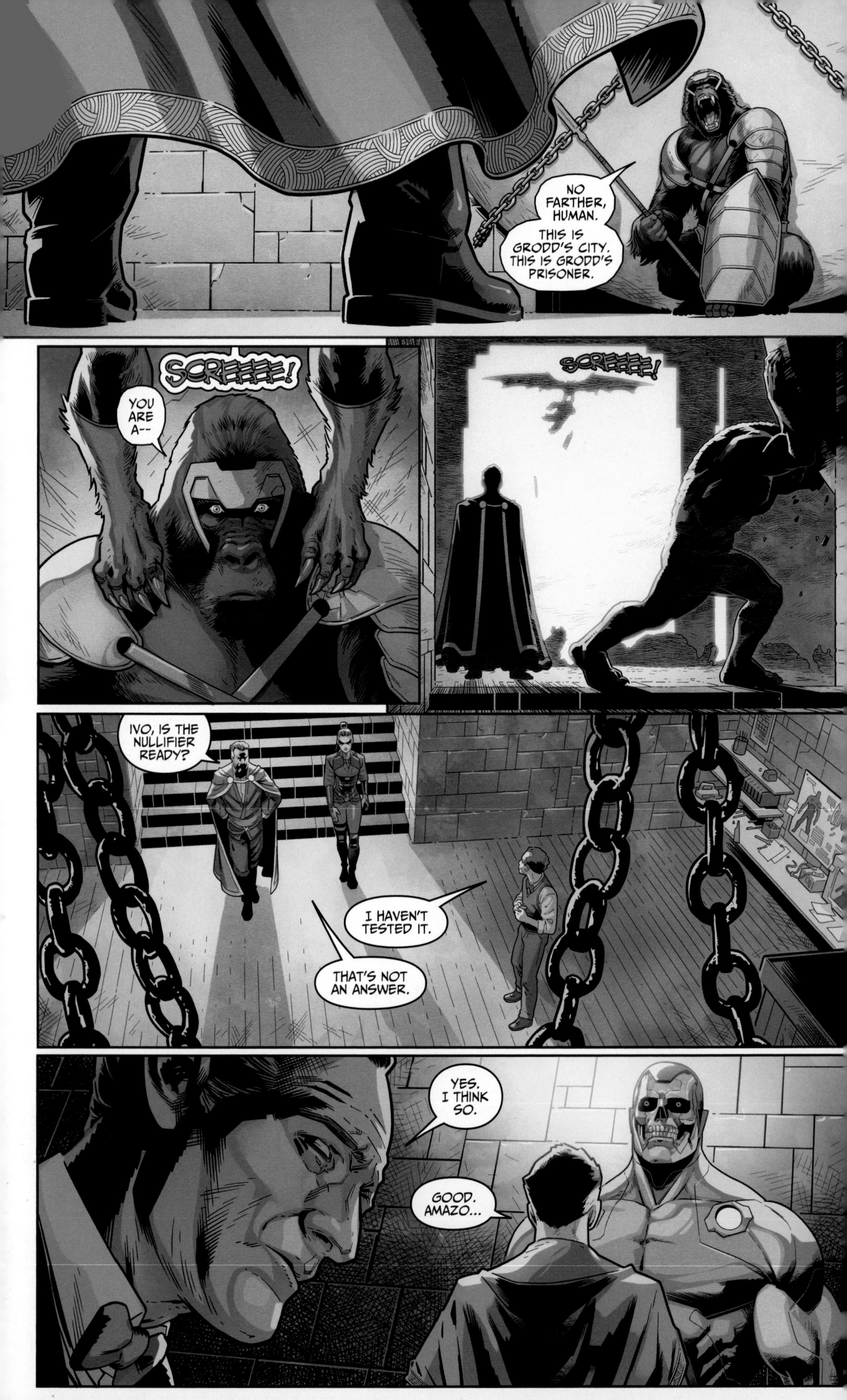
NO FARTHER, HUMAN.
THIS IS GRODD'S CITY. THIS IS GRODD'S PRISONER.
SCREEEEE!
YOU ARE A--
SCREEEEE!
IVO, IS THE NULLIFIER READY?
I HAVEN'T TESTED IT.
THAT'S NOT AN ANSWER.
YES. I THINK SO.
GOOD. AMAZO...

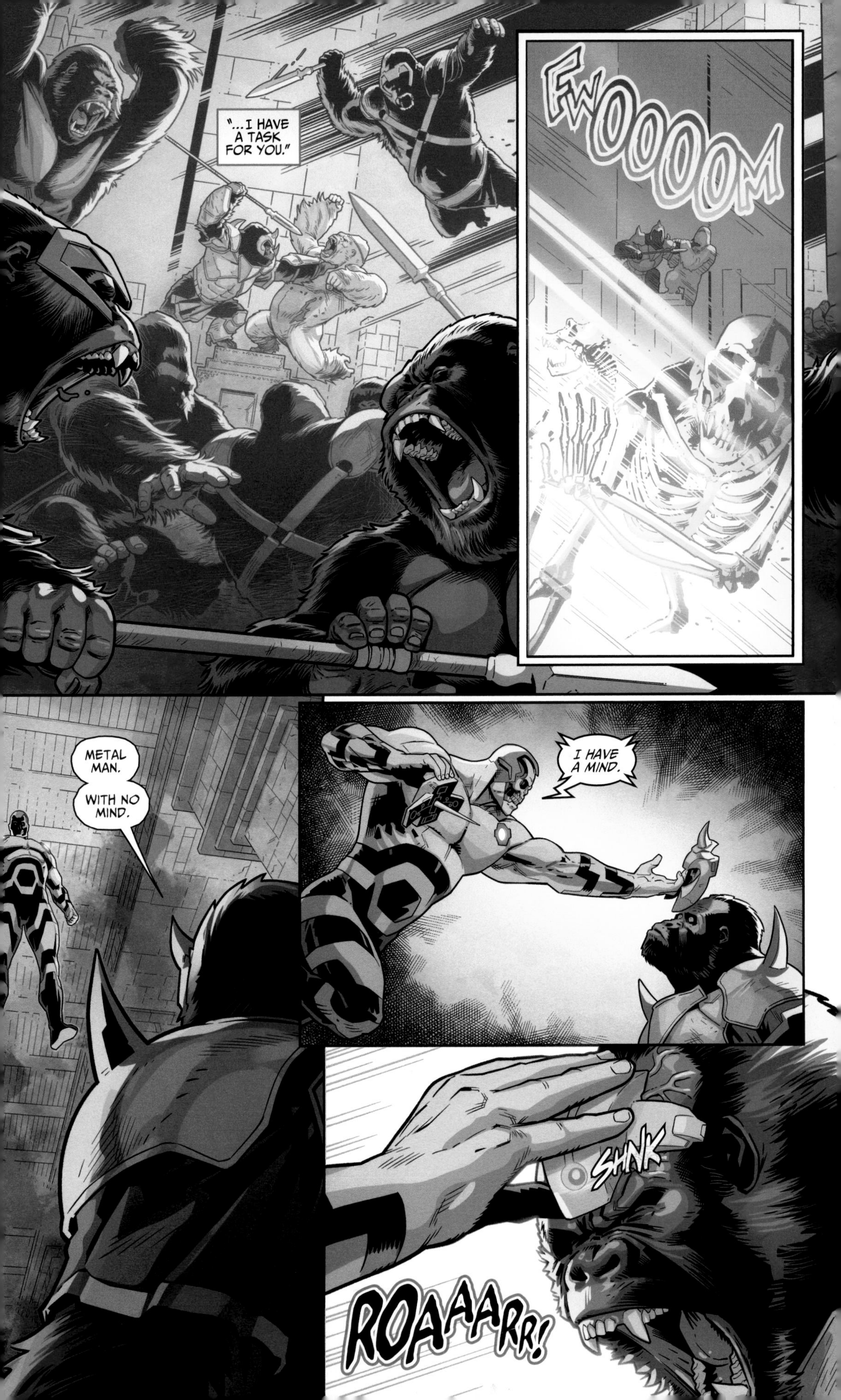
"...I HAVE A TASK FOR YOU."
FWOOOOOM
METAL MAN.
WITH NO MIND.
I HAVE A MIND.
SHNK
ROAAAARR!

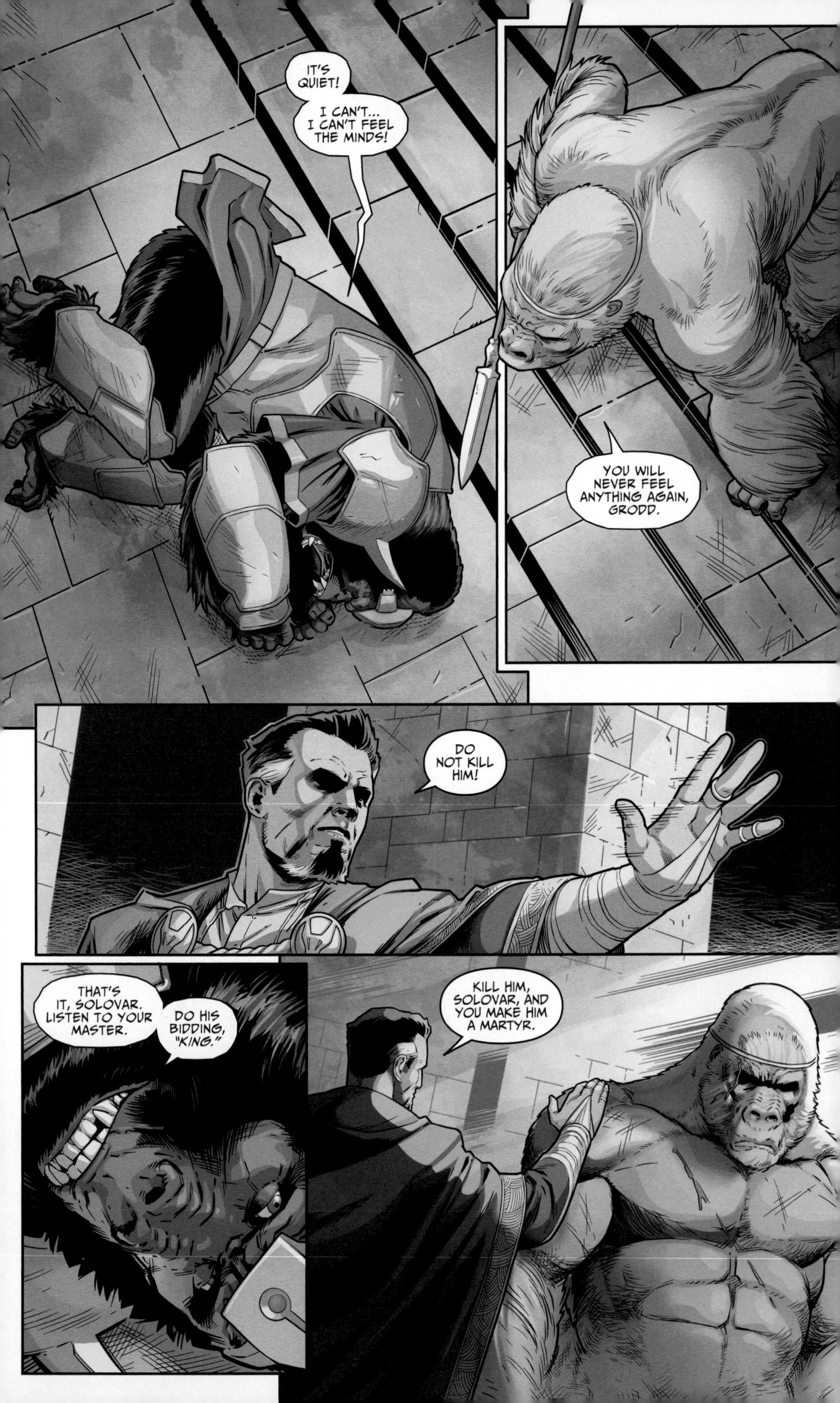
IT'S QUIET!
I CAN'T... I CAN'T FEEL THE MINDS!
YOU WILL NEVER FEEL ANYTHING AGAIN, GRODD.
DO NOT KILL HIM!
THAT'S IT, SOLOVAR. LISTEN TO YOUR MASTER.
DO HIS BIDDING, "KING."
KILL HIM, SOLOVAR, AND YOU MAKE HIM A MARTYR.

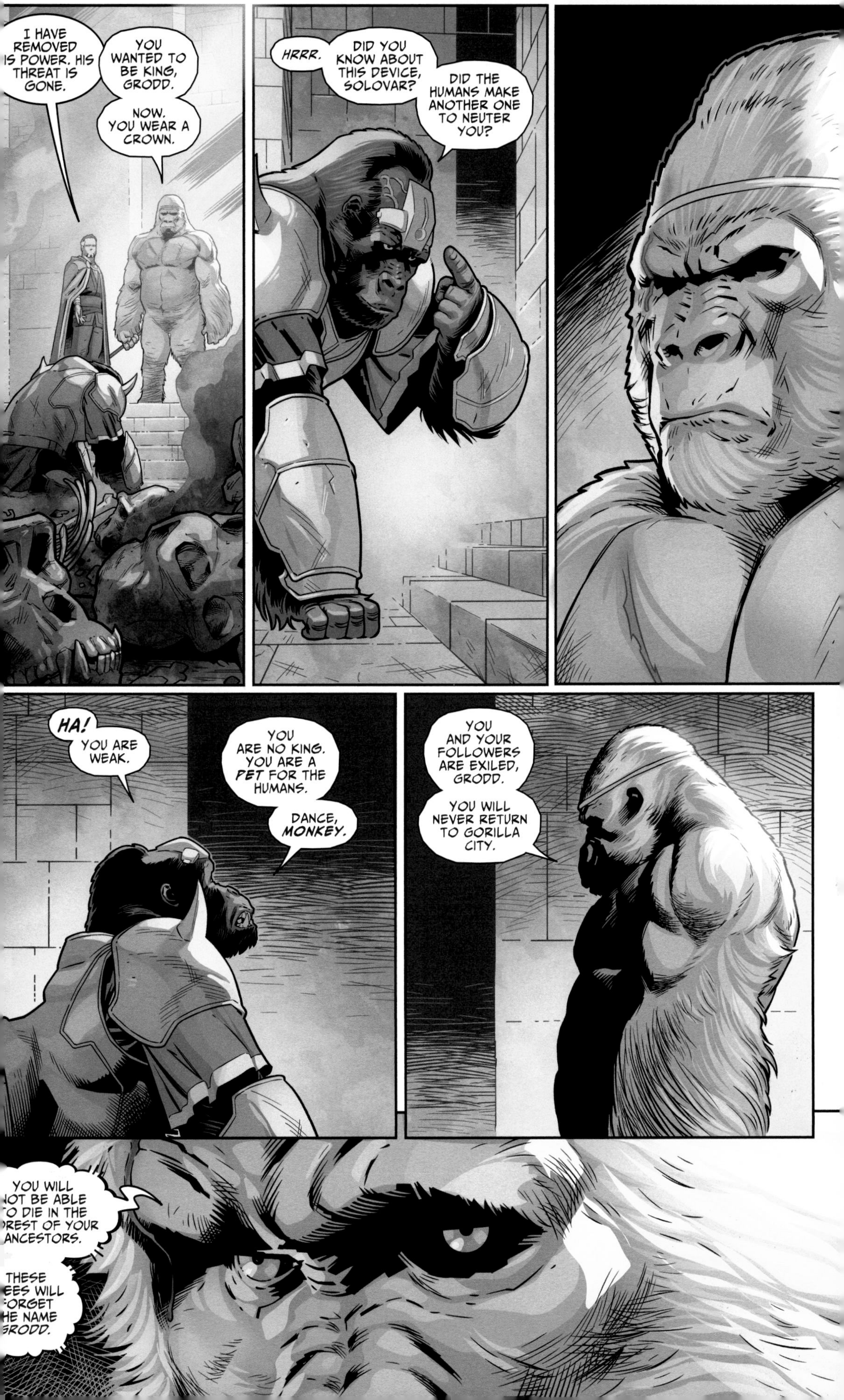
I HAVE REMOVED IS POWER. HIS THREAT IS GONE.
YOU WANTED TO BE KING, GRODD.
NOW. YOU WEAR A CROWN.
HRRR.
DID YOU KNOW ABOUT THIS DEVICE, SOLOVAR?
DID THE HUMANS MAKE ANOTHER ONE TO NEUTER YOU?
HA! YOU ARE WEAK.
YOU ARE NO KING. YOU ARE A PET FOR THE HUMANS.
DANCE, MONKEY.
YOU AND YOUR FOLLOWERS ARE EXILED, GRODD.
YOU WILL NEVER RETURN TO GORILLA CITY.
YOU WILL OT BE ABLE O DIE IN THE OREST OF YOUR ANCESTORS.
THESE EES WILL ORGET HE NAME GRODD.

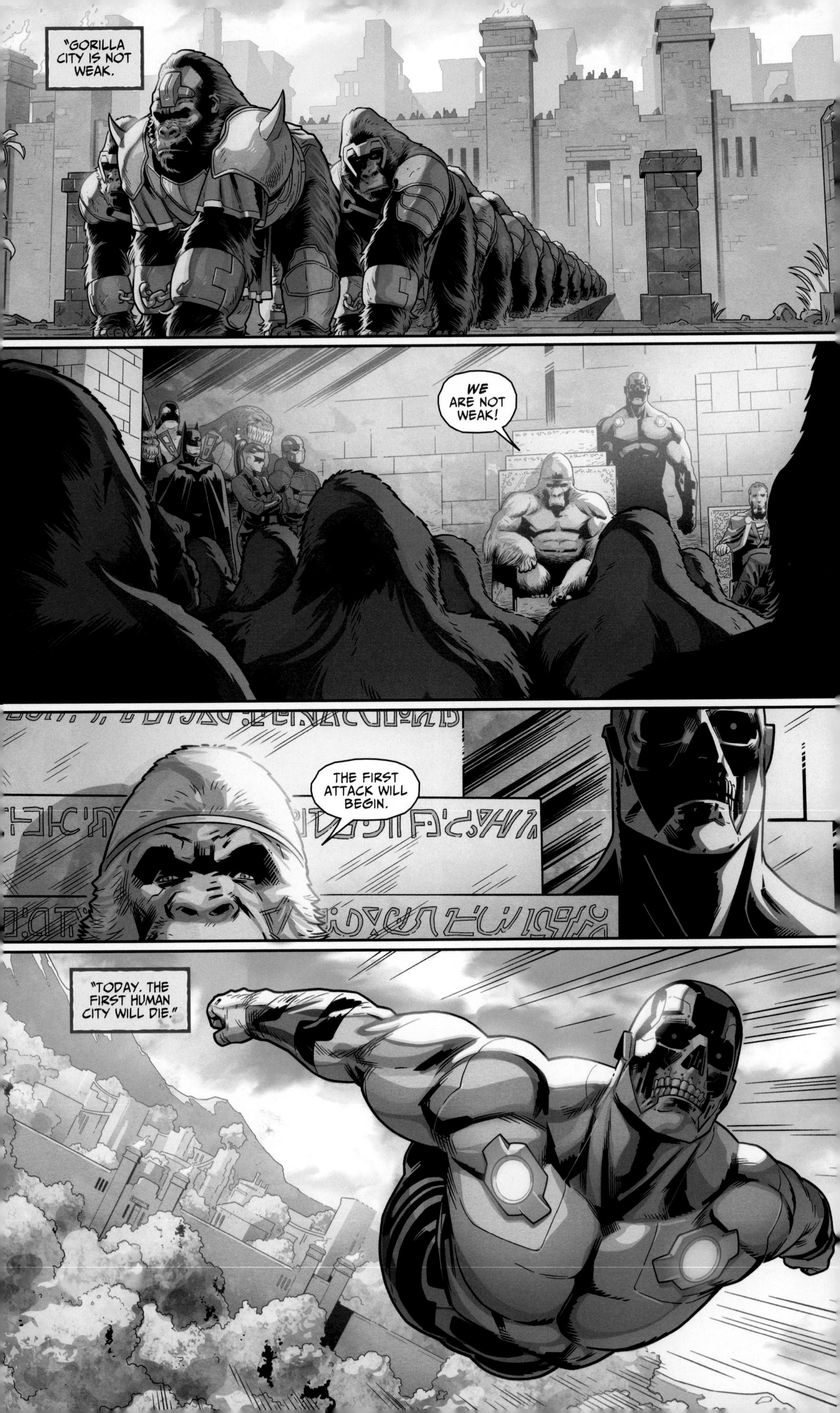
"GORILLA CITY IS NOT WEAK.
WE ARE NOT WEAK!
THE FIRST ATTACK WILL BEGIN.
"TODAY. THE FIRST HUMAN CITY WILL DIE."

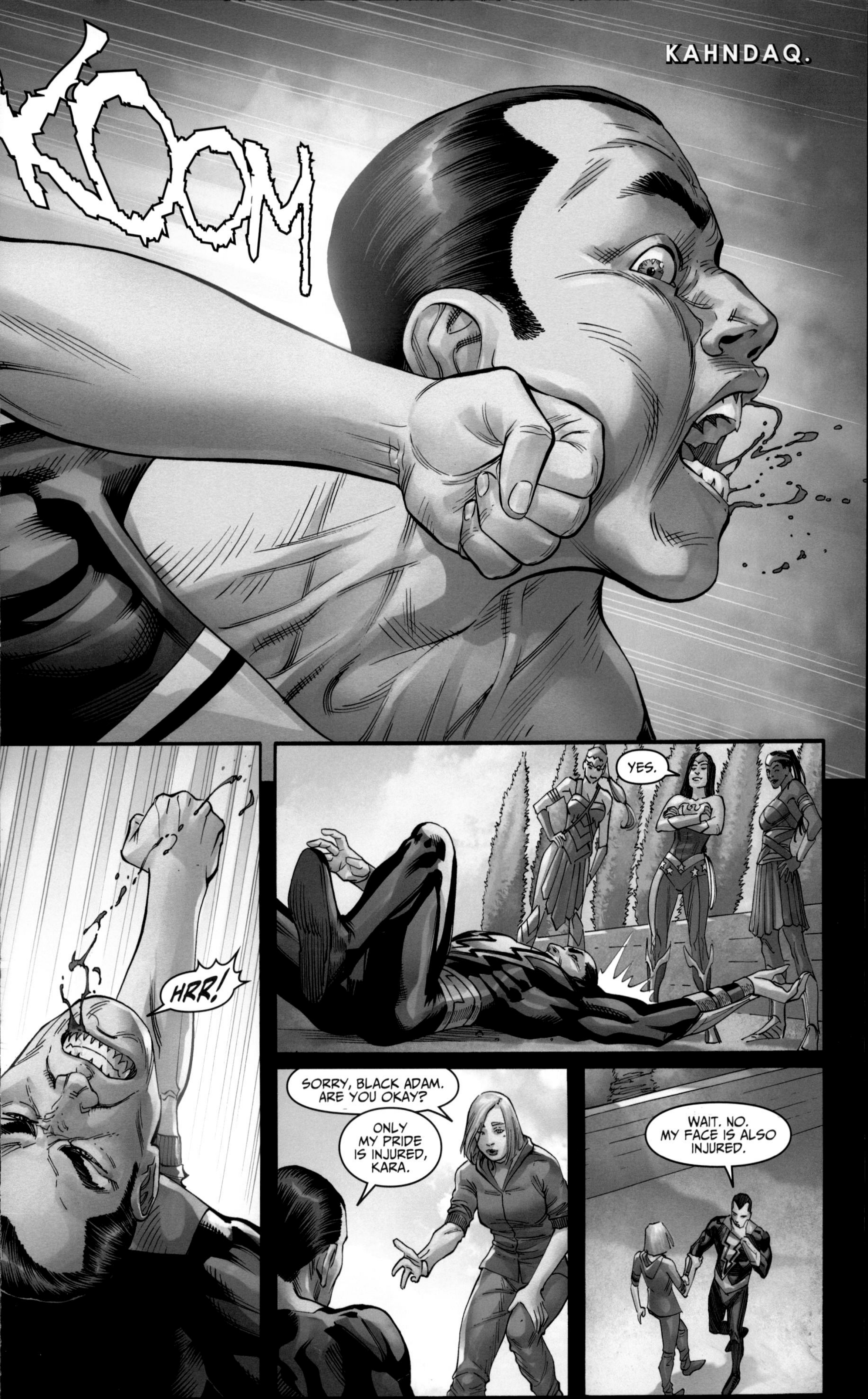
KAHNDAQ.
KOOM
HRR!
YES.
SORRY, BLACK ADAM. ARE YOU OKAY?
ONLY MY PRIDE IS INJURED, KARA.
WAIT. NO. MY FACE IS ALSO INJURED.

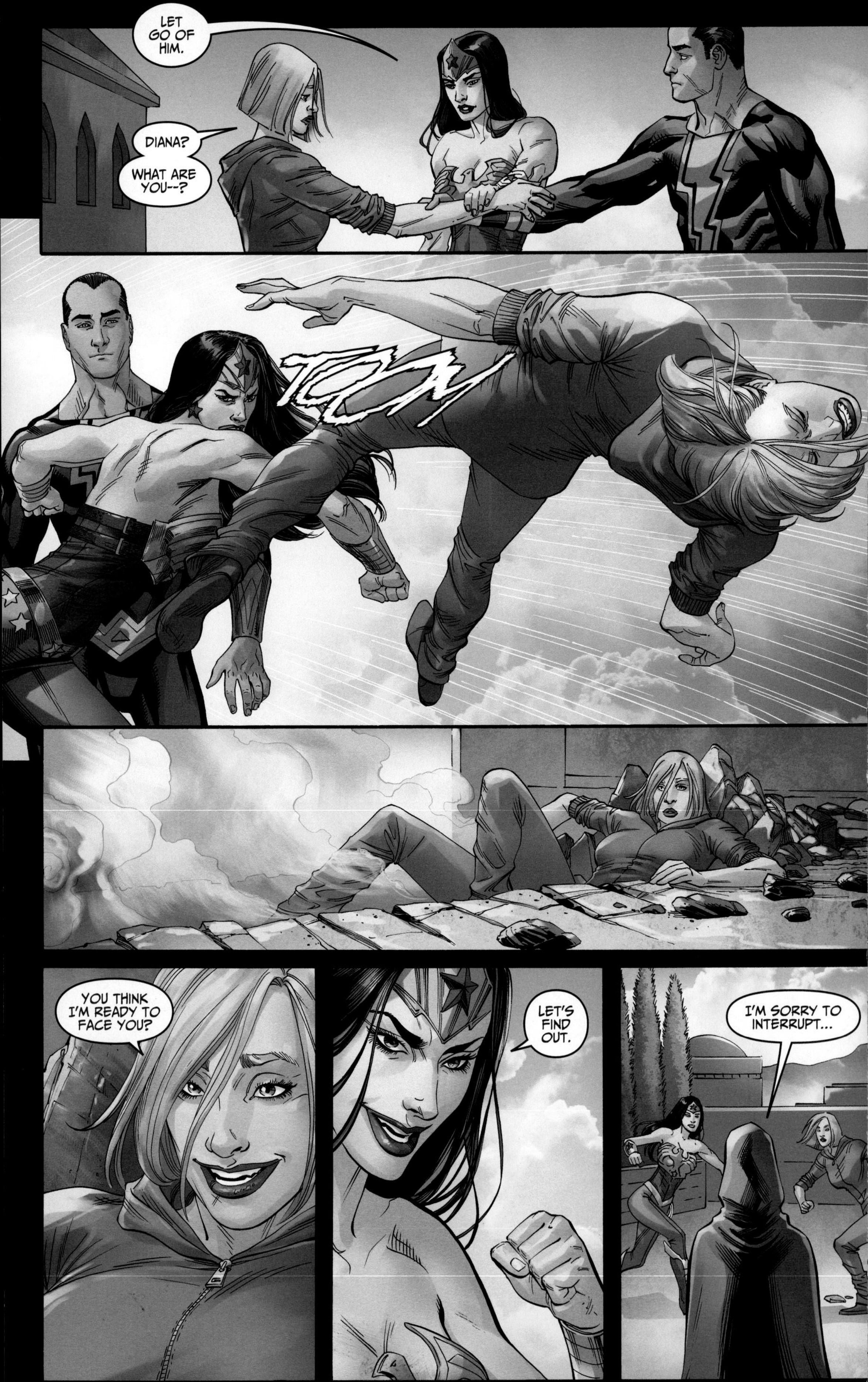
LET GO OF HIM.
DIANA?
WHAT ARE YOU--?
TOOM
YOU THINK I'M READY TO FACE YOU?
LET'S FIND OUT.
I'M SORRY TO INTERRUPT...

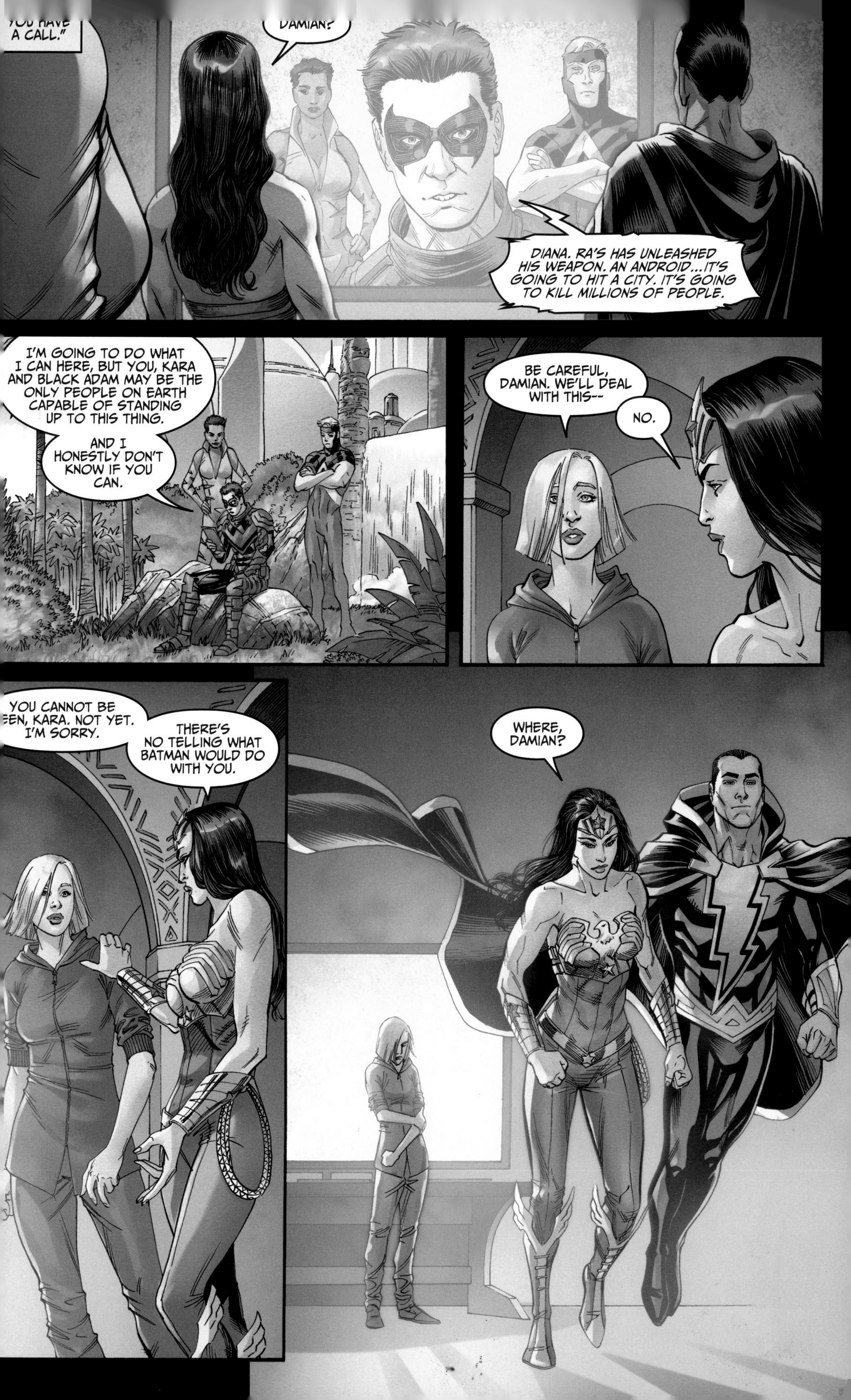

YOU HAVE A CALL."
DAMIAN?
DIANA. RA'S HAS UNLEASHED HIS WEAPON. AN ANDROID...IT'S GOING TO HIT A CITY. IT'S GOING TO KILL MILLIONS OF PEOPLE.
I'M GOING TO DO WHAT I CAN HERE, BUT YOU, KARA AND BLACK ADAM MAY BE THE ONLY PEOPLE ON EARTH CAPABLE OF STANDING UP TO THIS THING.
AND I HONESTLY DON'T KNOW IF YOU CAN.
BE CAREFUL, DAMIAN. WE'LL DEAL WITH THIS--
NO.
YOU CANNOT BE SEEN, KARA. NOT YET. I'M SORRY.
THERE'S NO TELLING WHAT BATMAN WOULD DO WITH YOU.
WHERE, DAMIAN?

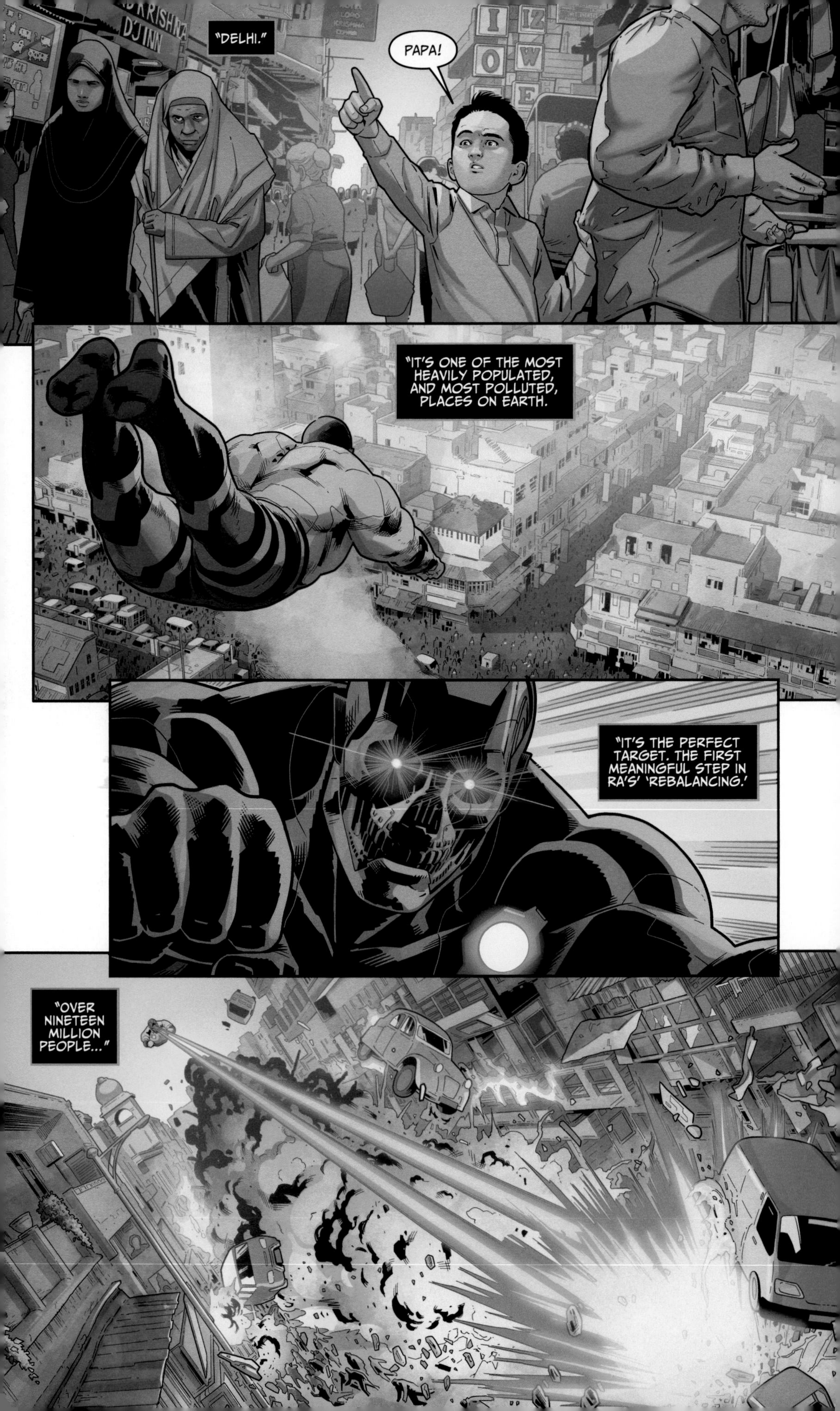
D'JINN
"DELHI."
PAPA!
"IT'S ONE OF THE MOST HEAVILY POPULATED, AND MOST POLLUTED, PLACES ON EARTH.
"IT'S THE PERFECT TARGET. THE FIRST MEANINGFUL STEP IN RA'S' 'REBALANCING.'
"OVER NINETEEN MILLION PEOPLE..."

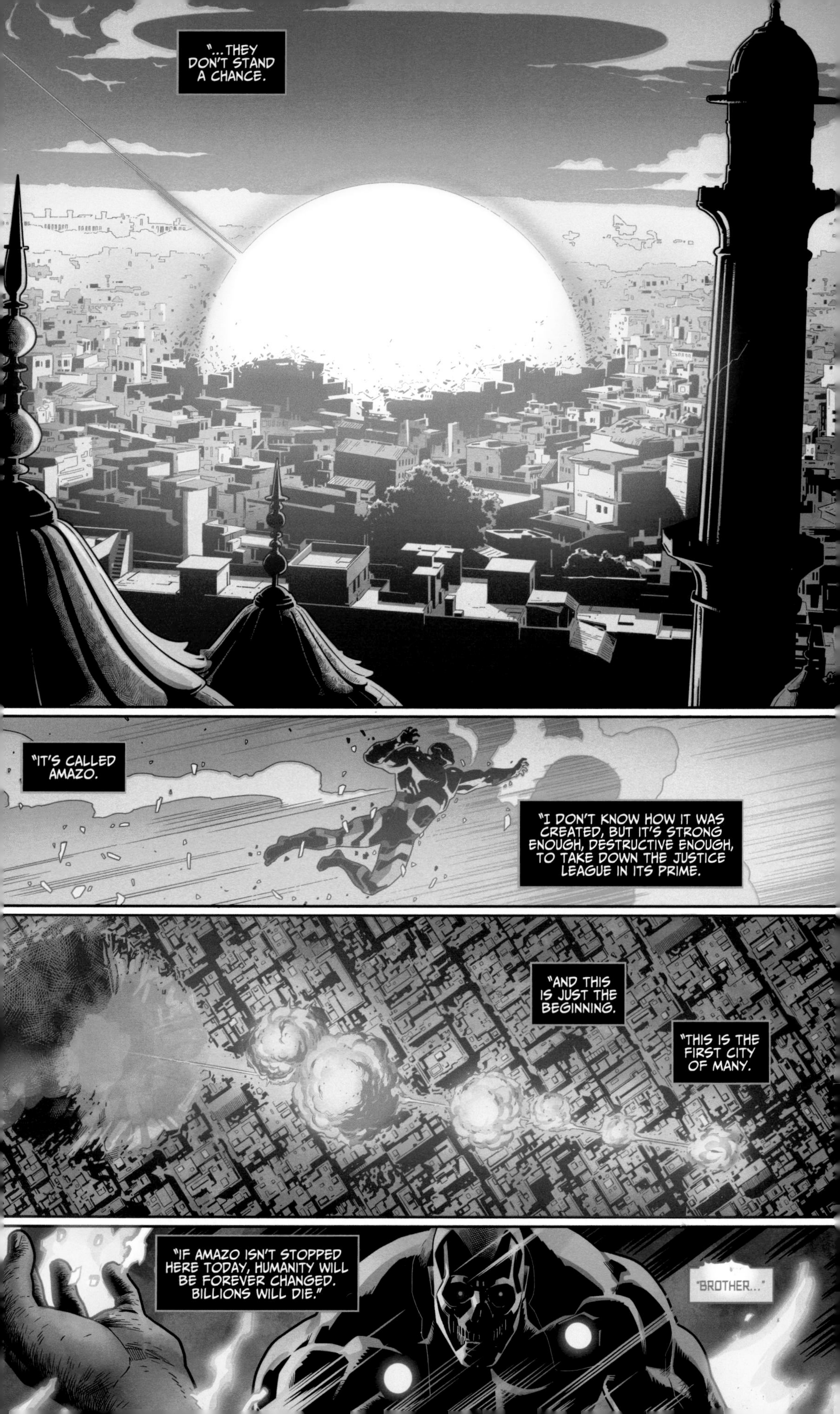
"...THEY DON'T STAND A CHANCE.
"IT'S CALLED AMAZO.
"I DON'T KNOW HOW IT WAS CREATED, BUT IT'S STRONG ENOUGH, DESTRUCTIVE ENOUGH, TO TAKE DOWN THE JUSTICE LEAGUE IN ITS PRIME.
"AND THIS IS JUST THE BEGINNING.
"THIS IS THE FIRST CITY OF MANY.
"IF AMAZO ISN'T STOPPED HERE TODAY, HUMANITY WILL BE FOREVER CHANGED. BILLIONS WILL DIE."
"BROTHER..."

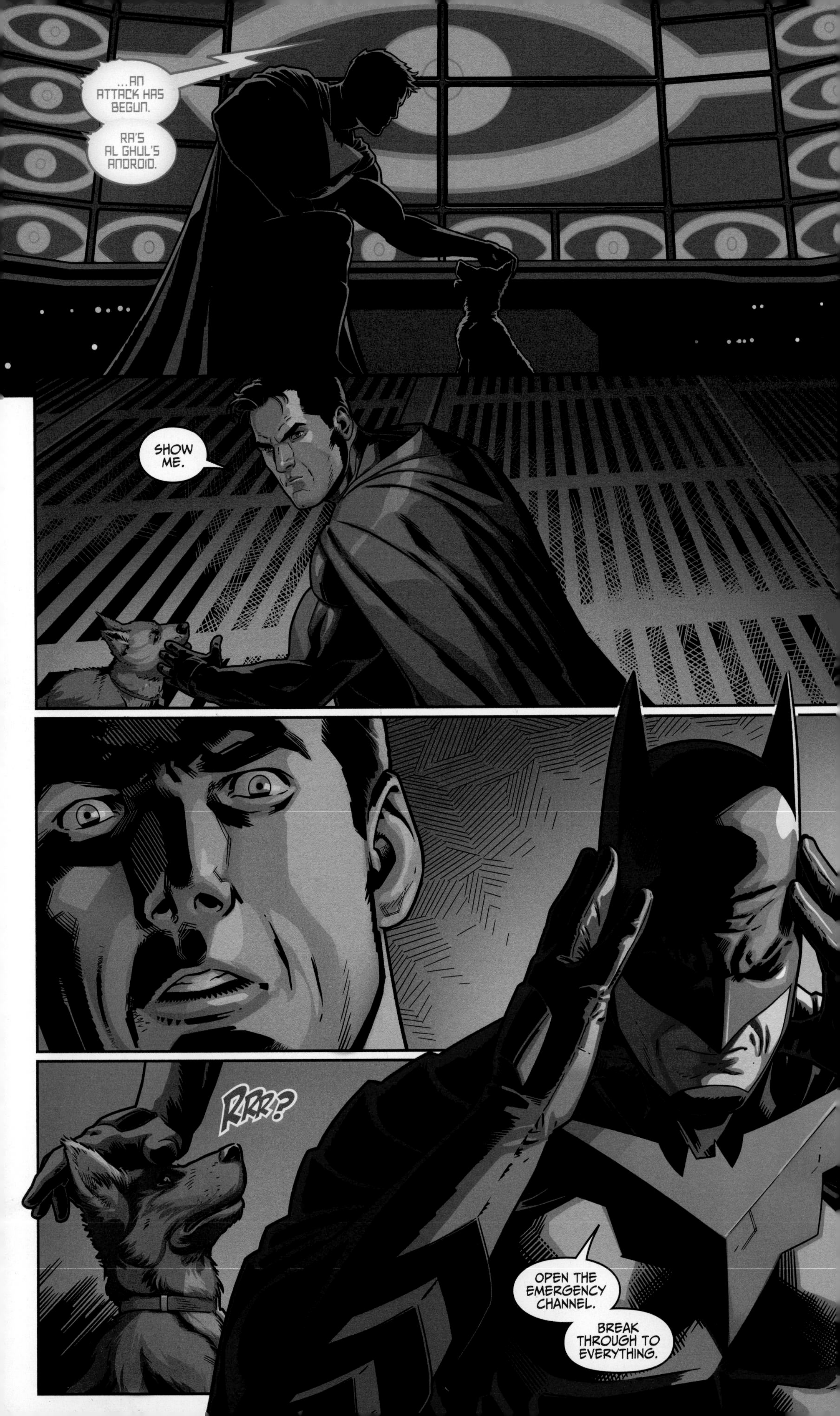
...AN ATTACK HAS BEGUN.
RA'S AL GHUL'S ANDROID.
SHOW ME.
RRR?
OPEN THE EMERGENCY CHANNEL.
BREAK THROUGH TO EVERYTHING.

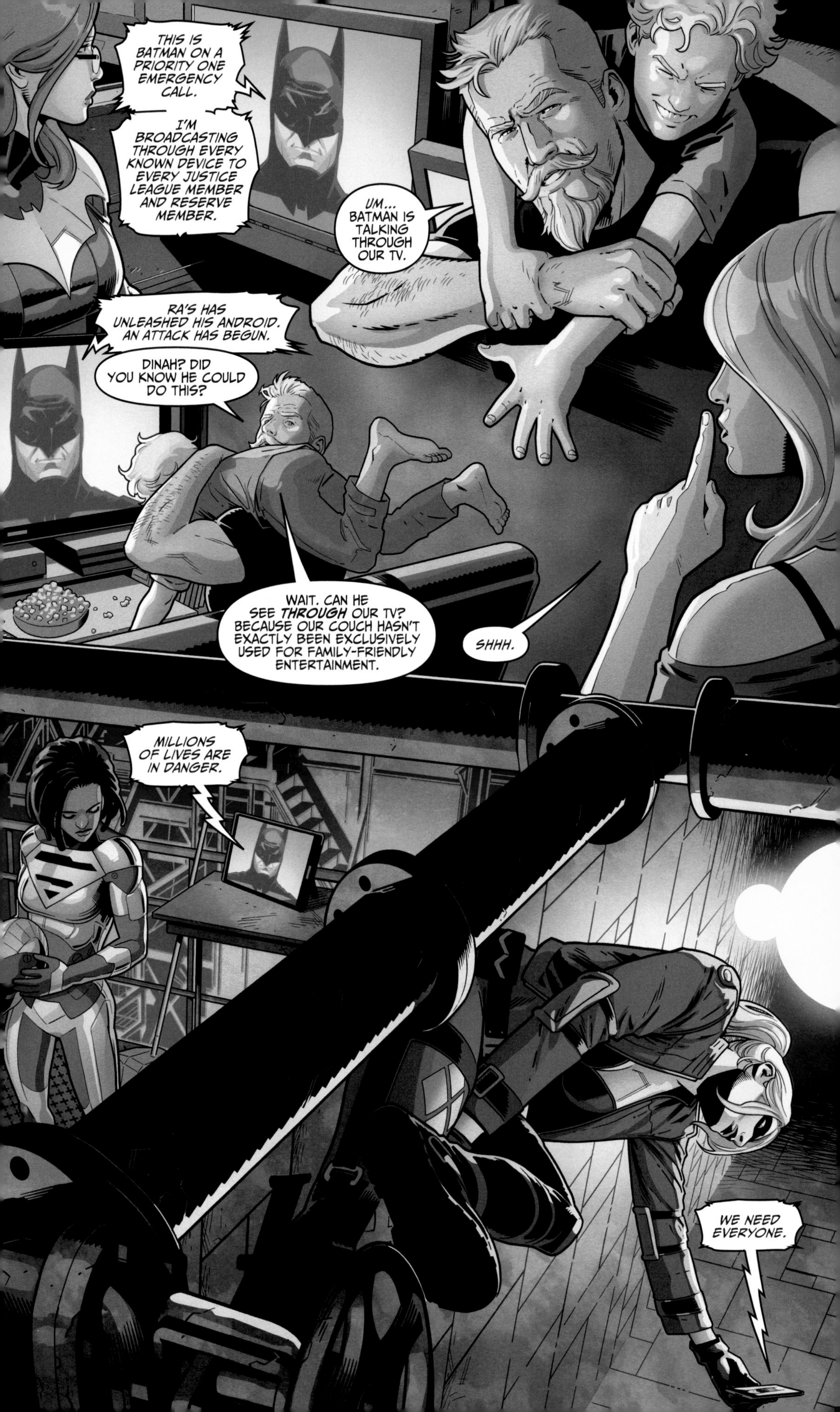
THIS IS BATMAN ON A PRIORITY ONE EMERGENCY CALL.
I'M BROADCASTING THROUGH EVERY KNOWN DEVICE TO EVERY JUSTICE LEAGUE MEMBER AND RESERVE MEMBER.
UM... BATMAN IS TALKING THROUGH OUR TV.
RA'S HAS UNLEASHED HIS ANDROID. AN ATTACK HAS BEGUN.
DINAH? DID YOU KNOW HE COULD DO THIS?
WAIT. CAN HE SEE *THROUGH* OUR TV? BECAUSE OUR COUCH HASN'T EXACTLY BEEN EXCLUSIVELY USED FOR FAMILY-FRIENDLY ENTERTAINMENT.
SHHH.
MILLIONS OF LIVES ARE IN DANGER.
WE NEED EVERYONE.

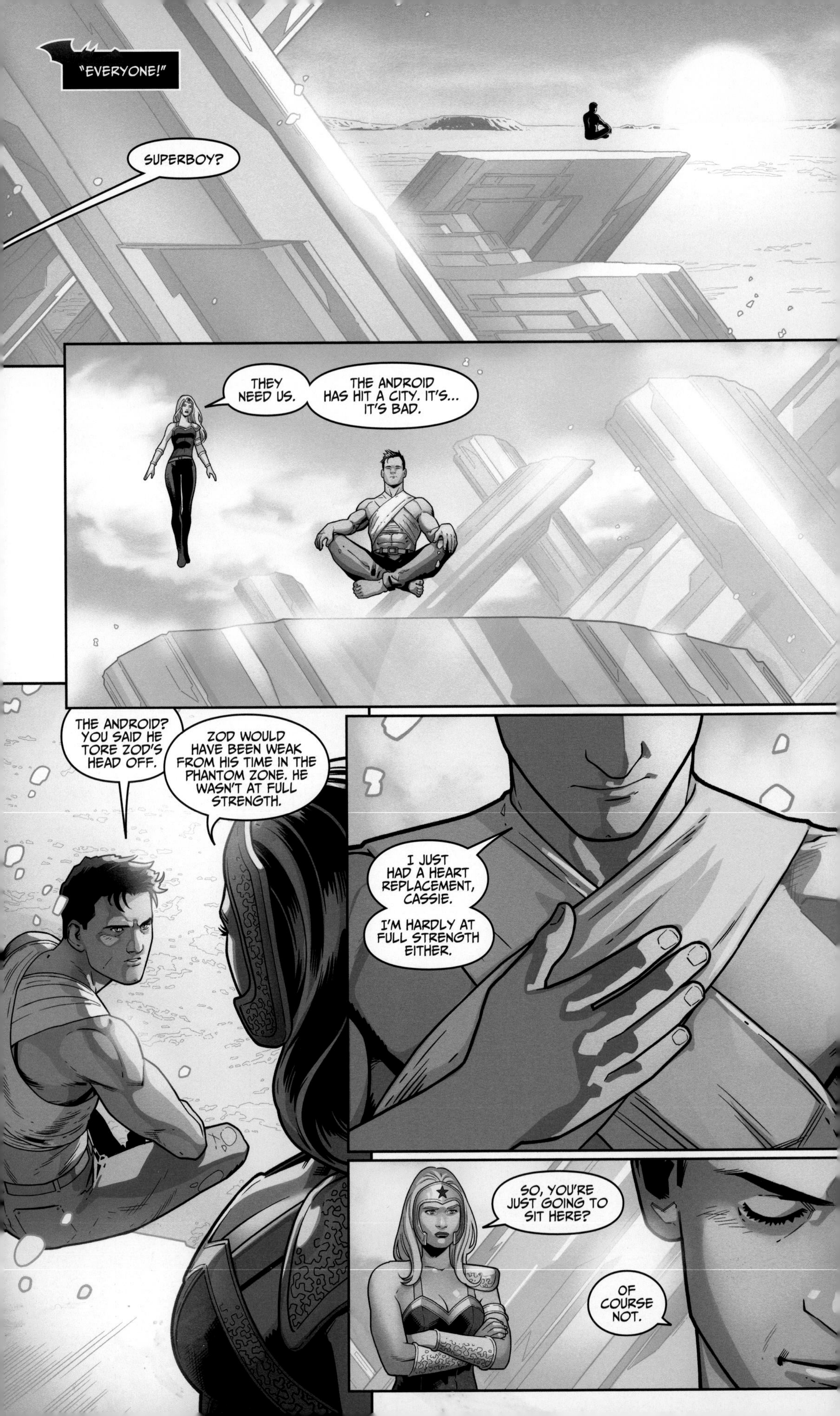
"EVERYONE!"
SUPERBOY?
THEY NEED US.
THE ANDROID HAS HIT A CITY. IT'S... IT'S BAD.
THE ANDROID? YOU SAID HE TORE ZOD'S HEAD OFF.
ZOD WOULD HAVE BEEN WEAK FROM HIS TIME IN THE PHANTOM ZONE. HE WASN'T AT FULL STRENGTH.
I JUST HAD A HEART REPLACEMENT, CASSIE.
I'M HARDLY AT FULL STRENGTH EITHER.
SO, YOU'RE JUST GOING TO SIT HERE?
OF COURSE NOT.

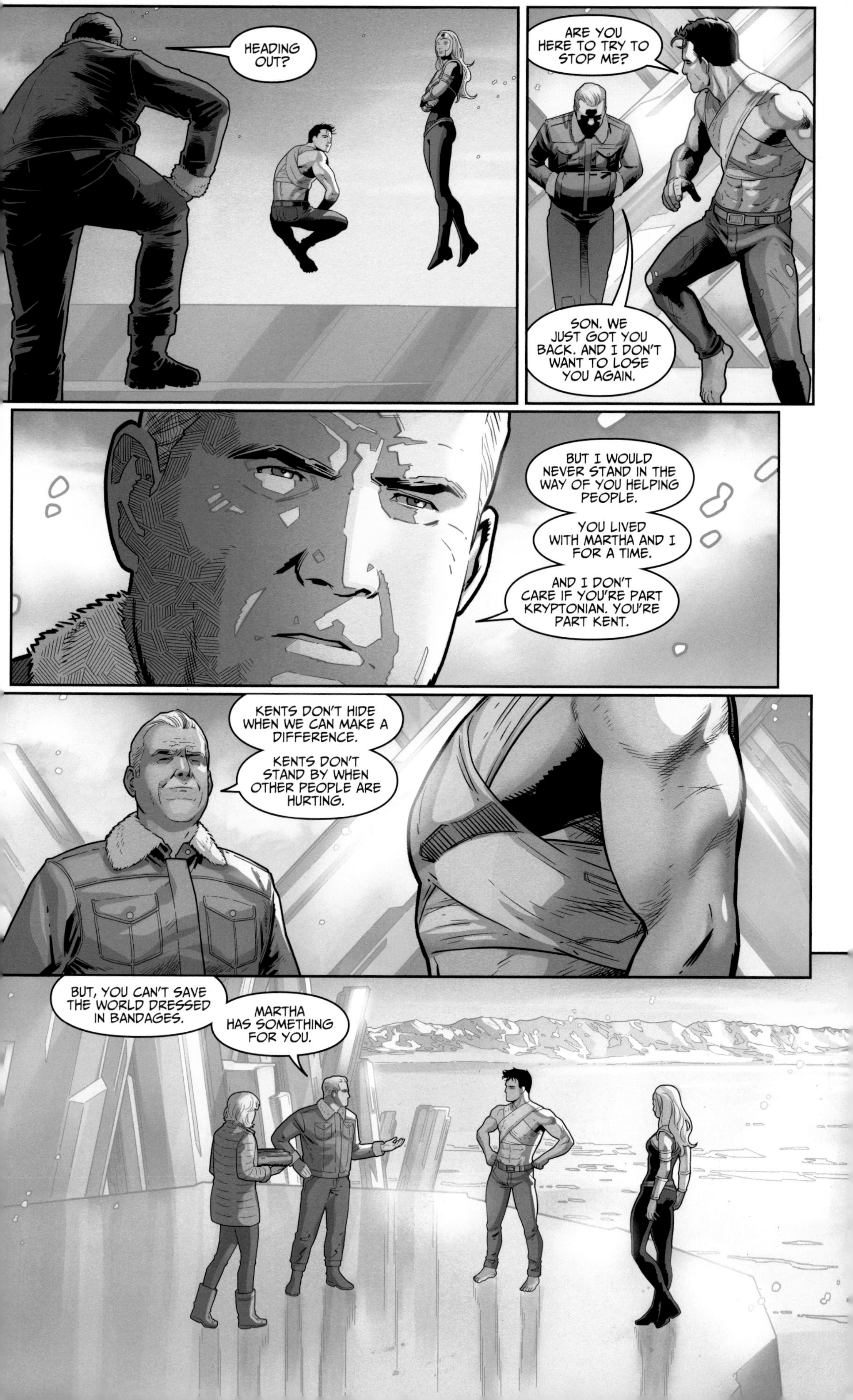
HEADING OUT?
ARE YOU HERE TO TRY TO STOP ME?
SON. WE JUST GOT YOU BACK. AND I DON'T WANT TO LOSE YOU AGAIN.
BUT I WOULD NEVER STAND IN THE WAY OF YOU HELPING PEOPLE.
YOU LIVED WITH MARTHA AND I FOR A TIME.
AND I DON'T CARE IF YOU'RE PART KRYPTONIAN. YOU'RE PART KENT.
KENTS DON'T HIDE WHEN WE CAN MAKE A DIFFERENCE.
KENTS DON'T STAND BY WHEN OTHER PEOPLE ARE HURTING.
BUT, YOU CAN'T SAVE THE WORLD DRESSED IN BANDAGES.
MARTHA HAS SOMETHING FOR YOU.

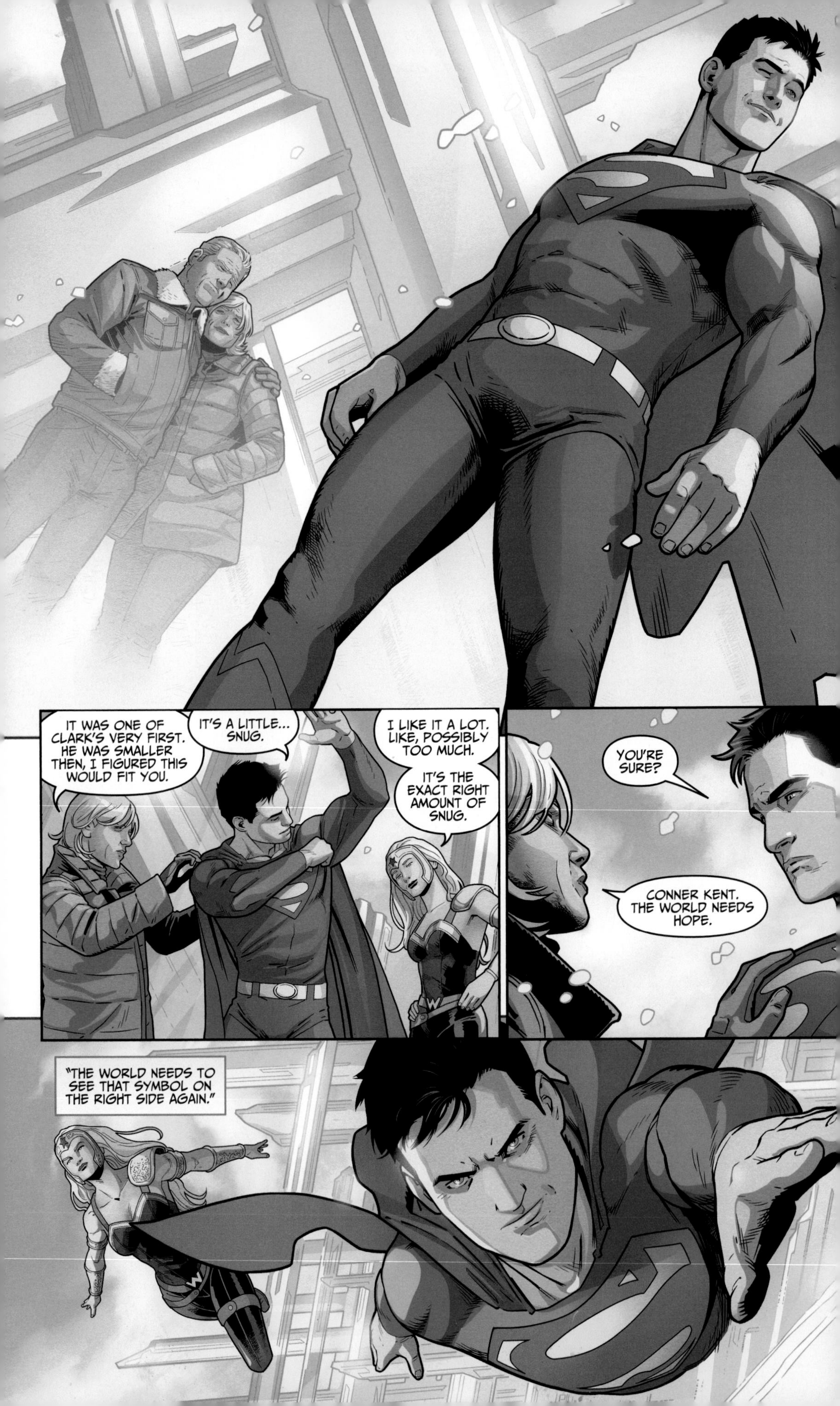
IT WAS ONE OF CLARK'S VERY FIRST. HE WAS SMALLER THEN, I FIGURED THIS WOULD FIT YOU.
IT'S A LITTLE... SNUG.
I LIKE IT A LOT. LIKE, POSSIBLY TOO MUCH.
IT'S THE EXACT RIGHT AMOUNT OF SNUG.
YOU'RE SURE?
CONNER KENT. THE WORLD NEEDS HOPE.
"THE WORLD NEEDS TO SEE THAT SYMBOL ON THE RIGHT SIDE AGAIN."

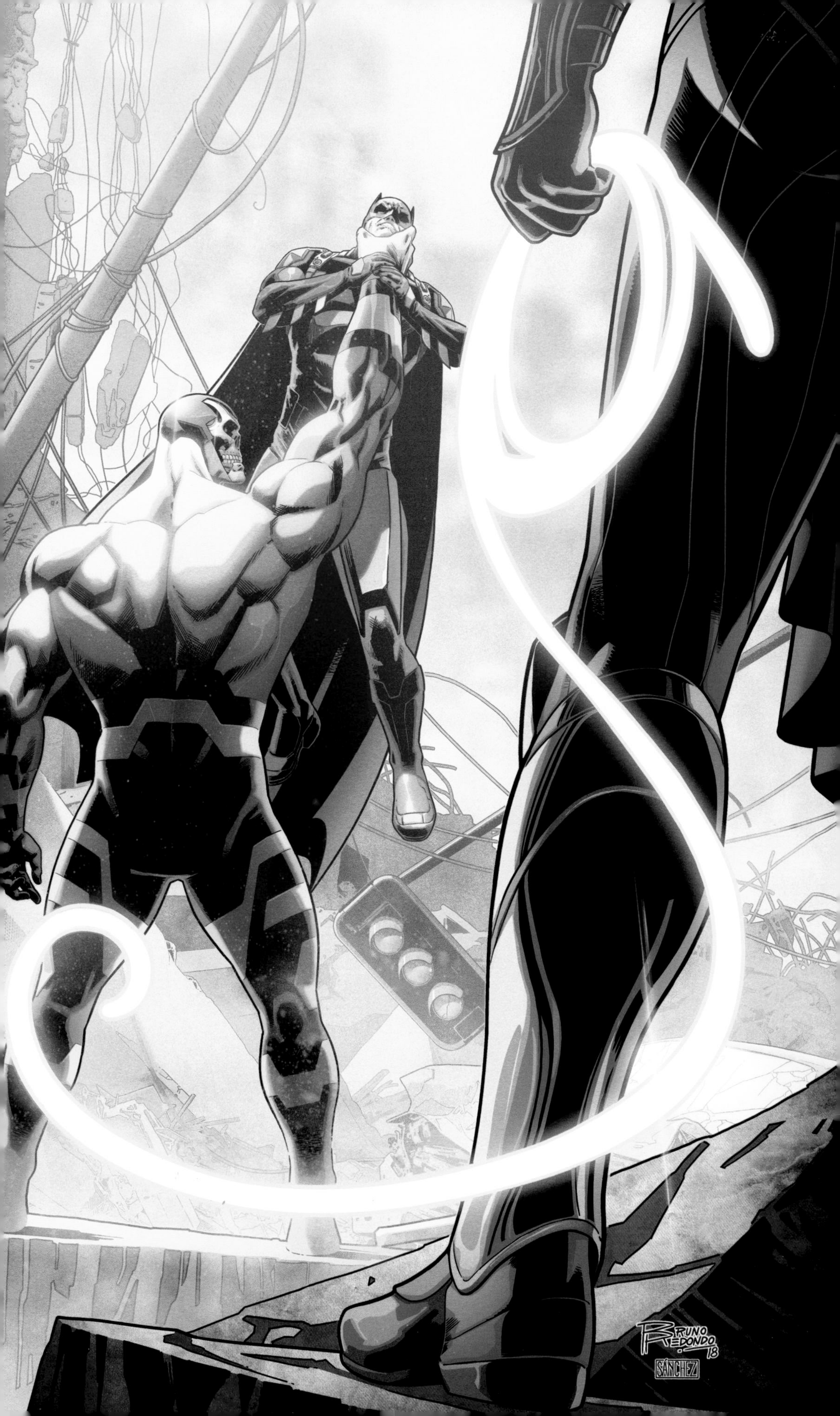
BRUNO REDONDO '18
SÁNCHEZ

"City Killer"

Tom Taylor Writer **Daniel Sampere** Penciller **Juan Albarran** Inker **Rex Lokus** Colorist **Wes Abbott** Letterer

Cover art by **Bruno Redondo** and **Alejandro Sanchez**

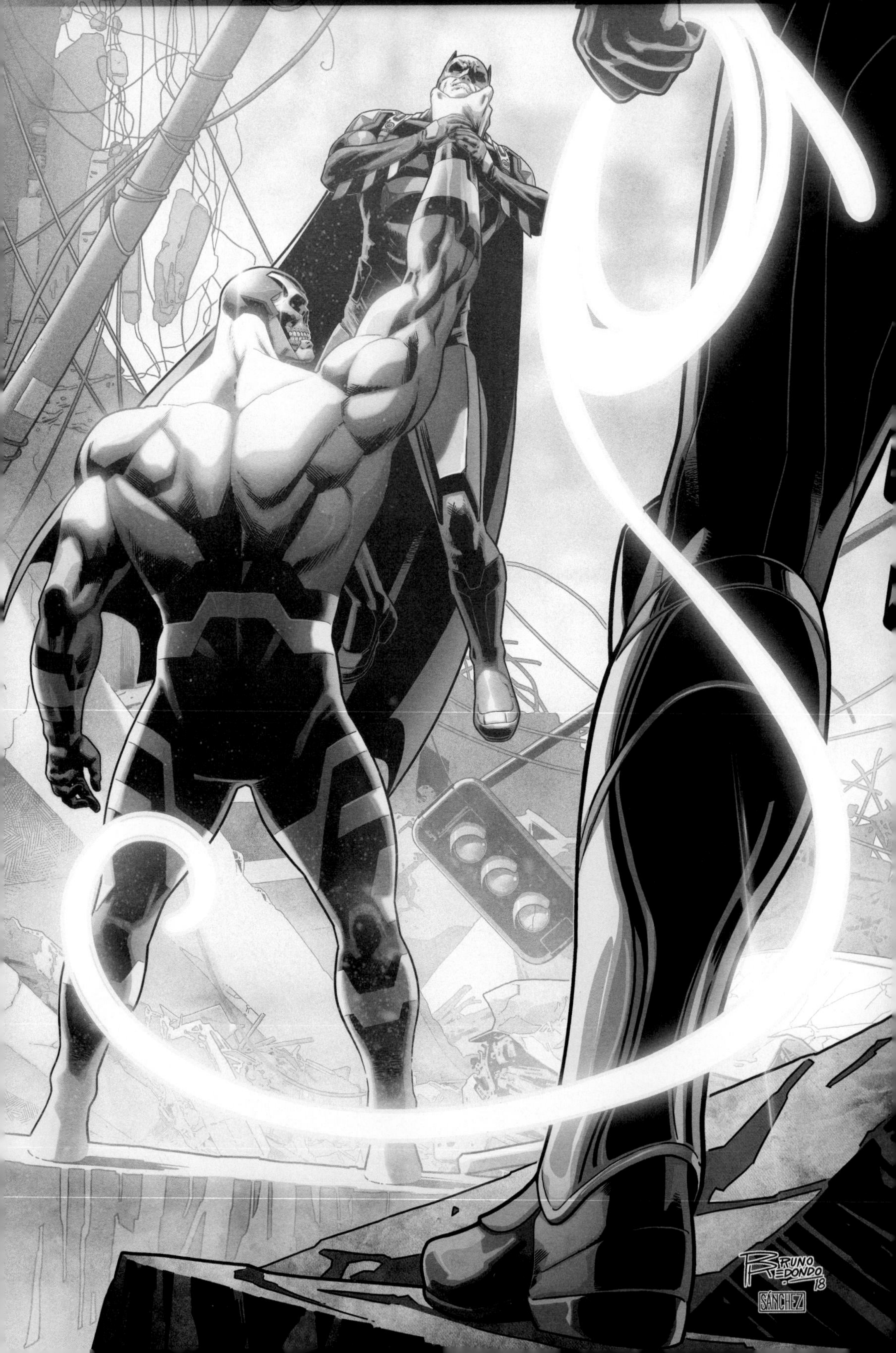

BRUNO REDONDO '18
SÁNCHEZ

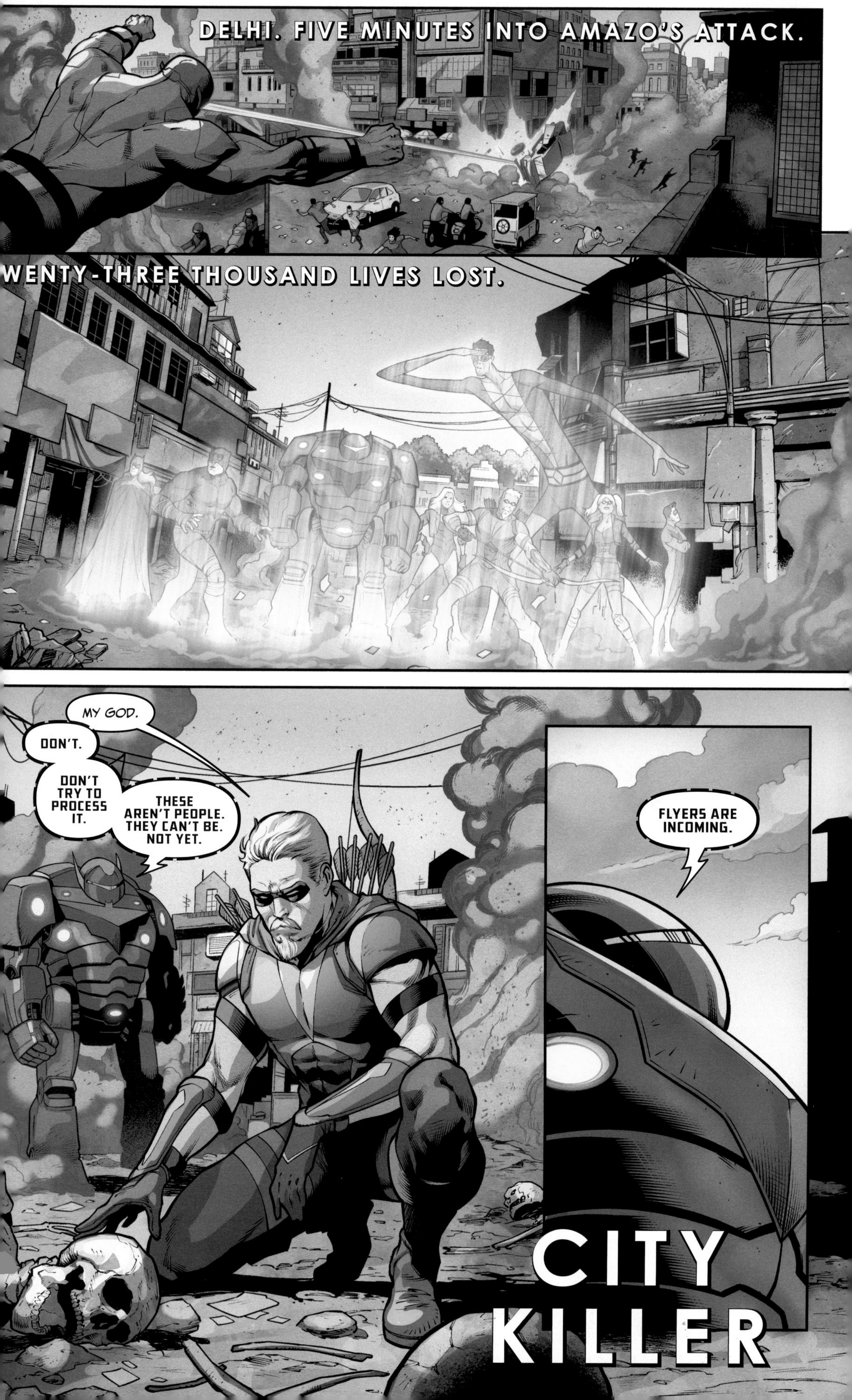

DELHI. FIVE MINUTES INTO AMAZO'S ATTACK.
WENTY-THREE THOUSAND LIVES LOST.
MY GOD.
DON'T.
DON'T TRY TO PROCESS IT.
THESE AREN'T PEOPLE. THEY CAN'T BE. NOT YET.
FLYERS ARE INCOMING.
CITY KILLER

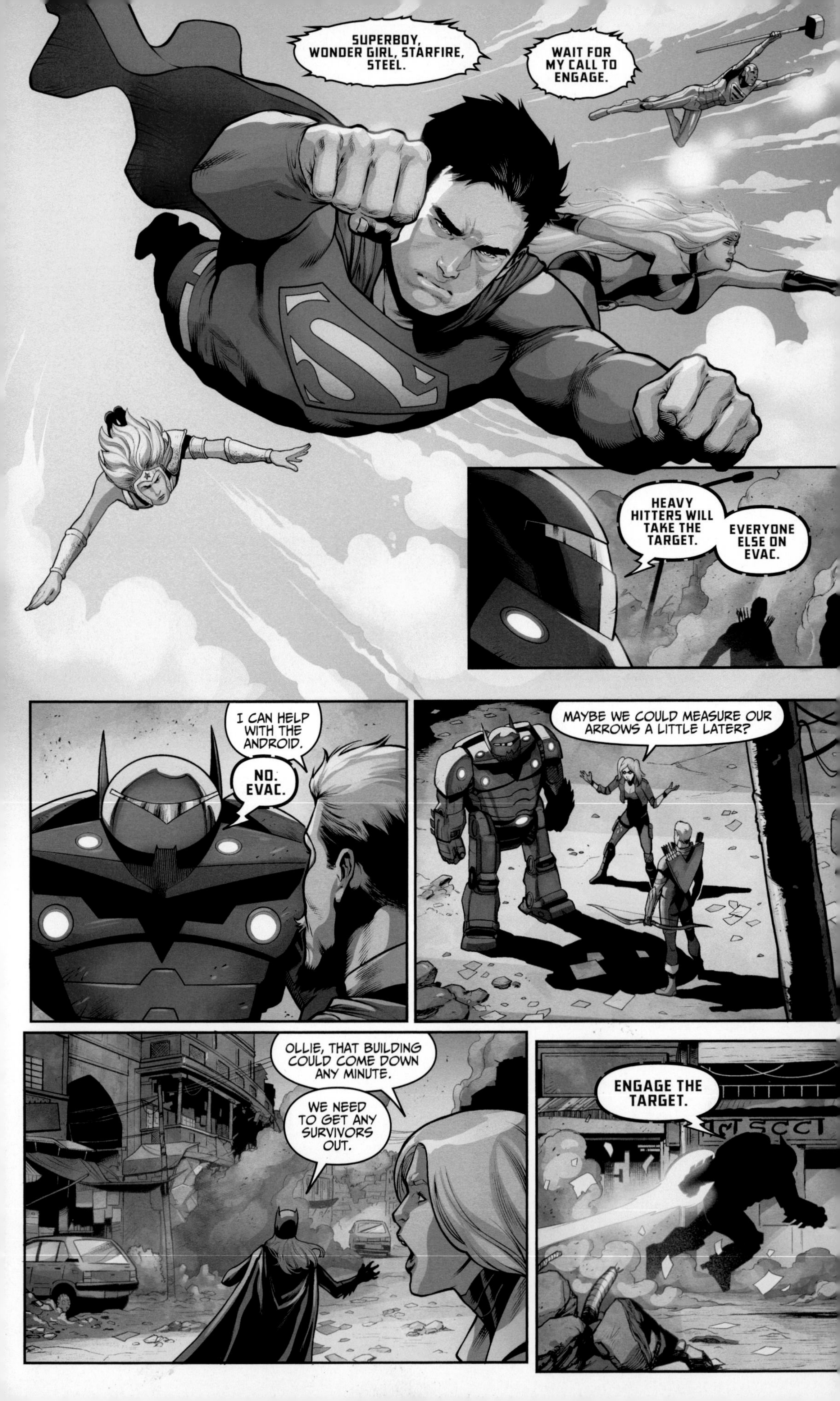
SUPERBOY, WONDER GIRL, STARFIRE, STEEL.
WAIT FOR MY CALL TO ENGAGE.
HEAVY HITTERS WILL TAKE THE TARGET.
EVERYONE ELSE ON EVAC.
I CAN HELP WITH THE ANDROID.
NO. EVAC.
MAYBE WE COULD MEASURE OUR ARROWS A LITTLE LATER?
OLLIE, THAT BUILDING COULD COME DOWN ANY MINUTE.
WE NEED TO GET ANY SURVIVORS OUT.
ENGAGE THE TARGET.

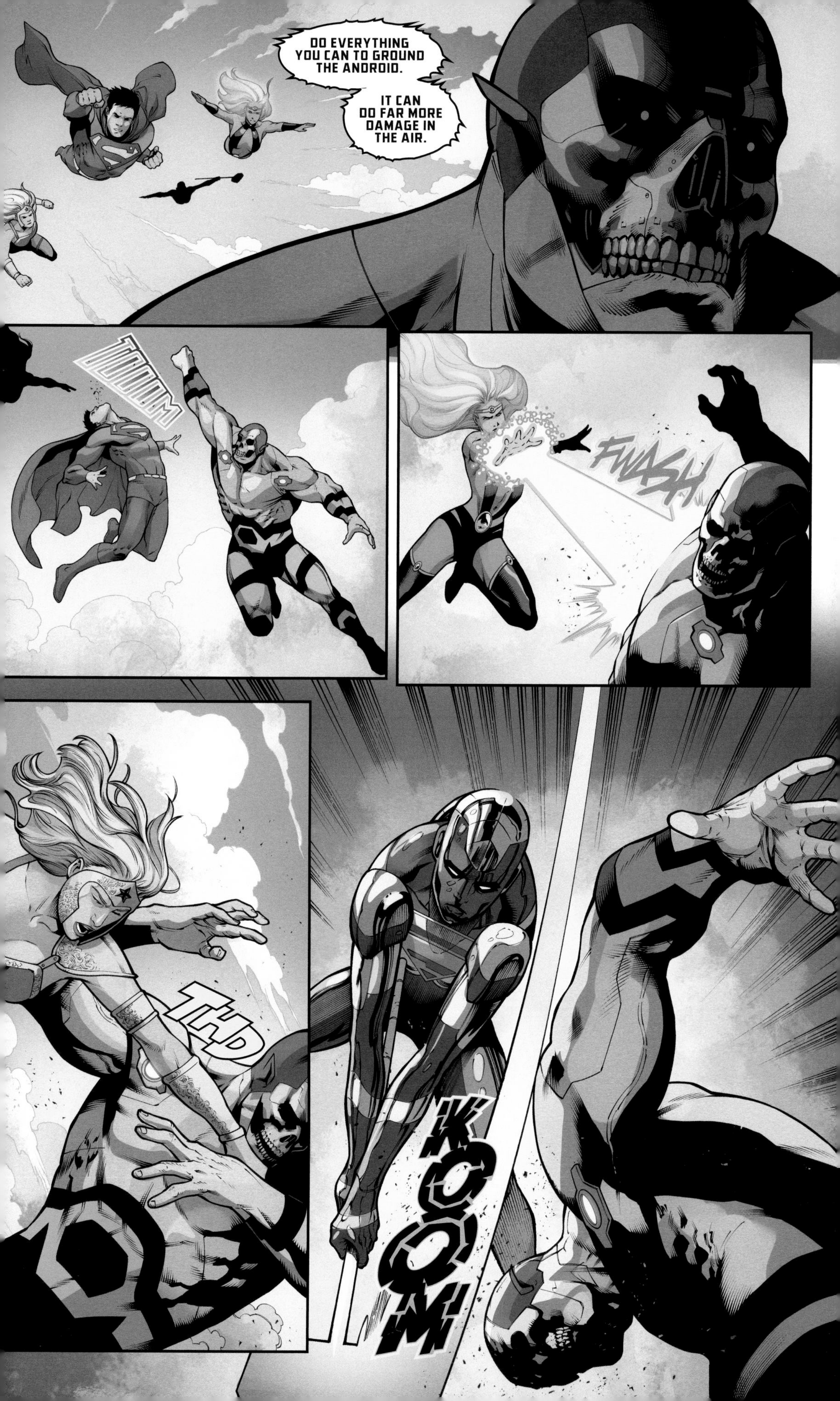
DO EVERYTHING YOU CAN TO GROUND THE ANDROID.
IT CAN DO FAR MORE DAMAGE IN THE AIR.
THOOOM
FWASH
THD
KOOOM!

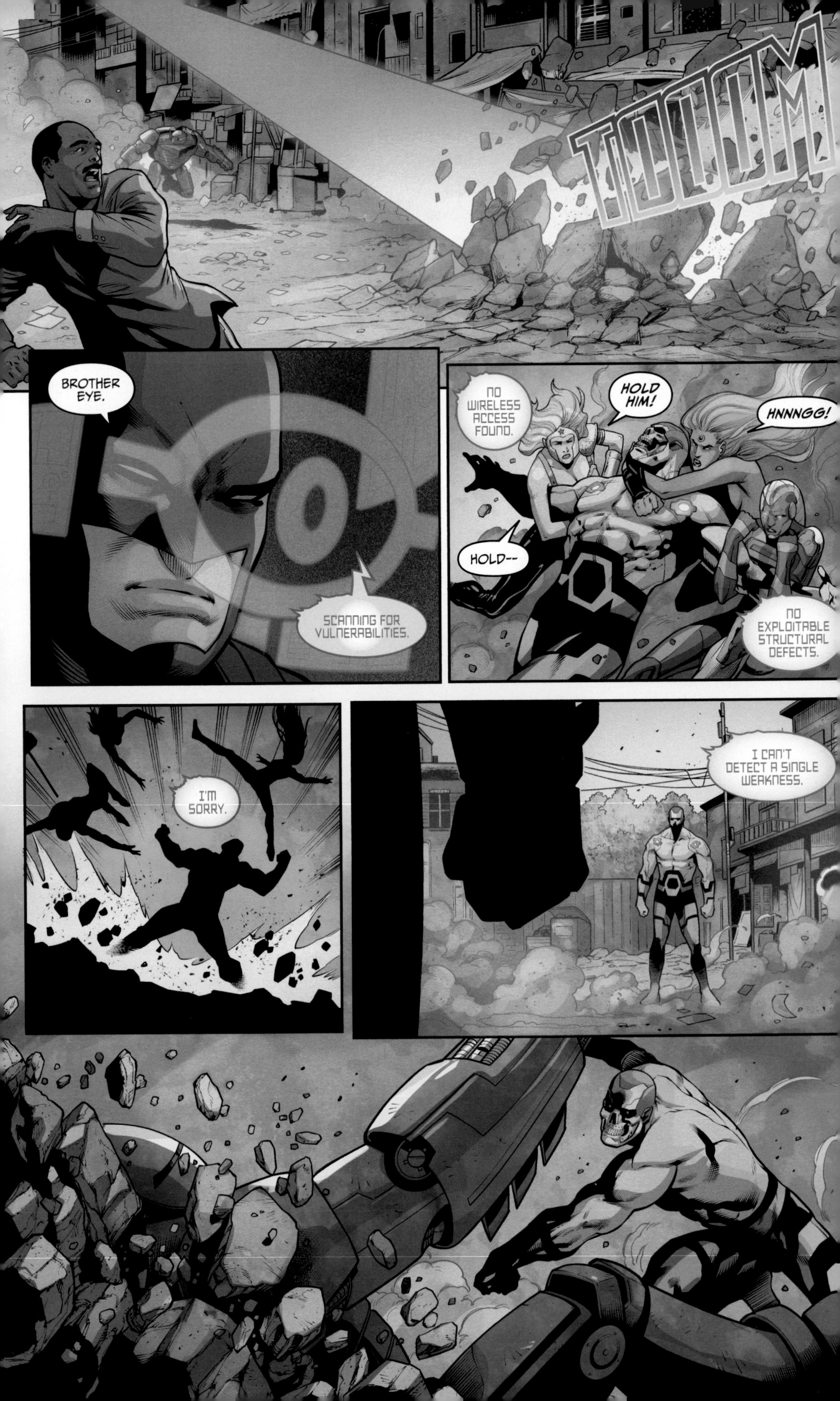
TOOOM
BROTHER EYE.
SCANNING FOR VULNERABILITIES.
NO WIRELESS ACCESS FOUND.
HOLD HIM!
HNNNGG!
HOLD--
NO EXPLOITABLE STRUCTURAL DEFECTS.
I'M SORRY.
I CAN'T DETECT A SINGLE WEAKNESS.

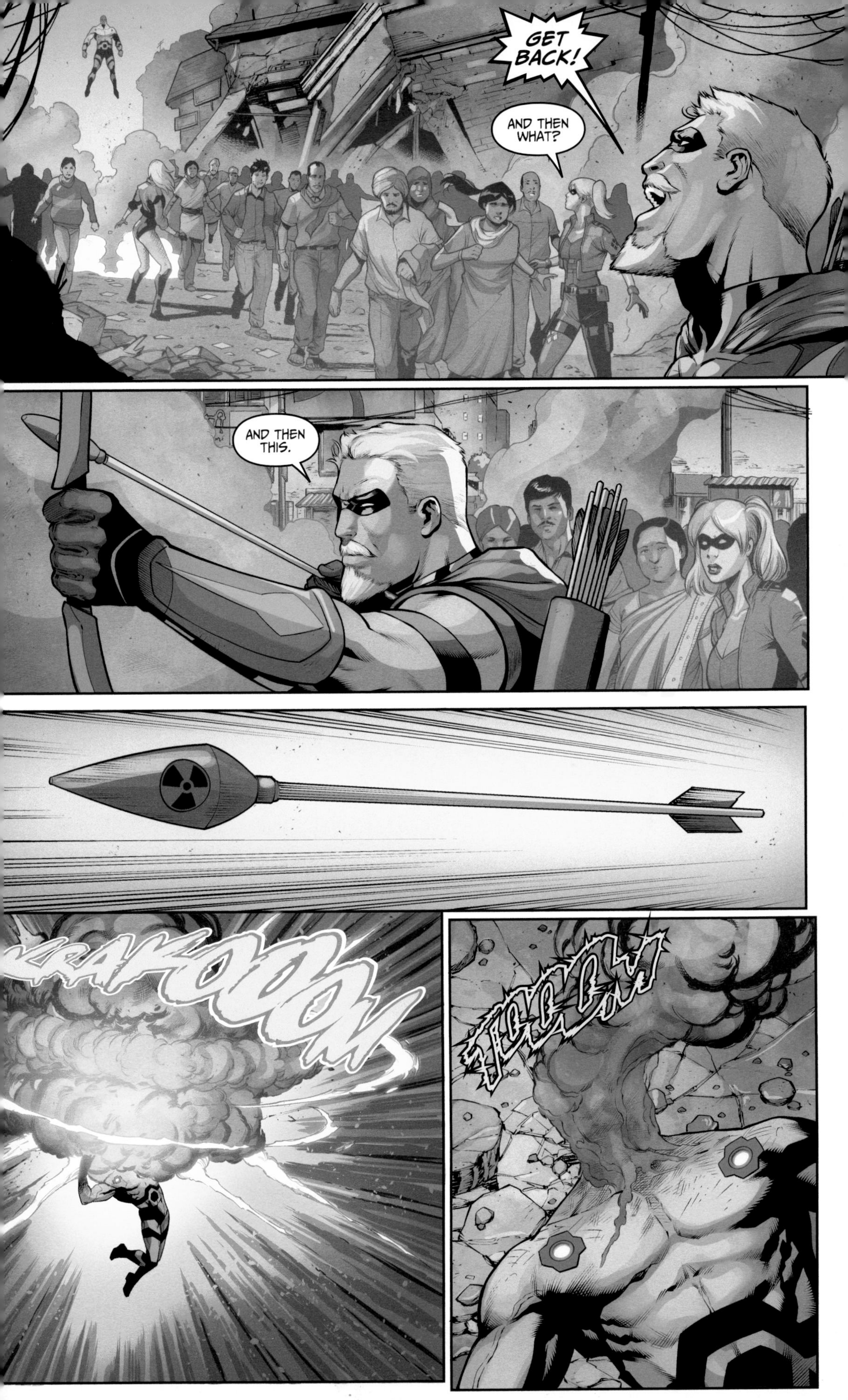

GET BACK!
AND THEN WHAT?
AND THEN THIS.
KRAKOOOOM

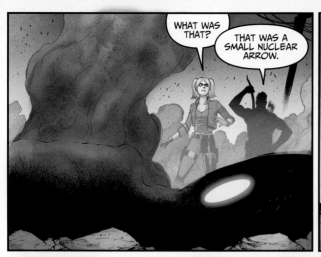

WHAT WAS THAT?

THAT WAS A SMALL NUCLEAR ARROW.

YOU CARRIED THAT ON YOUR *BACK*?

YEAH?

YOU HAD THAT IN OUR *HOUSE*?

WITH OUR *CHILD*?

I PUT IT ON A HIGH SHELF...

GUYS!

FWOOOM

NO!

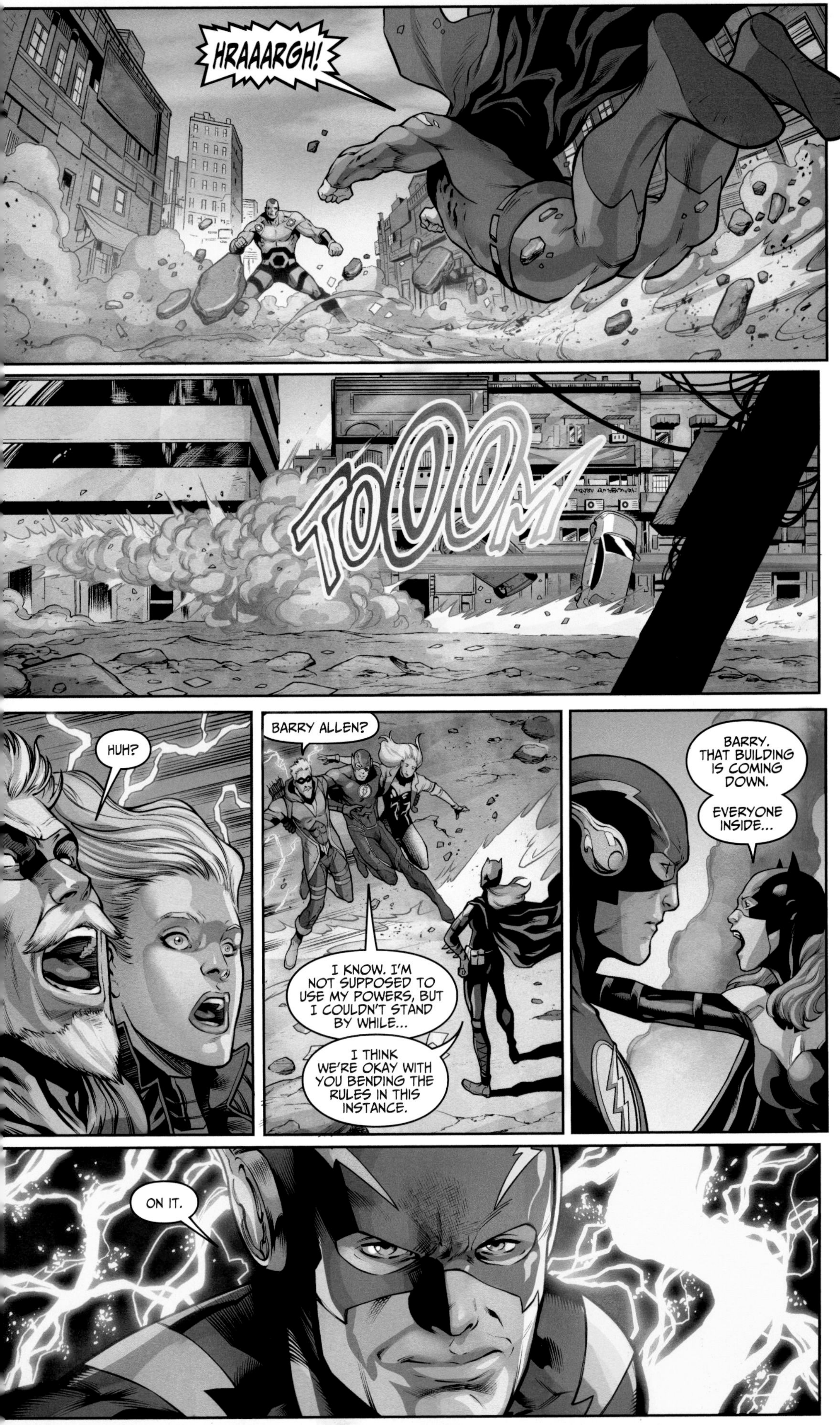
HRAAARGH!
TOOOM
HUH?
BARRY ALLEN?
I KNOW. I'M NOT SUPPOSED TO USE MY POWERS, BUT I COULDN'T STAND BY WHILE...
I THINK WE'RE OKAY WITH YOU BENDING THE RULES IN THIS INSTANCE.
BARRY. THAT BUILDING IS COMING DOWN.
EVERYONE INSIDE...
ON IT.

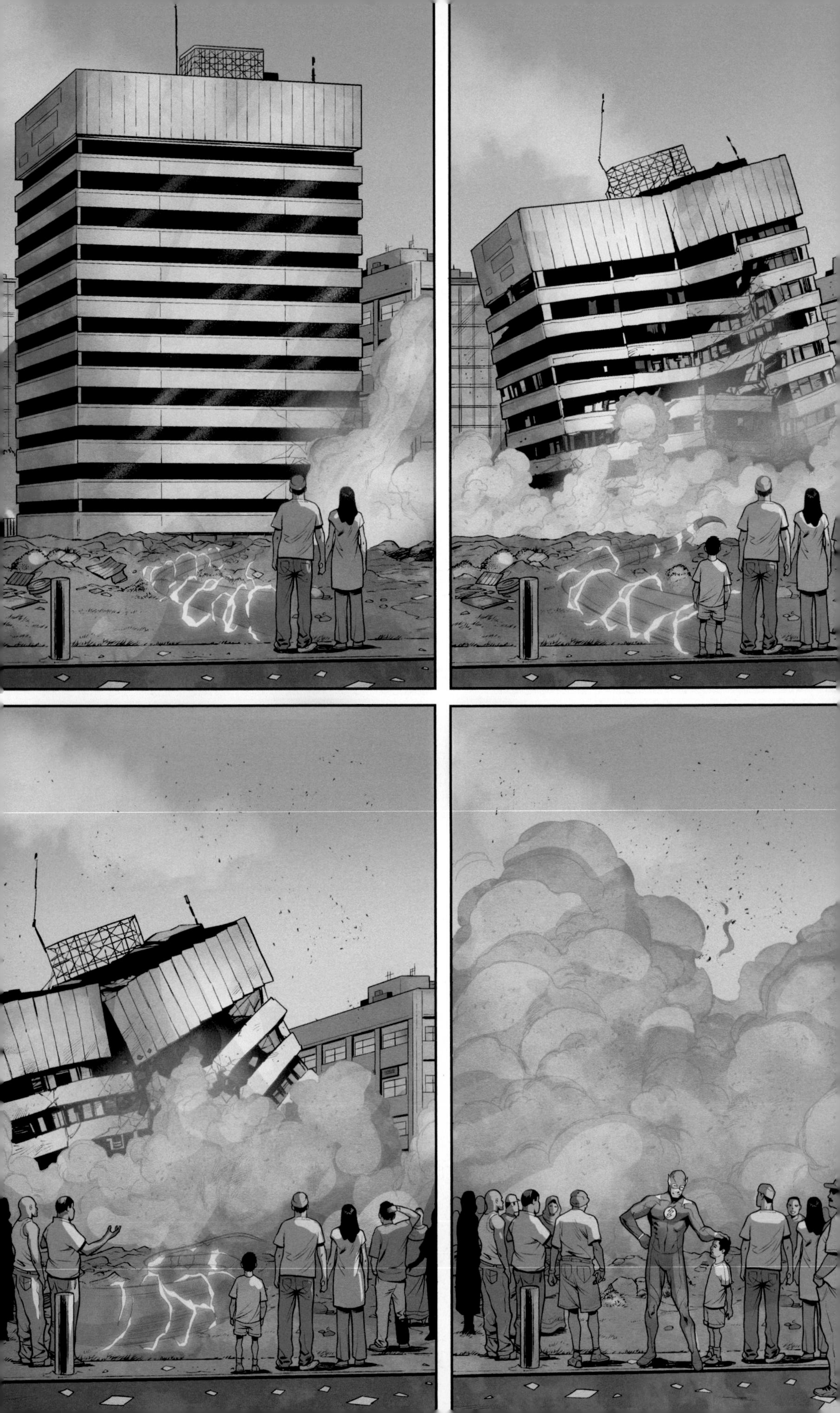

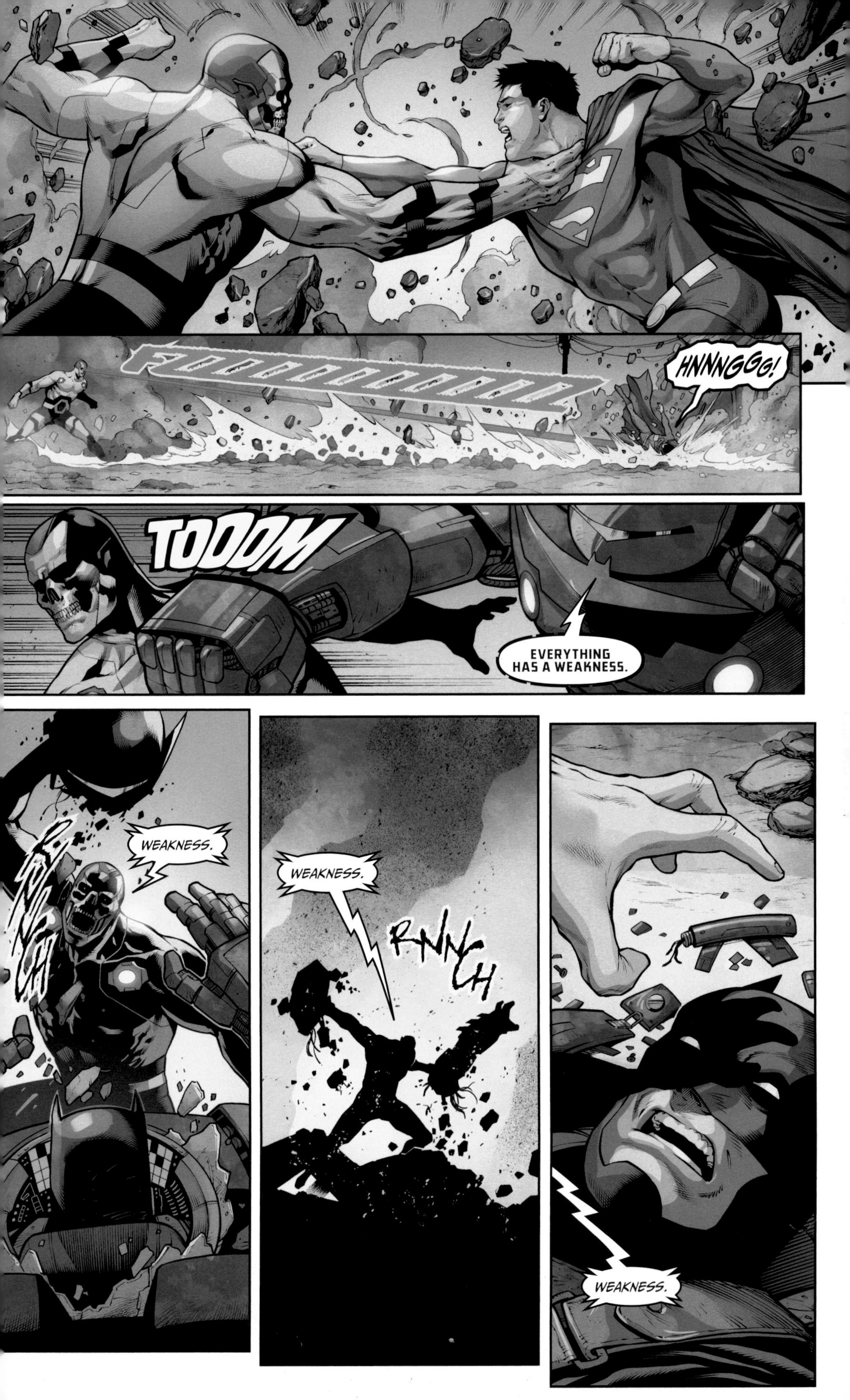
HNNNGGG!
TOOOM
EVERYTHING HAS A WEAKNESS.
WEAKNESS.
WEAKNESS.
RNNCH
WEAKNESS.

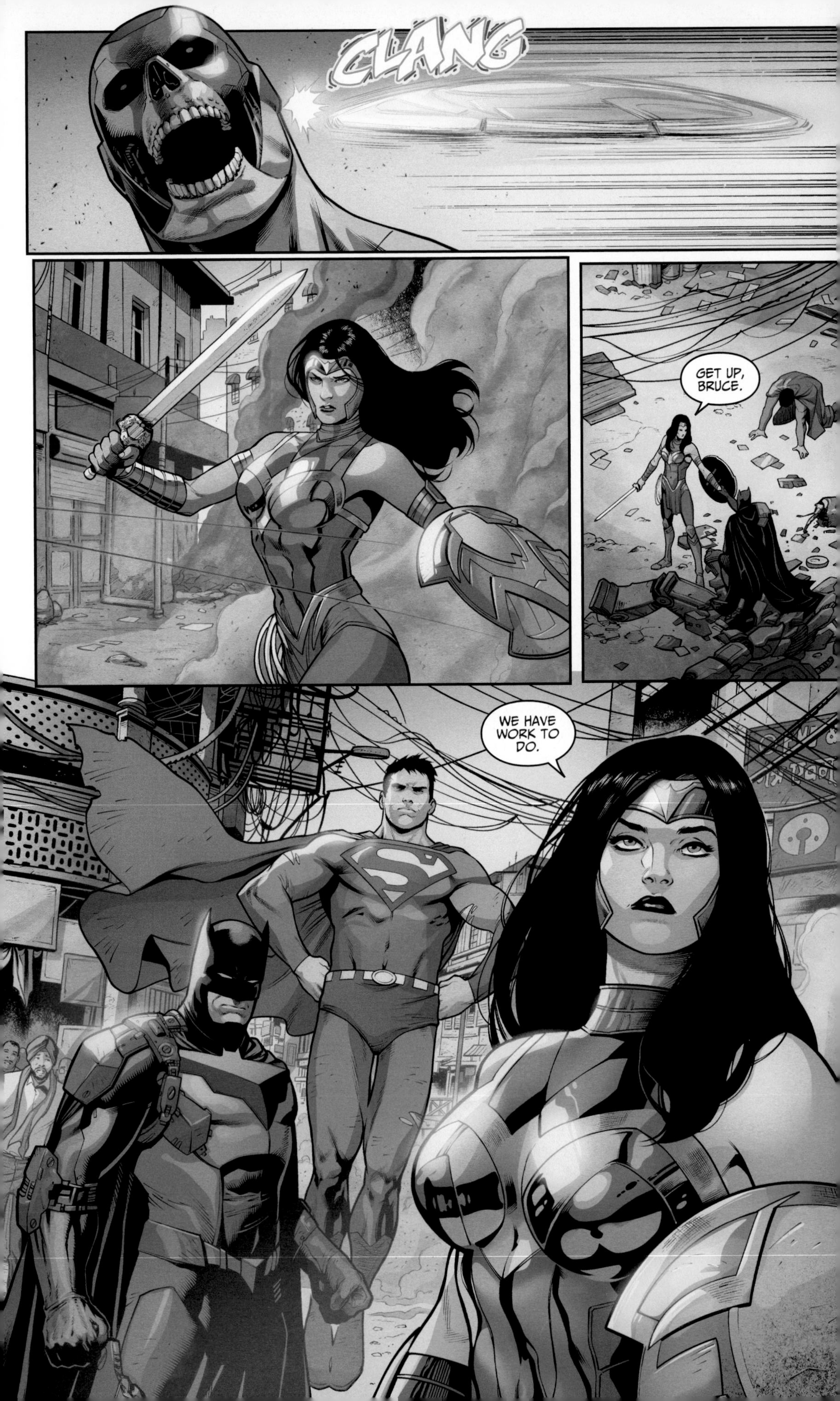
CLANG
GET UP, BRUCE.
WE HAVE WORK TO DO.

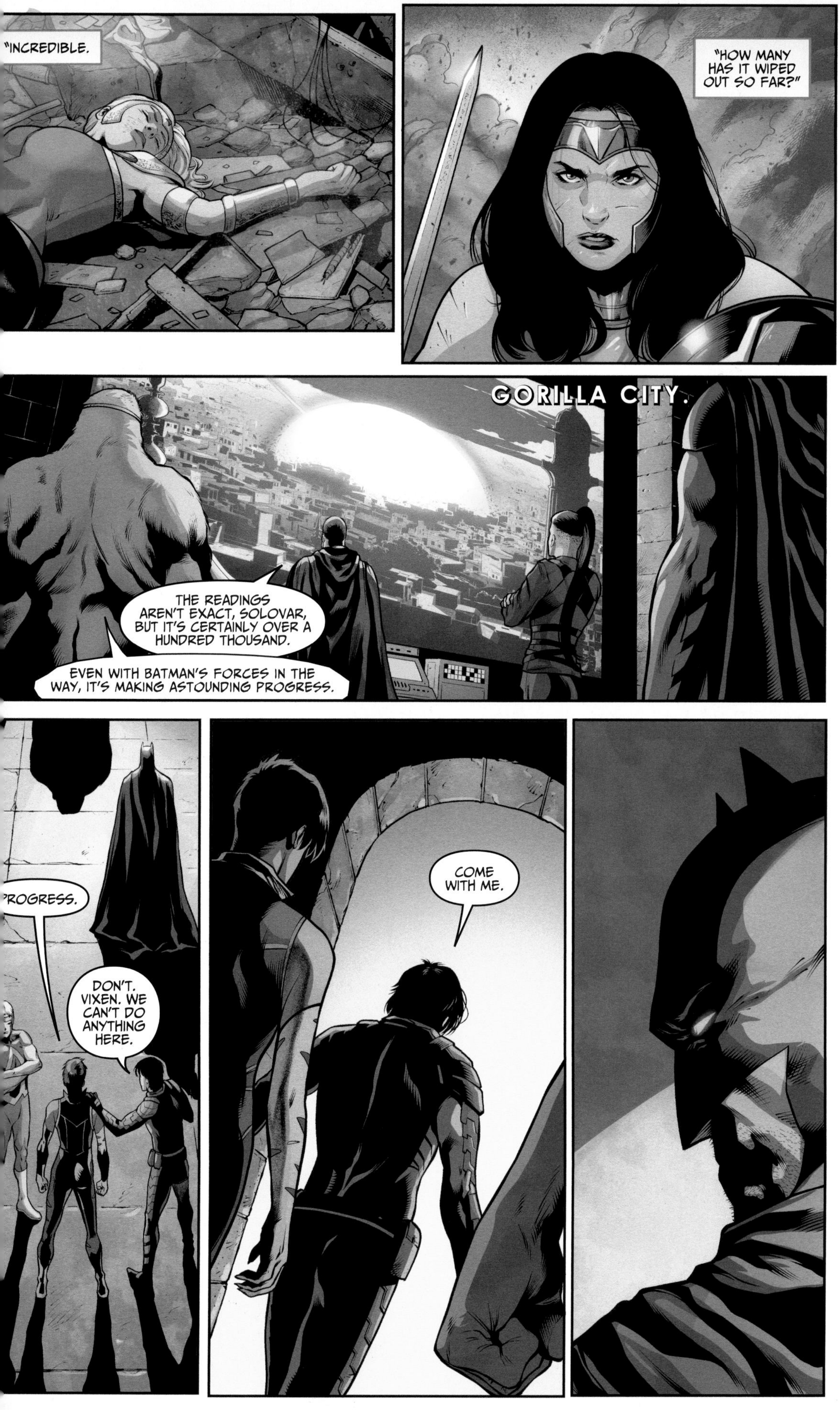
"INCREDIBLE.
"HOW MANY HAS IT WIPED OUT SO FAR?"
GORILLA CITY.
THE READINGS AREN'T EXACT, SOLOVAR, BUT IT'S CERTAINLY OVER A HUNDRED THOUSAND.
EVEN WITH BATMAN'S FORCES IN THE WAY, IT'S MAKING ASTOUNDING PROGRESS.
PROGRESS.
DON'T. VIXEN. WE CAN'T DO ANYTHING HERE.
COME WITH ME.

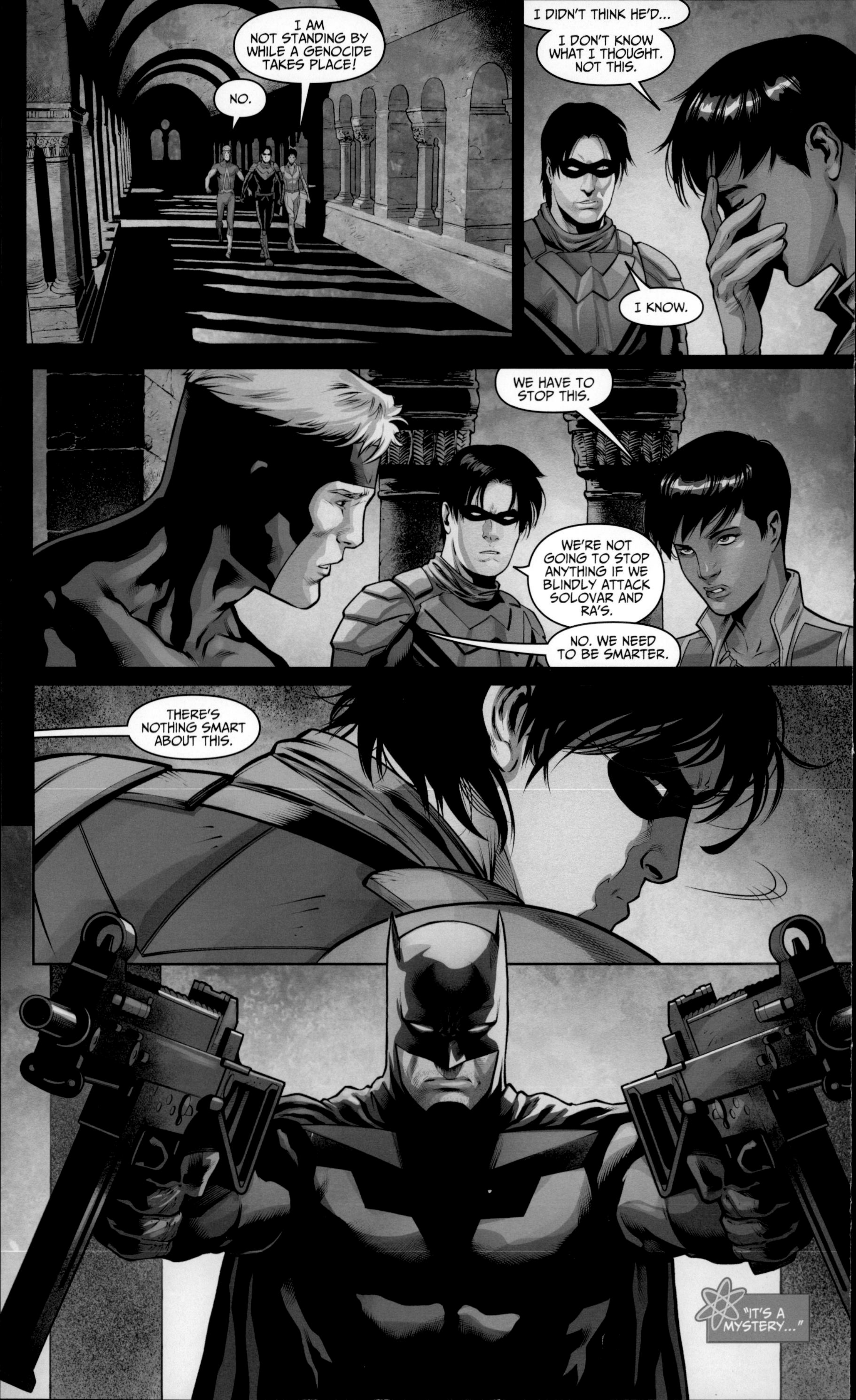
I AM NOT STANDING BY WHILE A GENOCIDE TAKES PLACE!
NO.
I DIDN'T THINK HE'D...
I DON'T KNOW WHAT I THOUGHT. NOT THIS.
I KNOW.
WE HAVE TO STOP THIS.
WE'RE NOT GOING TO STOP ANYTHING IF WE BLINDLY ATTACK SOLOVAR AND RA'S.
NO. WE NEED TO BE SMARTER.
THERE'S NOTHING SMART ABOUT THIS.
"IT'S A MYSTERY..."

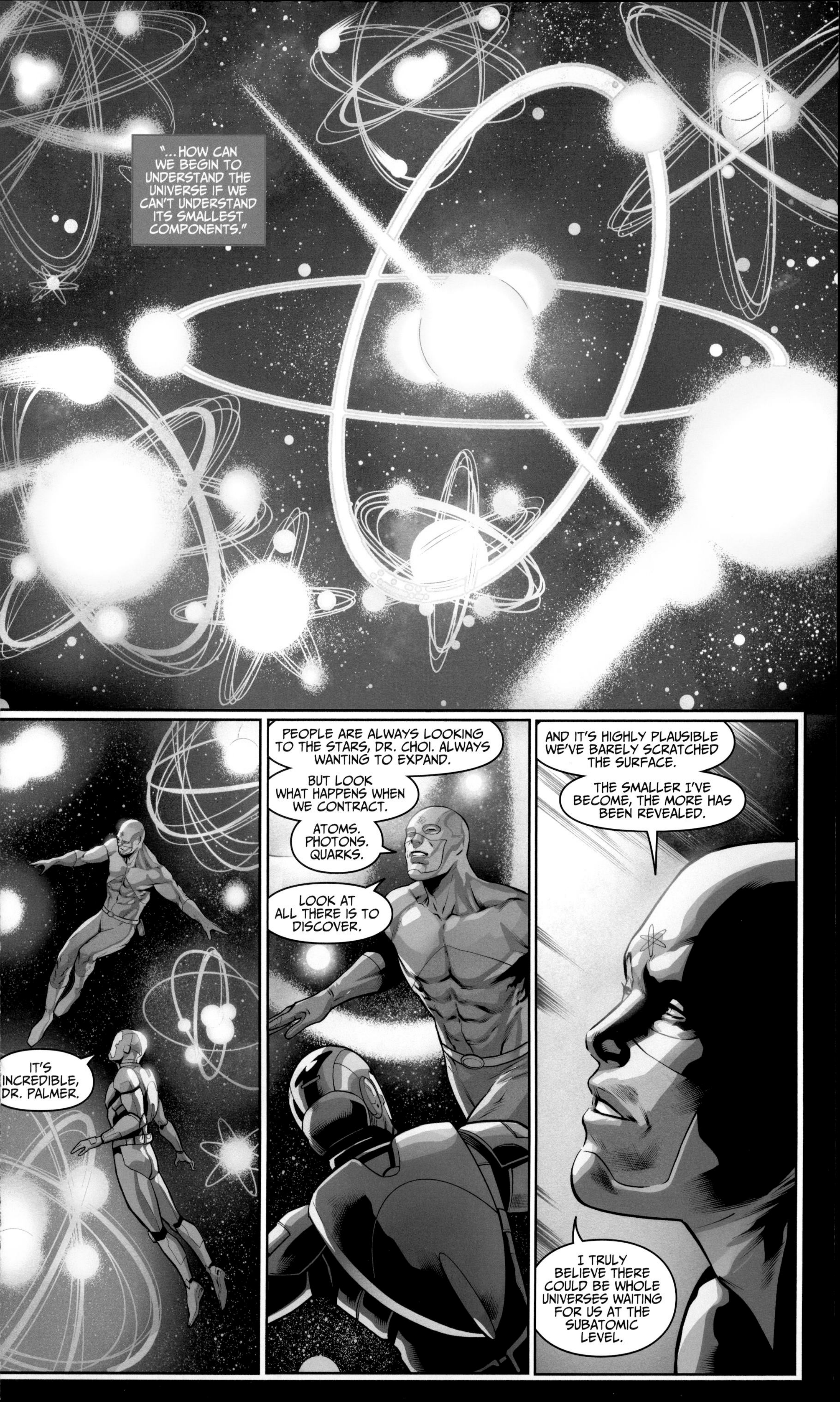
"...HOW CAN WE BEGIN TO UNDERSTAND THE UNIVERSE IF WE CAN'T UNDERSTAND ITS SMALLEST COMPONENTS."
IT'S INCREDIBLE, DR. PALMER.
PEOPLE ARE ALWAYS LOOKING TO THE STARS, DR. CHOI. ALWAYS WANTING TO EXPAND.
BUT LOOK WHAT HAPPENS WHEN WE CONTRACT.
ATOMS. PHOTONS. QUARKS.
LOOK AT ALL THERE IS TO DISCOVER.
AND IT'S HIGHLY PLAUSIBLE WE'VE BARELY SCRATCHED THE SURFACE.
THE SMALLER I'VE BECOME, THE MORE HAS BEEN REVEALED.
I TRULY BELIEVE THERE COULD BE WHOLE UNIVERSES WAITING FOR US AT THE SUBATOMIC LEVEL.

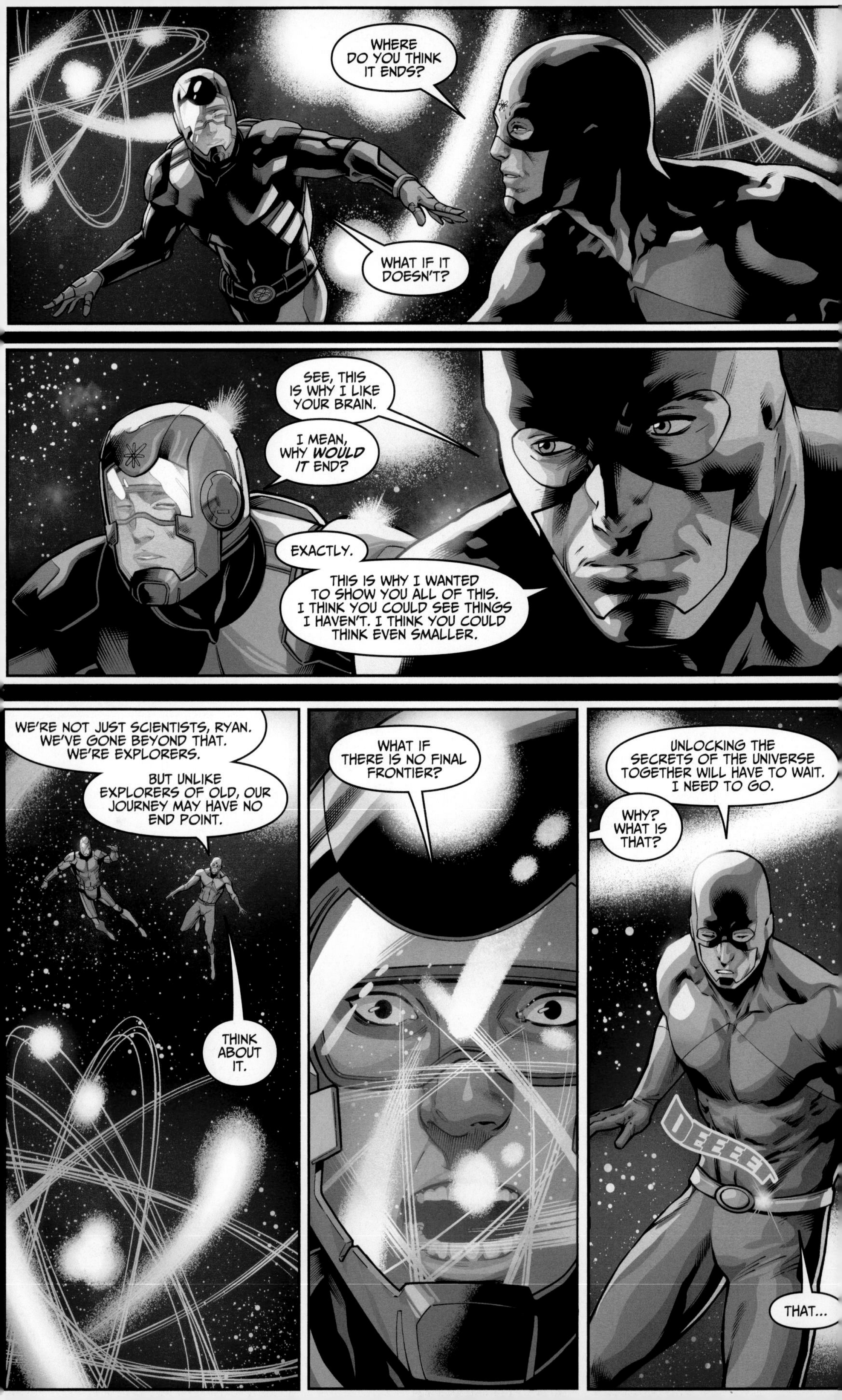

WHERE DO YOU THINK IT ENDS?
WHAT IF IT DOESN'T?
SEE, THIS IS WHY I LIKE YOUR BRAIN.
I MEAN, WHY *WOULD IT* END?
EXACTLY.
THIS IS WHY I WANTED TO SHOW YOU ALL OF THIS. I THINK YOU COULD SEE THINGS I HAVEN'T. I THINK YOU COULD THINK EVEN SMALLER.
WE'RE NOT JUST SCIENTISTS, RYAN. WE'VE GONE BEYOND THAT. WE'RE EXPLORERS.
BUT UNLIKE EXPLORERS OF OLD, OUR JOURNEY MAY HAVE NO END POINT.
THINK ABOUT IT.
WHAT IF THERE IS NO FINAL FRONTIER?
UNLOCKING THE SECRETS OF THE UNIVERSE TOGETHER WILL HAVE TO WAIT. I NEED TO GO.
WHY? WHAT IS THAT?
DEEEEE
THAT...

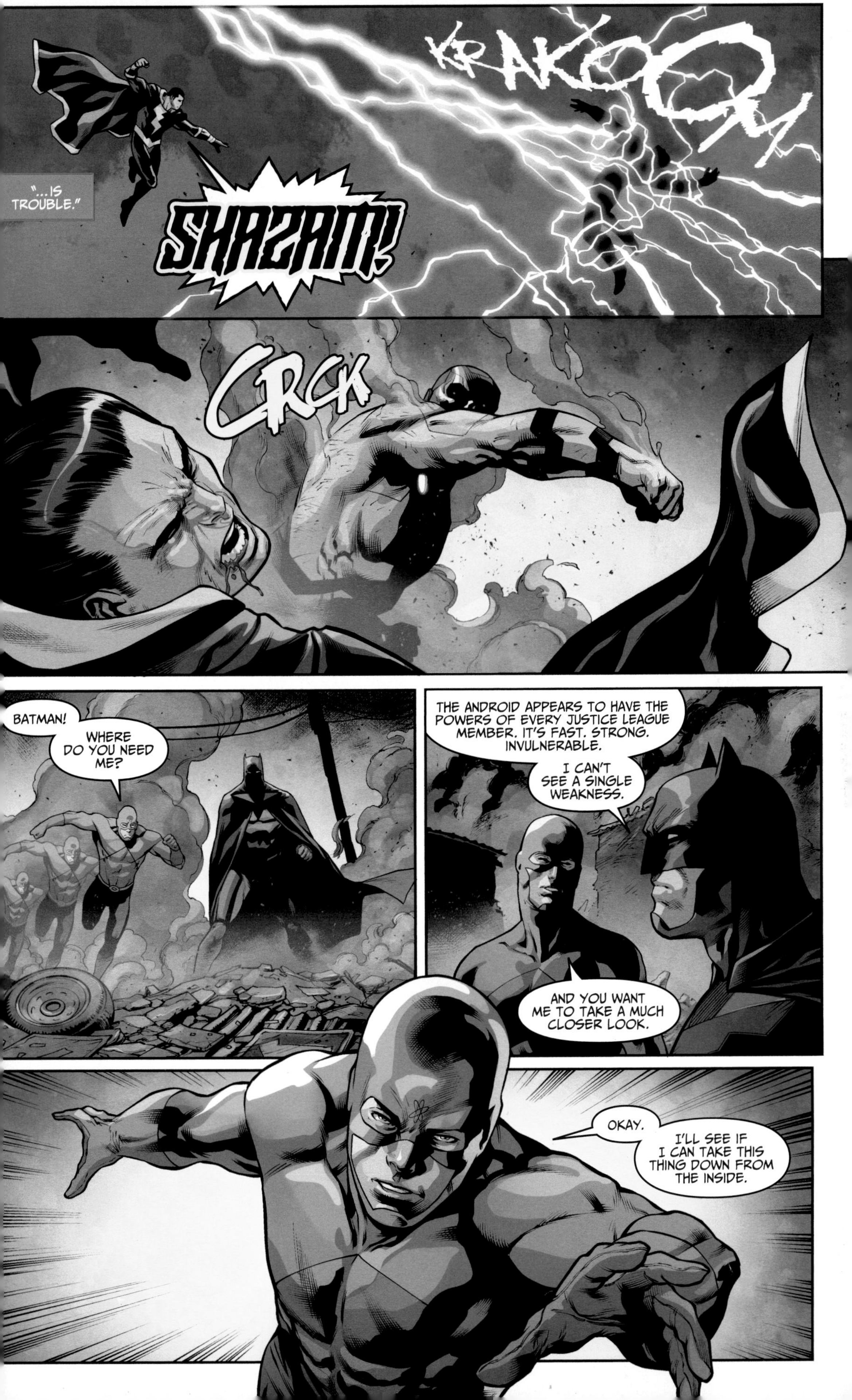
KRAKOOM
"...IS TROUBLE."
SHAZAM!
CRCK
BATMAN!
WHERE DO YOU NEED ME?
THE ANDROID APPEARS TO HAVE THE POWERS OF EVERY JUSTICE LEAGUE MEMBER. IT'S FAST. STRONG. INVULNERABLE.
I CAN'T SEE A SINGLE WEAKNESS.
AND YOU WANT ME TO TAKE A MUCH CLOSER LOOK.
OKAY.
I'LL SEE IF I CAN TAKE THIS THING DOWN FROM THE INSIDE.

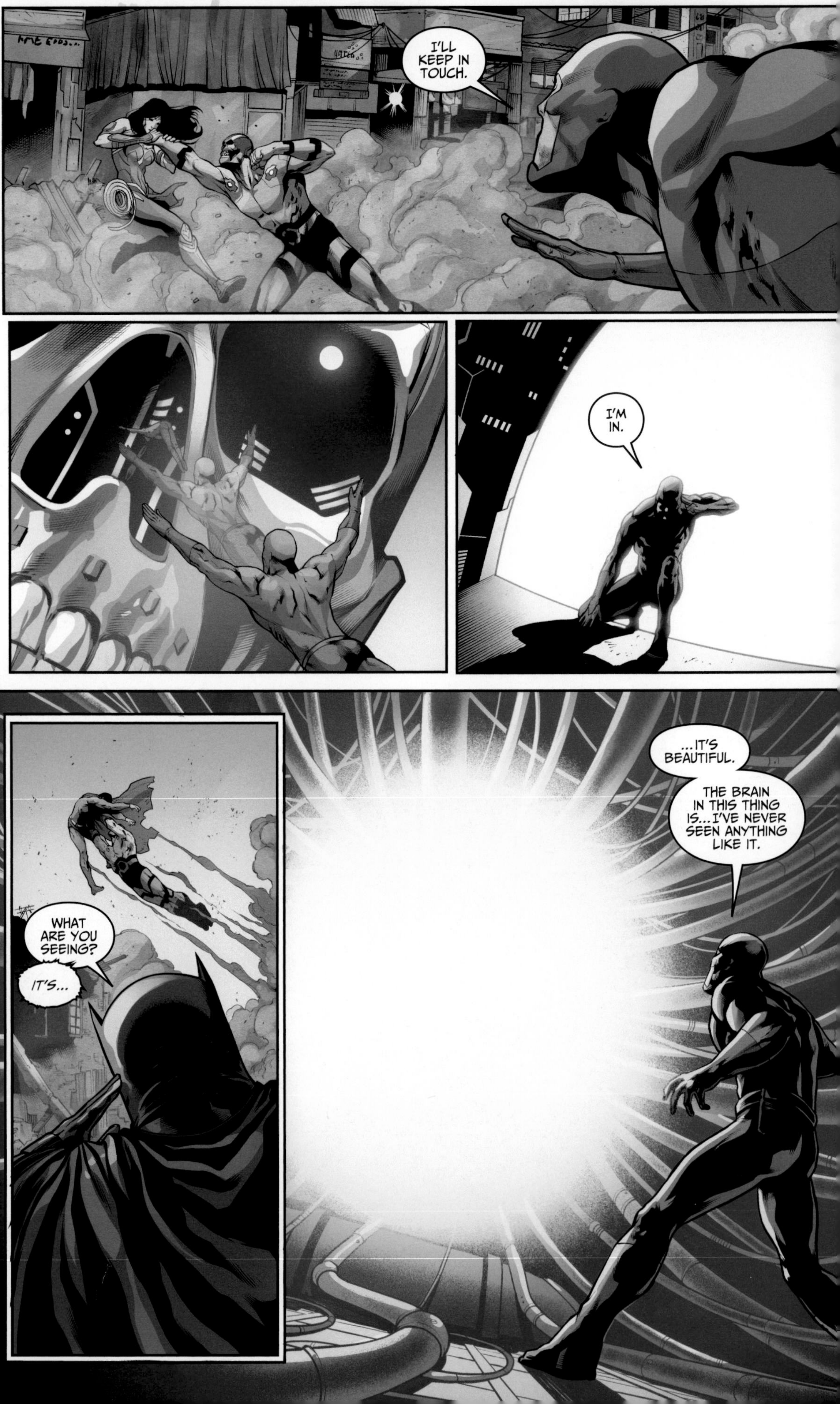

I'LL KEEP IN TOUCH.
I'M IN.
...IT'S BEAUTIFUL.
THE BRAIN IN THIS THING IS...I'VE NEVER SEEN ANYTHING LIKE IT.
WHAT ARE YOU SEEING?
IT'S...

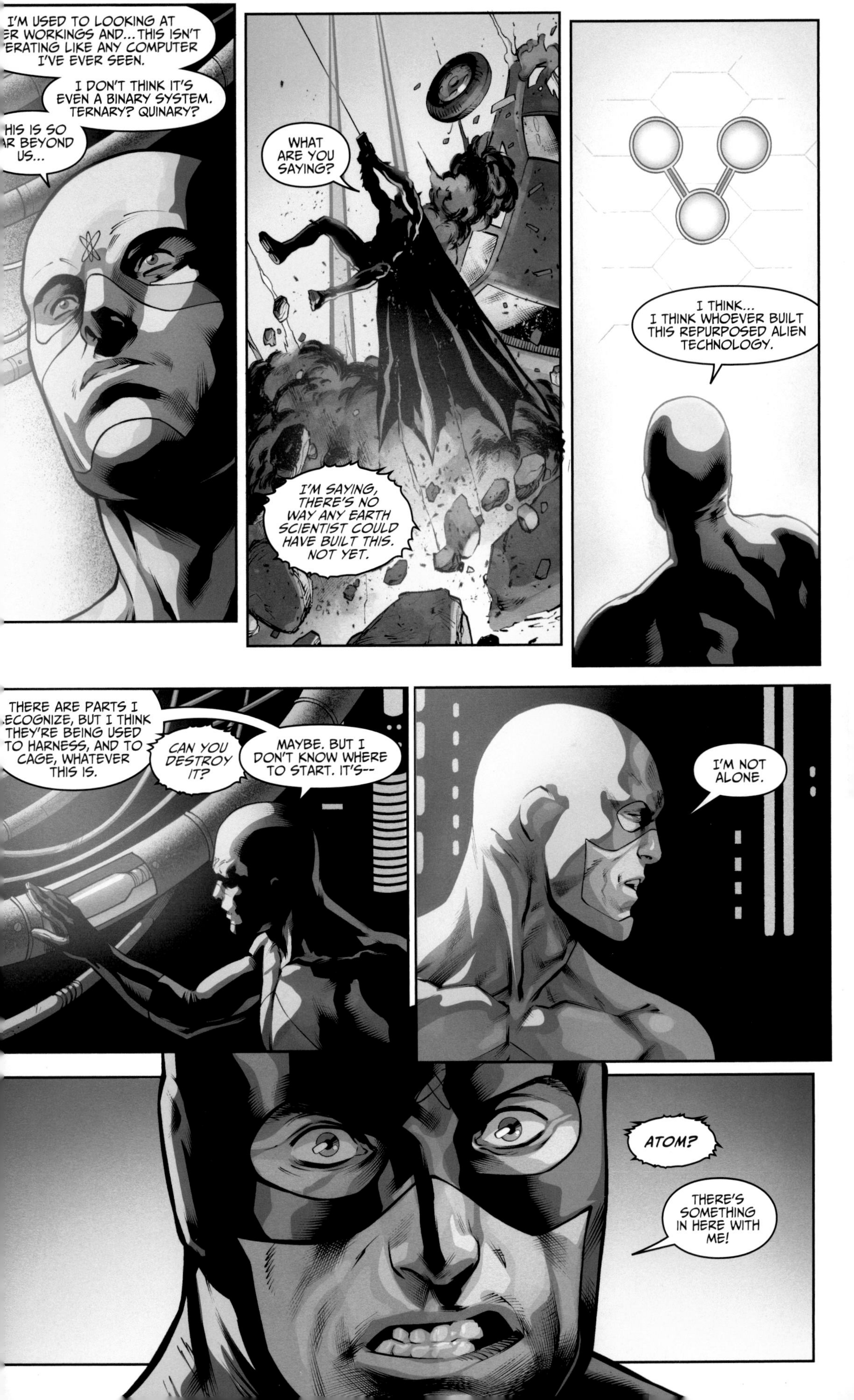
I'M USED TO LOOKING AT
ER WORKINGS AND...THIS ISN'T
ERATING LIKE ANY COMPUTER
I'VE EVER SEEN.
I DON'T THINK IT'S EVEN A BINARY SYSTEM. TERNARY? QUINARY?
HIS IS SO
AR BEYOND
US...
WHAT ARE YOU SAYING?
I'M SAYING, THERE'S NO WAY ANY EARTH SCIENTIST COULD HAVE BUILT THIS. NOT YET.
I THINK... I THINK WHOEVER BUILT THIS REPURPOSED ALIEN TECHNOLOGY.
THERE ARE PARTS I
ECOGNIZE, BUT I THINK
THEY'RE BEING USED
TO HARNESS, AND TO
CAGE, WHATEVER
THIS IS.
CAN YOU DESTROY IT?
MAYBE. BUT I DON'T KNOW WHERE TO START. IT'S--
I'M NOT ALONE.
ATOM?
THERE'S SOMETHING IN HERE WITH ME!

NANITES!

WHAT?

THEY KNEW I WAS COMING!

HAVE TO GET SMALLER. THEY--

ARGHHH!

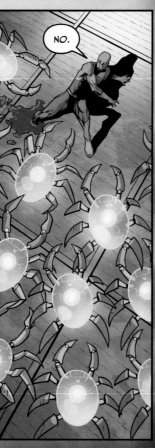

NO.

RAY!

"TAKE HIM..."

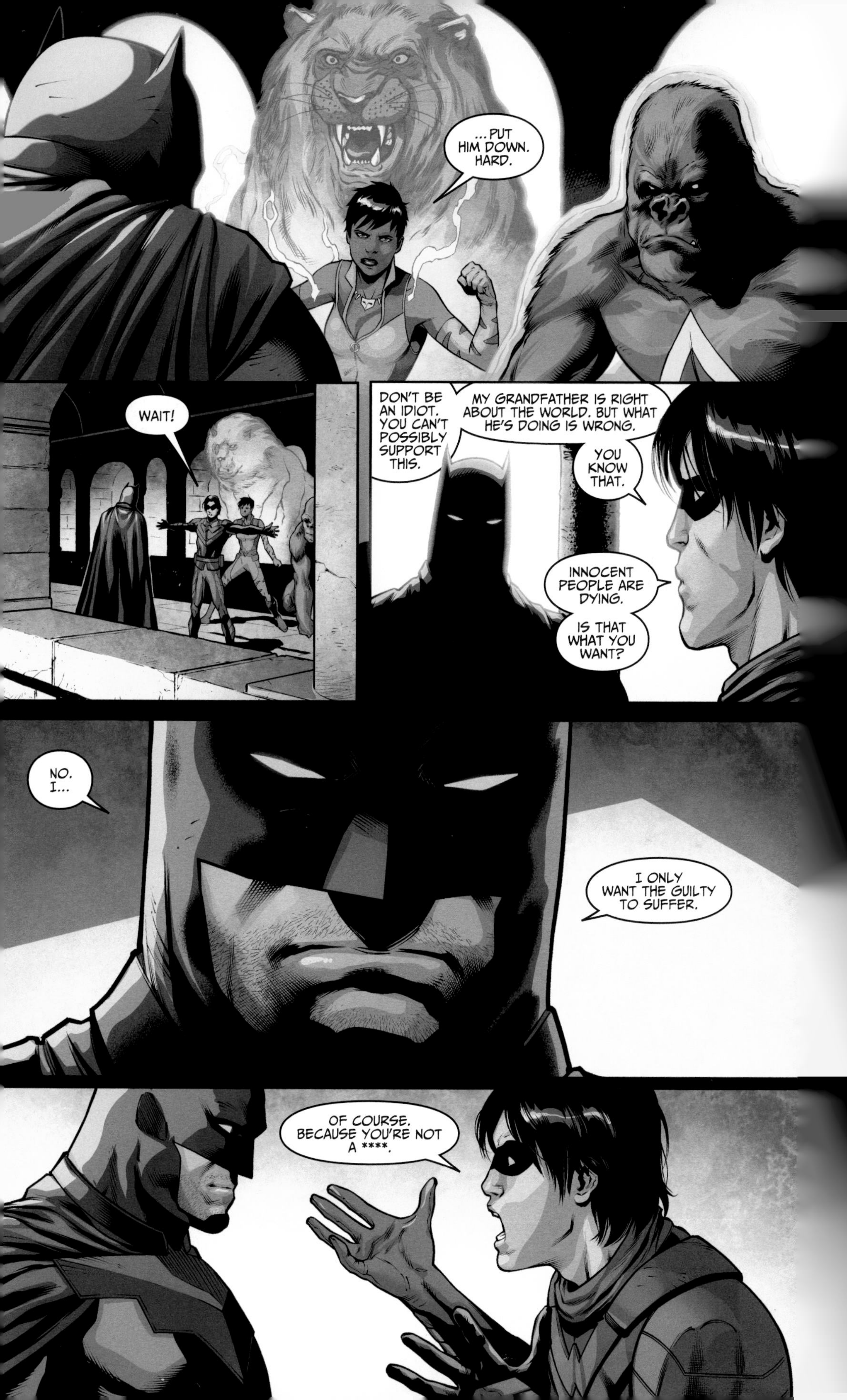
...PUT HIM DOWN. HARD.
WAIT!
DON'T BE AN IDIOT. YOU CAN'T POSSIBLY SUPPORT THIS.
MY GRANDFATHER IS RIGHT ABOUT THE WORLD. BUT WHAT HE'S DOING IS WRONG.
YOU KNOW THAT.
INNOCENT PEOPLE ARE DYING.
IS THAT WHAT YOU WANT?
NO. I...
I ONLY WANT THE GUILTY TO SUFFER.
OF COURSE. BECAUSE YOU'RE NOT A ****.

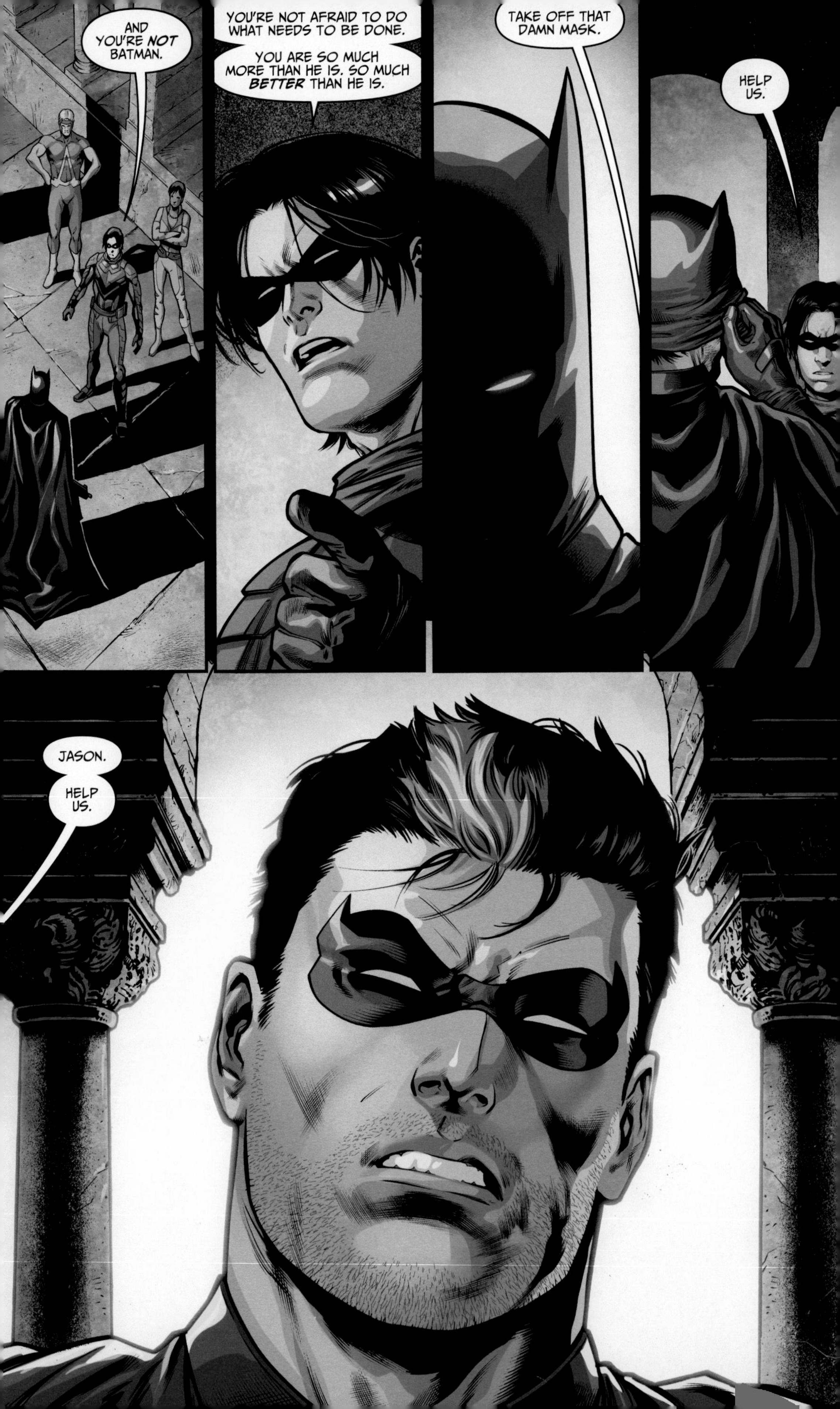

AND YOU'RE NOT BATMAN.
YOU'RE NOT AFRAID TO DO WHAT NEEDS TO BE DONE.
YOU ARE SO MUCH MORE THAN HE IS. SO MUCH BETTER THAN HE IS.
TAKE OFF THAT DAMN MASK.
HELP US.
JASON.
HELP US.

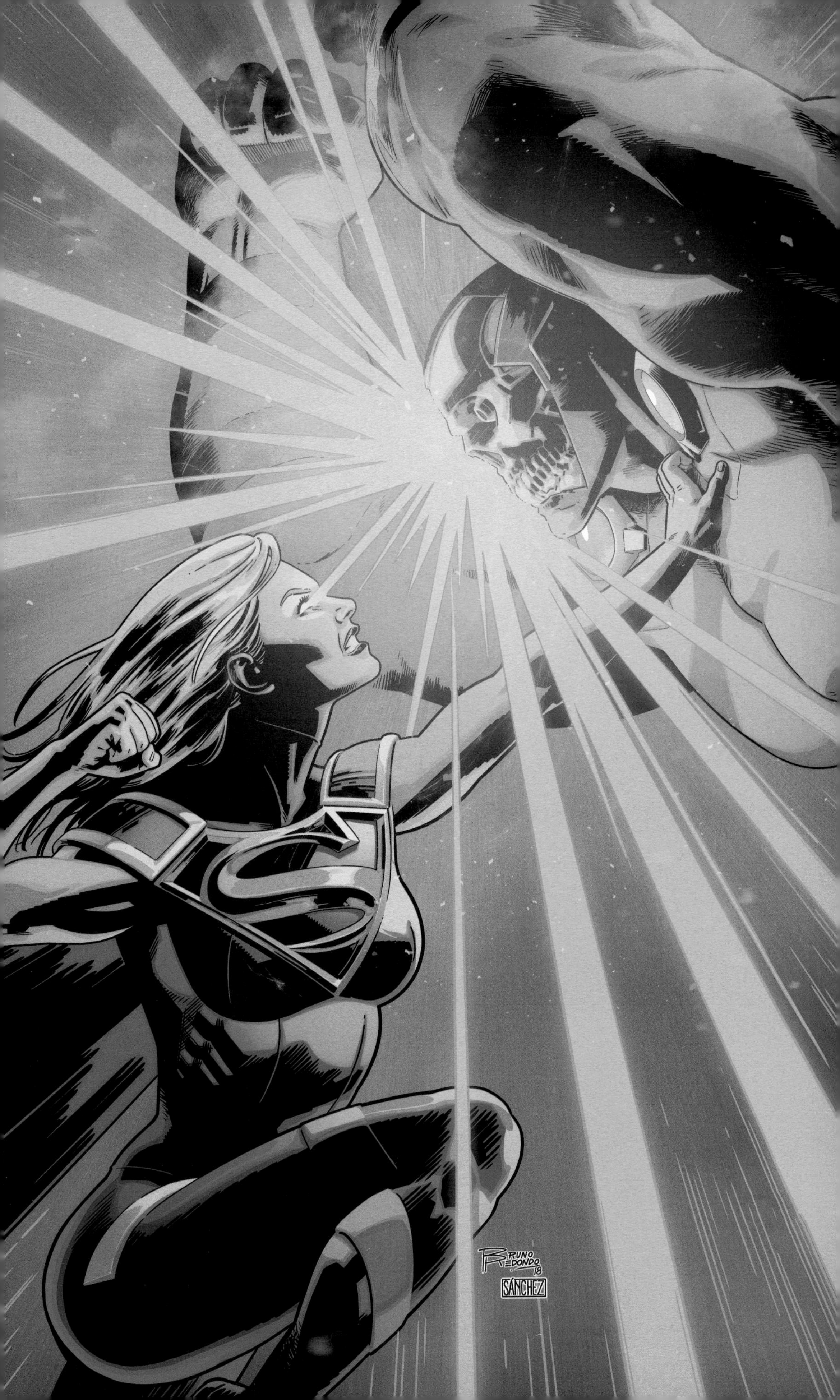

BRUNO REDONDO '18
SÁNCHEZ

"Up and Away"

Tom Taylor Writer **Bruno Redondo** Penciller **Juan Albarran** Inker **Rex Lokus** Colorist **Wes Abbott** Letterer

Cover art by **Bruno Redondo** and **Alejandro Sanchez**

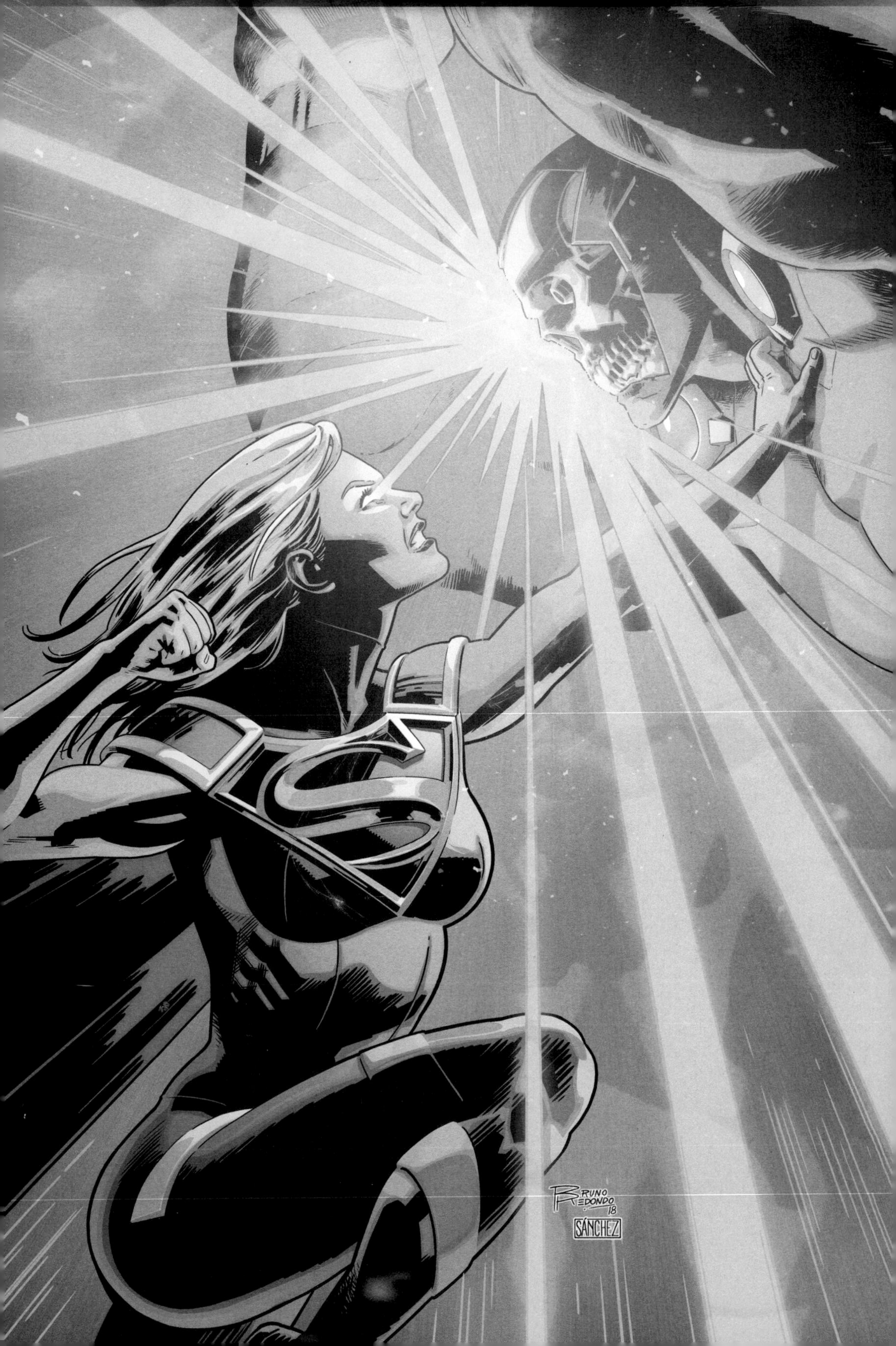
BRUNO REDONDO '18
SÁNCHEZ

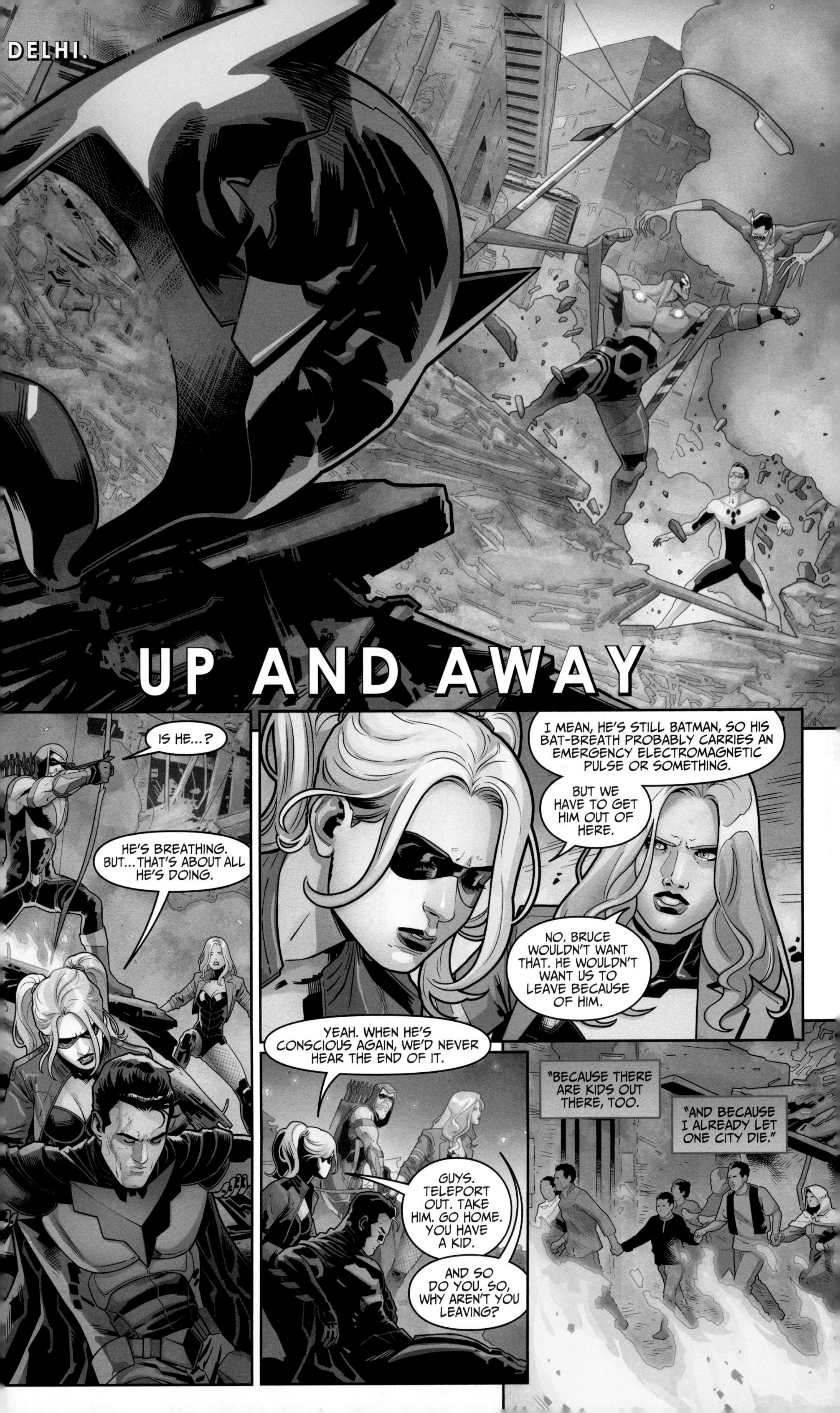
DELHI.
UP AND AWAY
IS HE...?
HE'S BREATHING. BUT...THAT'S ABOUT ALL HE'S DOING.
I MEAN, HE'S STILL BATMAN, SO HIS BAT-BREATH PROBABLY CARRIES AN EMERGENCY ELECTROMAGNETIC PULSE OR SOMETHING.
BUT WE HAVE TO GET HIM OUT OF HERE.
NO. BRUCE WOULDN'T WANT THAT. HE WOULDN'T WANT US TO LEAVE BECAUSE OF HIM.
YEAH. WHEN HE'S CONSCIOUS AGAIN, WE'D NEVER HEAR THE END OF IT.
GUYS. TELEPORT OUT. TAKE HIM. GO HOME. YOU HAVE A KID.
AND SO DO YOU. SO, WHY AREN'T YOU LEAVING?
"BECAUSE THERE ARE KIDS OUT THERE, TOO.
"AND BECAUSE I ALREADY LET ONE CITY DIE."

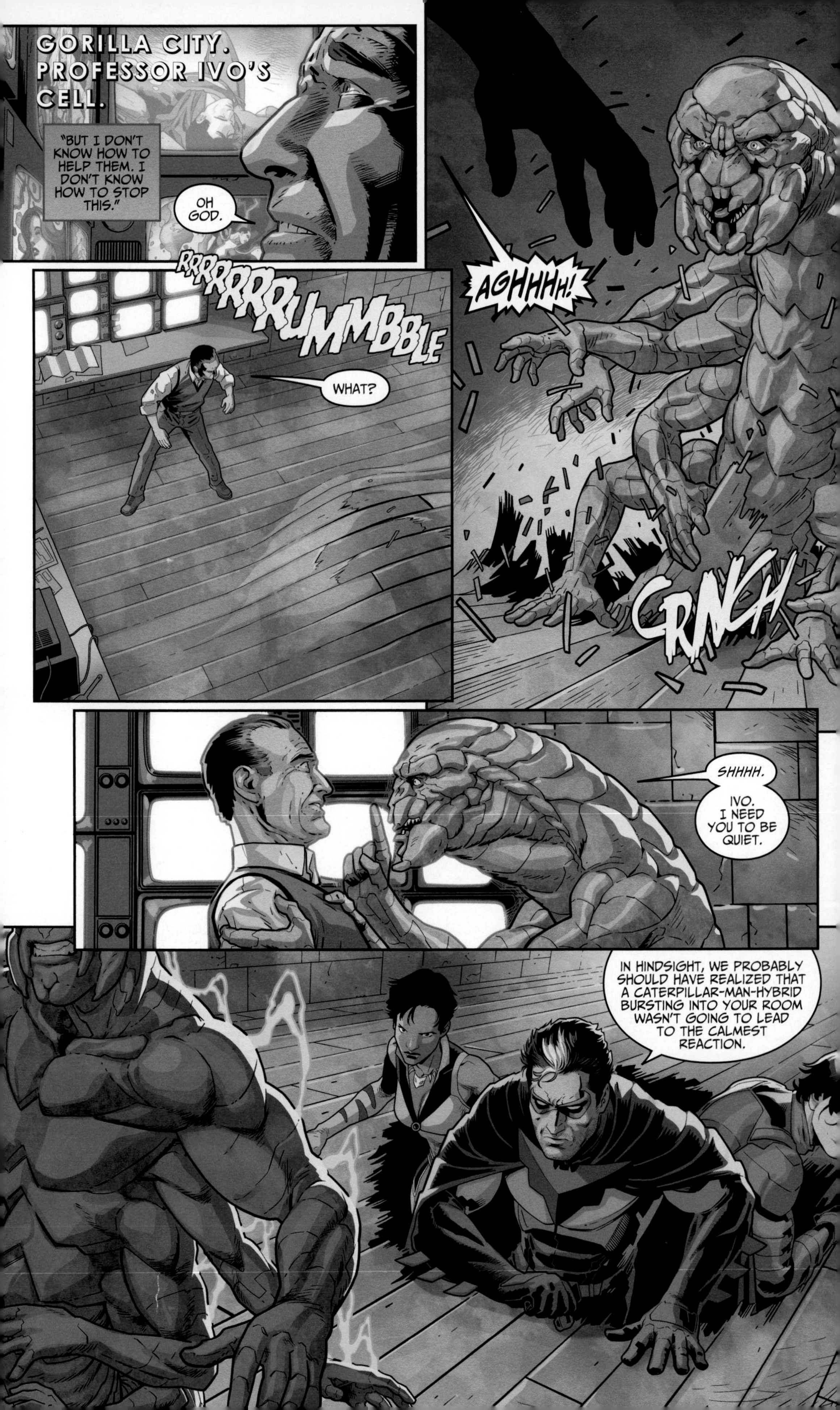
GORILLA CITY. PROFESSOR IVO'S CELL.
"BUT I DON'T KNOW HOW TO HELP THEM. I DON'T KNOW HOW TO STOP THIS."
OH GOD.
RRRRRRRUMMMBBLE
WHAT?
AGHHHH!
CRNCH
SHHHH.
IVO. I NEED YOU TO BE QUIET.
IN HINDSIGHT, WE PROBABLY SHOULD HAVE REALIZED THAT A CATERPILLAR-MAN-HYBRID BURSTING INTO YOUR ROOM WASN'T GOING TO LEAD TO THE CALMEST REACTION.

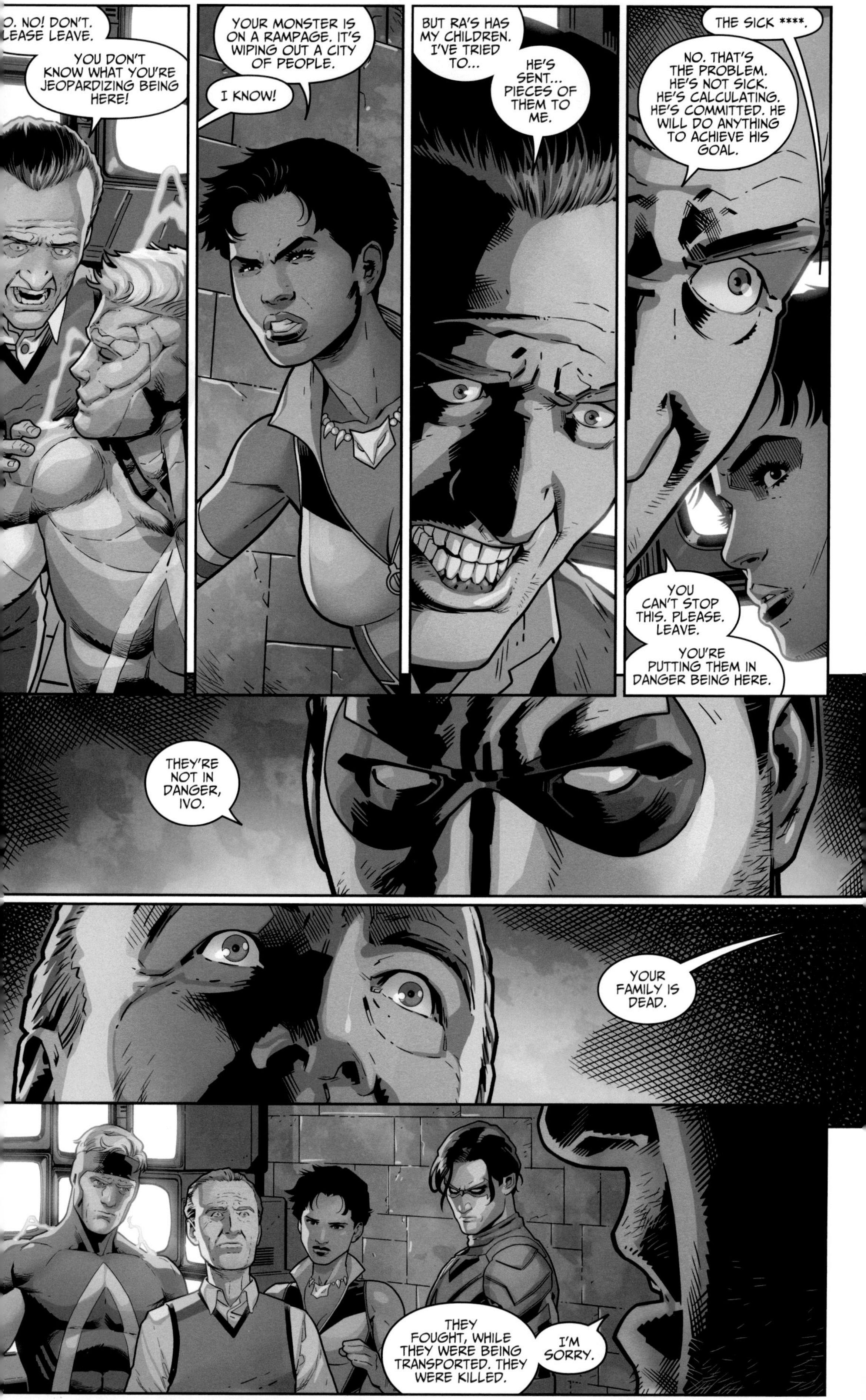
O. NO! DON'T. LEASE LEAVE.
YOU DON'T KNOW WHAT YOU'RE JEOPARDIZING BEING HERE!
YOUR MONSTER IS ON A RAMPAGE. IT'S WIPING OUT A CITY OF PEOPLE.
I KNOW!
BUT RA'S HAS MY CHILDREN. I'VE TRIED TO...
HE'S SENT... PIECES OF THEM TO ME.
THE SICK ****.
NO. THAT'S THE PROBLEM. HE'S NOT SICK. HE'S CALCULATING. HE'S COMMITTED. HE WILL DO ANYTHING TO ACHIEVE HIS GOAL.
YOU CAN'T STOP THIS. PLEASE. LEAVE.
YOU'RE PUTTING THEM IN DANGER BEING HERE.
THEY'RE NOT IN DANGER, IVO.
YOUR FAMILY IS DEAD.
THEY FOUGHT, WHILE THEY WERE BEING TRANSPORTED. THEY WERE KILLED.
I'M SORRY.

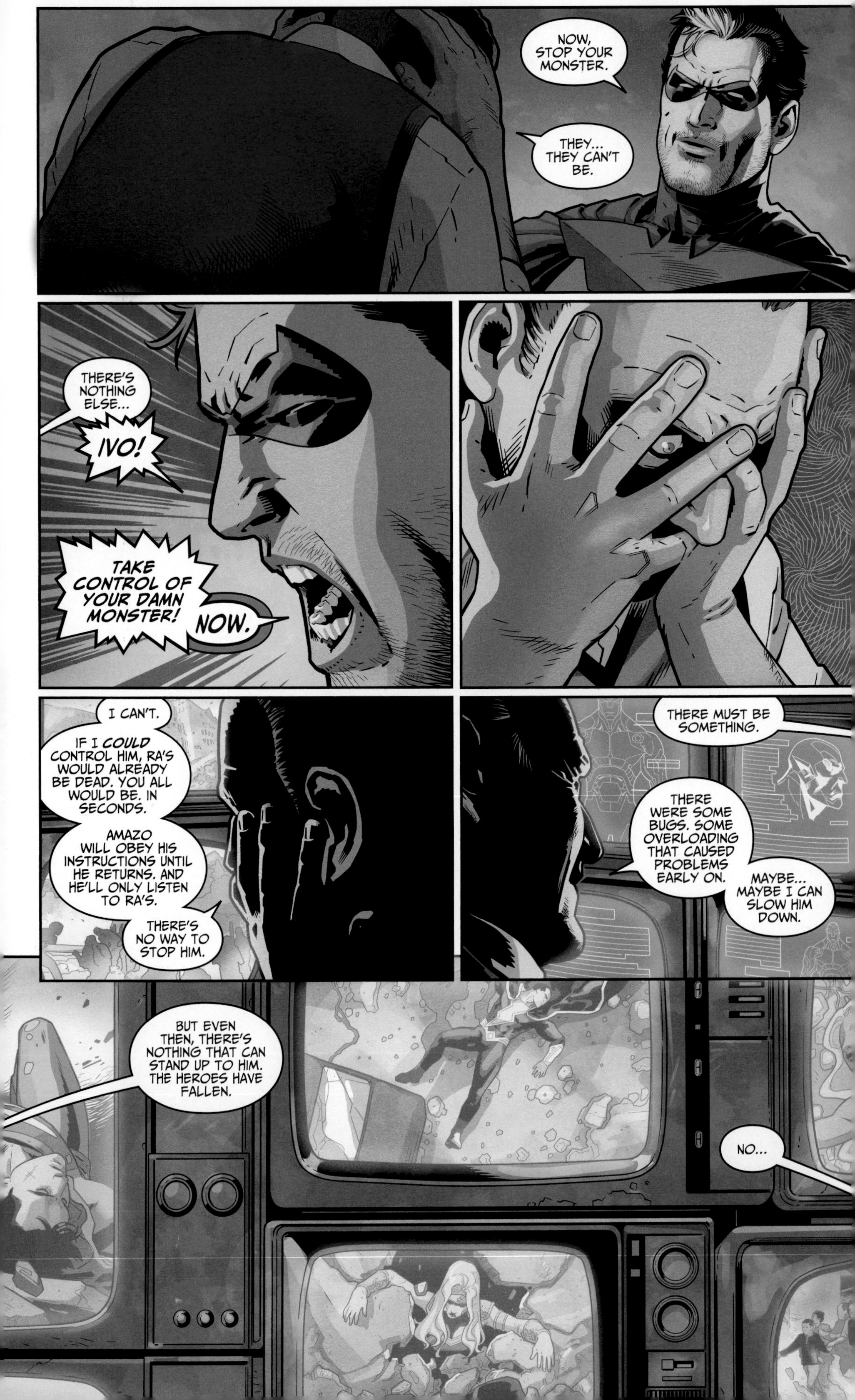

NOW, STOP YOUR MONSTER.
THEY... THEY CAN'T BE.
THERE'S NOTHING ELSE...
IVO!
TAKE CONTROL OF YOUR DAMN MONSTER!
NOW.
I CAN'T.
IF I COULD CONTROL HIM, RA'S WOULD ALREADY BE DEAD. YOU ALL WOULD BE. IN SECONDS.
AMAZO WILL OBEY HIS INSTRUCTIONS UNTIL HE RETURNS. AND HE'LL ONLY LISTEN TO RA'S.
THERE'S NO WAY TO STOP HIM.
THERE MUST BE SOMETHING.
THERE WERE SOME BUGS. SOME OVERLOADING THAT CAUSED PROBLEMS EARLY ON.
MAYBE... MAYBE I CAN SLOW HIM DOWN.
BUT EVEN THEN, THERE'S NOTHING THAT CAN STAND UP TO HIM. THE HEROES HAVE FALLEN.
NO...

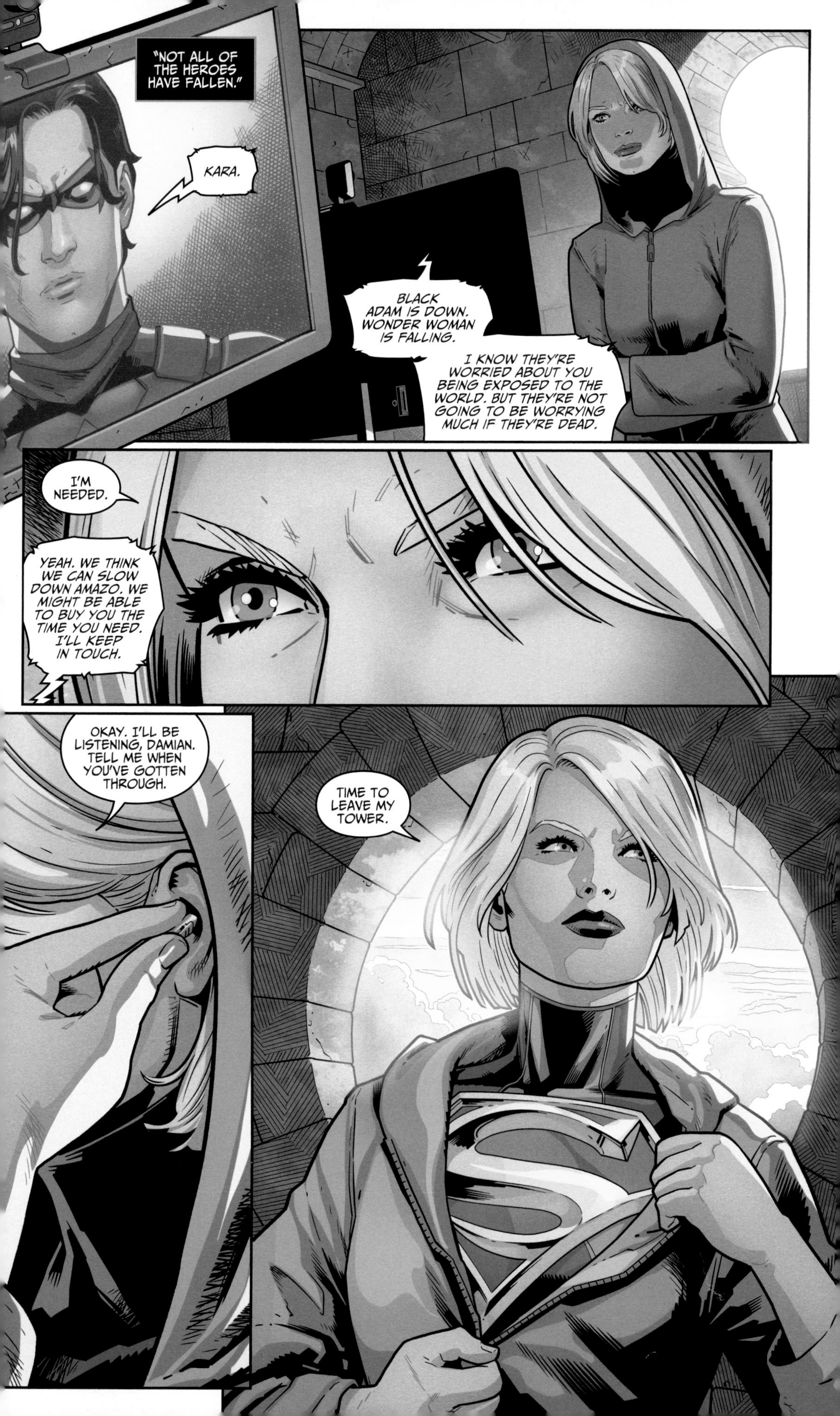
"NOT ALL OF THE HEROES HAVE FALLEN."
KARA.
BLACK ADAM IS DOWN. WONDER WOMAN IS FALLING.
I KNOW THEY'RE WORRIED ABOUT YOU BEING EXPOSED TO THE WORLD. BUT THEY'RE NOT GOING TO BE WORRYING MUCH IF THEY'RE DEAD.
I'M NEEDED.
YEAH. WE THINK WE CAN SLOW DOWN AMAZO. WE MIGHT BE ABLE TO BUY YOU THE TIME YOU NEED. I'LL KEEP IN TOUCH.
OKAY. I'LL BE LISTENING, DAMIAN. TELL ME WHEN YOU'VE GOTTEN THROUGH.
TIME TO LEAVE MY TOWER.

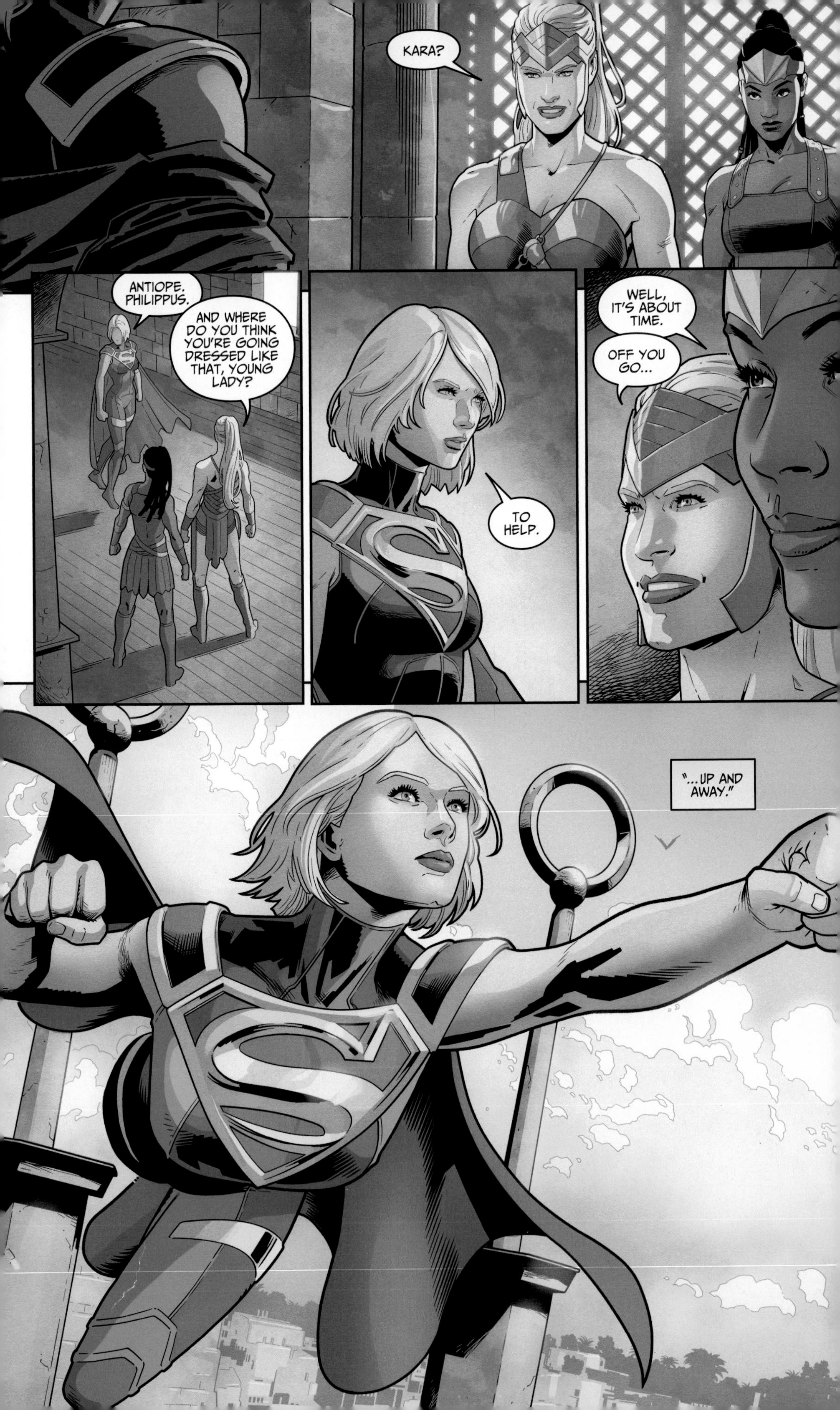
KARA?
ANTIOPE. PHILIPPUS.
AND WHERE DO YOU THINK YOU'RE GOING DRESSED LIKE THAT, YOUNG LADY?
TO HELP.
WELL, IT'S ABOUT TIME.
OFF YOU GO...
"...UP AND AWAY."

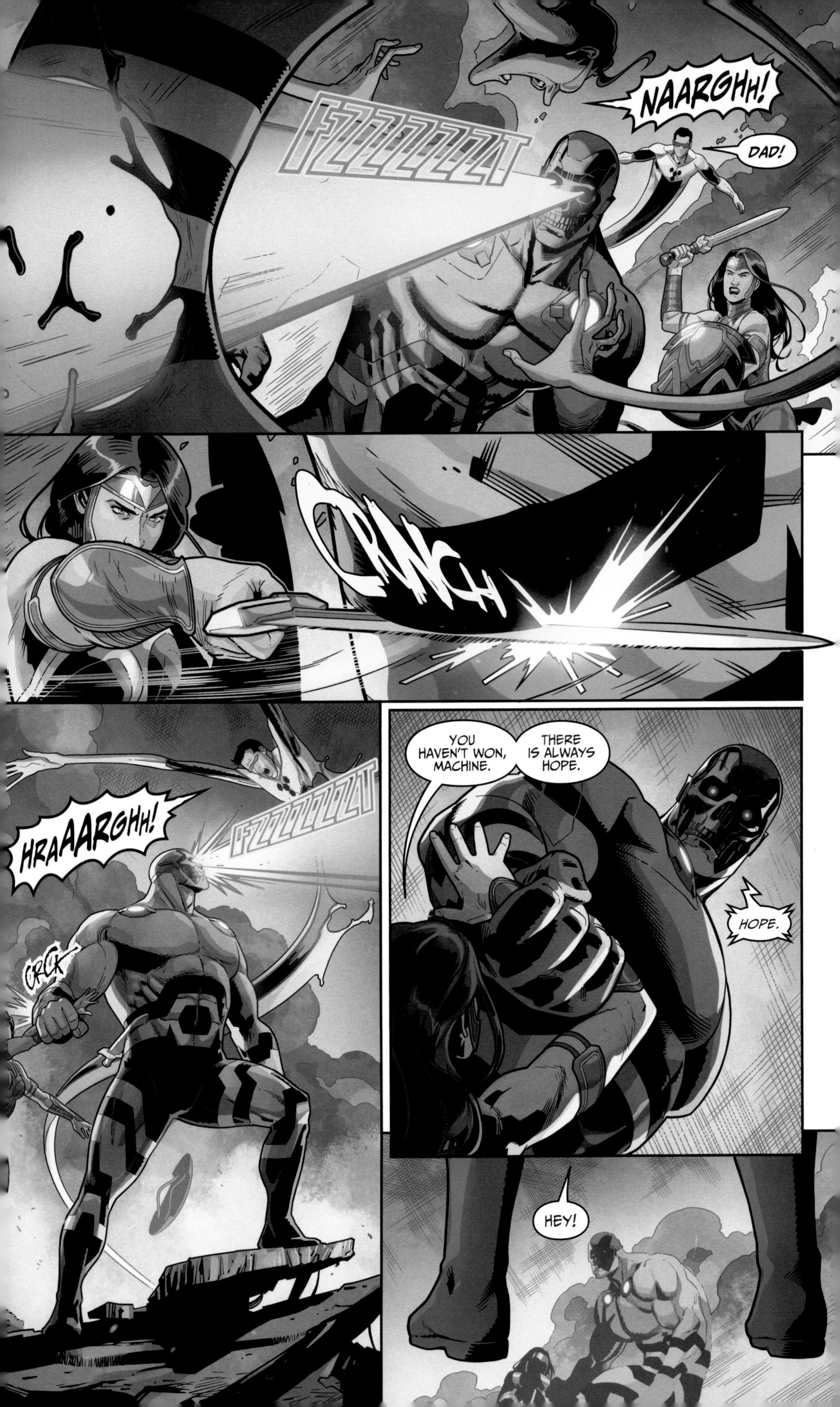
FZZZZZZZT
NAARGHH!
DAD!
CRNCH
HRAAARGHH!
FZZZZZZT
CRCK
YOU HAVEN'T WON, MACHINE.
THERE IS ALWAYS HOPE.
HOPE.
HEY!

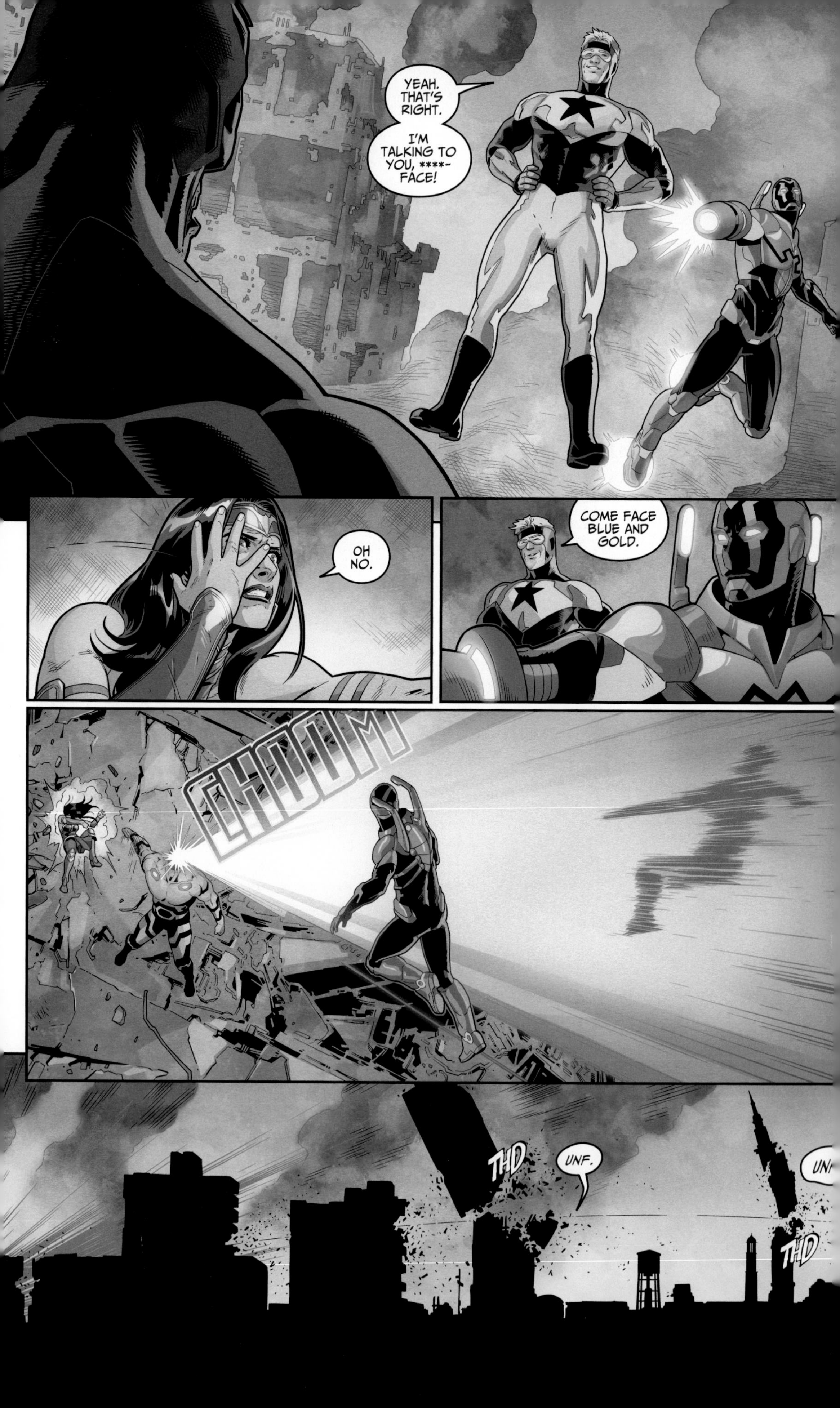

YEAH. THAT'S RIGHT.
I'M TALKING TO YOU, ****-FACE!
OH NO.
COME FACE BLUE AND GOLD.
CHOOM
THD
UNF.
THD

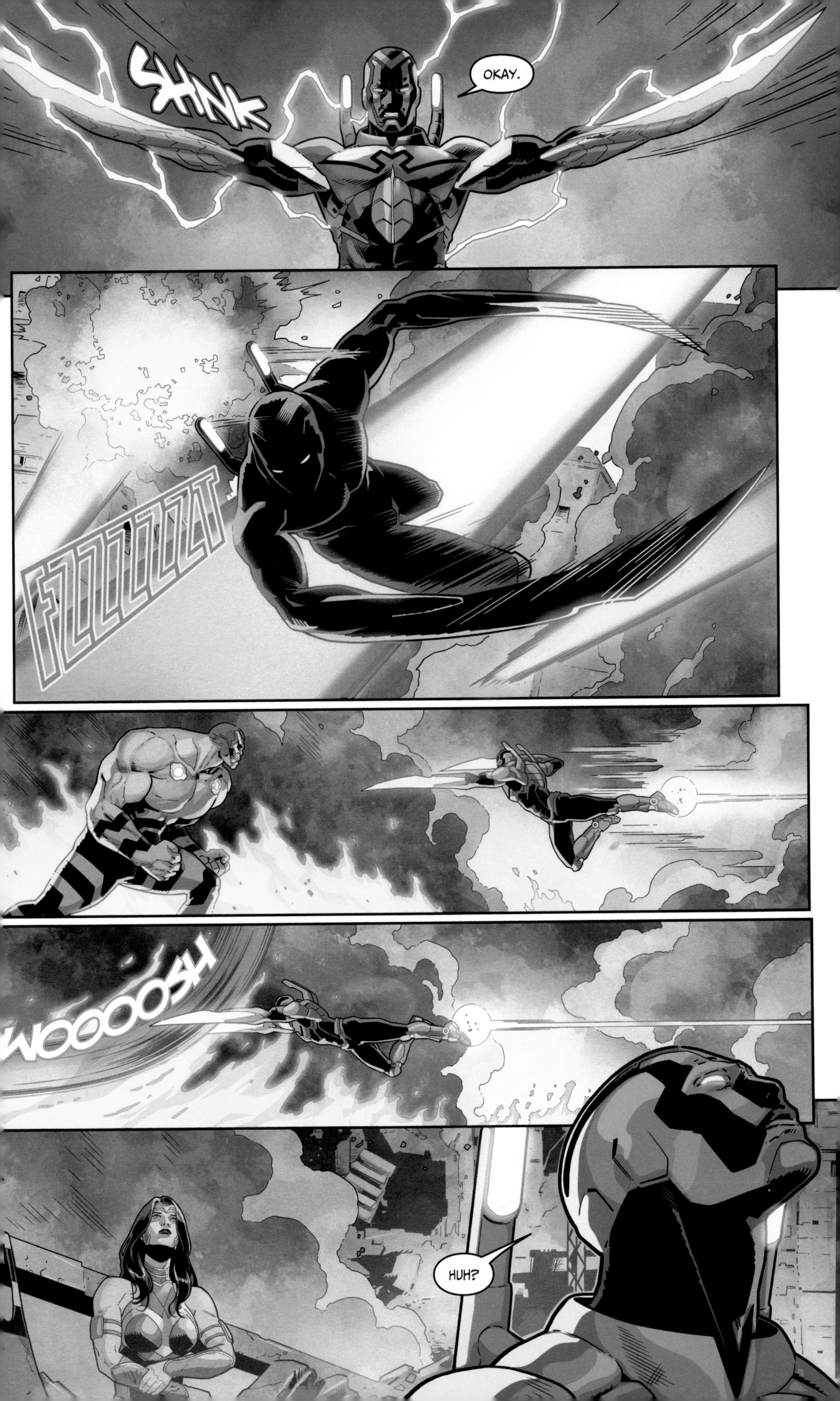
SHNK
OKAY.
FZZZZZT
WOOOOOSH
HUH?

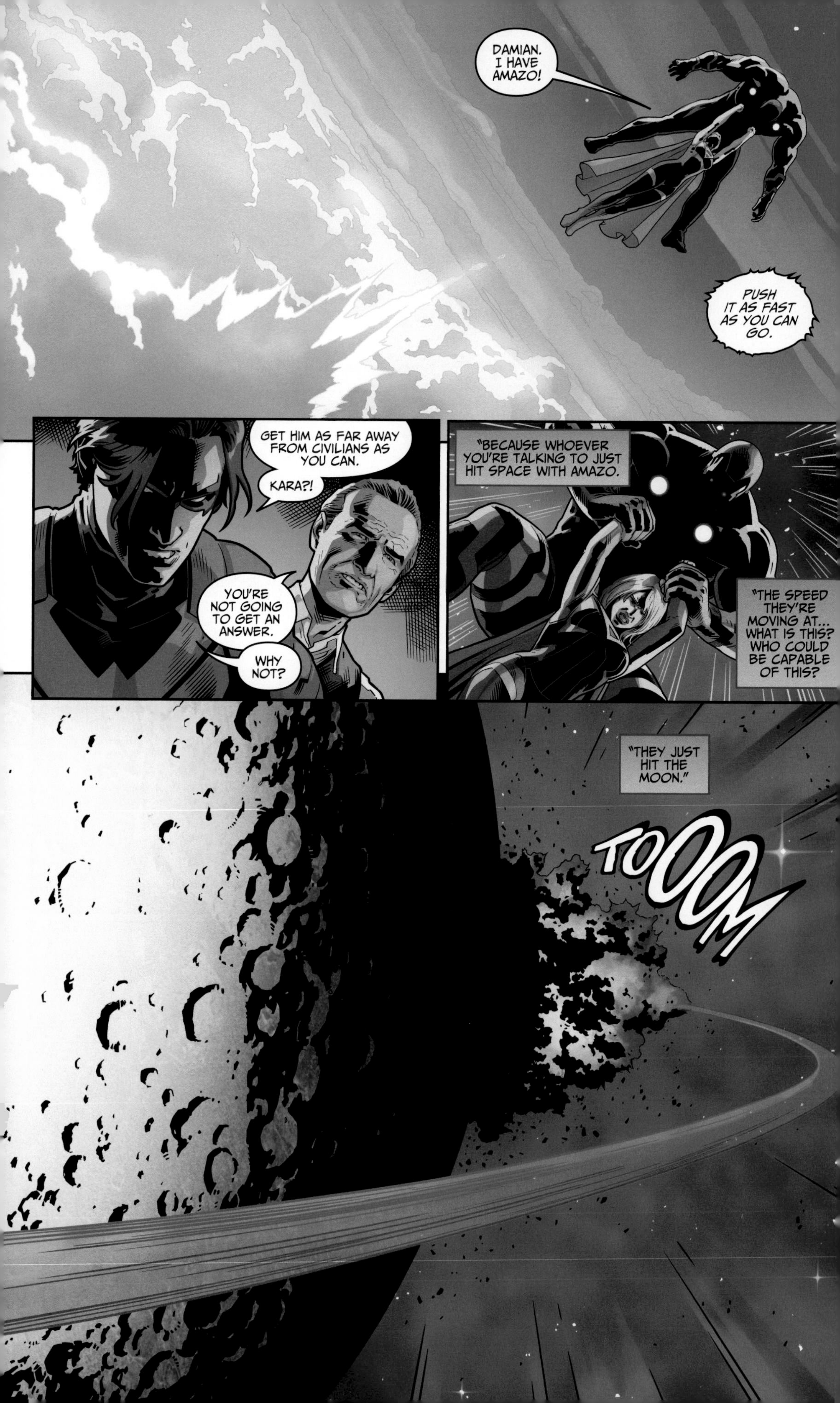

DAMIAN. I HAVE AMAZO!
PUSH IT AS FAST AS YOU CAN GO.
GET HIM AS FAR AWAY FROM CIVILIANS AS YOU CAN.
KARA?!
YOU'RE NOT GOING TO GET AN ANSWER.
WHY NOT?
"BECAUSE WHOEVER YOU'RE TALKING TO JUST HIT SPACE WITH AMAZO.
"THE SPEED THEY'RE MOVING AT... WHAT IS THIS? WHO COULD BE CAPABLE OF THIS?
"THEY JUST HIT THE MOON."
TOOOM

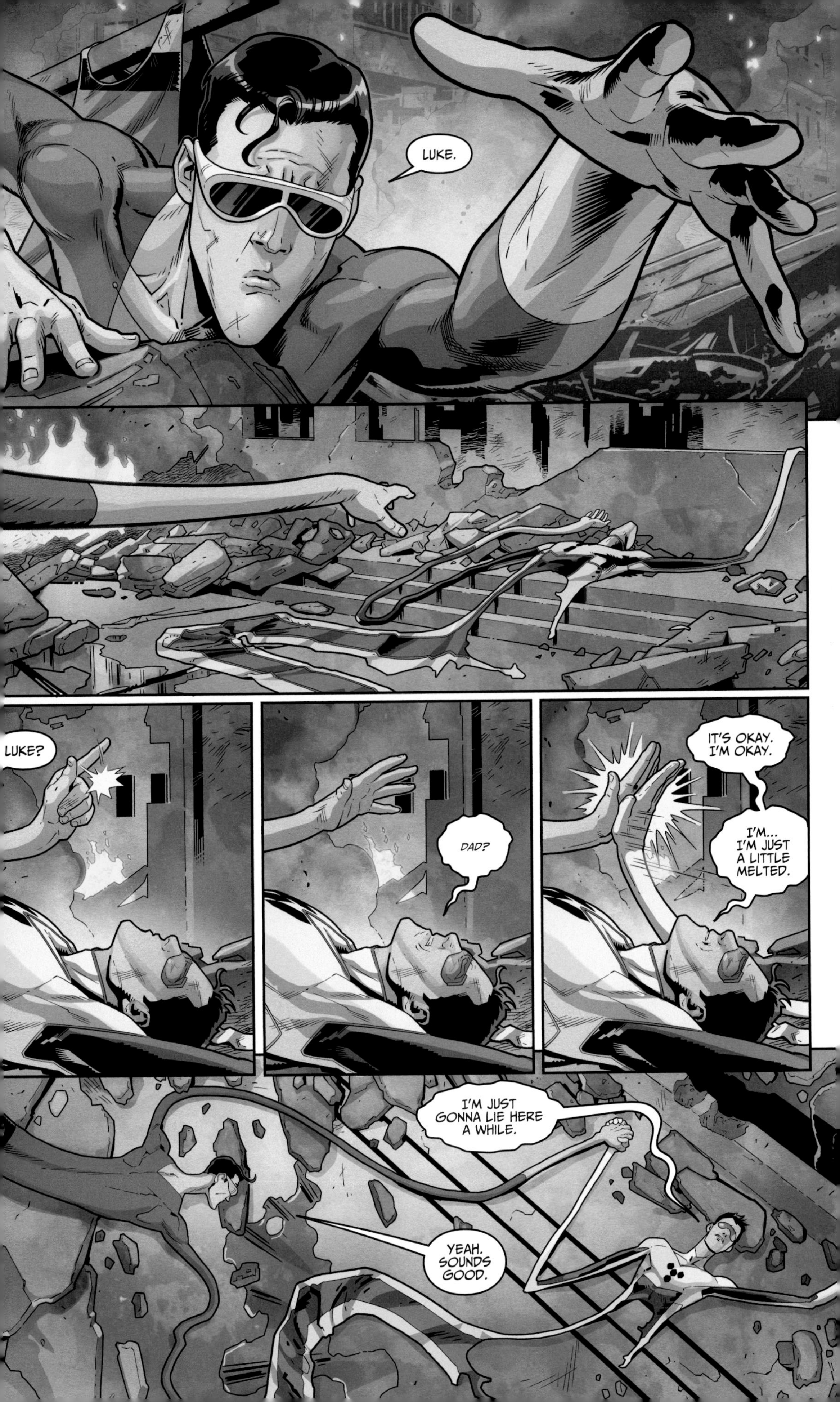
LUKE.
LUKE?
DAD?
IT'S OKAY. I'M OKAY.
I'M... I'M JUST A LITTLE MELTED.
I'M JUST GONNA LIE HERE A WHILE.
YEAH. SOUNDS GOOD.

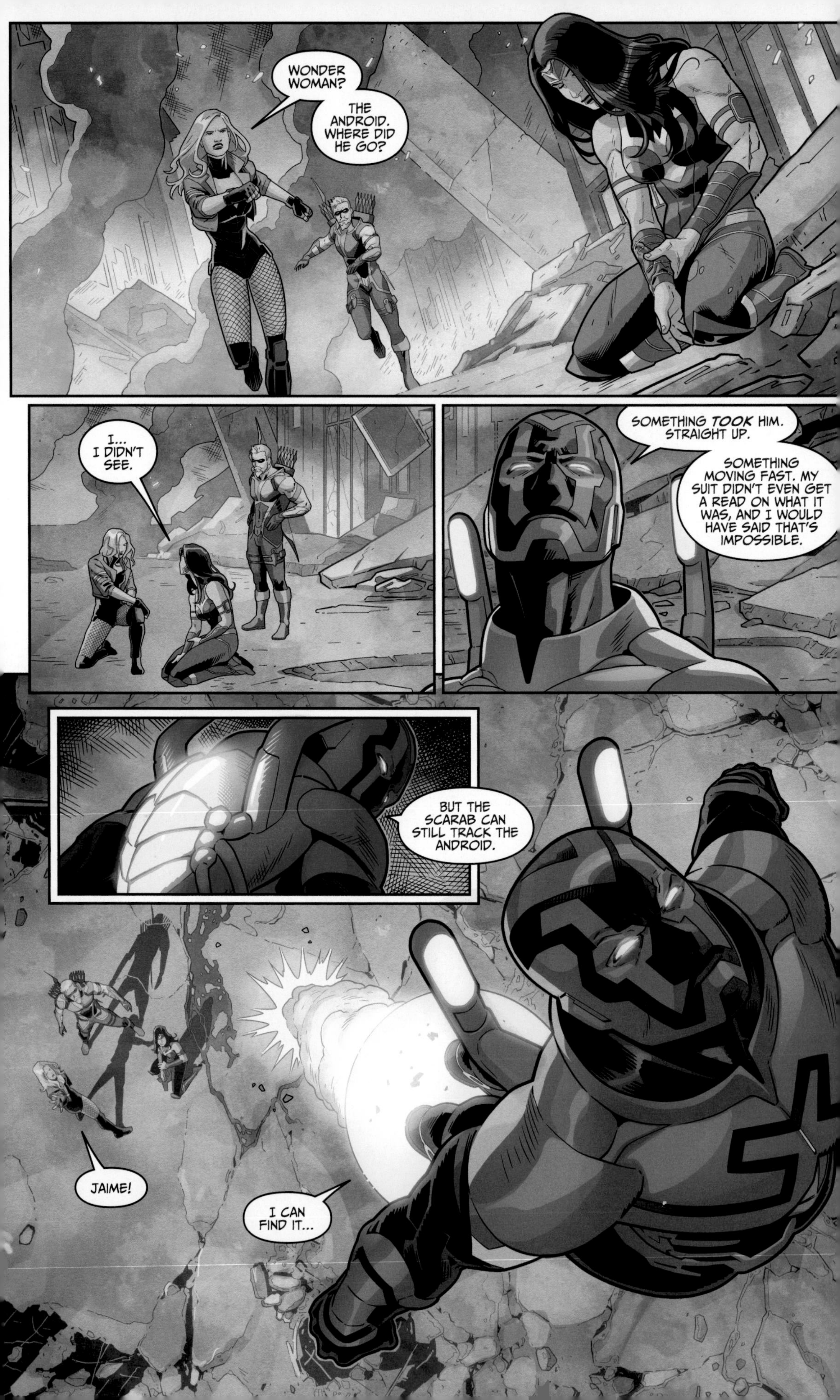

WONDER WOMAN?
THE ANDROID. WHERE DID HE GO?
I... I DIDN'T SEE.
SOMETHING *TOOK* HIM. STRAIGHT UP.
SOMETHING MOVING FAST. MY SUIT DIDN'T EVEN GET A READ ON WHAT IT WAS, AND I WOULD HAVE SAID THAT'S IMPOSSIBLE.
BUT THE SCARAB CAN STILL TRACK THE ANDROID.
JAIME!
I CAN FIND IT...

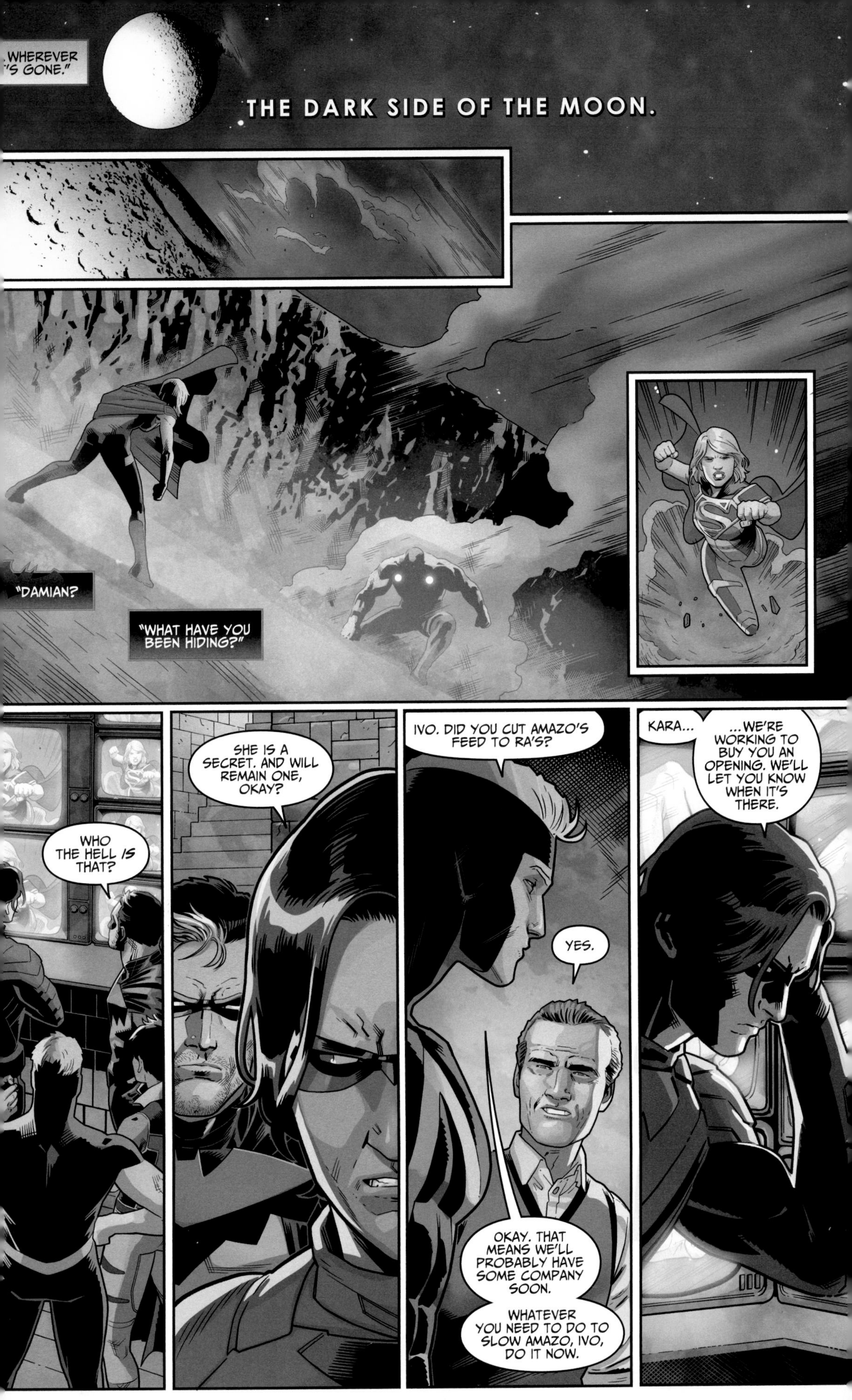
...WHEREVER
'S GONE."
THE DARK SIDE OF THE MOON.
"DAMIAN?
"WHAT HAVE YOU BEEN HIDING?"
WHO THE HELL *IS* THAT?
SHE IS A SECRET. AND WILL REMAIN ONE, OKAY?
IVO. DID YOU CUT AMAZO'S FEED TO RA'S?
YES.
OKAY. THAT MEANS WE'LL PROBABLY HAVE SOME COMPANY SOON.
WHATEVER YOU NEED TO DO TO SLOW AMAZO, IVO, DO IT NOW.
KARA...
...WE'RE WORKING TO BUY YOU AN OPENING. WE'LL LET YOU KNOW WHEN IT'S THERE.

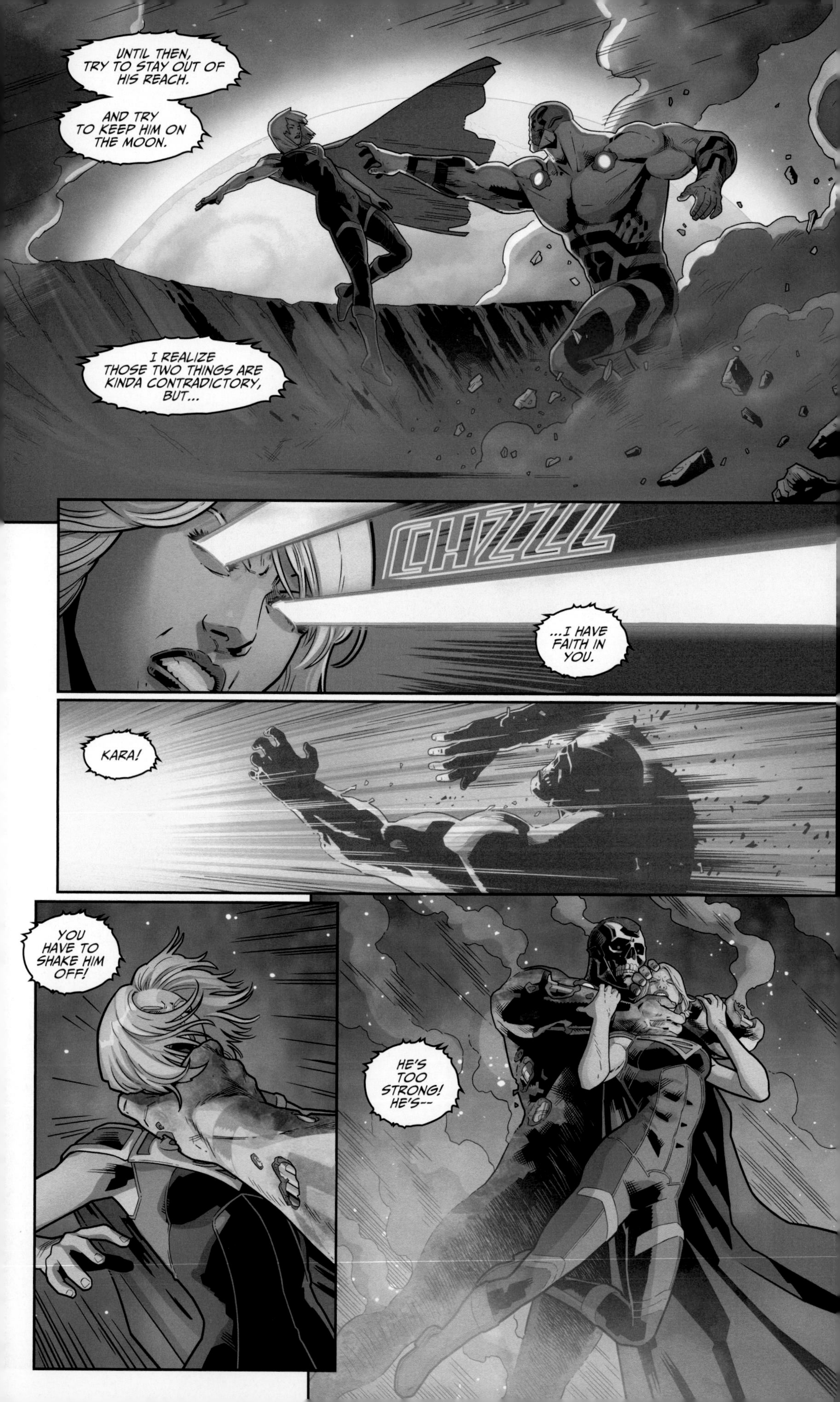
UNTIL THEN, TRY TO STAY OUT OF HIS REACH.
AND TRY TO KEEP HIM ON THE MOON.
I REALIZE THOSE TWO THINGS ARE KINDA CONTRADICTORY, BUT...
CHZZZZ
...I HAVE FAITH IN YOU.
KARA!
YOU HAVE TO SHAKE HIM OFF!
HE'S TOO STRONG! HE'S--

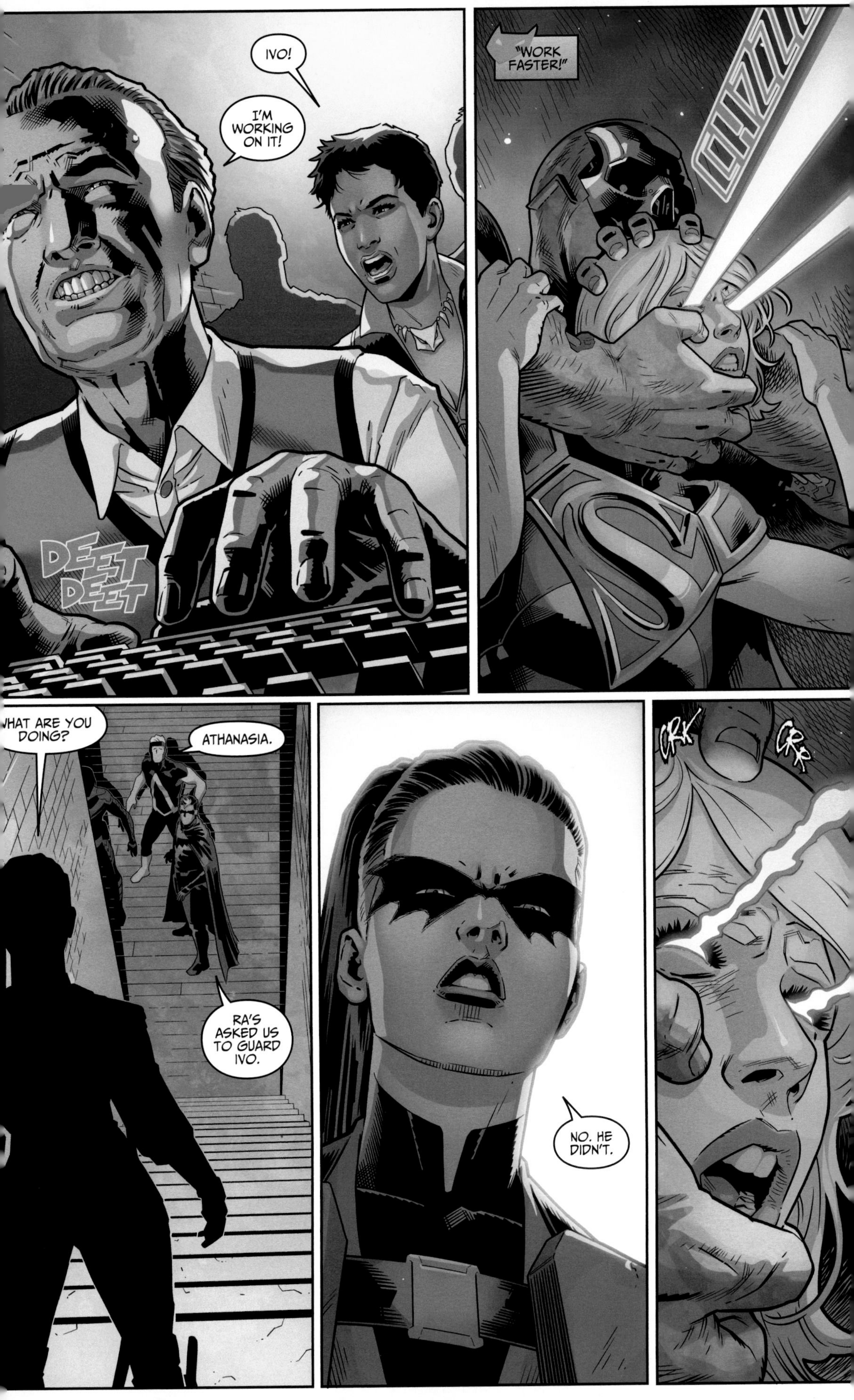
IVO!
I'M WORKING ON IT!
DEET DEET
"WORK FASTER!"
WHAT ARE YOU DOING?
ATHANASIA.
RA'S ASKED US TO GUARD IVO.
NO. HE DIDN'T.
CRK
CRK

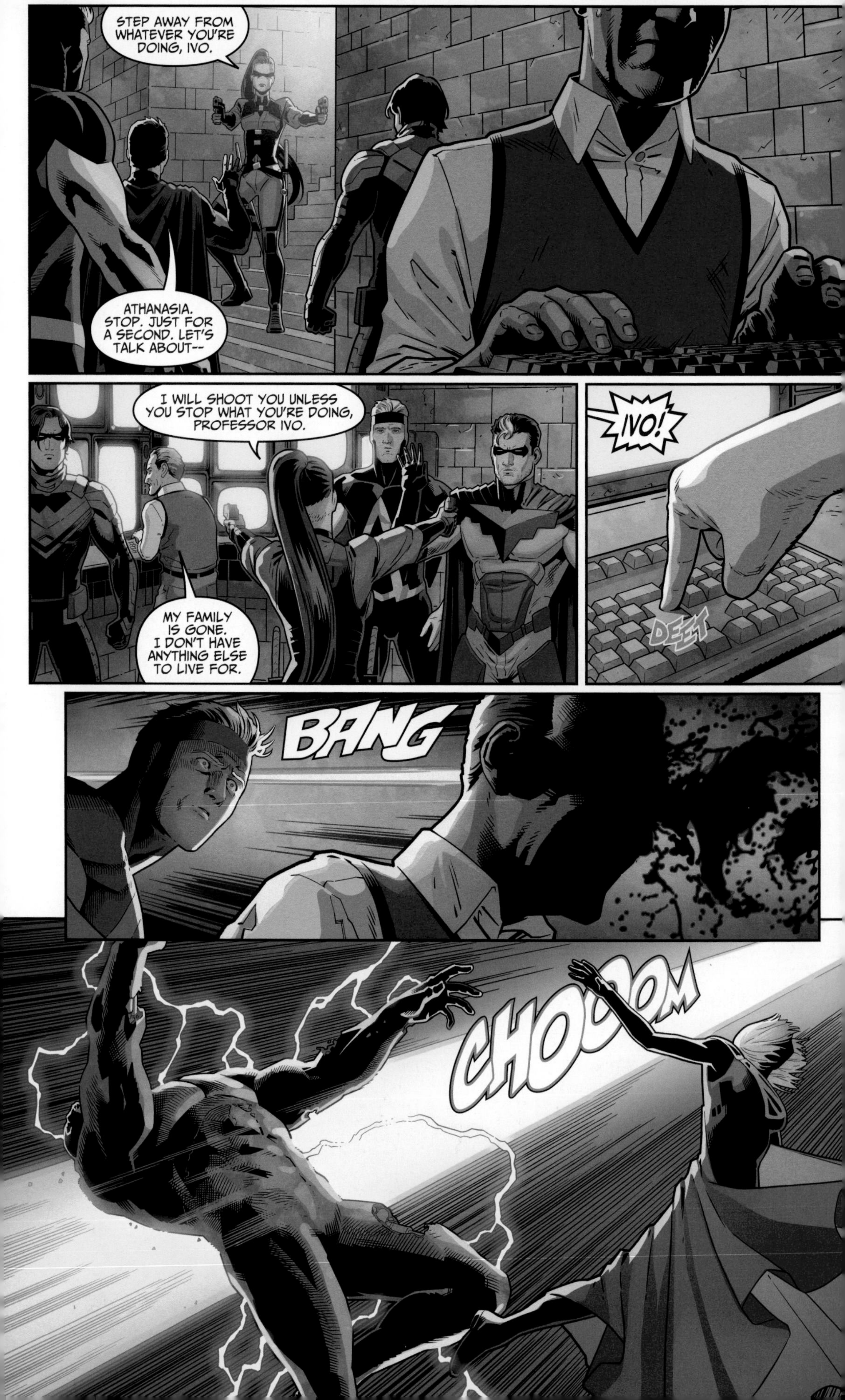
STEP AWAY FROM WHATEVER YOU'RE DOING, IVO.
ATHANASIA. STOP. JUST FOR A SECOND. LET'S TALK ABOUT--
I WILL SHOOT YOU UNLESS YOU STOP WHAT YOU'RE DOING, PROFESSOR IVO.
MY FAMILY IS GONE. I DON'T HAVE ANYTHING ELSE TO LIVE FOR.
IVO!
DEET
BANG
CHOOOOM

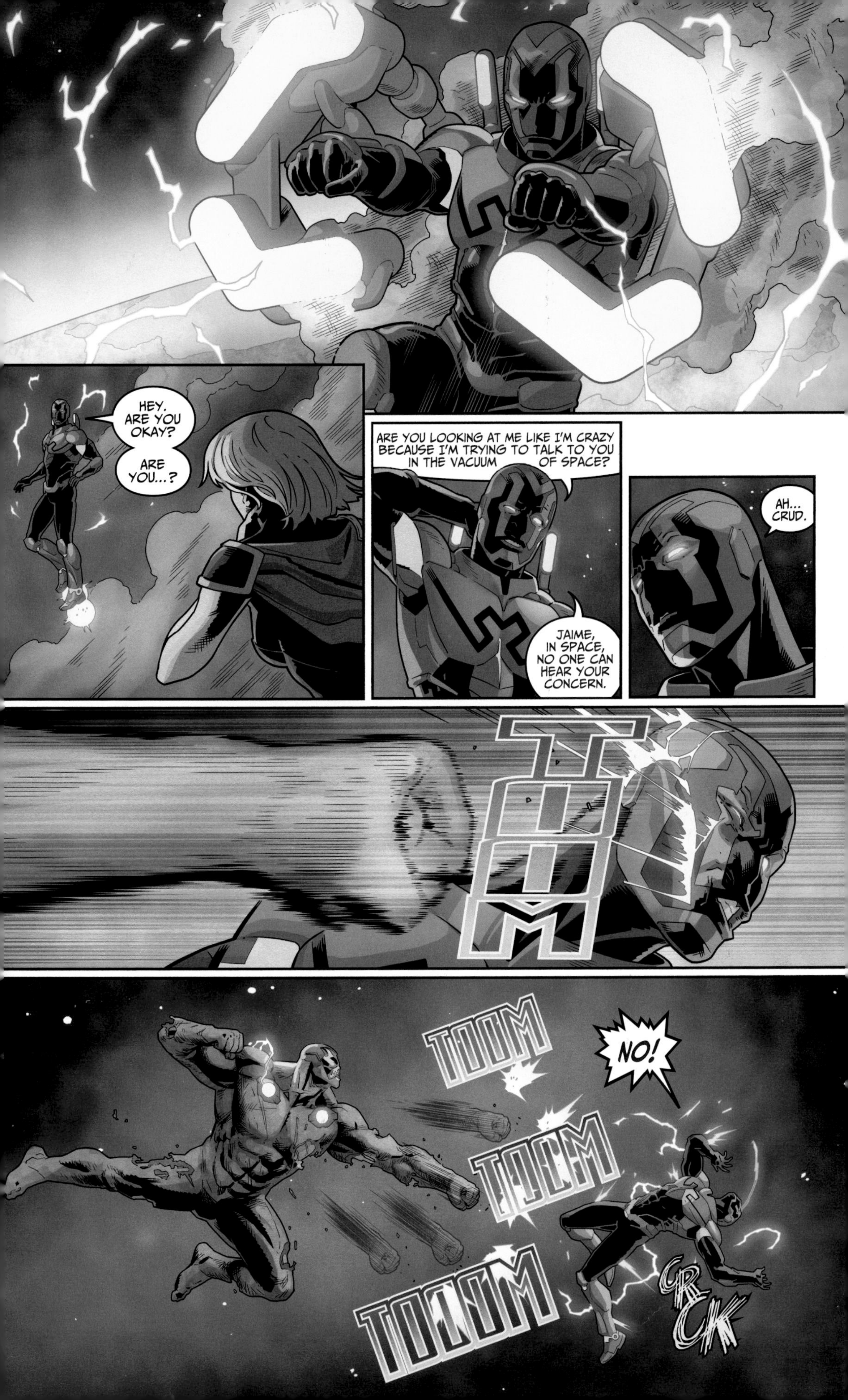
HEY. ARE YOU OKAY?
ARE YOU...?
ARE YOU LOOKING AT ME LIKE I'M CRAZY BECAUSE I'M TRYING TO TALK TO YOU IN THE VACUUM OF SPACE?
JAIME, IN SPACE, NO ONE CAN HEAR YOUR CONCERN.
AH... CRUD.
TOOM
TOOM
NO!
TOOM
TOOOM
CRCK

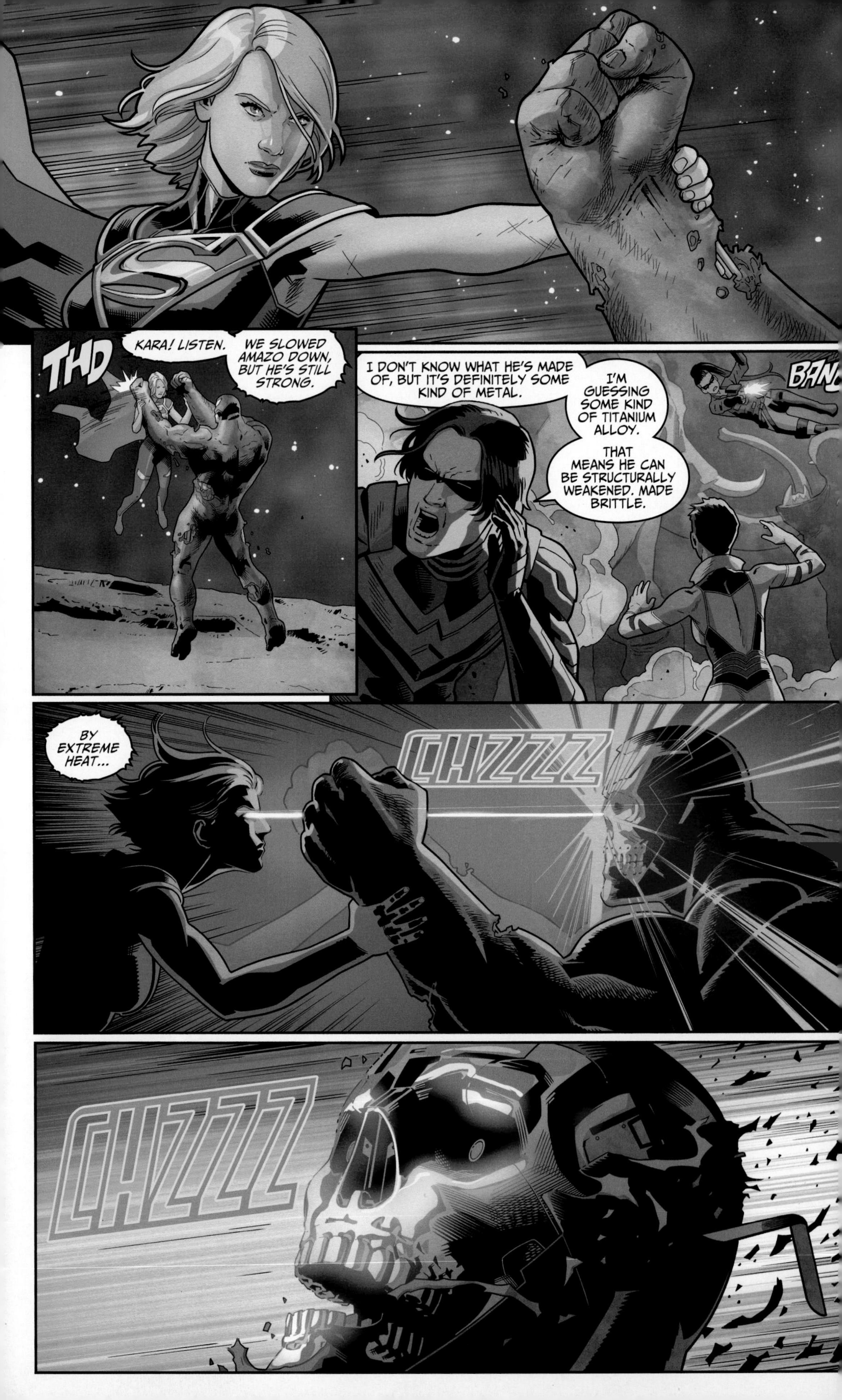

THD
KARA! LISTEN.
WE SLOWED AMAZO DOWN, BUT HE'S STILL STRONG.
I DON'T KNOW WHAT HE'S MADE OF, BUT IT'S DEFINITELY SOME KIND OF METAL.
I'M GUESSING SOME KIND OF TITANIUM ALLOY.
THAT MEANS HE CAN BE STRUCTURALLY WEAKENED. MADE BRITTLE.
BY EXTREME HEAT...
CHZZZZ
CHZZZZ

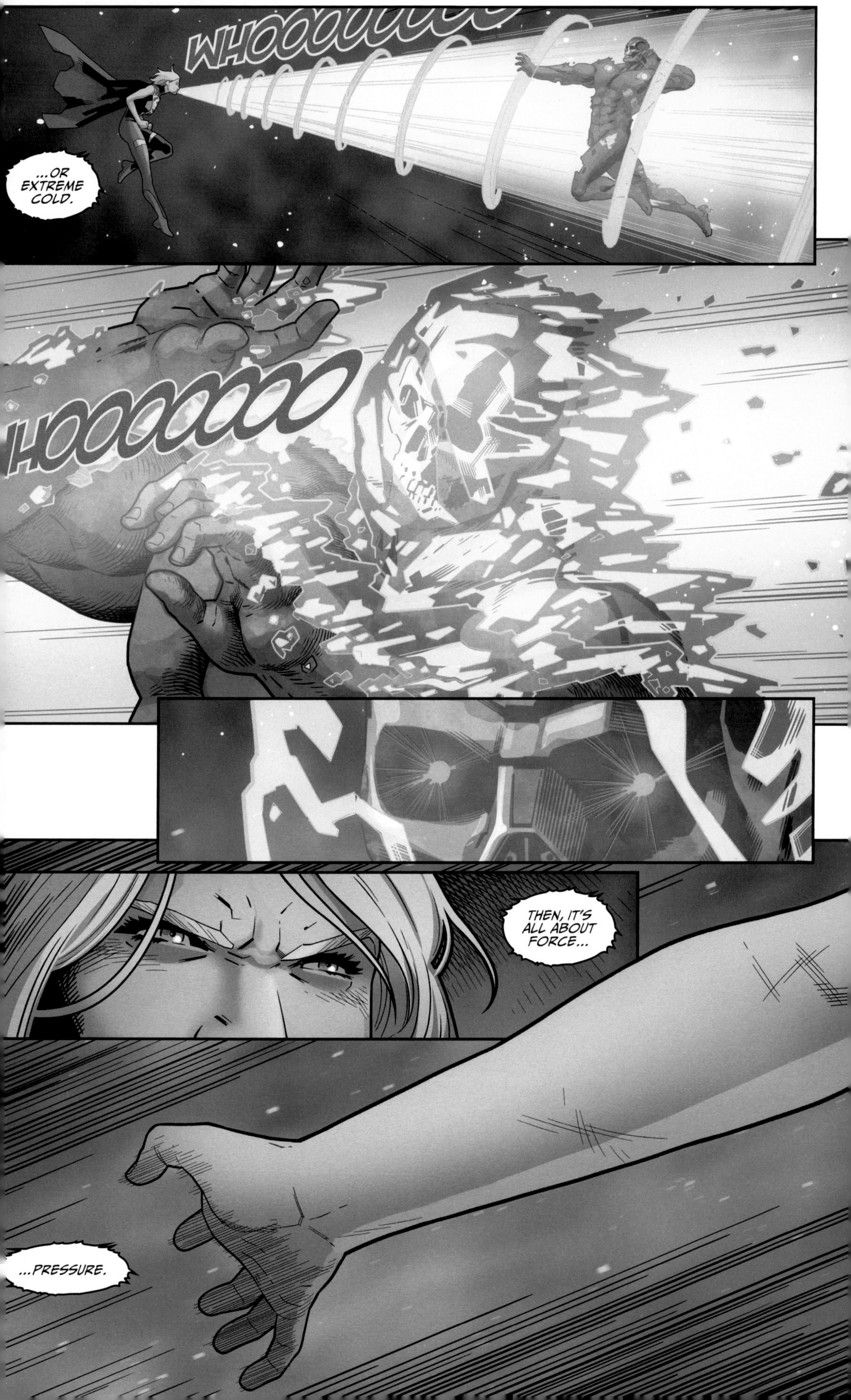
WHOOOOOOOO
...OR EXTREME COLD.
HOOOOOOO
THEN, IT'S ALL ABOUT FORCE...
...PRESSURE.

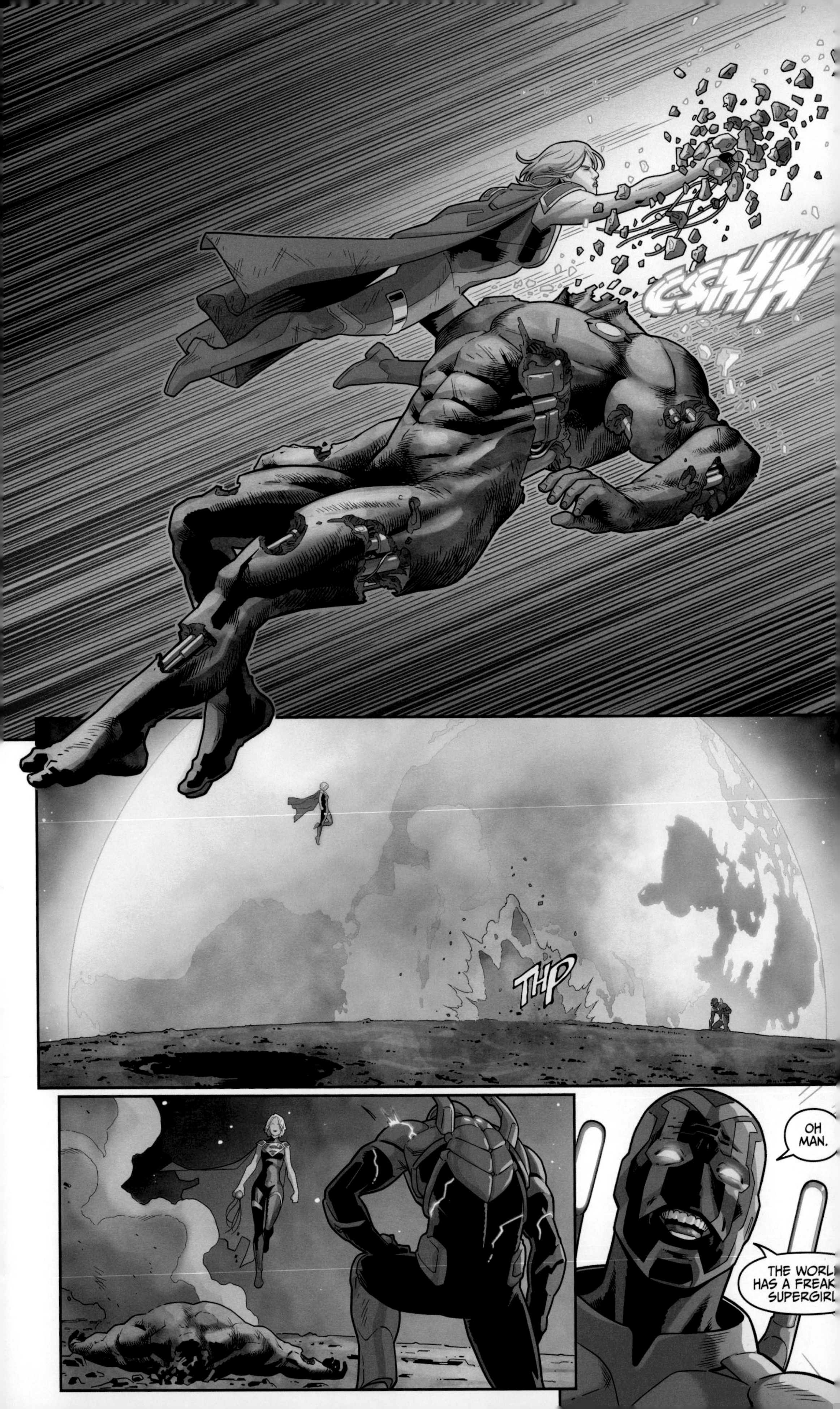
CSHHH
THP
OH MAN.
THE WORL
HAS A FREAK
SUPERGIRL

Character Designs by Bruno Redondo

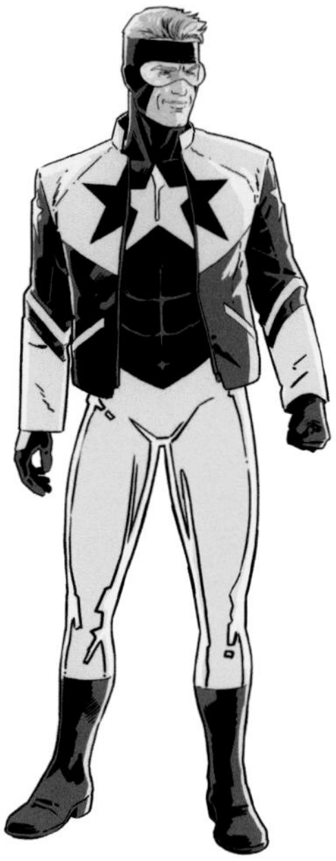

BOOSTER GOLD - INJ2

BRUNO REDONDO 18

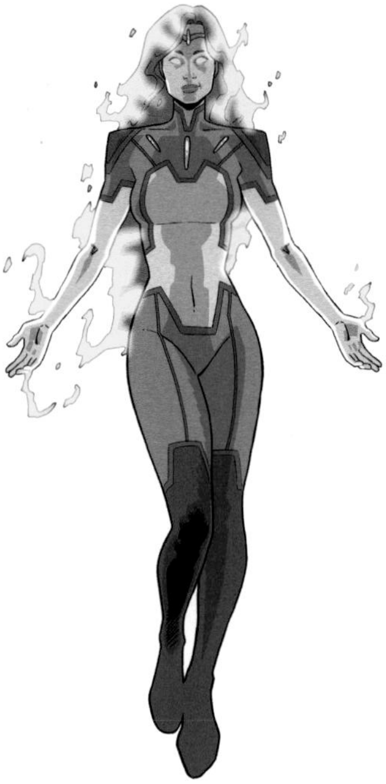

STARFIRE - INJ 2

BRUNO REDONDO 18

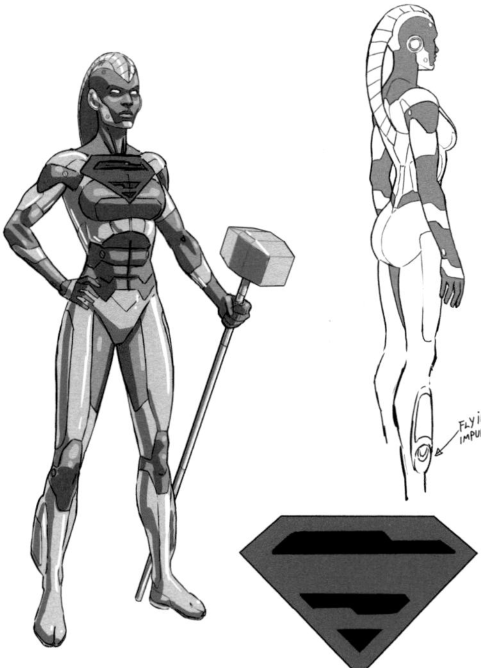
FLYING IMPULSE

STEEL - INJ 2

BRUNO REDONDO 17

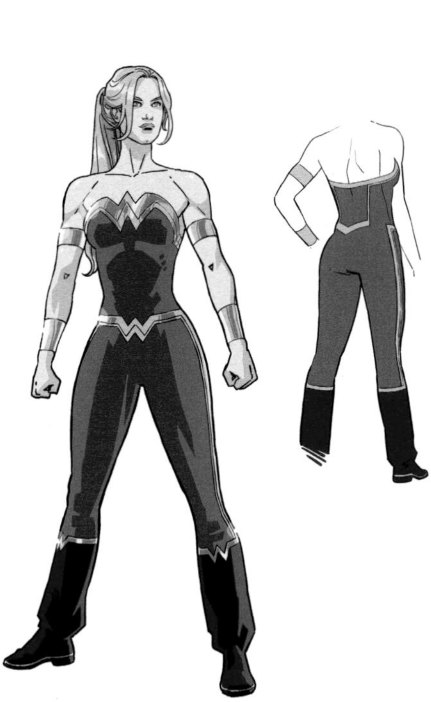

WONDER GIRL - INJ 2

BRUNO REDONDO 18

WONDER WOMAN character design by Bruno Redondo
ERADICATOR character design by Xermanico
ZOD character design by Daniel Sampere

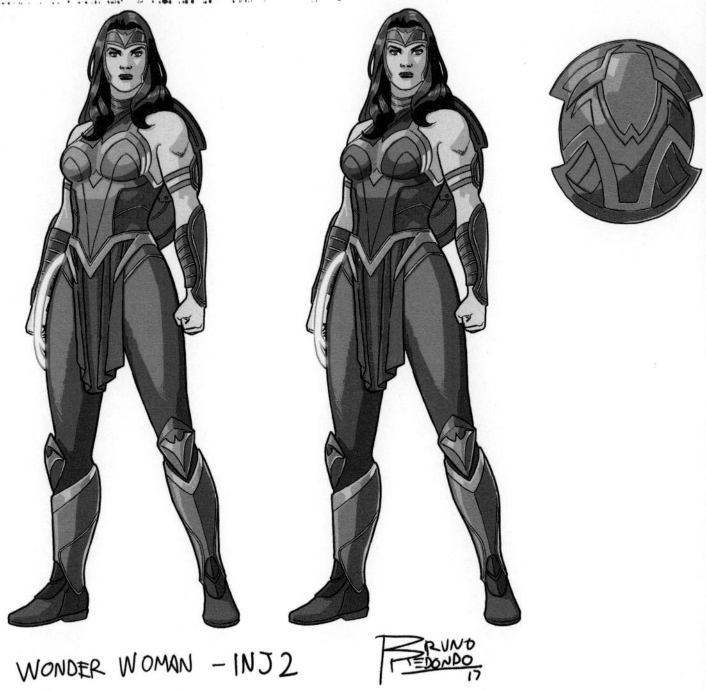
WONDER WOMAN - INJ2
BRUNO REDONDO 17

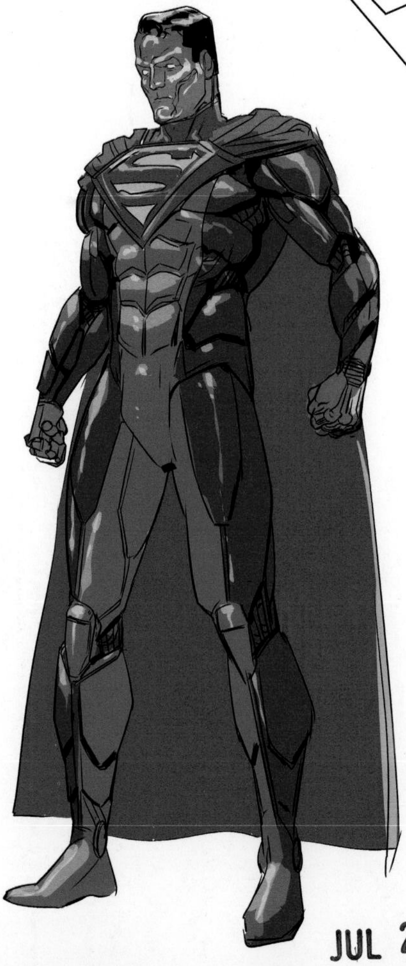

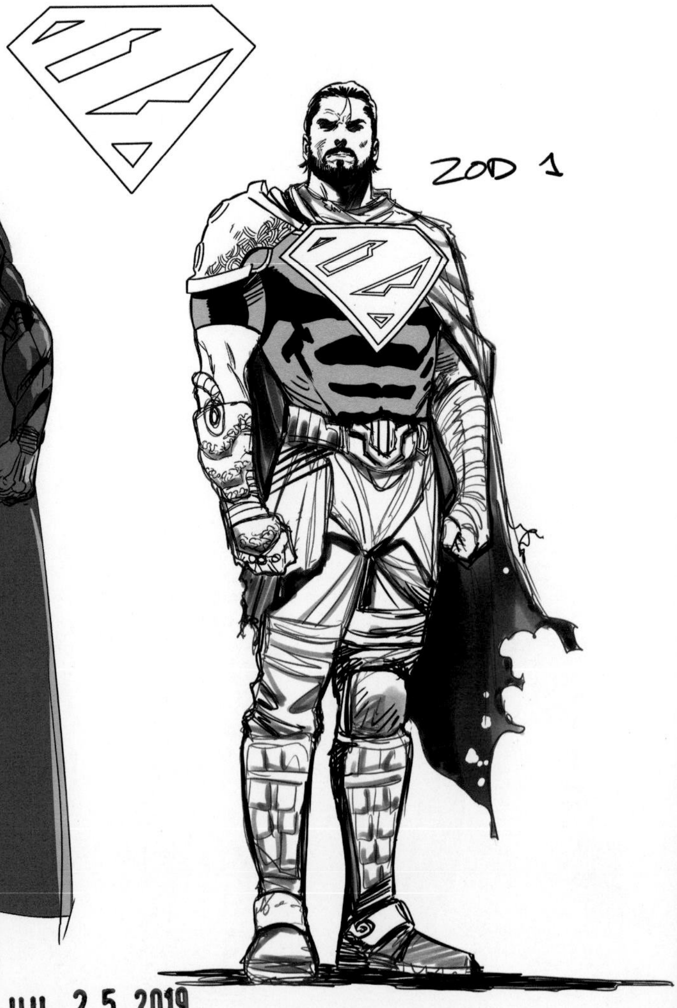
ZOD 1